FROM DONNE TO MARVELL

THE EDITOR

Boris Ford is the General Editor of the *New Pelican Guide to English Literature* (in 11 vols) which in its original form was launched in 1954. At the time it was being planned he was Chief Editor and later Director of the Bureau of Current Affairs. After a spell on the Secretariat of the United Nations in New York and Geneva, he became Editor of the *Journal of Education* and also first Head of Schools Broadcasting with Independent Television.

Following a period as Education Secretary at the Cambridge University Press, Boris Ford, until he retired in 1982, was successively Professor of Education at the universities of Sheffield, Bristol and Sussex – where he was also Dean of the School of Cultural and Community Studies. He edited *Universities Quarterly* from 1955 until 1986. He is General Editor of *The Cambridge Guide to the Arts in Britain* (in 9 vols, 1988–91), and of a forthcoming series of 8 volumes on the arts and civilization of the western world.

From Donne to Marvell

VOLUME

3

OF THE NEW PELICAN GUIDE TO
ENGLISH LITERATURE

EDITED BY BORIS FORD

PENGUIN BOOKS

PENGUIN BOOKS

Published by the Penguin Group
Penguin Books Ltd, 27 Wrights Lane, London W8 5TZ, England
Viking Penguin, a division of Penguin Books USA Inc.
375 Hudson Street, New York, New York 10014, USA
Penguin Books Australia Ltd, Ringwood, Victoria, Australia
Penguin Books Canada Ltd, 2801 John Street, Markham, Ontario, Canada L3R 1B4
Penguin Books (NZ) Ltd, 182–190 Wairau Road, Auckland 10, New Zealand

Penguin Books Ltd, Registered Offices: Harmondsworth, Middlesex, England

First published in *The Pelican Guide to English Literature* 1956
Revised and expanded edition published 1982
in *The New Pelican Guide to English Literature* in Pelican Books
This revised edition published in Penguin Books 1990
1 3 5 7 9 10 8 6 4 2

Printed and bound in Great Britain by
Cox and Wyman Ltd, Reading, Berks.
Filmset in Monophoto Bembo

Illustrations by
Albany Wiseman, pages 173, 176, 178, 180, 184, 185
Jeremy Ford, pages 174, 175, 183

CONTENTS

CONTENTS

PART IV

GENERAL INTRODUCTION

The publication of this *New Pelican Guide to English Literature* in many volumes might seem an odd phenomenon at a time when, in the words of the novelist L. H. Myers, a 'deep-seated spiritual vulgarity ... lies at the heart of our civilization', a time more typically characterized by the Headline and the Digest, by the Magazine and the Tabloid, by Pulp Literature and the Month's Masterpiece. Yet the continuing success of the *Guide* seems to confirm that literature – both yesterday's literature and today's – has a real and not merely a nominal existence among a large number of people; and its main aim has been to help validate as firmly as possible this feeling for a living literature and for the values it embodies.

The *Guide* is partly designed for the committed student of literature. But it has also been written for those many readers who accept with genuine respect what is known as 'our literary heritage', but for whom this often amounts, in memory, to an unattractive amalgam of set texts and school prizes; as a result they may have come to read only today's books – fiction and biography and travel. Though they are probably familiar with such names as Pope, George Eliot, Langland, Marvell, Yeats, Dr Johnson, Hopkins, and the Brontës, they might hesitate to describe their work intimately or to fit them into any larger pattern of growth and achievement. If this account is a fair one, it seems probable that very many people would be glad of guidance that would help them respond to what is living and contemporary in literature, for, like the other arts, it has the power to enrich the imagination and to clarify thought and feeling.

The *Guide* does not set out to compete with the standard Histories of Literature, which inevitably tend to have a lofty, take-it-or-leave-it attitude about them. This is not a *Bradshaw* or a *Whitaker's Almanack* of English literature. Nor is it a digest or potted version, nor again a portrait gallery of the Great. Works such as these already abound and there is no need to add to their number. What it sets out to offer, by contrast, is a guide to the history and traditions of English literature, a contour map of the literary scene. It attempts, that is, to draw up an ordered account of literature as a direct encouragement to people to read widely in an informed way, and with enjoyment. In this respect the *Guide* acknowledges a considerable debt to those twentieth-century writers and critics who have made a determined effort to elicit from literature what is of living value to us today: to establish a sense of literary tradition and to define the standards that this tradition embodies.

The *New Pelican Guide to English Literature* consists of ten volumes:

1, Part One. *Medieval Literature*: *Chaucer and the Alliterative Tradition* (with an anthology)

   Part Two. *Medieval Literature*: *The European Inheritance* (with an anthology)

2. *The Age of Shakespeare*
3. *From Donne to Marvell*
4. *From Dryden to Johnson*
5. *From Blake to Byron*
6. *From Dickens to Hardy*
7. *From James to Eliot*
8. *The Present.*
9. *The Literature of the United States*
   A Guide for Readers

Though the *Guide* has been designed as a single work, in the sense that it attempts to provide a coherent and developing account of the tradition of English literature, each volume exists in its own right and sets out to provide the reader with four kinds of related material:

(i) *A survey of the social context of literature* in each period, providing an account of contemporary society at its points of contact with literature.

(ii) *A literary survey* of the period, describing the general characteristics of the period's literature in such a way as to enable the reader to trace its growth and to keep his or her bearings. The aim of this section is to answer such questions as 'What kind of literature was written in this period?', 'Which authors matter most?', 'Where does the strength of the period lie?'.

(iii) *Detailed studies* of some of the chief writers and works in the period. Coming after the two general surveys, the aim of this section is to convey a sense of what it means to read closely and with perception; and also to suggest how the literature of a given period is most profitably read, i.e. with what assumptions and with what kind of attention. This section also includes an account of some non-literary artist (here Inigo Jones) who particularly flourished at the time, as perhaps throwing a helpful if indirect light on the literature itself.

(iv) *Finally an appendix of essential facts for reference purposes*, such as authors' biographies (in miniature), bibliographies, books for further study, and so on.

Thus each volume of the *Guide* has been planned as a whole, and the contributors' approach to literature is based on broadly common assumptions; for it was essential that the *Guide* should have cohesion and should reveal some collaborative agreements (though inevitably, and quite rightly, it reveals disagreements as well). They agree on the need for rigorous standards and have felt it essential not to take reputations for granted, but rather to examine once again, and often in close detail, the strengths and weaknesses of our literary heritage.

BORIS FORD

NOTES

Notes designated by an asterisk or glosses by a
letter are given at the foot of each
page. Numbered notes are given at
the end of each chapter.

PART I

THE BACKGROUND TO ENGLISH LITERATURE: 1603–60

MARJORIE COX

Elizabethan and Seventeenth-Century

The relationship between literature and the society in which it is created eludes any easy definition or even description. In different periods, different aspects of the life of society will constitute the relevant historical 'background' of literature. Economically, the period 1603–60 is not sharply divided from the reign of Elizabeth I, but it was distinguished by vigorous colonial expansion and settlement. The excitement of the discoveries was still felt and the imagery of the New World is found in writers as diverse as Donne, Browne and Glanvill. The price rise which had set the economic pace of the later sixteenth century continued, though at a diminishing rate, and brought, as before, opportunities for the adventurous and difficulties for the conservative all along the social scale. The most dynamic point in the economy was still in foreign trade: it was here that the greatest fortunes were made and the speediest. But from the second quarter of the century domestic and foreign misfortunes, particularly the dislocation of the European markets by war, produced chronic depression in the all-important cloth export trade: the period has been characterized as 'the lean years'. The cloth industry remained, despite setbacks from James I's interference, the most widespread source of industrial wealth, but the chances for projectors lay rather in heavier industries such as coal and metals, and in newer enterprises such as alum and glass, where royal monopolies gave protection as they had done under Elizabeth. Industry as a whole revealed the same mixture of traditional and new methods of organization as had distinguished it in the later sixteenth century; only a small proportion was carried on by capitalist employers and workmen, the bulk remaining in the hands of small masters.

Agriculture, which employed the overwhelming mass of the population, showed none of the striking features of the Tudor or

Augustan ages. Although enclosure seems to have continued, it had not the dramatic quality of the Tudor movement, and only feeble echoes of the great anti-enclosure risings were heard in the Midlands in 1607. Improvements in technique were the theme of many books from Elizabeth's reign onwards, but despite the introduction of some new crops and more efficient farming for markets, especially in districts within range of London's expanding demand, there was no general change of methods and small-scale subsistence farming was the common occupation. The most impressive innovation was the draining of fenlands in East Anglia, sponsored chiefly by the Earl of Bedford using Dutch engineers. For the most part cultivation was on traditional lines, even if estate management had to be tightened up to meet an inflationary situation and the food supply was always precarious, depending critically each year on the yield of the harvest.

English society in the early seventeenth century showed a distinctive combination of hierarchy and fluidity. The social structure was organized by rank and status and pervaded by the generally accepted notion of 'degree', classically stated by Shakespeare in *Troilus and Cressida* (1602) and invoked by preachers, Puritan and non-Puritan alike, and by official pronouncements. The significant dividing line was between 'gentlemen' (and above) and those below that rank. Nevertheless this distinction was not equivalent to the continental one between noble and commoner. In spite of the cult of heraldry and genealogy there was no aristocratic or even 'gentle' *caste*. By means of the acquisition of land the *nouveau riche* was soon absorbed into the gentry, if not so easily into the aristocracy, as witness the objections to Lionel Cranfield's peerage. Landownership gave social status and political authority. Burghley's statement, 'Gentility is nothing else but ancient riches' was a recognition of a fact of English social life.

The landowning gentry was constantly recruited from the more successful yeomen below and from city merchants and lawyers. Nothing like the urban patriciates of Italy or the Netherlands had developed in England, and the rigid contrasts of *rus* and *urbs* and of landowning and trade were absent. The working of primogeniture and the absence of the French rule of *dérogeance* sent the younger sons of the gentry as apprentices into trade; financial needs led to marriages with city heiresses; city men invested in land; and landowners were involved in industrial and commercial enterprises. The Puritan squires and peers of the Providence and Massachusetts ventures, among them John Pym, can be paralleled by the Royalist Edmund Verney's investments in monopoly patents and drainage schemes or the Catholic Sir Thomas Tresham's highly commercialized agriculture. This mobility was not new in England, but there are indications that the tempo had quickened in this period. Contemporaries were aware of this, and it gave them a sense of the shifting of social and moral foundations; historians at present lay the emphasis on the upward movement of those immediately below the gentry – yeomen, merchants, citizens. The very active debate among historians over the 'rise' or 'decline' of the gentry or the 'crisis' of the aristocracy is now over. The terms of the debate no longer seem relevant, but it produced a wealth of information about the multiple movements (up and down and over generations) within society and the variety of their causes.[1]

It is in politics rather than in the social and economic spheres that the period has a distinctive character; a summary description, covering a highly complex development, is 'the winning of the initiative by the House of Commons'. Alternatively, it can be described as the crisis of the 'mixed constitution', the ancient constitution which was supposed to issue in harmony. Its climax was in civil war and an interregnum, followed by the restoration of a monarchy fundamentally modified though superficially the same. Many of those who lived through the early Stuart reigns contrasted them sadly with the glories of Elizabeth's; opposition M.P.s measured the royal foreign policy by an Elizabethan yardstick and found it wanting; conservative statesmen like Clarendon and Newcastle saw in the Civil War a judgement on departure from Elizabethan methods. Yet in many ways the change of sovereign in 1603 merely exacerbated difficulties already present during the nineties. Only Elizabeth's peculiar skill could have produced from the situation of 1601 her 'Golden Speech' celebrating the mutual love of prince and subjects. In fact, she left to her successors a legacy of unsolved problems: the Crown's financial position, the meaning of the Commons' privilege of free speech, and the precise nature of the Church of England, of which the sovereign was head. In religion and in politics, questioning and the desire for definition grew with the century. But to recognize that there were problems is not to admit the inevitability of breakdown, certainly not of civil war. These domestic problems had as their background the rising diplomatic tension on the continent, culminating in the outbreak in 1618 of the politico-religious struggle of the Thirty Years' War. By 1635 all the major European powers were involved, with the exception of England. To James and Charles the interests of a daughter and a sister were at stake, but to numerous frustrated Englishmen the survival of Protestantism itself seemed in the balance, while England pursued a policy of non-intervention.

Whereas the Victorian habit was to see the decisive change in the history of thought in the Renaissance of the fifteenth and sixteenth centuries, contemporary historians find it rather in the seventeenth century. Nothing is more difficult to plot than a change in habits of thinking, for its penetration can only be very gradual. The 'new philosophy' was already a catchword at the beginning of the century, and by the Restoration scientific experiment was achieving a fashionable status. The first half of the seventeenth century is a critical stage in the replacement of one total framework for viewing the universe by another – a movement, it must be emphasized, which was European, and of which the English flowering came in the later seventeenth century. Although the change was far from complete by the end of our period, there was a growing momentum compared with the age of Elizabeth. Scholasticism, that medieval synthesis of the Christian and Aristotelian traditions, had produced a durable, inter-dependent structure of thought, at once physical and metaphysical, based on ancient observations, on assumptions and above all on logic. It provided a convincing and satisfying theory of the nature of the whole universe as organic, ordered, teleological and geocentric, which had been elaborated over the centuries. This now had the status of an orthodoxy resting on 'authoritative' texts, and questioning any part of it threatened the whole structure.

The change to the Newtonian 'world-picture' was at once fundamental and very gradual. Newton's abstruse *Principia Mathematica* (1687) unified into an authoritative and intellectually satisfying whole the fruits of a series of brilliant scientific discoveries. To over-simplify: physics and metaphysics were separated, the universe, now heliocentric, was seen not as organic and teleological, but as mechanical and matter-based; in Galileo's words the book of the universe was 'written in mathematical language'. This change was achieved by means of a new mode of inquiry into nature, based not on accepted authorities (nor on mere observation) but on the mathematical–physical experimental method. The process took over a century and a half and was extremely complex: discoveries – some themselves only hypotheses – nibbled at the scholastic totality, but could not win universal acceptance, since, though calling into question aspects of existing explanation (but not always with proved alternatives), they could not provide a similar comprehensive theory. This was especially true of astronomy, the study of the heavens visible to all, where the old Ptolemaic system was not finally satisfactorily challenged until Galileo's *Dialogue on the Two Great World Systems Ptolemaic and Copernican**★ (1632), but had lost ground to new hypotheses on planetary motion – that of Copernicus (1543), modified by Kepler's, and by Tycho Brahe's compromise, which retained geocentricity. In England John Wilkins wrote defending the Copernican theory in 1640, and acceptance of it filtered through society from the *savants*.

Science or 'natural philosophy' in this period is full of contradictions and complexities. Lacking accepted touchstones of proof, educated men could hold what we see as inconsistent beliefs and theories. Interwoven with the rational and experimental in Copernicus's and Kepler's astronomy and in William Gilbert's great work on magnetism are strange strands of mysticism deriving from Plato and the neo-Platonists. Astrology retained its reality for many, including Tycho, while chemistry, developed by the empiric Paracelsus, still had semi-magical aspects. Curiously, too, the major English scientific figures of this period, William Gilbert (magnetism) and William Harvey (the circulation of the blood) both functioned in the neo-Aristotelian, Galenist, Royal College of Physicians. Is it surprising that there are signs among educated men of scientific, particularly cosmological, confusion? William Drummond of Hawthornden conveys it: 'thus sciences are become opinions, nay Errores, and leave the Imagination in a thousand labyrinths'. Confusing it may have been, but less fundamentally unsettling than might have been

---

★ Translated into English after the Restoration.

expected: stimulating it certainly was, opening educated minds to awareness and questioning of authorities.

Galileo epitomizes the scientific revolution in his combination of the conceptual and mathematical with the practical experimental method. Sir Henry Wotton, writing to the Earl of Salisbury in 1610, immediately recognized the significance of Galileo's observations of the moon and planets, just published in *Siderius Nuncius*, and his telescope quickly became a symbol. In other areas of knowledge practical experiment played the dominant part. For William Gilbert the search for knowledge was not in books but in things themselves. From the late sixteenth century much scientific activity and invention in London was stimulated by the needs of trade and navigation. Gresham's College was set up in the City in 1598 with seven chairs, three of which were in Geometry, Physics and Astronomy. The professors, drawn from the universities, lectured in English as well as Latin, and their mathematical teaching had a strong practical bias: knowledge of Napier's discovery of logarithms, for example, was at once spread by Henry Briggs, and the slide rule was invented by Edmund Gunter. There was thus, besides the refusal to give unquestioned acceptance to old authorities which characterized the whole scientific movement, a practical utilitarian cast of mind which both encouraged and was encouraged by the 'new philosophy'.[2]

The role of Francis Bacon (1561–1626) in the intellectual changes of the seventeenth century has been the subject of much dispute. The sheer bulk of the philosophical work (much of it in Latin), its unfinished, sometimes fragmentary state, and its odd publishing history complicate the just weighing of his thoughts and encourage argument based on selectivity. Debate continues on the relation of his thought to Aristotle (despite the explicit challenge of the title of his *Novum Organum*, 1620), to the new experimental method, to the great creative mathematical and conceptual foundations of the 'new philosophy', and to the utilitarian side of science. Challengingly antischolastic, he yet retained many of the old Aristotelian assumptions and methods. A champion of experiment, he was ignorant of many of the important contemporary discoveries, and did not fully grasp the combination of hypotheses and the experimental method. He lacked contact with the Renaissance Platonic tradition, and so did not appreciate the fundamental role of mathematics in changing man's understanding of the universe. 'Janus-headed' he has been called, and in this he was characteristic of his age.

Nevertheless he thought of himself as '*buccinator novi temporis*' (the herald of a new age):

Those, therefore, who determine not to conjecture and guess but to find out and know ... to look into and dissect the nature of this real world must consult only things themselves.

His significance for his contemporaries and later generations was as the 'bell which called the wits together'. The dynamism, the optimism, the Faustian urge, the 'inspired dream' of the man who as early as 1592 had announced that he had 'taken all knowledge to be [his] province' played a decisive part in discrediting scholastic philosophy and shaping new attitudes. The English version of *The Advancement of Learning* (1605), 'well tasted', he later wrote, 'in the universities here and the English colleges abroad', was turned in 1620 into the expanded Latin version *De Augmentis Scientiarum* to give it international currency.

The trenchant prose and educated breadth of reference, coming from one who held the highest office, gave Bacon's work a general currency denied to more original experimenters like Gilbert. The radical reformers (at once utilitarian and visionary) who were active in the public sphere in the Civil War and Interregnum, the intellectuals who in that period held their private meetings from which discussion of religion and politics was banned, the scientifically curious dilettanti gentlemen, the 'virtuosi', Thomas Sprat in his *History of the Royal Society* (1667) and Cowley in his introductory ode to it, all looked back to Bacon as their inspiration. Even if his grand classified scheme of knowledge and inquiry, the uncompleted *Instauratio Magna* (The Great Renewal), was semi-Aristotelian and not the way forward, his uniting of the hitherto separated liberal and mechanical arts and his idea of co-operative scientific research were immensely fruitful and helped to alter the conditions of investigation. The nature of the influence exerted by his works outran his own presuppositions and beliefs. The utilitarian emphasis of his philosophy, reacting against scholastic abstraction, was not of such a narrow kind as it appeared in a later seventeenth-century setting. His doctrine of the 'double truth', the universe shown in God's word and in God's works, had not for him the secularist colour which it later assumed. To have a just understanding and appreciation of Bacon, we must view him in his own lifetime.

The Milieu of Literature, 1603–42

Without entering into the vexed question of the extent of literacy, we can none the less find evidence of a widening reading public. There was a considerable increase in the number of new books printed annually: romances, histories, sermons, handbooks on manners and on business, broadside ballads and the early beginnings of newspapers fed the popular demand, and during the Civil War the pamphlet explosion, especially in London (2,000 published in 1642 alone), testified to the large number of readers.[3] Comenius, visiting London in 1641, was astounded at the output of books and the number of bookshops. It was a time of educational expansion, which affected all but the lowest strata of society. However, many of the works considered in later chapters circulated for a long time in manuscript among the authors' friends and acquaintances; during their authors' lifetimes the poems of Donne and Herbert were read chiefly in manuscript, while Browne's *Religio Medici* was printed only through a friend's indiscretion. These facts are a reminder of the intimacy of the cultivated society within which much of the literature was produced. A surprising number of the well-known men of letters, of politics, and of religion were friends or at least habitual acquaintances. The 'tribe of Ben' formed a strong nucleus, and the circles were linked by a central figure like Sir Henry Wotton, ex-ambassador and Provost of Eton, a close friend of Donne, a friend of Izaak Walton, and an acquaintance of Milton. Clarendon's autobiography reveals the large London circle to which he belonged as a young man at the Middle Temple – Jonson, Selden, Sir Kenelm Digby, Thomas May, and Thomas Carew – and his links with the Great Tew circle and with Edmund Waller, cousin of John Hampden and frequenter of Penshurst, the home of the Sidneys.

Writers of this period, and not merely the most famous, reveal an astonishing versatility and range of knowledge. Versatility was, of course, an accepted social ideal, but what made possible the varied intellectual activities of Ralegh, Bacon, Selden, Burton,

Browne, Sir Kenelm Digby, and many others was the relative compactness of their world of knowledge; politics, law, history, philosophy, poetry, and science could all be touched, and those who wrote on such diverse subjects shared a common classical heritage and training. But breadth of learning was matched by breadth of experience; most writers were not solely men of letters but had careers in the political, academic or clerical worlds.

The concentration of cultivated society followed from the overwhelming and growing predominance of London. No other English town approached its population of perhaps a quarter of a million, and its increase was not materially checked by plague. To meet the increased demand for houses, mainly by nobility, gentry, courtiers and professional men, London was expanding westwards towards Westminster. Though for the most part it remained the haphazard, overcrowded town described by Stow in 1598, the Italianizing of London's architecture began under the leadership of Inigo Jones. The bulk of England's foreign trade passed through the port of London; the great trading companies were based on the city; the hub of the major English industry – the cloth trade – was there, at Blackwell Hall; and also the chief market for raising loans and buying and selling land.

The reasons for the magnetic influence of London were not only economic, but political, social and legal. Every session of Parliament at Westminster brought over 400 members, sometimes with their families, to London. More regularly the Common Law and Prerogative courts brought numerous suitors and their witnesses to town. Contemporaries were well aware of the significance for London shopkeepers of the legal terms. The Inns of Court, the city schools and certain famous schoolmasters drew many, and finally there were those who came to the capital for pleasure. Judging by the complaints of contemporaries, this habit was on the increase; King James was only one among many who denounced 'those swarms of gentry, who through the instigation of their wives ... did neglect their country hospitality and cumber the city'. The beginnings of the London season can be found in the early seventeenth century; parks, pleasure gardens, theatres, and transport (hackney coaches and sedan chairs existed under Charles I) were developed to meet the demand. It is impossible to say what proportion of the nobility and gentry frequented London, but in 1632 some 250 were prosecuted in the Star Chamber for disobeying the King's proclamation to return to their estates. Perhaps Sir Humphrey Mildmay, a country gentleman of Essex with Court connections, was unusual in spending between four and six months a year in London, but his diary gives a typical round of pleasures. Besides swimming and boating on the Thames, dicing and card-playing and going a-maying in Hyde Park, he went to wrestling matches and to the theatre (sometimes two or three times a week), seeing Shirley's *The Gamester*, Fletcher's *The Pastoral*, and in 1635 *Othello*. Like the citizens of London, he watched the spectacles of Court and city activity: the reception of an ambassador, the progress of a Knight of the Garter, and the Lord Mayor's Show.

London was prominent among the *milieux* of literature; some writers were born there, Milton the son of a scrivener, Donne of a prosperous ironmonger, Herrick of a goldsmith; more were drawn there by its attraction as an economic, social and intellectual centre. But London was only part of the background of cultivated society: most of the men of letters of this period, and many of their contemporaries of the 'political nation', shared with the Earl of Clare in 'all the ornaments the University, Inns of Court, Court, Camp, travel, and language could enrich him with'.[4] It is this common social and cultural ground which must be explored now.

No single modern institution provides an analogy to the Court of the early seventeenth century. The Court had still a central and magnetic position in society; contact with it could give power, office and wealth. Royal favour alone raised George Villiers, of a minor Leicestershire family, to a dukedom and his relatives to wealth and influence. This was a spectacular demonstration of the ways of the Court, and it is small wonder that the ambitious and needy alike flocked to it. George Herbert, while Public Orator of the University of Cambridge, was haunted by 'Court-hopes', seldom looking 'towards Cambridge unless the King were there, but then he never fail'd'; Richard Baxter, the son of an obscure Shropshire freeholder, was urged 'to go to London and get acquaintance at Court and get some office as being the only rising way'.

The Court took its tone from the personal character and tastes of the sovereign. In this period, therefore, the machinery remained the same – the royal household with its increasing number of officials subsisting largely on perquisites from suitors and its waste and extravagance in catering – but with the change from James to Charles the atmosphere of the Court changed. 'Two sorts of men King James had never kindness for', wrote a contemporary, 'those whose hawks and dogs flew and run as well as his own, and those who were able to speak as much reason as himself'. Hunting and scholarship were his dominant interests. In many ways shrewd, good-humoured and approachable, he lacked Tudor dignity and political sense. His Queen's taste for luxury in dress and entertainment and his own lavish gifts to favourites and general fecklessness in money matters raised Court expenditure to unprecedented heights. In 1617 James travelled farther north than Elizabeth had ever done, but in general royal progresses declined. Moreover, Elizabeth had never submitted herself so abjectly to her favourites.

The accession of Charles, 'temperate, chaste, and serious', brought a change. Although Court expenditure remained such as to astonish Rubens, the sprawling lavishness of James disappeared; the Court and household were better ordered, and something more than the dignity of Elizabeth's Court was regained, though without its popular appeal. The decline of royal progresses continued, and there was increasingly a private or coterie quality in the Court; Van Dyck's portraits (confined almost entirely to the Court circle) reveal, if nothing more, the way in which Charles and his Court liked to be portrayed. The fashionable interest, led by the King, was now largely in the visual arts; the collecting of pictures, begun by Arundel, was continued by Charles with genuine taste, and at amazing expense in view of his financial straits. Living artists, too, especially Rubens and Van Dyck, were patronized. This dominant aesthetic interest formed a link between Charles and various continental Courts. The missions of papal representatives to Charles were accompanied or masked by gifts, including a Titian and a bust of Charles by Bernini. Courtiers like the dubious Balthazar Gerbier, the Roman Catholic Tobie Mathew, and Endymion Porter with his Romanist wife, were used as middle-men in transactions with Catholic states, mingling diplomacy and art-collecting. These links with the Continent and with Rome were tightened by Henrietta Maria. Partly through her influence conversions to Rome became frequent in the Court circle, despite Charles's disapproval. The politics and taste of her own group, including Jermyn, Mathew, and Suckling, were influenced by her French origin, and her interests ran to drama and the masque. Court life under her influence seems to have been dignified if frivolous.

Behind this Court, at its zenith in the thirties, lay the 'personal rule' of Charles. It was made possible by some dubious fiscal expedients, and by others legally correct but politically unwise. Under this rule the integrity of the judges became suspect: even Strafford, though unsparing in the enforcement of royal policy, profited by his position, and lesser men more intimately associated with the Court made corrupt profits. When such a régime championed the social welfare of the lower classes, it could not but be suspected of using this as a pretext for actions against its political opponents among the upper classes. This political bias and the Roman Catholic aura clinging to the Court tended to isolate it from many Englishmen. During the 1620s the opposing political terms 'Court' and 'Country' had gained currency, but in the thirties poets like Carew, Fanshawe and Townshend fostered the royal illusion of national contentment.[5]

The two universities were at this period well within the orbit of Crown and government; both were within easy distance of London, and both owed to James their exemption from subsidies and their representation in Parliament. The reigns of the first two Stuarts saw an increase in royal interference not only in the universities, in the election of Chancellors (Buckingham and Holland at Cambridge, and Laud at Oxford), but also in the colleges. Just as the pulpits were 'tuned', so the discipline and curriculum of the universities (teaching, not research, institutions) were matters of concern to the Crown; they were, in an age of religio-political crisis, 'the nurseries of our religion' and as such had to be safeguarded.

The university population in this period seems to have been somewhat over 5,000, and the average age of undergraduates entering the colleges about sixteen. From the middle of the sixteenth century to 1642 enrolment rose rapidly and with it the proportion of sons of the nobility and gentry, although the universities were always less socially exclusive than the Inns of Court. Scholarly training became a gentlemanly ideal, even if degrees were not always taken. To meet this changed function the undergraduate curriculum was modified to give more emphasis on the humanist subjects, grammar and rhetoric; logic, however, retained pride of place. Severe criticisms of university life and education were made by many contemporaries: those of Bacon and Milton are well known. At both universities, though, there were innovations: at Cambridge the anti-Aristotelian logic of Petrus Ramus was used, and there was an endowment for the study of ancient history in 1628; at Oxford geometry was introduced into the undergraduate course with the foundation in 1619 of the Savilian Chair of Geometry and Astronomy, whose holder was to lecture taking into account Copernican views, while in the 1630s Greek and Arabic were prescribed. Oxford, too, received Sir Thomas Bodley's munificent gift in 1605 of a library which became second only to that of the Vatican. At both universities there is some evidence in the mid-seventeenth century of a widening of reading and studies under college tutors. Nevertheless the framework remained the statutory curriculum and Aristotle remained dominant throughout the seventeenth century, whether in Laud's Oxford statutes of 1636, where his authority was described as paramount, or in the teaching of an (advanced) Cambridge college tutor in the 1650s, James Duport. The dominance of Aristotle and his later commentators was in content and in method. In content, its apriority was most objectionable in physics, but generally the weight of authority might be stultifying. In method, Latin disputations and declamations remained the universities' means of training and testing, and their highly verbal, speculative and dialectical character shaped educated minds of the period. It was, perhaps, a more lively educational tool than has been thought, and large numbers of learned, cultivated and intellectually adventurous men emerged from this environment.[6]

Although theology was not part of the undergraduate curriculum, and the universities were not merely clerical seminaries, nevertheless university life, even more than the life of society, was pervaded by religious concern and theological debate. Attendance at college chapel, daily religious observance, 'diting' of sermons were part of undergraduate life, even for those for whom the university was but one phase of a liberal education leading on to a more or less cultivated life of squirearchical responsibilities. This characteristic was strengthened by the role of the university as a central element in training for holy orders: the tone was set by bachelors going on to the M.A., intending divines and fellows of colleges. Controversial theology dominated the Cambridge of the thirties, for instance, when among the fellows were Jeremy Taylor at Caius, Crashaw and Joseph Beaumont at Peterhouse, and Cleveland at St John's. Native and foreign observers noted also the prominence of ecclesiastical controversy. The party alignment which was growing in the country was naturally earlier and sharper in the clerical university world. At Cambridge, Peterhouse under Matthew Wren and Cosin, and Pembroke under Lancelot Andrewes and his successors, led the high church group, while the Puritan strongholds were Emmanuel, the college of so many preachers who emigrated to the New World, and Cromwell's college, Sidney Sussex. At Oxford, by tradition less Puritan, the division crystallized round the academic career of Laud, and religious controversy was exacerbated by personal ambitions and acrimony. By Laud's efforts as Chancellor, high church doctrine took hold of Oxford, giving it the character it retained after the Restoration.

London gained something of the character of a university town from the Inns of Court, probably accommodating about a thousand members. The four Inns were the means of entry into the profitable and expanding profession of common lawyers, and their students consequently increased rapidly in this period. Like the universities, however, they were filled increasingly by the sons of the nobility and gentry. For a future J.P. or perhaps M.P., and equally for a future landowner, some knowledge of the tortuous ways of the common law in a highly legalistic age was desirable, though it is debatable how much mastery of this exceptionally difficult subject could be acquired by 'non-professional' students. But it was not merely for their 'black-letter learning' that Ben Jonson (admittedly in a dedication) praised the Inns as 'the noblest nurseries of humanity and liberty in the kingdom'. Pre-eminently in this period from the late sixteenth century to the Civil War, the Inns acted as metropolitan academies or finishing schools for 'gentlemen of the best qualities'. The young student could polish himself by taking lessons in music, dancing and fencing: he would 'buy an Ovid with a Littleton',* or, according to a satirist, show a marked preference for 'Shakespeare's plaies instead of my Lord Coke'.[7] Meanwhile the regular exercises of his legal training (case-putting, bolts and moots), like those of the

* Thomas Littleton's treatise *Of Tenures* was the indispensable textbook on the law of real property.

universities, sharpened his memory and verbal aptitude. The general education owed its quality to the society to be found at the Inns; 'the liveliest, the most intelligent, and certainly the most influential society England could furnish', it has been called.[8] Eminent lawyers, such as Bacon and Coke, remained in close touch with their Inns, while the majority of their famous contemporaries had been at one of the Inns: Selden, Strafford and Hampden at the Inner Temple; Campion and Suckling at Gray's Inn; Whitelocke, Hyde and Carew at the Middle Temple; Quarles, Benlowes, Donne and Prynne at Lincoln's Inn. The society described in their autobiographies by Hyde and Whitelocke was obviously stimulating and absorbing. The preachers at the Inns were among the best in the country: Donne, for whose sermon in 1623 at the consecration of the new chapel of Lincoln's Inn there was such a crowd that 'two or three were ... taken up dead for the time', or the Puritan Richard Sibbes at Gray's Inn, one of whose sermons, bought at the door from a pedlar, converted Baxter. The Inns delighted in dramatic entertainments combining music, poetry and spectacle. If nothing in this period came up to *Twelfth Night*, performed in 1602 in the Middle Temple, there were masques by Chapman and Francis Beaumont to celebrate the wedding of Elizabeth of Bohemia, and the exceptionally magnificent masque, with music by William Lawes, presented to the King and Queen in 1634 by all four Inns. It is no wonder that Hyde in his student days found it difficult to tear himself away from 'study and conversation' in London.

Despite its urban aspects, English society was rooted in the land. The rhythms of society corresponded with those of agriculture, the long vacations of universities and law courts coinciding with harvesttime. In such a society the locality had a reality and attraction for its inhabitants, and the term 'my country' during the century commonly meant 'my county'. The county was the significant unit, socially and politically as well as administratively. The role of localism is being increasingly explored and understood by historians.

Although some of the nobility and gentry were acquiring town houses, the centre of life and work remained for most of them the country house with its park and estates. Notwithstanding the economic situation, many houses (of office-holders especially) were built or extended in this period: Audley End, Hatfield, Castle Ashby,

Wilton and Bolsover are among the famous; but the mixed Jacobean and the purer Italianate styles are found in numerous country houses, large and small. There were already 'prodigy houses', but an old house like Penshurst, celebrated by Ben Jonson, or a new one like Fairfax's Nun Appleton, rebuilt on the old plan, had a lay-out fitting the old ways and relationships.[9] The government insisted strongly on the duties of the landowner to his neighbourhood: not only did he maintain order and provide employment, but his household was often a social and educational centre. Noblemen and frequently gentry had in their households chaplains, tutors, pensioners, 'gentlemen', and boys from neighbouring families sent to them for a training, though not everyone could make his table, like the Earl of Clare's, 'a continued *Convivium Philosophale*'. How far the absentee landlordism and the decay of 'hospitality', of which both government and moralists complained, had gone it is impossible to say. Probably it was most marked in the home counties, but in many districts the old 'hospitality' continued.

No generalization can hope to apply to all the nobility or to the 500 knights and 16,000 gentlemen (the estimate of Thomas Wilson in 1600). The incomes within a social class varied immensely; variations arose out of the different ways in which estates were utilized and land cultivated; the gentry of the home counties close to the economic and intellectual influences of London had a different environment from those of remote northern districts; those within the orbit of the Court differed from those outside it. It is a far cry from the Dorset squire, Henry Hastings, as portrayed by his famous neighbour Shaftesbury, his house littered with the apparatus of hunting, hawking, smoking, and dicing, his staple books the Bible and the *Book of Martyrs*, to the learned, cultivated Kentish gentry – the Twysdens, Sandys, Filmers, Derings, Culpepers and Digges, who followed in the steps of the historian Lambarde. The gentry and nobility covered the whole of this range: many were denounced as boorish, many kept abreast with current learning and literature, science and philosophy, took an interest in exploration, and wrote verses in their leisure. Among the nobility, the Earl of Newcastle patronized poets and dramatists, wrote verses and treatises on horses, made chemical experiments at Bolsover, and discussed problems of optics with Hobbes. Poetry, drama and philosophy were missing from the predominantly theological library of the fifth Earl of Bedford; interest in alchemy and American voyages was reflected in that of the ninth Earl of Northumberland. Among the gentry, 'to get learning' was common advice from father to son; libraries were becoming more common, and though the stock volumes were of theology, history, and law, literary works old and new were often there.

The normal picture is one of mixed occupations in the country: care of the estate and tenants, building, the duties of a J.P. or other commissioner of the Crown, hunting and hawking (there is a glimpse in the Knyvett letters of Thomas Knyvett, a Norfolk squire, discussing the ship-money levy with a neighbour while out hunting), entertaining, bowls and cards, music and reading. The correspondence of the Kentish Oxinden family, in the years up to the Civil War, reflects the day-to-day routine; the additions to the manorhouse, the trees and hedges planted (a tree for the birth of every child), the problems of education, careers, and marriage, the hereditary service on the estate, the portrait painting by Cornelius Janssen, and the letter-writing spiced occasionally with a quotation from one of Donne's poems. This country life was still the foundation of the cultivated society to be found in London, at Court, and in the universities and Inns of Court, forming the *milieu* of most literature before the Civil War.

Religion before the Civil War

Religion dominated both national and personal life in the early seventeenth century; in both it was a matter of life and death. Religious unity was judged essential to the welfare of society and its enforcement, therefore, the duty of the state. 'Whosoever bringeth in innovation in religion is a capital enemy of the Commonwealth', the House of Commons resolved in 1629; among individuals many, like Baxter, were 'serious and solicitous about my soul's everlasting state'. An intense interest in theological controversy, and to some extent in books of devotion, was common to almost all ranks of society. Probably nearly half of the books published between 1600 and 1640 were on religious topics. Their readers ranged from the nobility, through the gentry (Sir John Strode enjoined his son to read 'especially the book of God') to the yeomen, in whose inventories the books most commonly mentioned are the Bible and Foxe's *Book of*

Martyrs, the citizens, and the apprentices, of whose reading and debates Lilburne and the Baptist Kiffin have left records. In such a society, virtually without newspapers, the pulpit played an outstanding part. Contemporaries were at one in seeing this; Charles I and Laud in their attempts at censorship, the Puritans in their attempts to evade this by financing 'lecturers'*, and in their attacks on preachers like Mainwaring and Sibthorpe. To all the pulpit had a political as well as a religious significance; it was a way of reaching the vast bulk of the population. Church-going was legally enforceable, but equally sermons were a genuine popular interest.

The Church of England was still an inclusive Church, numbering, except for the Roman Catholics and a few Separatists, the whole nation. Under the Elizabethan compromise it had leaned towards Calvinism in its doctrines and theology, but retained in its structure and rites traditional elements and ambiguities differentiating it from the continental Reformed Churches. These were its two points of strain at the beginning of the century. Hooker's *Ecclesiastical Polity* had already marked out the Anglican road, vindicating that Church's position in relation to both Rome and Geneva, and establishing it on the basis of history and tradition as well as of Scripture. His influence helped to make Anglicanism a favourable environment for learning and scholarship. There were, too, elements in Anglican thought making for tolerance; Anglican controversialists tended to show a lack of dogmatism, disclaiming infallibility and exclusive salvation for their Church, while the spread of Arminian† views on free will and salvation softened the Calvinist conception of God. Laud himself hated this conception for its denial of mercy, and showed intellectual tolerance in some theological debates. Anglicans of the school of Lancelot Andrewes, Cosin and Laud sought for outward beauty in churches: altars were moved to the east and railed round; stained glass, candlesticks and organs were introduced to promote a dignity of ceremonial as 'the great witness to the world that our heart stands right'. The chapels at Peterhouse, at Little Gidding, and at Herbert's Bemerton showed also a new order and aesthetic awareness.

* These were clergymen, usually of Puritan leanings, who held no benefices and were appointed in market-towns and elsewhere, solely to preach. They were frequently paid by local corporations, and were virtually free from episcopal control.

† Deriving from the Dutch theologian, Jacob Arminius, d. 1610.

Much in this Anglicanism was Catholic: the stress on tradition and the return to the early Fathers; the comparative neglect of Protestant Reformers' writings; the beautifying of the churches, and the prime emphasis on the altar and the sacramental system rather than on the pulpit and the Scriptures. But intrinsically there was nothing Roman in it; although high Anglicans writing against Rome were ready (unlike their Puritan counterparts) to see in it a true if erring Church, a deep gulf lay between them and Rome. It is possible, however, to see reasons besides the sheer confusion of Catholic with Roman why their Puritan critics identified them with Popery. Laud's friend, Sir Kenelm Digby, returned to the religion of his birth; Chillingworth, Laud's godson, was a temporary convert to Rome, and numbers who moved with him in the royal circle went over. The Puritans noted that the Arminian minority among the clergy rose to power, not through weight of numbers but through favour with a king married to a French Roman Catholic. Laud epitomized this ecclesiastical monopoly; theoretically liberal, he had, nevertheless, inflexible ideas on uniformity or worship which he enforced by means of state machinery. Busy and officious in many spheres, social and political as well as religious, he roused peculiar hatred among Puritans, and irritation among non-Puritan Anglicans like Falkland, Hyde, George Digby and Verney. With high ideals, in practice he was unimaginative and unable to comprehend his opponents' position or even their honesty, so that his fiercest punishments were for attacks on himself and his fellow bishops.

The distinctive feature of the history of the Church before the Civil War was the growth and rise to power of Laudianism, but throughout there was an Anglicanism which was neither Laudian nor Puritan. It has been cogently argued that, although Arminian ideas were present from the late sixteenth century, until the 1620s most Anglicans, including bishops and 'mainstream Puritans', shared a common belief in the Calvinist doctrines of Predestination and Election, and that Arminianism, as it developed in the setting of the Anglicanism of the Elizabethan Settlement, was an innovatory and divisive force.[10] This new theological division caused heightened tension, which added to the former differences on ceremonies and church government. It fuelled resentment of the new pronounced Crown patronage of Arminian clergy and by Charles I's suppression of debate on the burning doctrinal issues. Under the goad of Laudian interference moderate Anglicans followed Puritan leadership, but the threat to the Prayer Book (as distinct from that to the bishops) in September 1641 rallied them against the Puritans. During the Civil War and Interregnum the persecution of the clergy and the suppression of the liturgy reversed this trend. Despite all the controversy, often bitter, we should perhaps recall the fact that the religious poems of George Herbert* were prized by men as diverse as Charles I, Richard Baxter and Cromwell's chaplain, Peter Sterry.

Undoubtedly the main swing of opinion up to the Civil War was with Puritanism. The definition of the word 'Puritan' puzzled contemporaries and still exercises historians.[11] 'Puritanism' covers a great diversity of people and represents rather a temper of mind within the Church of England than the nonconformity with which it is now associated. Political and economic frustration swelled the following of the Puritan leaders, and this Puritanism was based, like the early 'Protestantism' of Luther, on great negatives. But for many there was a positive core in the teachings of Calvin, and for some in the example of Geneva. The Calvinist scheme of Predestination and Election, deduced from the Scriptures, provided a framework for life. The convinced Puritan emerged from the despair of his doubt and remorse with a sense of salvation and of special insight into the ways of God, encouraging claims to infallibility. Such a pattern of Puritan spiritual development is revealed in many diaries, autobiographical writings, and speeches. The rigidity of this Calvinist theology gave a sense of security in dangerous times. To some, further reformation of the Church was needed; to others, the clean break of Geneva with the hierarchy and ritual of the past seemed the only sure defence of the nation against a Rome seen as Antichrist. In the face of the European conflict of Catholic and Protestant, Laudian Anglicanism seemed a perversion of the Elizabethan Church and a betrayal of Protestant unity. Alarm and irritation grew during the thirties, a period of Habsburg victories after the death of Gustavus Adolphus and of political impotence for the domestic opposition in Church and State.

A note of fanaticism, even of hysteria, appeared among the Puritan critics of Laud at this time. If his authoritarian methods justified some

* His disquiet at the 'debates and fretting jealousies' in the Church is mentioned by C. V. Wedgwood in *Poetry and Politics under the Stuarts*, p. 54.

of these protests, their tone often deserved his scathing references to 'the vulgar sort'. William Prynne is the typical Puritan of the text-book; between 1627 and 1640 he published nearly a score of pamphlets, among the most virulent of their kind, and spent at least six years in prison. Drinking, the drama, 'the Unloveliness of Lovelocks', and breaking of the Sabbath alike came under his indiscriminate denunciation. Plays were 'the very poison and corruption of men's minds and manners'; while in sanctioning the 'Book of Sports',* the bishops had done no more than Beelzebub, were he an archbishop, could have done 'to make it [the Sabbath] the Devil's day instead of the Lord's day'. Prynne was not alone in making such extravagant charges against the bishops: Milton's pamphlets of 1641 descend to coarse and unreasoned abuse, and significantly one of the Elizabethan Marprelate tracts was reprinted in 1642, and was followed by several imitations.

Yet to take Prynne as typical of the Puritans is to do injustice to the scope of Puritanism and the variety of Puritans. Puritanism has gained during the course of centuries a strong emotional connotation; its manifestations in New England, or in England in the nineteenth century, have drawn attention to its hostility to the arts, its intolerant morality, and its dull sabbatarianism. For many men, however, in this period, a Puritan temper was an understandable reaction to popular ignorance, indifference, and immorality; if they were serious in outlook, they often took pleasure in the arts and in sport. Cromwell's bowls, his hunting and hawking and delight in music, Milton's love of music and classical poetry, John Hutchinson's enjoyment of music, painting, and tennis suggest the need for qualifications. Nevertheless, there was the danger that the intense seriousness of the Puritan outlook would drive out what Baxter called 'the sins which go under the name of pastimes', and with them the pursuit of the arts. The attacks on traditional country celebrations like May-day games and wakes before the Civil War were followed under Puritan rule by the ban on organs in churches and the closing of the theatres.

---

* This royal declaration authorizing certain sports on Sundays after divine service was first issued in 1617 to settle a dispute in Lancashire, but, in face of opposition, not generally enforced by James. In 1633 it was reissued by Charles, who insisted that it should be read by the clergy in every church, many clergymen were penalized for disobedience.

The complexity of Puritanism is seen in its ambiguous relation to liberty and toleration. In its pre-Civil War form it was a protest on behalf of the individual conscience against the authority of lordly bishops; John Lilburne's championship of liberty had a direct source in his Calvinist convictions. But it was not a general assertion of liberty of conscience; the Grand Remonstrance of the Commons in 1641 gave the assurance that 'it is far from our purpose or desire to let loose the golden reins of discipline and government in the church'. Already there was among the Puritans a strong element inclining to an authoritarian uniformity, reminiscent of Laud's, which was expressed in the alliance with Scottish Presbyterianism. The more substantial Puritan contribution to liberty of thought lay with a different element, that of the sects. Their rise to power came later, out of the confusion of the Civil War, and their very multiplication furthered a toleration which was only slowly and partially willed for its own sake.

A small tributary to the main stream of religious thought flowed from Great Tew, near Oxford. Here. separate from both Laudians and Puritans, but linked with Anglicanism of the Hooker tradition, was a small group of men, meeting regularly during the thirties at the country house of Lord Falkland. Falkland provided for his friends a civilized background to their discussions; as his interests changed, literary men such as Jonson, Carew, and Waller were succeeded in the Great Tew circle by philosophers and theologians, several from Oxford – including John Earle, who professed to have learned more at Great Tew than ever he had at Oxford. The essential spirit of Great Tew can be gauged from Falkland's frequent quoting from Erasmus. The writings of the members of the circle, Falkland, Chillingworth, and, above all, John Hales of Eton College, show the reaction of thoughtful religious men to the bitter denominational controversy so characteristic of the age. 'Nothing troubled him more than the brawls which were grown from religion,' wrote Edward Hyde (one of the circle) of Hales. The sight of the disputes between Dutch Calvinists and Arminians at the Synod of Dort had caused him to 'bid good night to John Calvin'. Intolerant dogmatism and human claims to infallibility in religion seemed to Great Tew alien to the Christian spirit of charity, and a defect of the Protestant Reformers as much as of Rome. The Christian humanism of the circle led to

Chillingworth's plea for religious toleration by law and Hales's for unity among all kinds of Christians on the basis of the common elements in their beliefs. Such solvents of intolerance had their echo in fashionable society; Suckling, if he lamented that Falkland was 'gone with religion', wrote, about 1637, *An Account of Religion by Reason*. Like that of Great Tew, the thought of George Herbert's brother, Lord Herbert of Cherbury, must be seen against the background of religious controversy reflected in Donne's third satire. Even Chillingworth, according to Hyde, in face of the rival claims to infallibility, 'contracted such a habit of doubting that by degrees he grew confident of nothing'. Lord Herbert in his search for a common denominator went outside the Christian religion. His *De Veritate*, published in 1624, was an attempt to formulate a 'natural religion' commanding universal assent. This foreshadowing of eighteenth-century deism had, as far as can be judged, little influence, but such as it was it contributed to the gradual undermining of the bases of religious intolerance in the century as a whole.

The Civil War: Disintegration and Reform Projects

The mounting opposition to the government in Church and State found vent in the Long Parliament of 1640. For its first few months the Commons were united in a 'Country' opposition, future Royalists and Parliamentarians joining to curb prerogative government and establish a common law monarchy. It was, however, impossible to achieve the mutual trust between King and Houses of Parliament essential for such a monarchy. The Commons started from an ingrained fear and hatred of Popery and an immovable belief in a large-scale Popish plot. The intrigues of Henrietta Maria, the Army Plot of Goring and Suckling, and, above all, the Irish massacre of November 1641, fed this conspiratorial theory. On his side Charles showed little political sense and some duplicity, although the first approach to violence, the execution of Strafford, had come from the Commons. Fear and distrust, reinforced by radical, popular pressure in London, led Pym and the majority during the autumn of 1641 into novel and revolutionary claims, which alienated a substantial minority of their fellow members. This minority had appeared earlier in certain ecclesiastical debates, and now based itself not only on the Prayer Book but on the existing constitution.

Gradually, and almost in spite of Charles's own unwise activities, including the attempted arrest of the five members, this minority became the King's party. Its constitutional stand was strengthened by arbitrary actions on the part of the majority (the imprisonment of the Kentish champions of the Church, among them Lovelace, antagonizing many) and by apprehension of social anarchy.

The departure of the King and Queen from London in January 1642 closed a chapter: although a Court existed later at Oxford, it could not reproduce the atmosphere of the thirties, and for eighteen years Whitehall ceased to be the hub of society. Slowly, with extreme reluctance and continued negotiation, the parties aligned themselves during the summer. No single or simple explanation will account for the way the men divided; political and religious issues, social distinctions played their part, but equally, personal characteristics, family traditions, and local feuds. Each county had its own variations on the theme of civil division. The broad division into Royalist north and west and Parliamentarian south and east obscures the substantial minorities in each area. Among the peers, about eighty followed Charles, some thirty supported Parliament, and another twenty took no part; the division among the M.P.s elected between 1640 and 1642, about three hundred Parliamentarians and about two hundred and thirty Royalists, reflected the very real division among the gentry. Tenants usually followed their lords, but freeholders might act independently, often for Parliament. The indecision and changes of side at the beginning and the splits within so many families were of the essence of the English Civil War; so were the large number of neutrals and the local neutrality agreements.[12] London was a conspicuous exception to this temper, and the determination of its trained bands prevented a speedy Royalist victory. On both sides there were a few leaders with military experience gained as volunteers on the Continent, but the trained soldiers to follow them were almost completely lacking. During the early campaigns, therefore, amateur warfare was the rule. Although volunteers were plentiful at first, both sides were reduced to impressment by 1643, and altogether no more than 60,000 or 70,000 took part in the war on each side. Soon the outcome of the war was seen to depend on which side could first organize an efficient army. Cromwell's drive gave this advantage to Parliament in the raising of the New Model Army. Regular pay, centralized control not deflected by local considerations, recruitment in strongly Puritan areas, and a single-minded concern for efficiency on the part of its commanders, gave it the decisive victory of the First Civil War at Naseby.

To estimate the effects on Caroline society of the ten years of war from 1642 to 1652 is a very difficult task, for which the materials are as yet incomplete. The fighting, if not very intensive (much of it was in skirmishes, raids, and sieges of towns, castles and country houses), extended to practically every county. The number of country houses destroyed or damaged was considerable, while the pillaging and free quartering of soldiers injured whole districts. Interference by both sides with communications affected trade, and in some areas, in the south and south-west particularly, there was industrial depression. The removal of strict central control, together with the war itself, led to a breakdown of the poor law administration in many areas and the increase of distress. Even if recovery was comparatively swift in the fifties, there had been real dislocation of the economy during the forties.

The Caroline Court circle had been swiftly broken; as early as 1641 Jermyn and Suckling had fled abroad. In the first Civil War the talents of poets like Cleveland and Denham were used in satirical Royalist propaganda.[13] Suckling died in 1642, 'little Sid' Godolphin was killed in 1643, and by the late forties Fanshawe, Davenant, and Denham were in exile. Great Tew also was dispersed: Falkland was killed at Newbury; Chillingworth died in 1644 after capture by the Parliamentarians at the siege of Arundel Castle; Hammond and Earle were deprived of their livings and Hales of his Fellowship, while Hyde spent his exile working for a restoration and writing his *History of the Rebellion*. In the universities, too, there was upheaval: after military vicissitudes, religious and political tests were imposed on the Fellows and many were expelled. Crashaw, ejected from Peterhouse in 1643, went abroad and became a Roman Catholic; Cowley, expelled from Trinity, became cipher-secretary to Henrietta Maria; at Cambridge a majority of the Fellows and heads of Colleges was ejected, and at Oxford a total of about four hundred members of foundations. Yet if the personnel changed, the traditions of learning were upheld to a remarkable degree.

Among the aristocracy and gentry as a whole there were the

casualties of war, and among the Royalists, the financial oppression of taxes, fines, and confiscations. Many had already made heavy sacrifices for the King, if not on the scale of the Marquis of Worcester's £700,000. As Parliament extended its control, taxation and heavy fines for 'delinquency', levied after sequestration of their estates, forced many Royalists to sell land; later the Commonwealth government confiscated the lands of seven hundred prominent 'delinquents'. The large-scale public sales of lands – royal, episcopal, and private – benefited especially London merchants, Parliamentarian officials, and army officers, but the gentry had a substantial share. The total picture should not be made over-tragic, though it left a legacy of revenge to the Restoration period; there were many legal subterfuges whereby Royalists evaded the full penalties. Though some families were ruined by the war, many were able to weather the storm, somewhat impoverished, but by judicious sacrifice retaining the bulk of their lands. The misfortunes of the Verney family, including deaths, exile and loss, can be curiously compared with the wartime Grand Tour of John Evelyn, who on his return bought back his father-in-law's confiscated estate and began, literally, to cultivate his garden at Deptford.

Broadly the forties saw the destruction of the traditional framework of authority in Church and State. In the Church the abolition of the High Commission removed the strongest disciplinary sanction; Laud was executed in 1645, and about a third of the parish clergy were ejected from their livings. The attempt, during the Parliamentary alliance with the Scots, to replace the Anglican order by the Presbyterian discipline had only a limited success, and Milton's 'new Presbyter' was by no means everywhere 'old Priest writ large'. In the secular sphere, if taxation ('the sinews of war') had never been so efficiently collected as in the areas under Parliamentary control, in general there was a breakdown of old controls. Without the Star Chamber central control over the localities was weakened, while for three years the traditional censorship of the Press lapsed. The symbolic climax was the execution of the King and the abolition of the House of Lords.

This unprecedented opportunity for reform and rebuilding encouraged a widespread visionary Utopianism; hopes ran high of making this 'a truly happy and wholly free nation'. Religious inspiration lay behind this reforming idealism, and an extraordinary number of men were gripped by the conviction of the imminence of Christ's kingdom. Cromwell opened the 'Parliament of Saints' in 1653 with the words, 'Why should we be afraid to say or think, that this way may be the door to usher in the things that God hath promised and prophesied of?' Such vivid consciousness of the Scriptures was common; the Puritan domination of the pulpit for the past half-century had encouraged the popular study of the Bible, and the fruits of that impulse appeared as the traditional controls and inhibitions were loosened. From 1641 complaints appeared of 'mechanick preachers': craftsmen of all kinds, apprentices, yeomen, labourers, found each his own personal inspiration in the Scriptures. George Fox recorded characteristically how 'I would get into the orchard, or the fields, with my Bible by myself'. The widespread and undirected study of the Bible added to the Puritan elevation of the individual conscience – 'conscience obliging above or against human and outward constitutions' – multiplied the sects and encouraged movement by individuals from one to another. By 1646 a Presbyterian opponent had counted sixteen groups and over two hundred 'heresies' of recent growth. This vigorous, if at times eccentric, religious life could not be contained within the Presbyterian 'conscience prison'. Among the Puritans of the left the belief that God's truth was still being revealed and that they should 'stand ready to receive further light' made for liberty of conscience and toleration. The doctrine of the 'inner light' and the reaction against Predestination encouraged a shift from dogmatic religion towards a more rational theology and a more humane religion. Yet at times there was only the noise of shrill and bitter controversy between opposing dogmatists.

In social terms, the religious activity of the forties meant that elements of society, hitherto silent, were becoming vocal in preaching, organizing, and writing. The spate of pamphlets was unprecedented: the bookseller George Thomason collected 20,000 published during the Civil War and Interregnum. The artificial conditions of the New Model Army and its atmosphere of religious enthusiasm encouraged the voice of the common people. 'The consciences of common men', wrote A. S. P. Woodhouse, 'were a new phenomenon in politics', and nowhere did they find clearer expression than in the debates of the Army Council in 1647–9, at which the rank and file were represented. Fundamentals of politics were discussed in the open; the debate between the conservative Ireton and the radical Rainborough moved the latter to this assertion: 'I do think that the poorest man in England is not at all bound in a strict sense to that government that he hath not had a voice to put himself under.'

The zeal for radical reform which had its roots in religion was soon applied to secular concerns, and many aspects of society came under debate. As Baxter saw, Church democracy led on easily (though not invariably) to State democracy. The heterogeneous Levellers, led by the first-class publicist John Lilburne, had strong democratic tendencies. In their tenets, Lilburne's Calvinist-based individualism and his vein of historicism derived from Coke mingled with William Walwyn's rational tendencies coming from classical writers and Montaigne. The Levellers demanded a broad franchise, a fairer distribution of Parliamentary seats, and the protection of the people's rights by a fundamental law binding their representatives. Despite their name, they were not social egalitarians; the reform of the economic order as distinct from the political was the hope of the small group of Diggers. Their programme was essentially agrarian: first common lands and then private estates were to become common property, but not by violence. The earth, their leader Winstanley wrote, was to become 'a common treasury again' by all men 'acting in righteousness one to another'. Winstanley's communism seems to have sprung almost wholly from his study of the Bible, combined with a mystical temper very close to that of the Quakers. The ferment of reforming idealism found a wide variety of outlets, some surprisingly modern such as suggestions for woman's suffrage and free medical service for the poor. There was a strong movement for simplifying the complexities of the law and, as might be expected, education was radically debated. Pamphlets abounded on improving and up-dating education, and Parliament went so far as to make provision in Wales for state-aided schools. Milton's contribution to the debate (1644) took the form of a letter to Samuel Hartlib, one of an influential trio of reformers who came over from the war-torn continent. The most original was Comenius (Jan Amos Komenský), the eminent Bohemian educationist, who was invited to England in 1641 to forward reform. Baconian influence and a visionary Millenarianism combined in his large plans for universal knowledge and Protestant unity. After his brief stay in England his views were propagated by his fellow-Baconians, John Dury and the indefatigable Hartlib, a man of wide English and continental contacts, constantly advocating ambitious schemes (some Utopian) for educational and social reform, the advancement of learning and the promotion of improvements in agriculture and industry.[14]

Towards Stability

An attempt at stabilization was inevitable sooner or later. With the return to something approaching normality in the mid-fifties, the pressure behind the vigorous, optimistic radicalism of the forties gradually relaxed. The end of serious fighting came at Worcester in 1651, and Cromwell, by then the key-figure, turned to the problems of peacetime organization. The Digger experiment in Surrey had been broken up in 1649, and the Leveller movement in the army had been crushed at Burford, even if Lilburne remained the irrepressible champion of a civilian remnant. Puritan Millenarianism of an undemocratic kind – rule by the elect, not by the elected – found short-lived expression in the 'Parliament of Saints'. When the moderate members voted its dissolution they coincided with Cromwell's disillusion and later, looking back, he could refer to it as a product of 'my simplicity', 'a story of my own weakness and folly'. Milton shared this disillusion after his earlier exaltation when he expected 'the jubilee and resurrection of the state' and believed that 'God shakes a Kingdom with strong and healthful commotions to a general reforming', but to the last he was faithful to 'the good Old Cause'.

There had been no social revolution during the Civil War; the Diggers from a practical point of view had been insignificant, and the bulk of the Levellers strongly upheld the rights of private property. Confiscated property had been sold chiefly in large lots to comparatively wealthy purchasers including speculators. Moreover, the traditional checks on enclosure were weakened, and a new plan to safeguard copyhold tenants from exploitation failed. Under the Protectorate the country gentry and lawyers in Parliament became more influential, although the civilian groups never superseded the army. Four years before the Restoration of the King there was a return to the older forms of government; a second chamber was restored and the Commons' privileges were guaranteed in the traditional way. Cromwell's refusal of the offer of the crown did not prevent him assuming many of its attributes, including the hereditary succession of his son. The Puritan zeal for righteousness led him still to attempt forcible moral reform, but on the whole he worked for the ideal he set before his last Parliament, to be 'the repairers of breaches, and the restorers of paths to dwell in'.

Intellectual life continued with a vigour surprising in view of the purges of church and universities. Some of it was perforce in exile: Hobbes wrote some of his major works in Paris and had as friends the scientific philosophers Mersenne and Gassendi, while Kenelm Digby, a friend of Descartes, continued his philosophical writings and scientific experiments. At home, at first chiefly in London, groups with scientific interests were active in the late forties. There were Hartlib's ambitious Comenian schemes for the dissemination of scientific information, the 'Invisible College', which attracted the youthful Robert Boyle for its philosophy which 'values no knowledge, but as it hath a tendency to use', and, most important, the group inspired by Theodore Haak, a refugee from the Palatinate. This met from about 1645 at Gresham College and elsewhere, to discuss 'Physick, Anatomy, Geometry, Astronomy, Navigation, Statics, Magneticks, Chymicks, Mechanicks, and Natural Experiments with the state of these studies at home and abroad', and excluded from debate theology and state affairs. Among its members were the Copernican, John Wilkins, and the mathematician, John Wallis, both clergymen, and various leading physicians. From 1648 several active members moved to academic posts at Oxford, replacing ejected Royalists. Wilkins, the Warden of Wadham College (subsequently Cromwell's brother-in-law, and later Bishop of Chester), became the key figure of a brilliant and fertile group which met regularly to perform experiments according to the 'new philosophy', 'conversing in quiet ... without being engaged in the passions and madness of that dismal age'. By 1652 the thirty members included Parliamentarians like the moderate Wilkins himself, John Wallis, Savilian Professor of Geometry, once decoder of Royalist despatches, and William Petty, Professor of Anatomy and originator of 'political arithmetic'. But there were also the Royalist, Seth Ward, Professor of

Astronomy and future Bishop of Salisbury, and younger men such as Robert Boyle, 'the father of modern Chemistry', son of the Earl of Cork, and Christopher Wren, as yet a scientist and not an architect, from a Royalist clerical family. New posts took several members away from Oxford in the late fifties, but meetings continued there and in London, drawing in new, interested *virtuosi*, like John Evelyn.[15]

At Cambridge, where Wilkins went in 1659, the group of philosophers and moralists known as the Cambridge Platonists was active. Almost all belonged to the Puritan Emmanuel College and were opposed to 'mere speculation' in religion as in science. They had affinities with the Great Tew circle in their tolerance and rational leanings, but they were more concerned with the impact of science on religion, for they faced the implications of the philosophical systems of Descartes and Hobbes. They combined a rationalism which fostered the Latitudinarianism of churchmen of the later seventeenth century with a mysticism of Platonist origin.

The focal point of the development of the 'new philosophy' was, however, to be in London. Immediately after the Restoration, the *virtuosi*, resuming their meetings there after the upheavals of 1659, formally instituted a society which gained Charles II's interest and patronage. In 1662 the Royal Society 'for the Improving of Natural Knowledge' was incorporated, its motto, *Nullius in verba*,* challenging the old philosophy's dependence on authorities. John Wilkins was joint secretary and there were 115 fellows of varying political and denominational pasts ranging from Kenelm Digby to Theodore Haak. The number grew as royal favour made membership fashionable. The distinguishing aim of the Royal Society was 'raysing a new Philosophy' in a systematic, long-term way by co-operative effort, 'the joynt force of many men', engaged in original scientific experiments, which, from 1665, were recorded in the Transactions. The Society aimed 'to overcome the mysteries of all the works of Nature' and to apply that knowledge 'for the benefit of human life'. In tackling the whole range of scientific knowledge, the old

---

*Part of a quotation from Horace: '*Nullius addictus jurare in verba magistri*', freely translated by E. N. da C. Andrade in his life of Isaac Newton as 'We don't take anybody's word for it'.

distinction between the 'liberal' and the 'mechanic'* sciences was abandoned: in accordance with Bacon's vision, hand and mind were joined. Equally, though some of the early experiments were purely utilitarian (cider-making, for example) and some trivial and eccentric, earning the satire of Samuel Butler, Bacon's 'light-bearing' as well as his 'fruit-bearing' experiments were the ideal. The *History of the Royal Society* (1667) by Thomas Sprat (later Bishop of Rochester), at once history, defence and propaganda, embodies the ethos – the triumphant optimism of the 'New Philosophy', the 'Real Philosophy'. For him the Society was trying to free its activities from the 'humours and passions of the Sects'. The language of experimental philosophy was to be of a 'mathematical plainness', not that of 'wits and scholars' or the scholastic, word-spinning disputations, but resembling that of 'the artisan, the countryman, the merchant'. None the less, he asserted, the great majority of the Society's members were not tied by utilitarian pursuits, but were 'gentlemen, free and unconfin'd'.

The Restoration, celebrated (according to C. V. Wedgwood) by more poems and ballads than any other event of the century, restored a king already educated by exile and later by the example of France. Charles II's experiences had left him with an indifference to religion predisposing him to tolerance, but also a strong determination never to go on his travels again. In the Royal Society Sprat pointed to 'an unusual sight to the English Nation, that men of disagreeing parties, and ways of life, have forgotten to hate, and have met in the unanimous advancement of the same Works': this was a rational ideal among the *virtuosi*. In a broader context, Samuel Butler's satire on the Puritans, *Hudibras* (1662), which delighted the King and achieved nine editions within a year, reflected and intensified a general reaction which made 'fanatic' a term of opprobrium and 'enthusiasm' suspect. Although in the long run this reaction was to make for tolerance, its immediate expression was the desire for revenge and restitution in

* The word is used here to refer to the classical and medieval educational distinction between subjects requiring intellectual and manual ability. It covers Bacon's use of it to mean pertaining to craftsmen and artisans. It must not be confused with the 'mechanic' or 'mechanical' philosophy, which saw the universe as a mechanism. Christopher Hill, in pursuit of his argument in *Intellectual Origins of the English Revolution*, 66, n. 2, assimilated the two meanings, but in *The World Turned Upside Down*, 237, confessed to the confusion.

Church and State on the part of displaced clergy and injured cavaliers. The failure of negotiations for a comprehensive church of the old type and the subsequent punitive legislation changed the nature of English religious and social life by transforming Puritans into a recognized but separate and excluded non-conformity, subject, until 1689, to intermittent persecution. The painful and complex experience of the Civil War and its aftermath cast a long shadow forward over individuals, state and society.

NOTES

1. A useful brief appraisal of the 'gentry controversy' is in the admirable Introduction to *The Origins of the English Civil War*, ed. C. Russell (1973), which has good bibliographies.

2. The history of science in this period is a complex and much debated subject. There are good general accounts in A. R. Hall, *The Scientific Revolution 1500–1800* (1954), A. C. Crombie in the *New Cambridge Modern History*, Vol. IV, and H. F. Kearney, *Science and Change* (1971). The older books, E. C. Burtt, *The Metaphysical Foundations of Modern Physical Science* (1925, rev. 1932) and B. Willey, *The Seventeenth-Century Background* (1934) are still illuminating. More recently, the attempt by Christopher Hill in *Intellectual Origins of the English Revolution* (1965) to relate science to other aspects of thought and society stimulated much criticism and lively debate: see the articles in *The Intellectual Revolution of the Seventeenth Century*, ed. C. Webster (1974) and H. F. Kearney's 'Scientists and Society' in *The English Revolution*, ed. E. W. Ives (1968). K. V. Thomas, *Religion and the Decline of Magic* (1971), provides a wealth of material to be taken into account in this context as in others.

3. D. Bush, *English Literature in the Earlier Seventeenth Century* (2nd edn 1962), 27, quotes figures showing that between 1500 and 1630 the annual production of books rose from about 45 to about 460, and by 1640 approached 600. Between 1640 and 1660 the number greatly increased. For the size of editions and impressions see H. S. Bennett, *English Books and Readers 1558–1603*, 297–8 and K. V. Thomas, 294.

4. Quoted from Gervase Holles, *Memorials of the Holles Family*, 111.

5. R. Ashton in *The English Civil War: Conservatism and Revolution 1603–49* (1978) warns against a too rigid contrasting of the 'two cultures', Court and Country, and stresses the intertwining of the two.

6. See W. T. Costello, *The Scholastic Curriculum at Early Seventeenth-Century Cambridge* (1958) and M. H. Curtis, *Oxford and Cambridge in Transition 1558–1642* (1959), together with Hill's criticisms of Curtis in the Appendix to *The Intellectual Origins of the English Revolution*.

7. Quoted by W. R. Prest, *The Inns of Court under Elizabeth I and the Early Stuarts 1590–1640* (1972), 138 and 156.

8. By G. M. Young, 'Shakespeare and the Termers', *Proceedings of the British Academy*, XXXIII.

9. See G. R. Hibbard, 'The Country House Poem of the Seventeenth Century' in *Journal of Warburg and Courtauld Institutes*, XIX (1956) and A. Everitt, 'The County Community' in *The English Revolution*, ed. E. W. Ives.

10. N. Tyacke, 'Puritanism, Arminianism and Counter-Revolution' in *The Origins of the English Civil War*, ed. E. Russell and R. Ashton, *The English Civil War*. Historians have reacted against polarization and now stress the moderates and the middle ground, but the picture is confused and complex.

11. See Christopher Hill, 'The Definition of a Puritan' in *Society and Puritanism in Pre-Revolutionary England* (1964).

12. Continuing study of the divisions in the Civil War has emphasized neutralism and the complexity and local individuality of the subject. See A. M. Everitt, *The Local Community and the Great Rebellion* (1969) and the summary of recent work given by R. Ashton.

13. See C. V. Wedgwood, *Poetry and Politics under the Stuarts* (1960), ch. III.

14. See the lively account of them by H. R. Trevor Roper, 'Three Foreigners: The Philosophers of the Puritan Revolution' in his *Religion, the Reformation and Social Change* (1967).

15. The nature and composition of these groups and their relationship to the Royal Society form an area of continuing debate between historians. The issue is linked with differing views about the general connection of scientific development with religious, political and social alignments. See the books mentioned in n. 2 and the bibliography in *The Interregnum, The Quest for Settlement 1646–60*, ed. G. E. Aylmer (1972). Like other controversies referred to in these notes, this one is fuelled by the unavoidable use of categorization of individuals: each label (e.g. gentry, bourgeois, country, Puritan, even Royalist and Parliamentarian), as Lawrence Stone has said, is 'valid for certain analytical purposes, none adequate as single all-embracing characterization', *The Causes of the English Revolution* (1972), 34.

PART II

A SURVEY OF LITERATURE FROM
DONNE TO MARVELL

R. G. COX

It is an undisputed fact of literary history that the first half of the
present century saw a greatly increased interest in the period from
Donne to Marvell and especially in the poetry of metaphysical wit.
This was to a considerable extent connected with the rise of a new
poetic movement in the work of Eliot, Pound and the later Yeats,
and the attendant reaction against the lingering habits and assumptions of late Victorian romanticism. The metaphysicals seemed to
provide an example of poetry open to a wide range of thought and
experience and free from restricted conventional notions of the
'poetical'. This sense of illuminating rediscovery, with its sometimes
exaggerated view of the affinity between the two ages, was particularly marked in the period between the wars, and in the post-war
decades there were those who would have dismissed it as merely a
temporary reaction. To a remarkable degree, however, the revaluation has survived later changes of taste and fashion, and there seems
no danger of a reversion to earlier attitudes. No one today would
be likely to dispute the value of this literature in its own right, or to
doubt its importance as reflecting a crucial stage of development from
the medieval to the modern world.

Elizabethan and Seventeenth-Century

When Donne began to write, about 1592, much of Spenser's work
was still to come; when Marvell died, in 1678, Milton had been
dead four years, and Dryden was almost half-way through his literary
career. Given that all 'periods' of literature are to some extent arbitrary divisions, that they inevitably overlap and are blurred at the
edges, there remains a reasonable case for considering the intervening
decades as a separate age. A division about the time of the Restoration,
between the period of the Renaissance and that of the 'eighteenth
century', is traditional and seems natural. At the other end a division

between the Elizabethan age and the 'seventeenth century', within the general development of Renaissance literature, is harder to fix and calls for many exceptions and qualifications; yet the difference between the age of Spenser, Sidney, Marlowe, and Hooker and that of Herbert, Marvell, Milton, and Browne seems sufficiently marked.

It cannot be claimed, however, that homogeneity is one of the main characteristics of the period. Even more than most, it deserves to be called an age of transition; here, if anywhere, medieval touches modern in all spheres of life and thought. The age inherited views of the order and structure of the universe, of the laws governing political and economic activity, of the spiritual and physical nature of man, which had their origins far back in the Middle Ages.

In recent years scholars have been busy reconstructing for us what has come to be known as the Elizabethan 'world-picture'. The universe was still conceived, according to the old Ptolemaic astronomy, as a vast system of concentric spheres with the earth as the centre. The spheres carried the moon, the sun, the planets, and the stars; the substance of these celestial bodies increased in refinement and purity in proportion to their distance from the earth, and beyond the outermost sphere lay empyrean heaven, the abode of God. The whole system was bound together in a divinely appointed order, always thought of as hierarchical. From mere matter up to God there stretched a continuous 'chain of being' in which man formed the vital central link: below him animals, vegetables, and inanimate matter, above him celestial intelligences and the orders of angels. A complicated harmony was manifest in constant correspondences between different planes of existence: the order of the cosmos was paralleled in the order of the State: the State, or 'body politic', was an organic unity analogous to man himself: and man was the 'microcosm', a little world reflecting in miniature the organization of the whole universe. As the whole universe was composed of different combinations of the four elements, fire, air, water, and earth, so human temperament was the result of varying blends of the four corresponding bodily fluids or 'humours', choler, blood, phlegm, and melancholy (black bile). In such a conception of the world and man's place in it, physics, physiology, psychology, philosophy, and religion seem to the modern mind to be hopelessly intermingled; they have not yet been recognized as completely separate studies with distinct disciplines. Yet at the beginning of our period these ideas were still receiving serious and eloquent expression by, for example, Ralegh and Shakespeare, and they were to remain for many years a commonly accepted background to thought. Knowledge was still based to a considerable extent on the authority of earlier writers, on deduction from traditional theory, or on the ingenious working out of analogies, rather than on observation and experiment. The road to learning was still the traditional one of grammar, rhetoric, and logic, and university education was still largely medieval in conception and method. Above all, Faith and Reason were not commonly set in opposition to each other, and their spheres were not sharply distinguished.

At the end of the period, very different assumptions prevail. Empirical science has emerged and is claiming the whole material universe as its field; the territory of Faith is coming to be strictly limited and fenced off so as to leave all the rest to Reason; exact measurement and scientific law are replacing the older arguments from analogy and authority. It is the age of Hobbes's deterministic psychology, and of the mathematical philosophy of Descartes. There is a conscious modernity in the air, a deliberate anti-medieval movement, so that 'scholasticism' becomes almost a term of abuse. The political upheaval of the Civil War has hastened many economic and social movements that had begun earlier. London, which has doubled its population, is rapidly developing towards the urban civilization of the Augustans. Economic individualism is becoming more a virtue than a vice; and 'political arithmetic', impersonal calculation based on statistics, is coming to seem more significant than the older organic sense of the 'body politic' and its relationships.

The transformation was of course gradual. In spite of much obvious continuity, certain signs of change appear about the beginning of the century. There are grounds, in fact, for distinguishing between the Jacobean and the Elizabethan temper, though it would be absurd to suggest that the new reign was marked by an immediate reversal of mood or outlook. Rather, certain tendencies which had been developing almost parallel with the trends towards expansiveness and idealism in the Elizabethan sensibility began to appear more prominently in the later nineties and continued to grow after 1600. Much of the Jacobean expression and discussion of melancholy may be dismissed as a passing fashion, a literary exaggeration. It remains true, nevertheless, that the Renaissance delight in new human potentialities was necessarily followed by a sharper sense of the contrast with the unchanging limitations of human existence, and that signs of this kind of disenchantment are frequent in the early seventeenth century. In political and economic life, too, there were maladjustments connected with the recent growth of capitalism and industrial enterprise, and others leading to unemployment and frustration among the more thoughtful and articulate groups – scholars, writers, aspiring courtiers, and would-be public servants – while the ending of war abroad removed one obvious outlet for unused energies. At a more philosophical level, the orthodox world-picture might also be interpreted pessimistically, laying stress on man's corruption as a result of the Fall and on the ageing and decline of a world which was thought to be drawing towards its end. Moreover, the whole grand system was undermined by Copernicus and the 'new philosophy', though the effect of this was delayed; even after Galileo's verifying experiments, the new conception of the solar system was liable to be regarded as merely one theory among others. More insidious was the effect of the amoral attitude of Machiavelli, with his naturalistic political philosophy, or Montaigne's sceptical probing of human personality and behaviour. Montaigne contributed to a new interest in psychology, which helped to give more precise expression to complex and divided states of mind.

The early years of the seventeenth century, then, show an increase in scepticism, introspection, self-consciousness, and self-criticism. The specifically literary signs are a growing emphasis on satire and realism, a deeper and more inward apprehension of tragedy, and an acuter analysis of human moods and experiences. Moreover, corresponding styles were also developed: the older rhetorical method in verse with its copiousness and formal elaboration gave way to a more concentrated manner, following more closely the diction and rhythms of speech, to what were called at the time 'strong lines' and to what became known later as 'metaphysical' wit. In prose there was a reaction away from Ciceronian eloquence as a model towards the packed terseness of Seneca and Tacitus. The first can be seen in the tragedians and Donne, the second in Bacon's essays. As so often, the old and the new continued for a long time side by side.

Poetry and the Tradition of Wit

The primary aim of Elizabethan poetry was not the spontaneous outpouring of emotion, whatever effects of simplicity, sensuousness, and passion may be found in its best products. It was a conscious art, rhetorical in method, concerned above all to impose form and order upon experience, working equally through the senses, the emotions, and the reason, and directed (at least in theory) at the will.[1] Wit and the play of mind, argumentation, and logical development were therefore not foreign to it: artifice and convention were accepted as natural and desirable: fluency, copiousness of language, and easy regularity of verse were positive virtues. Such an art has its notable successes where true feeling informs the idealistic conventions and the rhetorical craftsmanship, or where the stylization is related to a way of life. But it is unfitted for certain kinds of directness, economy, concentration, and realistic force, and for expressing the subtler kinds of introspection and psychological analysis. It was when the need for these came to be felt that the new style began to appear, notably, of course, in the amazing development of Shakespeare's dramatic verse from *Henry VI* to *Hamlet*, and to some extent also in the verse of his sonnets, but also in the non-dramatic poetry of Donne and others. This development started, in fact, before half the best-known examples of the older manner were in existence: when Donne began to write, such typically Elizabethan vogues as those of the sonnet sequence and the Ovidian tale of classical mythology were barely established.

Certainly many poets kept up something like the earlier style well into the reign of James I, and some even beyond. Drayton, who survived until 1631, was an Elizabethan to the end, antagonistic to the new poets and their exclusiveness. Daniel, again, who lived until 1619, owed little to new fashions. These were contemporaries of Shakespeare and almost of Spenser, but there were also younger men who may be grouped together as Spenserians. William Drummond of Hawthornden (1585–1649) cultivated the Italian and French poets, from Petrarch and the Pléiade downwards, who had been the Elizabethans' chief models. His own work, which Ben Jonson judged 'not after the fancy of the time', is bookish and elaborately ornamented, ranging from love sonnets and madrigals to *Flowers of Sion*, with its eloquent sonnet on John the Baptist. William Browne (*c.*1591–*c.*1643) and George Wither (1588–1667) were pastoralists, expressing a feeling for country life in a vein of fluent prettiness. More important were the brothers Giles (*c.* 1588–1623) and Phineas (1582–1650) Fletcher. Phineas is chiefly known for his elaborate allegory of the human body, *The Purple Island*. Giles's *Christ's Victorie and Triumph* adapts the Spenserian style to the story of the Temptations; his verse has a warmer quality and a fondness for paradoxical wit that connect him with such Catholic poets as the Elizabethan Southwell and the Caroline Crashaw. The Fletchers form an important link between Spenser and Milton.

Much Elizabethan verse had been inseparable from music, and the association proved a conservative force for some time. Songs from masques and plays and from the numerous books of madrigals, airs, and ballets continued in the Jacobean period to be conditioned by their purpose; often the poet and composer were one, as with Thomas Campion (1567–1620). The effect of writing with music in view was to preclude complexity of mood, rapid shifts of tone, or a freedom of movement suggesting the speaking voice. Simple and obvious emotions, developed one at a time, and expressed in a lucid and formally regular style, gave the most effective opportunities to the composer. The limitations are obvious, but within them the Elizabethan lyric achieved an extraordinary freshness and grace, and in the early seventeenth century Campion was still developing new subtlety and delicacy in its treatment. Verse of this kind needs, of course, its musical setting to complete the effect.

These various survivals do not alter the fact that marked changes of style and interest were taking place during the 1590s. They are suggested in some of Ralegh's poems, with their personal melancholy and intensity of argumentation; in the energetic philosophizing of Sir John Davies's *Nosce Teipsum*; in Chapman's seriousness, intellectual temper, and explicit defence of obscurity; in some of Shakespeare's sonnets, where the movement and the imagery approach the vitality of his mature dramatic style; in the general development of verse in the theatre towards freedom and flexibility; and in the vogue for satire which produced the work of Hall and Marston. But outside the theatre the main agents of change and the dominant moulders of the new tradition were John Donne (1572–1631) and Ben Jonson (1572–1637), and Donne's originality was by far the more spectacular.

As far as we can tell, it appeared at once: if Donne's juvenilia included specimens of conventional Elizabethan verse, they have not survived. His work of the 1590s must have included, besides most of the satires and elegies, a number of what were later collected under the title *Songs and Sonets*, but there are here no sonnets in the strict sense, and the word 'songs' at once points to unusual qualities. For whether or not Donne thought that these lyrics might be set to music, he seldom allowed that possibility to control their diction, movement, or form, much less their theme, attitude, or general development. It is the directness and familiar tone of speech that at once strike us:

> Busie old foole, unruly Sunne
> Why dost thou thus,
> Through windowes, and through curtaines call on us?
> Must to thy motions lovers seasons run?
> Sawcy pedantique wretch, goe chide
> Late schoole boyes, and soure prentices,
> Goe tell Court-huntsmen, that the King will ride,
> Call countrey ants to harvest offices;
> Love, all alike, no season knowes, nor clyme,
> Nor houres, dayes, moneths, which are the rags of time.

The movement of this stanza from *The Sunne Rising* is inseparable from the tone and meaning; we cannot read it unless we recognize the lover's mood of humorous exasperation and allow its scornful emphases to play against the verse pattern – '*Busie* old foole', – '*Through windowes* and *through curtaines*' (doubling the sense of officious prying) – 'Must to *thy* motions...?' – 'houres, dayes, moneths, which are the *rags* of time'. Stress, intonation, gesture almost, are imposed on us as we read; we have the sense of a living speech, individual and intimate, not of formal or public utterance. The diction has a popular, colloquial vigour; the imagery is chosen for its effect of surprise and compression – 'countrey ants', 'the rags of time' – and sound effects such as assonance and alliteration are used to reinforce the tone and feeling rather than simply to create a pattern of verbal melody. The rhythmical effect belongs rather to the whole stanza than the single line, and it is subordinate to the expression of the meaning and the general air of dramatic realism. One aspect of Donne's originality, in fact, is that he gave to the short lyric something of the flexibility, the urgent and profound expressiveness that came to be developed in dramatic blank verse.

Donne's poetry is further remarkable for its fusion of passionate feeling and logical argument. Progression by reasoning was nothing new in Elizabethan poetry, but what distinguishes Donne from, say, Sidney in this respect is the subtlety, incisiveness, and range of his thought, together with the sense that the play of intellect tended to become for him an emotional experience, and that, conversely, when deeply moved his mind only worked more rapidly. Thus parting and consolation lead him to contemporary beliefs about the universe, the scale of beings, the human soul, and the nature of matter, to remote astronomical phenomena and the malleable properties of gold; but the surprising argument only heightens the feeling:

> Moving of th' earth brings harmes and feares,
>   Men reckon what it did and meant,
> But trepidation of the spheares,
>   Though greater farre, is innocent.
>
> Dull sublunary lovers love
>   (Whose soule is sense) cannot admit
> Absence, because it doth remove
>   Those things which elemented it.
>
> But we, by a love so much refin'd
>   That our selves know not what it is,
> Inter-assured of the mind,
>   Care lesse, eyes, lips and hands to misse.
>
> Our two soules, therefore, which are one,
>   Though I must goe, endure not yet
> A breach, but an expansion,
>   Like gold to ayery thinnesse beate.

Some of Donne's dialectical acuteness may have derived from his Catholic upbringing and his study of scholastic philosophy; his employment of its concepts led later to the use of the term 'metaphysical' to define his wit and his particular type of conceit, and to its extension by Dr Johnson to describe his followers and imitators. Conceits and wit were a recognized part of the Elizabethan rhetorical apparatus for amplifying a theme, but Donne's characteristic use of them involves such an extraordinary range of ideas and experience with such startling connections between them, the whole process seems to work at a so much higher pressure, that in comparison the general Elizabethan use appears merely superficial and ingenious.[2] When it fails, the metaphysical conceit answers to Dr Johnson's account: 'the most heterogeneous ideas are yoked by violence together'.[3] When it succeeds one thinks rather of Coleridge's remark that imagination shows itself in 'the balance or reconciliation of opposite or discordant qualities'.

Donne's style was the natural expression of his sensibility, and its originality is reflected in his choice and treatment of subject. As he rejects the melodious fluency of Spenser's verse or the decorative use of classical mythology, so he turns from the Petrarchan conventions to analyse the experience of love in a variety of moods ranging from cynical sensuality to a profound sense of union, but always with the same realistic force and eager play of mind. When he turns to religious poetry later in life there is no change of style or method: the same variety and range of experience are drawn on, and the same dramatic power expresses his mental conflicts:

> Batter my heart, three person'd God; for, you
> As yet but knocke, breathe, shine, and seeke to mend;
> That I may rise, and stand, o'erthrow mee, and bend
> Your force, to breake, blowe, burn and make me new ..:
> (*Holy Sonnets*, XIV)

Throughout, his metaphysical wit was a means of bringing all sides of his experience into relation with the immediate subject.

The other great formative influence in seventeenth-century poetry was Ben Jonson. It is not so much that, as some older histories of literature used to assert, there was a 'school of Donne' and a 'school of Jonson'; rather that almost any seventeenth-century poet will show signs of having learnt from both, though the proportions and the nature of the blend may differ widely. Jonson's non-dramatic verse does not show such an obvious originality or such a decisive breach with contemporary fashion as Donne's; yet his different modification of the Elizabethan manner is almost equally significant. Even his songs have a greater neatness and point; they are more economical

in method, and the best of them achieve a striking sureness of movement, a kind of controlled *élan*, which is different from the limpid
Elizabethan flow, as in the 'Hymn to Diana' from *Cynthia's Revels*:

> *Queene*, and *Huntresse*, chaste and faire,
>   Now the *Sunne* is laid to sleepe,
> Seated in thy silver chaire,
>   State in wonted manner keepe:
> *HESPERUS* intreats thy light,
> Goddesse, excellently bright.

Apart from lyrics, including numerous songs from his plays and
masques, Jonson wrote chiefly occasional verse-epigrams, epitaphs,
odes, and epistles. He rejected equally the Petrarchan convention, the
Spenserian fluency and 'sweetness long-drawn out', and with rare
exceptions the sonnet form. For his models, he turned from the
French and Italian to the Latin lyric poems and epigrammatists,
especially Catullus, Horace, and Martial; from these he learned a
detached coolness of style which can unite with genuine feeling to
give it restraint, stability, and permanence, as in the epitaph on the
child actor, Solomon Pavy, who acted old men so well that the Fates
mistook him for one:

> So, by error, to his fate
>   They all consented;
> But viewing him since (alas, too late)
>   They have repented.
> And have sought (to give new birth)
>   In baths to steepe him;
> But being so much too good for earth,
>   Heaven vowes to keepe him.

Jonson's classicism was in no sense an escape from the contemporary world; in reaching after an ideal civilization he did not lose touch
with the interests of the life around him and a vigorous native idiom.
He translates Catullus into Elizabethan speech and English settings,
bidding Celia, after the first thousand kisses:

> ... unto the tother
> Adde a thousand, and so more:
> Till you equall with the store,
> All the grasse that *Rumney* yeelds
> Or the sands in *Chelsey* fields
> Or the drops in silver *Thames*

> Or the starres, that guild his streames
> In the silent sommer-nights
> When youths ply their stolne delights.
> (*To Celia*)

Similarly he can catch the Horatian tone of balanced moderation, the quiet acceptance of the human lot, as in *To the World*, with its characteristic close:

> Nor for my peace will I goe farre,
>   As wandrers doe, that still doe rome,
> But make my strengths, such as they are,
>   Here in my bosome, and at home.

Even the famous song 'Drinke to me onely with thine eyes' is made up of fragments from a late Greek prose writer; but it is Jonson's art which welds them into a whole with an effect of conversational ease and spontaneity.

When he fails, Jonson can be laboured and pedantic, but his characteristic successes achieve an urbane elegance which always suggests an underlying strength. Without attempting the obviously dramatic effect of Donne's broken rhythm, Jonson yet contrives within the smooth regularity of his verse a directness and energy of statement clearly related to speech. His detachment and his epigrammatic conciseness combine to produce an effect of wit, though it is not of the metaphysical kind and does not employ Donne's type of conceit. In *Discoveries*, his commonplace-book of critical notes, Jonson remarked that 'metaphors far-fet hinder to be understood', and the kind of strength he sought for was not to be achieved through obscurity or metaphorical complexity. If his work has 'wit', if his lines are 'strong', it is rather through the quality of 'tough reasonableness' which Eliot in his essay on Marvell noted as underlying the lyric grace of much poetry of this time. The further description of wit in the same essay as involving 'a recognition, implicit in the expression of every experience, of other kinds of experience which are possible', indicates the grounds on which both Donne and Jonson, for all their differences, may be seen as contributing to a common tradition.

That Donne and Jonson, in spite of obvious differences, have something akin, may be seen from the fact that there exists a group of elegies of which the authorship remains undecided between the two poets. The important fact for the student of seventeenth-century poetry, however, is that it was possible for the two styles to combine and interact. Some of the ways in which this might happen are foreshadowed already in such contemporaries as Donne's friend Sir Henry Wotton (1568–1639) or Lord Herbert of Cherbury (1583–1648), whose great *Ode upon a Question* ... combines Donne's intense philosophical argument and learned conceits with Jonson's smoothness and urbanity. They are clearly to be seen in younger poets, such as Donne's executor Henry King (1592–1669), remembered especially for his moving *Exequy* on his wife, in George Herbert (1593–1633), and the religious poets, and equally in Thomas Carew (1595?–1640?) and the Caroline lyrists.

The Metaphysical Manner and Religious Poetry

In its remarkable development of religious poetry the seventeenth century forms a striking contrast with the previous age, which has little of note in this field. An exception must be made for the poetry of the Jesuit martyr Robert Southwell (*c.* 1561–96), which shows an odd mingling of the earlier, more naïve Elizabethan rhetoric and the Counter-Reformation ardour, sensuousness, and love of paradox. If Catholic poets tended to look to Italian models, Protestants found theirs to some extent in Joshua Sylvester's translations of the didactic and encyclopaedic works of the Huguenot poet du Bartas, which appeared during the 1590s; but there was no doctrinal exclusiveness, and the strains often mingle. In the work of Phineas Fletcher, du Bartas's didacticism is married to Spenserian allegory; in that of his brother Giles, the Spenserian quality is modified by Italian warmth and paradoxical wit in a way that anticipates Crashaw and may be described as 'baroque'. Much religious poetry of this period was affected by the vogue of books of 'emblems', sets of allegorical pictures each accompanied by verses expounding its moral. The first emblem book in English had appeared in 1586, but the most significant examples of religious verse in this form were the collections of *Emblemes* by Francis Quarles (1592–1644). The indirect influence of the emblem may, however, be seen in the imagery of more important poets, such as Herbert and Crashaw.

The religious poetry of Donne shows the same qualities as his other work: the dramatic tone, the play of speech rhythms against the verse pattern, the dialectical subtlety, the startling imagery drawn from common life or from intellectual pursuits and the psychological penetration. The effects of thus applying metaphysical wit to religious subjects are almost as varied as in the love poetry: sometimes the ingenuity predominates, sometimes Donne's religious feelings seem to be indeed, as he described them, 'devout fits' coming and going 'like a fantastic ague'. With the *Holy Sonnets*, whatever their actual date of composition,[4] the note deepens; it is for the most part one of torment and struggle, and the style expresses this passionate conflict with dramatic vividness:

> I dare not move my dimme eyes any way,
> Despaire behind, and death before doth cast
> Such terrour . . .
>
> *(Holy Sonnets, I)*

Only in the last few hymns does Donne's religious poetry communicate the sense of assured faith:

> Since I am coming to that Holy roome,
>   Where, with thy Quire of Saints for evermore
> I shall be made thy Musique; as I come
>   I tune the Instrument here at the dore.
>   *(Hymne to God my God, in my sickness)*

Here no less than in the poems of conflict the characteristic style and imagery continue; once more, in the astonishing geographical figures which follow these lines, we feel the main theme brought into relation with the widest possible range of interests and experience.

The use of the metaphysical style in religious poetry by George Herbert (1593–1633) owes much to Donne, with whom he had early contacts, his mother being one of Donne's friends and patronesses. There are obvious contrasts: Herbert shows neither Donne's passionate and tortured casuistry nor his aggressive unconventionality of style. His courtly urbanity of language, his varied and musical verse forms, and a certain neatness and point, suggest the further influence of Ben Jonson. But it is from Donne that Herbert derives his wit and his conceits. Drawing upon ordinary experience and practical affairs rather than scholastic or scientific learning, Herbert's wit is often distinguished as 'homely', sometimes as 'quaint', and it does at times suggest simply the play of an ingenious fancy. In his best work, however, it has imaginative intensity and the effect of surprise:

The growth of flesh is but a blister.
(*Holy Baptism*)

But we are still too young or old;
    The Man is gone,
Before we do our wares unfold:
    So we freeze on,
Untill the grave increase our cold.
(*Employment*, II)

Often it serves to keep the religious experience close to everyday life, or it enables a sense of mental alertness to temper what might have become emotional excess, as in 'Love bade me welcome...' where, although there are no conceits, an effect of wit is achieved through the control of tone in the dialogue. Sometimes the conceit lies in a title suggesting the emblem (*The Collar, The Pulley*), or it may be extended into a short allegorical narrative, foreshadowing Bunyan (*Redemption, The Pilgrimage*). But there is always a controlling play of mind, a firm grasp of common experience, and a vivid, dramatic sense.

Herbert can suggest the speaking voice, not only with courtly politeness, but also with direct colloquial vigour:

Call in thy deathshead there: tie up thy fears.
(*The Collar*)

. . . as if none knew but he.
No man shall beat into his head,
That thou within his curtains drawn canst see.
(*Miserie*)

His purity of diction does not exclude proverbial and racy expressions like 'snudge in quiet', while the lyrical grace of his rhythms and stanza forms will usually be found to have an expressive relation to the meaning. In *The Collar* the movement effectively presents both the rebellious mood and the way it subsides; in *Aaron* two rhyme-sounds chiming through five stanzas suggest the bells which form one of the poem's dominant figures; elsewhere assonance and alliteration give extra emphasis and enforce the meaning in Donne's way (or Shakespeare's):

. . . there it [my heart] was dipt and dy'd
And washt and wrung: the very wringing yet
Enforceth tears.
(*Love Unknown*)

This realistic strength underlying Herbert's grace of style is related to the maturity of his emotional and religious life. The serenity of his faith was not achieved without suffering and conflict; while his poems do not show Donne's dramatic terrors and agonies, many of them convey a profound sense of dereliction and unworthiness:

> My mirth and edge was lost: a blunted knife
>> Was of more use than I.
> Thus thinne and lean without a fence or friend,
> I was blown through with ev'ry storm and winde.
> > > (*Affliction*, I)

Passages like this, by their intense honesty, add conviction to those expressing the resolution of conflict in faith and acceptance. At its most characteristic this acceptance is not mere resignation: it suggests mature choice and an enlargement of spirit, which is communicated most naturally in images of spring and renewal of life, as in *The Flower*. Herbert's best work embodies the religious temper of the seventeenth century at its finest and most humane.

Richard Crashaw (1612–49) called his 1646 volume *Steps to the Temple*, after Herbert's *The Temple*, but the two poets have little in common. In his use of conceits Crashaw has neither Donne's intellectual range nor Herbert's homely realism. He carries on rather from Southwell and Giles Fletcher, combining a fondness for paradox with sensuous warmth in the manner of the Italian poets of the Counter-Reformation, especially Marino and the Jesuit writers of Latin epigrams. Both influences lead towards a use of the conceit as isolated ornament rather than as an integral part of a poem's total meaning; *The Weeper*, with its variations on the theme of Mary Magdalene's tears, has been called a 'rosary of epigrams'. The characteristic warmth and lyrical glow appear in the operatic *Hymn of the Nativity*, where in contrast with Milton's more majestic celebration, they are linked with a tender humour:

> Poor WORLD (said I) what wilt thou doe
> To entertain this starry STRANGER?
> > Is this the best thou canst bestow?
> > A cold, and not too cleanly manger?

Even before his conversion to Rome about 1645, Crashaw was writing in a vein of voluptuous mysticism which suggests Italian and Spanish baroque art. He carries to extremes the traditional use of erotic metaphor to convey the ecstasies of adoration, and his uncontrolled lyric fervour sometimes collapses into an exclamatory verbal haze. Yet there are passages of eloquent and passionate conviction:

> Faith is my force. Faith strength affords
> To keep pace with those powrfull words.
> And words more sure, more sweet, than they
> Love could not think, truth could not say.
> (*The Hymne of Sainte Thomas*)

Where there is an obvious emblematic quality, or a close relation to liturgy, or both, as in some of the later poems, the conceits and paradoxes often take on a quality of formal ritual, which lessens their general poetic force. In various ways, therefore, Crashaw's poetry moves away from the tradition of Donne and Herbert, but at times, as notably in the *Answer* to Cowley's cynical poem *Against Hope*, or the lines to the Countess of Denbigh, an approximation to metaphysical wit adds strength and substance to his ecstatic lyricism.

Like Crashaw, Henry Vaughan (1622–95) wrote some secular verse in fashionable modes, but he is chiefly remembered for the religious poetry of *Silex Scintillans* (1655). Herbert's influence is marked in his work by many obvious echoes and borrowings. Where it is strongest, Vaughan usually suffers by the comparison; the effect is thinner and less concentrated. This is true even of comparative successes like *Regeneration*, which lacks Herbert's allegorical vividness though it shows something of Vaughan's special sensitiveness to natural beauty. The common assertion of Vaughan's greater imaginative power depends chiefly on effects of sudden illumination, like the opening of *The World*:

> I saw Eternity the other night
> Like a great *Ring* of pure and endless light . . .

or the first stanza of 'They are all gone into the world of light'. But *The World* has this quality only at the beginning and end, and 'They are all gone . . .' proves rather unequal as a whole. When Vaughan uses the conceits of a star 'confin'd into a tomb' or of 'the mists which blot and fill My perspective' (i.e. telescope) he suggests Donne, but when he makes light 'trample on my days' he is using language without the characteristic metaphysical precision, in a manner nearer to the Romantics.

Vaughan's poetry is less social, more removed from the world of action than that of Donne or Herbert; he has neither Herbert's attachment to the Anglican Church nor Crashaw's concern with Catholic ritual and dogma. His religious intuitions belong to a wider and vaguer tradition of neoplatonic mysticism, of solitary contemplation which turns to images from nature – sun and stars, winds and streams, the plant and the seed – to express the soul's aspiration to eternal light or the 'deep but dazzling darkness' of God. In his best work he can still use the metaphysical conceit effectively ('Bright shootes of everlastingness'), and this, with his fresh purity of diction, marks him of his age even when he handles Wordsworth's themes. But in single-minded concentration upon his personal vision he tends to lose that constant sense of other possible attitudes and experiences which gives the tradition of wit its peculiar strength.[5]

Most other religious poetry in the metaphysical manner may be roughly grouped round these four poets. Quarles is a kind of inferior Herbert; Benlowes (1603?–76) has some of Crashaw's ardour with a greater extravagance; Traherne (1637?–74) carries to an extreme Vaughan's neoplatonic mysticism, but fails for the most part to give his vision poetic embodiment. There is a Puritan sobriety in the religious feeling of Andrew Marvell (1621–78), but it is expressed in a characteristic blend of Donnean and Jonsonian wit. The poet of *The Coronet* cannot be dismissed as lacking in seriousness, but the *Dialogue between the Resolved Soul and Created Pleasure* can employ sophisticated and urbane epigram to present a morality as ascetic as that of *Comus*. Religion, in Marvell as in Herbert and Donne, is in touch with many sides of living experience.

Caroline Poets and the Courtly Lyric

The influence of the Court upon literature during this period varies with the different reigns. At Elizabeth's Court life had been stylized in the elaborate ritual of the cult of the Virgin Queen. Under her successor nothing quite took the place of this, with all its associated poetry of idealistic love; James I's Court seems to have lost much of the earlier ceremonial dignity, though in its luxury it was even more ostentatious. The masque, with its combination of poetry, music, and spectacle, became the most popular Court entertainment. Court influence on the drama tended in the direction of sophistication, exaggerated sentiment, and artificial heroics, especially in the work of Fletcher and his collaborators. Under Charles I and Henrietta Maria there was a partial return to the Elizabethan dignity and order: Court tastes acquired more refinement and wider aesthetic interests, especially in the visual arts. Much more than in the Jacobean period, it is possible to distinguish a school of courtly poetry, mainly in the form of songs and lyrics, but differing in many ways from its Elizabethan counterpart. The lyrics are more independent of music; even when obviously songs, their evolution is not so closely controlled by the needs of the composer. Their use of language is close to cultivated speech, their imagery is more intellectual and less sensuous, their method is often dialectical, and they aim at classical neatness and point. Between these poets and the Elizabethans, in fact, there stand Donne and Ben Jonson.

The leading representative of this group was Thomas Carew (1595?–1640?). If the label 'Cavalier poet' suggests that he was an elegant trifler, it hardly gives a fair notion of his best work. His elegy on Donne is both a moving tribute and a remarkable piece of criticism, successfully handling the pentameter couplet with Donne's argumentative energy. In his love poetry the Donnean conceit is usually embodied in more polished and regular verse:

> That killing power is none of thine,
> I gave it to thy voyce, and eyes:
> Thy sweets, thy graces, all are mine:
> Thou art my starre, shin'st in my skies;
> Then dart not from thy borrowed sphere
> Lightning on him that fixt thee there.
>
> (*Ingratefull beauty threatened*)

This graceful movement and logical neatness are Jonsonian, and the merging of the two influences is characteristic. The way in which a similar blend appears in many quite minor poets may be seen in the following lines from Godolphin:

> Though poorer in desert I make
> My selfe whilst I admire,
> The fuel which from hope I take
> I give to my desire.

> If this flame lighted from your Eyes
> The subject doe calcine,
> A Heart may be your sacrifice
> Too weake to be your shrine.
> ('*Noe more unto my thoughts appeare*')

A surprising number of minor poets were able to display these qualities in one or two poems; the names of Cartwright, Fanshawe, Habington, Hall, Kynaston, Randolph, and Stanley are a mere sample selection.

The two most often taken with Carew as Cavalier poets (though both stand well below him) are Sir John Suckling (1609–42) and Richard Lovelace (1618–53). Suckling borrows Donne's lighter themes and more cynical tone, usually embodying them in simple song metres with colloquial ease and informality. Lovelace is more unequal, but at his best a more serious poet. He has given us the most famous of all expressions of the Cavalier spirit in *To Lucasta on going to the Wars* and *To Althea from Prison*. A similar grade may be found in others of his love songs, and in such Horatian moralizings as *The Grasshopper*. The distinctive quality of the Caroline lyric comes out most clearly in a comparison with that of the Restoration; even when themes and attitudes are apparently the same, the tone of the later work has coarsened, and we miss the air of civilized grace. Even Suckling, who seems temperamentally indistinguishable from the Restoration wits, has still a slightly finer manner and a shade more purity of diction; certainly Lovelace could never be mistaken for one of the later group.

An attractive sidelight on the period is provided by a number of poems dealing with great houses and their rural neighbourhoods; they suggest that the Court was still aware of its roots in the country. Following Ben Jonson's praise of Penshurst, Carew writes of Saxham, Fanshawe of Charles I's proclamation 'commanding the gentry to reside upon their estates'. Similar themes appear in Randolph and later in Marvell. The poet who shows most obvious concern with rural culture is the conscious classicist Robert Herrick (1591–1674). Herrick's debt to Jonson is more superficial and less significant than that of Carew or Marvell; on the other hand, he owes little to metaphysical wit apart from an occasional conceit (night will 'make a seizure on the light'; the lover is 'thy Protestant'). In many ways he is nearer to the Elizabethan lyric. Writing of fairies and country customs, he recalls Drayton or *A Midsummer Night's Dream*; lamenting the transience of beauty he suggests Campion. His love songs ring the changes on the theme 'Gather ye rosebuds while ye may' with a fanciful charm which seldom sounds any imaginative depths.

Of course, the Caroline poets are smaller personalities than Jonson or Donne, and the assimilation of their influence could be only partial. But it is convincing and genuine, and the result is not merely imitative; up to a point the Cavaliers could share these modes of feeling and relate them to their own Court world. That world had its limitations, and it may be significant that the group contains no undoubted major poet. But it is reasonable to suppose that the finely poised urbanity of Caroline poetry at its best had some connection, however indirect, with actual living. Certainly the atmosphere was favourable to the full development of minor gifts; the dominant literary influences, combining with the last phase of true Court culture in English history, produced some of the best lyrical and occasional poetry in the language.

Later Developments of Wit in Poetry

The middle years of the century show metaphysical poetry undergoing various changes. With some poets the manner declines into eccentricity and extravagance; with others, wit takes on a different character in response to changes in contemporary sensibility. At the same time, the tradition shapes its last great poet in Andrew Marvell (1621–78).

Marvell's work has a central significance, gathering together many strands of seventeenth-century thought, feeling, and style. His special blend of wit includes the imaginative surprise of Donne and the civilized grace of Jonson, the gallantry of Carew and the grave delicacy of Herbert. His temperament has both Puritan sobriety and a classical sophistication more flexible than Milton's. In no poet are levity and seriousness more subtly mingled, though something of the same quality appears in Pope. The lightest pastoral may take on the resonances of religious allegory without losing its quality of delicate artifice (*Clorinda and Damon*); a playful love song will contain a quiet reminder of human transience, as in *The Mower to the Glow-worms*:

> Ye Country Comets, that portend
> No War, nor Princes funeral,
> Shining unto no higher end
> Than to presage the Grasses fall ...

and a fancifully elaborated comparison of garden flowers to soldiers on parade, in *Upon Appleton House*, can lead without the slightest incongruity to serious reflections on the Civil War. The wit that permits these transitions is essentially a wide-ranging play of mind which is continually making imaginative connections between different levels of experience. It appears not only in the learned paradoxes from which Marvell constructs his *Definition of Love*, but also in the vivid force of Fate's 'iron wedges'; not merely in the comic extravagance of the first paragraph of *To His Coy Mistress*, but also in the sudden intensity of 'Times winged Charriot' and the 'Desarts of vast Eternity', the qualified triumph over time asserted by the conclusion and the linking of these stages in connected argument.

Marvell returned to favour in the nineteenth century earlier than the other metaphysical poets, largely on account of his feeling for natural beauty. Whenever he touches this theme his verse has certainly a remarkable quality of freshness and moving intimacy, yet this is achieved without any exclusion of his usual intellectual agility or any change from the tone of mature sophistication. The tropical paradise of *The Bermudas* is related not only to political and religious interests but to art and civilization; the spring *enamels* everything, God sends the birds on *visits* and

> ... hangs in shades the Orange bright
> Like golden Lamps in a green Night.

Similarly the meadow grass of *Upon Appleton House* 'seems as green silks but newly washed'; artificial and natural beauty are not set in opposition, but illuminate each other. A sense of the emblematic possibilities of 'Nature's mystick Book' does not preclude a direct sensuous response, nor does the pleasure of the senses impede the profounder imaginative insights of the mind in *The Garden's* 'green shade'.

The classical quality in Marvell appears in his smooth polished verse, his precision and economy of phrase, and his balanced sense of human limitations. It is nowhere seen to better advantage than in his *Horatian Ode upon Cromwell's Return from Ireland*, which contemplates the events of the Civil War with an urbane detachment which is, nevertheless, far from cynicism or irresponsibility. Cromwell is accepted as an irresistible natural force, a minister of Destiny and the instrument of England's greatness, but the personal dignity of Charles and the pathos of his fate receive due emphasis, and the conclusion is clear-sighted:

> The same *Arts* that did gain
> A *Pow'r* must it *maintain*.

Marvell's concern with politics was to increase, and eventually to crowd poetry out of his life. After the Restoration he wrote little verse apart from political satire in rough doggerel. The change has a significance related to larger changes in the temper of the age; the culture of the Restoration was not of the kind which could feed Marvell's peculiar poetic genius.

Occasional examples of conceits running to fantastic extravagance can be found in almost all the metaphysical poets from Donne onwards, but they tend to multiply in the forties and fifties. Crashaw's faults in this kind are well known; the wit of Marvell himself sometimes becomes excessively self-conscious in its ingenuity, as with his notorious salmon-fishers who, 'like *Antipodes* in Shoes,/Have shod their Heads in their Canoes'. The work of Benlowes is notorious for its high proportion of extreme instances of the fantastic and obscure. But the real decadence of the style is seen when ingenuity is pursued for its own sake, with no informing imaginative pressure, as in most of the verse of John Cleveland (1613–58), and much of that of Abraham Cowley (1618–67). For Cleveland wit is a game, even in an elegy like that on Edward King (Milton's *Lycidas*), where he protests:

> I am no Poet here; my pen's the spout,
> Where the rain water of my eyes run out.

When he says of his mistress:

> . . . call her the square circle; say
> She is the very rule of Algebra.
> (*The Hecatomb to his Mistress*)

72

is is clear that we are dealing with something more superficial than Marvell's geometry in *The Definition of Love*. Dryden, distinguishing between Donne's satire and Cleveland's, said 'the one gives us deep thoughts in common language ... the other gives us common thoughts in abstruse words'. It is significant that Cleveland is at his best in political satire, a mode congenial to the next age.

Cowley, like Cleveland, had an immense contemporary reputation, which he has never regained. His work is extraordinarily representative of the changing taste of his age; it shows the wit of Donne turning into the wit of Dryden. He has all the analytical and logical skill of the earlier Metaphysicals, the same striking openings, the same elaborately extended comparisons, but he lacks any profound imaginative synthesis of experience; his intellect is employed in decorating a number of fairly simple ideas and sentiments. Wit, for Cowley, was a matter of rational comparison, with a common-sense basis to its ingenuity. The poem *Against Hope* provides a fair example:

> Thou bringst us an *Estate*, yet leav'st us *Poor*,
> By clogging it with *Legacies* before!
>   The *Joys* which we *entire* should wed,
>   Come *deflowr'd Virgins* to our bed;
> Good fortunes without gain imported be,
>   Such mighty *Custom's* paid to Thee.
> For *Joy* like *Wine* kept close does better tast;
> If it take air before, its spirits wast.

He had no use for the '*Cobwebs* of the *Schoolmen's* trade' which had furnished so many of Donne's conceits; he was interested in the new science, and wrote odes *To Mr Hobs* and *To the Royal Society*. These indications of Cowley's rational temper acquire an additional importance when we consider Hobbes's explicit pronouncements on current taste and the nature of poetry. In *Leviathan* Hobbes equates Imagination and Fancy as 'decaying sense': in his *Answer* to Davenant's *Discourse* on his poem *Gondibert* he attacks 'the ambitous obscurity of expressing more than is perfectly conceived, or perfect conception in fewer words than it requires'. The function of Fancy in poetry is simply ornamental:

Time and Education begets experience: Experience begets memory, Memory begets Judgement and Fancy; Judgement begets the strength and structure, and Fancy begets the ornaments of a Poem.

The new insistence is all on perspicuity and directness, on poetry as a social activity; wit is more and more limited by the claims of Good Sense, until we find Dryden in his *Apology* prefixed to *The State of Innocence* defining it as 'a propriety of thoughts and words'. All this was of course part of the general movement of thought, the swing towards mathematical demonstration and scientific logic: the aims of the new Royal Society, according to its historian, Thomas Sprat, were 'to separate the knowledge of Nature from the colours of Rhetorick, the devices of Fancy or the delightful deceit of Fables' in order to obtain for mankind 'a Dominion over *Things*'. At the same time the new society emerging from the upheaval of the Civil War was increasingly to encourage the public voice in poetry, whether as easy, direct statement or as lofty formal decorum, together with subject-matter of social and political interest. The metaphysical balance of passion and argument, imagination and reason, settles towards the rational side, and in Cowley's poetry (and in a less representative degree that of Sir William Davenant, 1606–68) we can see the process taking place. At the same time, Edmund Waller (1606–87) and Sir John Denham (1615–69) were beginning to cater for and confirm the new tastes.

Cowley was more than a decadent metaphysical: he established the neo-classic vogue of the 'Pindaric' ode in which lofty magniloquence is allowed a certain licence of verse form, strictly limited by convention, and in the *Davideis* he made the first attempt at an epic poem on classical principles. He is at his most effective, however, in a vein of personal feeling and simple good sense which both recalls his early admiration for Spenser and looks forward to certain elegiac strains of eighteenth-century poetry; of this the most notable example is *On the Death of Mr William Hervey*.

Milton: Humanist and Puritan

The development as a poet of John Milton (1608–74) is nothing if not individual. His early work shows, nevertheless, a variety of contemporary influences. At first he seems a Spenserian, related to Drummond, Browne, and the Fletchers, carrying on the Elizabethan manner of sensuous richness and mythological decoration, and employing, as in *On the Morning of Christ's Nativity* (1629), variations upon the Spenserian stanza form. This is a typically Renaissance poem in its mingling of classical deities and 'yellow-skirted Fayes' with the Bible story: the old tradition of Christ's birth silencing the oracles provides a plausible excuse. A more direct influence from Spenser can be seen in *Comus* (1634), and the verse paragraphs of *Lycidas* recall the marriage odes in their adaptation of the Italian *canzone*. According to Dryden, Milton himself acknowledged Spenser as 'his original'. Echoes of Ben Jonson, with something of his urbane grace and neatness, appear in *Arcades* and the *Epitaph on the Marchioness of Winchester*; but Milton's classicism was, in general, to take a different direction from Jonson's. Metaphysical wit makes an occasional appearance, used facetiously in the lines on Hobson the carrier or seriously in those on Shakespeare. A further influence comes from the Jacobean dramatists. Comus's great temptation speech:

> Wherefore did Nature powre her bounties forth
> With such a full and unwithdrawing hand ...

is Shakespearian in its varied liveliness of diction and its expressive interplay of sound, movement, and imagery, though not all of the masque has this dramatic quality.

Throughout the early poems Milton was developing his own personal voice and style. He came fairly soon to abandon both metaphysical wit and the decorative conceits of the Elizabethan or Italian kind. After *Comus* we do not find again the Jacobean dramatic complexity, or the pure lyricism of the songs which outdo Campion in exquisite verbal melody. What continues through to *Lycidas* and beyond is a type of sonorous musical eloquence already foreshadowed as early as the *Nativity* ode, especially in its rolling alexandrines:

> And all the spangled host keep watch in squadrons bright

> The wakeful trump of doom must thunder through the deep

and carried on in the sustained exaltation of *At a Solemn Musick*. In *Lycidas*, employing the elegiac pastoral conventions, Milton is concerned 'to sing and build the lofty rhyme' with ceremonial formality, even while exploring personal problems and conflicts. The characteristic Grand Style is emerging, what Tennyson called Milton's 'organ voice', which carries on through the eloquence of the sonnets to become the epic manner of *Paradise Lost*. The great power of this style is an incantatory grandeur and nobility unrivalled for the expression of large majestic conceptions and generalized or broadly simple feelings. This power was not achieved without sacrificing certain qualities of sensuous richness, flexibility, and sensitiveness present in the earlier work. A preoccupation with sonority tends to preclude subtler suggestions of the speaking voice; the pattern of sound is elaborated in a much broader and less direct relation to the meaning than in Comus's temptation speech. Milton's classicism played its part in the evolution of his style, not merely in encouraging learned allusiveness and the assumption of a formal vatic manner, but in an increasing tendency to handle English in a classical spirit, adopting Latin syntactical constructions, and using classically derived words in their strict etymological sense. This again tended to increase dignity and eloquence more than inwardness or vitality.

The development of Milton's style is related to his consciousness of vocation both as man and as poet. At nineteen he already wishes to employ his native language 'in some graver subject'; at twenty-three he laments his unproductiveness and dedicates his talents to God. In Comus he transforms the Caroline masque into a high-minded defence of chastity and temperance; in Lycidas the direction of his moral fervour against corrupt clergy suggests already the combination of religious seriousness and political ardour with which he greeted the Civil War. His prose works of the early forties share a jubilantly apocalyptic mood common on the Parliamentary side at this time. Disillusion was to follow, and a progressive rejection of one sect and party after another, but through all the controversy, often acrimonious, of the next twenty years, Milton never lost the sense of being a dedicated champion of true religion and liberty. Single-minded integrity, rather than flexibility and sensitiveness, is the mark of Milton's character and thought as of his style.

For the Renaissance humanist the ultimate triumph was to do for his own country what Homer and Virgil had done for theirs, to vindicate its language and culture in a Heroic poem. For the Puritan Milton this aim coalesced naturally with the propagation of moral truth. Before the various interruptions of the Civil War he had contemplated a national epic on the Arthurian theme; a little later he was planning a drama on the story of the Fall. For reasons which may have included disillusionment over national events and a feeling encouraged by the increasing rationalism of the time that national legends were 'delightful deceits' obnoxious to reason, whereas biblical stories had the sanction of revelation, Milton eventually planned his Heroic poem as *Paradise Lost*, and set out to

> ... assert Eternal Providence
> And justify the wayes of God to men.

Many critics of different schools have noted the difficulties involved in adapting the bibical story to the epic form, especially the prehistoric setting, the absence of truly human characters before the Fall itself, and the direct presentation of the Christian Deity in speech and action.[6] Milton exerts the full force of his art and learning to solve these problems, particularly in the width of reference and allusion permitted by epic simile, in the sonorous sweep of his verse and the sustained elevation of his style. All man's learning and achievement is brought into relation with the central event of the Fall; Milton keeps constantly before our minds the grandeur of human history and the romantic variety of lands, races, and civilizations. He draws particularly on the world of classical legend, so potent for the humanist in its suggestions of ideal beauty:

> Not that faire field
> Of *Enna*, where Proserpin gathring flours
> Her self a fairer Floure by gloomie *Dis*
> Was gatherd, which cost Ceres all that pain
> To seek her through the world; nor that sweet Grove
> Of *Daphne* by *Orontes*, and th' inspir'd
> *Castalian* Spring might with this Paradise
> Of Eden strive.

Yet few would undertake to defend altogether his treatment of God and Heaven, and it is still matter for critical debate how far the poetic presentation of Satan in Books I and II avoids a degree of interest inconsistent with the explicit degradation of him later and with the general theme. Even more important is the question whether in spite of its obvious triumphs Milton's epic manner does not sometimes involve a certain externality and insensitiveness as the complement of its formal grandeur. Many modern readers, who would not wish to deny that Milton is a great poet, have been led by considerations of this kind to question the nineteenth-century view of him as a twin peak with Shakespeare.[7]

In *Paradise Regained*, a poem of discussion and argument whose method recalls the Book of Job, and in the strict classical tragedy of *Samson Agonistes*, the theme of which symbolizes so much of Milton's fears and hopes for his country and the Puritan cause, we have the last stage of his style. This shows an austere concentration on bare dignity of statement, and in the dramatic choruses a formal elevation, which seem to have certain neo-classic affinities, though they are at the same time a logical culmination of Milton's whole artistic development.

Eloquence and Wit in Prose

The prose of the earlier seventeenth century is even more varied than its verse, and the lines are harder to distinguish. This is partly because of the more varied functions that prose has to serve – practical, informative, persuasive, rhetorical, artistic – functions which at this time were not clearly distinguished and some of which overlap those of verse; and partly because there was as yet no prose of everyday use as a norm from which significant variations could be made for special purposes. In some respects, nevertheless, the 1590s show developments in prose roughly parallel to the rise of metaphysical wit.

For the Elizabethans the great model of cultivated prose style had been Cicero, and the chief aim amplification and embellishment according to the rules of the classical and Renaissance rhetoricians. The new concern is with matter rather than manner, a desire for more concentration and weight, and a preference for the epigrammatic terseness of Seneca or Tacitus. It was felt, as Sir William Cornwallis put it in his essays of 1601, that 'reason ... wrapped in a few words hath the best tang'. As in verse, there was no simple succession of one style by another: Ciceronian amplitude continued well into the middle of the seventeenth century, but it is important to note the beginning of a new mode. The *Essays* of Francis Bacon (1561–1626) provide an obvious example of the new style, especially in their first version, that of 1597. Later revisions and additions were to relax somewhat the uncompromising sententiousness of these strings of aphorisms, and to give a little more continuity in the development of the thought and allow some metaphorical expansion, but the general character remains:

78

Crafty men contemne Studies; Simple Men Admire them; And Wise Men Use them. *(Of Studies)*

Fortune is like the *Market*; Where many times, if you can stay a little, the Price will fall. *(Of Delayes)*

I cannot call *Riches* better, than the Baggage of Virtue.

(Of Riches)

From the sententious aphorism it is an easy step to epigrammatic wit, as these examples show, and a neat and witty prose is employed in the early years of the century for a variety of purposes. It appears in such flippant exercises as Donne's *Paradoxes and Problemes*; it was naturally taken up by the dramatists, and obvious instances may be found in the comedies of Jonson or the tragedies of Webster. When a minor character in *The White Devil* is described as 'A new up-start: one that swears like a Falckner, and will lye in the Dukes eare day by day like a maker of Almanacks', Webster is using the manner of the 'character', another prose genre which encouraged and developed epigram and pointed wit. The 'character' was a brief description, often didactic or satirical, of a human type; its classical model was the series by the Greek Theophrastus, and the vogue may have owed something to the Latin translation of this in 1592. But many forms of character-sketch had come down from medieval literature, and various interests combined to make the form popular – the drama generally, the new concern with realism and satire, the doctrine of 'humours' and its development in psychological theory. The first English collection of 'Characters' in 1608 was by the satirist Joseph Hall, whose packed style earned him the title 'our English Seneca'. The most famous of the many imitations were those of 'Overbury' (1614, with enlarged later editions), which were really by a group of writers including Webster; and the *Microcosmography* of John Earle (1628). The former is as famous for its 'Fair and Happy Milkmaid' as for 'A Roaring Boy'; the latter ranged from the academic satire of 'A Critic' to the meditation on innocence of 'A Child', but always with a neat wit approaching the metaphysical: 'He is nature's fresh picture newly drawn in oil, which time, and much handling, dims and defaces'. The manner continues in Fuller's *Holy and Profane State* (1642), which mingles the 'character' form with maxims, essays, and biographies.

It is an important characteristic of this period that one of the most popular forms of prose writing was the sermon. Here, too, effective use was made of the new terseness and pointed antithesis; while, as in religious poetry, metaphysical wit proved an effective way of expressing the great paradoxes of faith. The most famous exponents of this kind of sermon oratory were Lancelot Andrewes (1555–1626) and Donne himself, though Donne's style has other qualities. Andrewes is intellectual and analytical, teasing every possible significance out of the words of his text and playing equally with meaning and sound: 'the word within a word, unable to speak a word'; 'if He had not *beene made*, we had beene marred': or employing startling metaphor from common life – 'the *Conduit pipes* of His *Grace*'. Donne combines this wit with a more expansive rhetoric, even approaching at times the looser kind of long period: the result is a greater emotional charge, a dramatic urgency and poetic power recalling his verse:

... though in the wayes of fortune, or understanding, or conscience, thou have been benighted until now, wintred and frozen, clouded and eclypsed, damped and benummed, smothered and stupefied till now, now God comes to thee, not as in the dawning of the day, not as in the bud of the spring, but as the Sun at noon to illustrate all shadows, as the sheaves in harvest, to fill all penuries, all occasions invite his mercies, and all times are his seasons.

(*Eighty Sermons*, 1640, Sermon II)

The mingling of wit and eloquence in Donne's oratorical style is like his highly individual verse, the expression of his mind and personality, in which scholastic learning, acute introspective analysis, and a restless intellect playing over the whole range of contemporary life and thought are inseparable from sensuous directness and passionate feeling.

A somewhat similar blend of epigrammatic wit with heightened eloquence may be seen in writers other than preachers. Robert Burton (1577–1640), in his encyclopaedic *Anatomy of Melancholy*, claimed to follow Seneca in respecting matter rather than words, but his habit of piling up learned references and examples, and his liking for strings of synonyms, made for long sentences which have been described as 'clause-heaps'. Sometimes these will approach the more elaborately articulated Latin sentence; more usually they seem shapeless and rambling. Burton can show at times a certain colloquial vigour, and his garrulity fits with his wide-ranging curiosity about human life and his immense reading. Sir Thomas Browne (1605–82) is chiefly famous as an exponent of sonorous eloquence and the swelling period, but in his earliest work, *Religio Medici*, there is something of colloquial familiarity and epigrammatic sententiousness, while a love of paradox and a kind of metaphysical wit appear in all his writings. Wishing to state that he limits his desire for wealth, he says, 'I have not Peru in my desires, but a competence'; in his soul he finds among his passions 'the battail of Lepanto', and man appears to him 'that great and true *Amphibium*, whose nature is disposed to live ... in divided and distinguished worlds'. Browne's own nature was certainly so disposed; he is constantly making unexpected connections between different fields of knowledge and experience – scholastic philosophy, classical legend and history, Christian and biblical tradition, contemporary scientific theory, individual observation and personal musings and emotions. Similarly he plays off against each other the Latin and Teutonic elements in the language, speaking of 'the funambulatory Track and narrow Path of goodness' or 'a vanity almost out of date, and superannuated piece of folly'.

But Browne is increasingly concerned with effects of sonority, rhythm, and cadence; and in any classification of seventeenth-century prose styles his place must be with the renewed turning to expansive eloquence apparent in the pamphlets of Milton and the sermons of Jeremy Taylor (1613–67). All these writers show a deliberate and conscious rhetorical art, with a marked use of Latinized diction and syntax and a preference for the long period. Milton, indeed, is the most notable Ciceronian in English, though the anti-Ciceronian reaction had set in long before his time. His *Areopagitica*, conceived as a classical oration addressed to the Lords and Commons of England, is a sustained and glowing plea for liberty of expression; through its swelling rhythms we feel the lofty hopes of the Puritan Revolution's more idealistic phase:

Methinks I see in my mind a noble and puissant nation rousing herself like a strong man after sleep, and shaking her invincible locks. Methinks I see her as an eagle mewing her mighty youth, and kindling her undazzled eyes at the full midday beam; purging and unscaling her long-abused sight at the fountain of heavenly radiance; while the whole noise of timorous and flocking birds, with those also that love the twilight, flutter about, amazed at what she means, and in their envious gabble would prognosticate a year of sects and schisms.

Such heightened eloquence could not, of course, be the staple manner of Milton's prose writings, though it maintains a generally formal and rhetorical level. The last lines of this extract suggest the vein of harshness and pedantry which sometimes appears in more heated passages of controversy; a certain inflexibility in the style makes the occasional excursions into colloquial directness seem forced and heavy. In his most memorable passages Milton handles prose as oratory or poetry. The third of these writers who preferred the long, constructed period, Jeremy Taylor, is equally a prose-poet, noted for his fluent vocabulary and copious metaphor. Like Browne he has affinities with metaphysical wit, but even more a love of sonority and cadence together with an ornate imagery of sensuous beauty. Neither Browne nor Taylor shows Donne's urgency and intensity.

In writers like Milton and the preachers, one might expect to find a considerable influence from the Authorized Version of the Bible (1611). This is obvious in direct allusion and echoes, or in the use of the parallelism and Oriental imagery of Hebrew poetry which fitted in well with seventeenth-century exuberance. But in stately and eloquent rhythms it is not always easy to distinguish the influence of the Bible from other contemporary factors, such as the general state of the language and the study of classical rhetoric. The Authorized Version was the work of a committee of scholars, which inevitably produced an impersonal style at times somewhat conservative in its dignity and elevation; nevertheless, many of the narrative passages had a more direct simplicity which was to blend easily with homely speech in some of the Puritan pamphleteers and in Bunyan.

The pursuit of eloquence and wit, either singly or in various combinations, made possible the expression of many fascinating or impressive examples of seventeenth-century thought and sensibility. But while genius had free play, there was no check upon eccentricity; the age had no standard prose for logical argument and no normal medium for ordinary discussion and communication. It was these intellectual and practical needs which were increasingly to discipline and restrict extravagances and to lead towards the emergence of a prose of everyday use after the Restoration.

Prose as an Intellectual Instrument

As the language of learning and thought, English at the beginning of the seventeenth century had to compete with Latin, still the universal language. Bacon planned his great unfinished *Instauratio Magna* in Latin, and Hobbes used Latin for *De Cive* and *De Corpore*, translating them later. Burton would have written in Latin had not his publishers dissuaded him, and Browne used English for *Pseudodoxia Epidemica* only on second thoughts. Works were often translated into Latin to give them a European circulation; among these may be mentioned Browne's *Religio Medici* and Hooker's *Ecclesiastical Polity* (translated by John Earle, the 'character' writer).

English prose of intellectual argument as we understand it today may be said to begin with Hooker's *Laws of Ecclesiastical Polity*, but it was Bacon who fully launched it, in *The Advancement of Learning* (1605). Here in a manner more connected and flowing than that of the *Essays*, yet equally concerned for 'matter' rather than 'words', he sets out the conditions of all rational investigation of nature and human life. Claiming that 'nothing parcel of the world is denied to man's enquiry and invention', he sees as 'the root of all error' 'too untimely a departure and too remote a recess from particulars'. He advocates a radical change in intellectual habits, a transfer of interest from abstract speculation to direct observation and experiment. Bacon was the great propagandist for a kind of knowledge which should lead to practical control of the world. Though not himself a scientist, he established the basic methods of science and furthered its rapid development later in the century; by the time of the Restoration, Cowley was hailing him as the Moses who had reached the border of the scientific Promised Land. With such preoccupations it is hardly surprising that Bacon developed a prose style recognized even in his own time as aiming rather at 'Masculine, and clear, Expression, than at any Fineness, of Affectation of Phrases'.[8] Without rejecting some degree of eloquent heightening, and without losing altogether the concrete force of popular speech, he develops particularly the rational possibilities of language, using metaphors primarily as vivid intellectual illustration, and showing some distrust of imaginative writing: poetry doth raise and erect the mind by submitting the shews of things to the desires of the mind; whereas reason doth buckle and bow the mind unto the nature of things.

(*The Advancement of Learning*, Book 2)

Here we have the beginnings of an attitude which was to grow more common later in the century, with important repercussions on prose style.

Prose appears as an instrument of thought about literature in the important fragments that survive of Ben Jonson's criticism. *Timber: or Discoveries* is a collection of notes from his wide reading in ancient and contemporary rhetoricians and critics, with original comments and examples. As elsewhere, Jonson makes his borrowings his own, and the considered conclusions on literature and life are expressed with a weight and authority recalling Bacon.

An approach towards a more scientific method and temper can be seen in various kinds of prose writing throughout this period. Ralegh's *History of the World* (1614) has an encyclopaedic or epic inclusiveness, beginning with the Creation and interpreting biblical and classical events and legends according to theological and philosophical beliefs still largely medieval. In marked contrast, Bacon's *History of the Reign of Henry VII* is an attempt at a coherent and rational interpretation of a limited period. Burton, in so many ways medieval and lacking in historical sense and scientific method, yet shows a genuine observation and understanding of human psychology: it is interwoven with religious beliefs, medieval philosophy, traditional medicine, popular superstition, literary interests, humour, and satire, but one strand in the complex fabric is a true scientific curiosity. Browne, again, shows himself in part a follower of Bacon; in the *Pseudodoxia Epidemica* or *Vulgar Errors*, he takes up a project of Bacon's own, and in so far as he refers common beliefs to the test of experiment, he is a true scientist. Experiment, however, is only one of Browne's weapons: he appeals also to general reason and learned authority, and he recognizes no separation of the fields of science and religious belief. Moreover, he often shows an imaginative interest in curious notions for their own sake; even in a work whose professed aim is scientific and practical. Browne does not feel it necessary to separate rational thought from poetic imagination, and his style reflects this freedom, varying between straightforward exposition and his more characteristic vein of eloquent meditation. A more single-minded and practical development along Baconian lines may be seen in the discussions during the forties and fifties, which led to the foundation of the Royal Society in 1660.

The tendency towards disengaging the quality of clear and logical argument from the various other possible uses of prose was not confined to scientists, professional or amateur. It appears in the writings of those more Latitudinarian divines who were concerned to demonstrate the rational and philosophical basis of religious truth; among these may be mentioned John Hales (1584–1656) and William Chillingworth (1602–44). The group known as the Cambridge Platonists shared the general preoccupation with reason, but for them right reason was inseparable from true faith, the two being reconciled in an idealistic philosophy which did not hand over all truth other than that of revelation to materialistic empiricism. This philosophy was often expressed in an ornate and poetic language, especially by Henry More (1614–87) and John Smith (1615–52); but the style of others of the group, such as Benjamin Whichcote (1609–83) and Ralph Cudworth (1617–88), partakes of the growing movement towards clarity and directness.

The movement of contemporary events provided a wide field for intellectual prose, and one extensively cultivated, in the discussion of politics. Here the more extended writings include the work of Sir Robert Filmer (1588?–1653) in defence of absolute monarchy; the *Oceana* of James Harrington (1611–77), a description of an ideal republic which bears upon the economic and agrarian causes of the Civil War, and the *Leviathan* of Thomas Hobbes (1588–1679). To these may be added the controversial pamphlets of Milton and of the left-wing theorists of the Commonwealth period, especially John Lilburne the 'Leveller' (1615–77) and Gerrard Winstanley (1609–after 1650), the leader of the 'Diggers'. Milton, as we have seen, expressed his political thought in mannered eloquence, and the revolutionary pamphleteers show at times a biblical fervour, but for the most part political discussion produced a plainer prose concentrating on logical exposition and argument.

Many of these movements of thought and style combine in the political and philosophical writings of Hobbes. As a philosopher, he carries further Bacon's empiricism, applying it to human psychology and developing a theory of knowledge as based on sense-impressions, which are themselves ultimately reducible to the impact of bodies in motion. From the standpoint of this thorough-going materialism and determinism, Hobbes surveys the world in general and more especially the constitution of society. In *Leviathan* he produces a tightly argued philosophical theory of absolutism, bringing the whole force of his logical and scientific mind to the task. It is only natural that for the expression of these ideas he should have evolved a strong and unadorned style which carried still further the concern with matter rather than manner, rejecting as far as possible all the emotional qualities of language and concentrating on rational lucidity. The following passage from *Leviathan* gives some idea of the geometrical logic with which his argument advances, though he does not always employ such a staccato brevity of sentence:

> To this war of every man, against every man, this also is consequent: that nothing can be unjust. The notions of right and wrong, justice and injustice, have there no place. Where there is no common power, there is no law: where no law no injustice. Force, and fraud, are in war the two cardinal virtues. Justice, and injustice are none of the faculties neither of the body, nor mind. If they were, they might be in a man that were alone in the world, as well as his senses, and passions. They are qualities, that relate to men in society, not in solitude ...

> (*Leviathan*, Part I, ch. 13)

By this stage, prose as an intellectual instrument has acquired both precision and force.

Familiar and Miscellaneous Prose

Apart from the prose of conscious art and serious intellectual discussion, this age saw a great expansion of the more miscellaneous and utilitarian types of writing: accounts of travels, biography, autobiography, diaries, letters, pamphlets, and the beginnings of journalism. Here there was a general movement away from such formal models as existed towards a simpler and more straightforward manner, and an increasing adjustment of style to the practical needs of ordinary communication. On the whole, this tendency fitted in easily with the growing intellectual concern for logic and clarity.

Among the travellers may be mentioned first the eccentric figure of Thomas Coryate (1577?–1617). The title *Coryat's Crudities Hastily gobled up in five Moneths travells* suggests the extent to which he was still a showman displaying his wit, in a manner related to the Elizabethan pamphleteers and the character-writers. Fynes Morison (1566–1630), in his *Itinerary*, wrote in a more straightforward manner of his travels in Europe. Captain John Smith (1580–1631), the historian of the founding of Virginia, was concerned primarily with communicating factual and practical information and recommending the cause of colonization. Samuel Purchas (1577–1631), no traveller himself, but devoted to the study of geography and the explorations of others, attempted to carry on the work of Hakluyt and planned a history of the world based on all existing travel literature in the vast compilation *Purchas his Pilgrims*. Generally speaking, accounts of travels tended to employ a plainer and more straightforward prose style.

The seventeenth century shows considerable development in the field of biography. In 1605 Bacon remarked that it was surprising how few lives of famous historical personages existed; by the end of the century this was no longer true, and the word 'biography' itself appeared in English soon after the Restoration. The chief starting-points for those attempting this genre were the classical model of Plutarch and the generalized 'character' depicting a social type. These influences combine in the short sketches of contemporary figures which appear in the work of historians of their own times like Arthur Wilson (1595–1652), Sir Philip Warwick (1609–83), and pre-eminently Edward Hyde, Earl of Clarendon (1609–74) in his *History of the Rebellion*. Fuller, in his *History of the Worthies of England*, mixes informal sketches and anecdotes with his biographical information in a characteristically unsystematic fashion. What may be called the first true English biographies are the *Lives* by Izaak Walton (1593–1683) of Donne, Wotton, Hooker, Herbert, and Sanderson. These were written at various times between 1640 and 1678, but even the earliest show a style which, though related to the sententious and witty manner, achieves a remarkable degree of simplicity and directness. After the Restoration, biographies multiplied; mention may be made of two whose materials were in process of collection earlier: one Puritan, the *Life of Colonel Hutchinson* by his wife Lucy (1620– after 1675); the other Royalist, the *Life of the Duke of Newcastle* by his second wife Margaret (1623?–73). Allied to biography was the report of conversation, exemplified in Drummond's notes of his talks with Ben Jonson, and in the *Table Talk* of the broad-minded lawyer and politician John Selden (1584–1654), recorded by his secretary.

Autobiography showed a similar progression towards a plainer style. Sir Kenelm Digby (1603–65) treats his *Private Memoirs* as a kind of romance, in a vein of artificial eloquence; Lord Herbert of Cherbury, on the other hand, writing his *Autobiography* in old age during the Civil War, employs a style that is informal and even negligent. Intimate accounts of the author's own tastes, opinions, and activities form part of the attraction of Walton's *Compleat Angler,* and Cowley's essay *Of Myself* shows the autobiographical interest expressed in measured conversational simplicity. Among the diaries that were to be published later, those of the Presbyterian Richard Baxter (1615–91) and the Quaker George Fox (1624–91) may be mentioned; after the Restoration come the more famous diarists Pepys and Evelyn.

Letter-writing, again, moves from rhetorical formality and elaborate wit towards a more straightforward manner. The letters of Donne show many of the qualities of his other prose, as do those of Bacon and other literary figures. Sometimes, as in the *Epistolae Ho-Elianae* of James Howell (1593?–1666), we find genuine letters mingled with an artificial use of the form to record miscellaneous reflections and observations; here the conscious art appears also in the style. But there survive from this period a large number of letters with no pretension to art, informal communications between scholars and men of affairs, practical information exchanged between soldiers and politicians of the Civil War, and the normal commerce of domestic life betweeen relations and friends. Some of these are preserved in family collections like the Verney papers. The increase of this kind of everyday writing naturally encouraged a style nearer to ordinary speech; the letters of Dorothy Osborne (1627–95) to William Temple, whom she married in 1654, embody her belief that 'all letters . . . should be as free and Easy as ones discourse'.

An important factor in the evolution of a plainer prose was the rise of journalism. Regular sheets of foreign news, called 'corantos', had begun to be published as early as 1620; at the beginning of the Civil War, in response to a natural demand, there appeared the first accounts of politics and events at home. Growth was rapid, and the Royalist *Mercurius Aulicus*, which continued from 1642 to 1645, had many imitators. Its chief political opponent was the *Mercurius Britannicus*, and later, during the fifties, the *Mercurius Politicus* had an official status under the government. At the same time a host of short-lived 'diurnals' and controversial pamphlets fed and developed the appetite for political discussion, and by their very nature encouraged a simple and forthright style, approximating ever more closely to the tone and movement of informal speech. The result may be seen in later pamphlets, like the anti-Cromwellian *Killing No Murder* by the notorious one-time Leveller Colonel Sexby (d. 1658) or the attack on Milton by Roger L'Estrange (1616–1704) called *No Blind Guides*.

The number of religious writings – sermons, controversial tracts, and spiritual autobiographies – from the various Puritan sects was no less than the political. Here the raciness and vigour of popular speech is usually modified by a strong biblical influence. How fruitful this mingling could be is shown pre-eminently in the work of John Bunyan (1628–88), whose mind was formed under the Commonwealth, though his written works appeared after the Restoration. Bunyan represents a different side of Puritanism from Milton the scholar and humanist. His strength is to a great extent that of a popular culture close to the soil, with a language of homely vitality which had earlier formed the basis of Elizabethan pamphleteering and much dramatic dialogue. It is a culture that has its roots in the Middle Ages on both the religious and the secular side; behind the vivid allegory of *The Pilgrim's Progress* lies a long line of popular preaching, with illustrations and examples drawn from common life and appealing to practical experience and shrewd folk wisdom. To this vigour and realism of conception and style the study of the Bible added dignity and eloquence, making possible the classic expression of a religious attitude to life which went deeper than doctrinaire Calvinism or the fanaticism of a sect. It has often been noted that Bunyan anticipated the novelists of the next century. This is true not only of his narrative power and dramatic dialogue, his lively portraits of characters like Mr By-ends and Mr Worldly Wiseman and the sombre realism of parts of *Mr Badman*, but also of his record and analysis of inner conflict, especially in *Grace Abounding*, which looks forward beyond Richardson to Rousseau's *Confessions* and the psychological novel of the nineteenth century.[9]

Towards the Augustan Age

It will be apparent that by the time of the Restoration various lines of development were converging to establish a new poetry and a new prose. In both, modifications of style were symptoms of change in sensibility, intellectual habits, the general orientation of culture, and the nature of society.

In poetry the taste for 'strong lines', highly charged with meaning and employing startling figures of speech, yields gradually to a desire for perspicuity, for clear general conceptions, appealing, so to speak, to the social rather than the inner ear. Metaphysical wit changes to an epigrammatic neatness based on polite rationality and Good Sense; passionate thought gives place to urbane argument, satire, or compliment, or to a formal eloquence and magniloquence for the loftier and graver themes. The most appropriate form of the expression of the new interests was found to be the sequence of self-contained pentameter couplets, handled with a smooth regularity that owed something to the more obvious qualities of Ben Jonson's lyrics. Waller and Denham were regarded by the Restoration critics as the pioneers of the new versification – 'Mr Waller', said Dryden, 'reformed our numbers' – though in fact they had forerunners, especially among translators like Fairfax (d. 1635) and Sandys (1578–1644). The new manner and the new interests are well illustrated in Waller's *A Panegyrick to My Lord Protector* (1655):

> Your never failing Sword made War to cease,
> And now you heale us with the arts of Peace,
> Our minds with bounty, and with awe engage,
> Invite affection, and restrain our rage:
> Less pleasure take brave minds in battles won,
> Than in restoring such as are undon.

The new social style and subject-matter fitted in easily with the existing strain of conscious classicism in seventeenth-century poetry, which was reinforced through the French contacts of the royal exile; the Court returned anxious to assert its modernity and civilization according to continental standards. Signs of the new tendencies appear in Marvell in his couplet verses on Cromwell and his turning to political satire. Reaction against Puritanism and the 'rule of the Saints' found a notable satirical voice in the work of Samuel Butler (1612–80), whose mock-heroic poem *Hudibras* had been started before the Restoration. An extreme and uniquely personal expression of the new rationalism and hedonism appears in the poems and satires of John Wilmot, Earl of Rochester (1647–80), who has been described as having rejected the new orthodoxy of Augustan civilization at its very outset.

In prose various causes were leading towards the emergence of a normal style of everyday use, of a kind which hardly existed at the beginning of the century. Eloquent persuasion and authoritarian assertion were giving way to a tone of polite discussion and the assumption that the reader would be a gentleman of equal status and amenable to rational argument. Similarly the lighter types of prose were moving away from the self-conscious exhibition of cleverness; wit was increasingly regulated by a sense of 'good form' and social decorum. The new scientific interests, too, helped to foster a plain prose of exposition and reasoning. Hobbes's limited view of figures of speech, and his assertion of the superiority of judgement to fancy, have already been mentioned. Sprat's much-quoted lines on the Royal Society's requirements in style should not be given an exaggerated importance, but they remain a significant pointer:

They have exacted from all their members a close, naked, natural way of speaking, positive expressions, clear senses, a native easiness, bringing all things as near the Mathematical plainness as they can, and preferring the language of Artizans, Countrymen, and Merchants, before that of Wits and Scholars.

At the same time the practical needs of political discussion, pamphleteering, and journalism under the Commonwealth, aided by social developments in the direction of an urban culture such as the rise of the coffee-house, all helped to encourage the growth of a plain prose of ordinary use. In prose as in poetry the effects of the Court exile helped to confirm developments at home. Familiarity with French prose certainly did not dispose the minds of the returning Royalists against the new plainer style, and it may have helped to add something of polish and urbanity.

In this survey the drama has received little attention, since its later

Jacobean and Caroline development is more appropriately considered in relation to the period of its triumph. But it is worth noting that the Restoration drama was not a completely new start. Marked developments towards both the comedy of manners and heroic tragedy can be seen in such writers as Fletcher, Massinger, and Shirley well before the closing of the theatres in 1642, and to a great extent the Restoration playwrights picked up the tradition from where it lapsed.

If the culture of the Restoration had its roots far back in the century, so equally a number of figures not usually thought of as 'Restoration' lived on well into the new reign – not only Bunyan, Milton, and Marvell, but also Browne, Herrick, Vaughan, Walton, and even Hobbes, who had been Bacon's secretary. It is convenient, nevertheless, to treat these as individual exceptions and to draw the general line at 1660, by which date the new spirit and the new modes of expression were reasonably well established.

NOTES

1. See the previous volume in this series: *The Age of Shakespeare*.
2. Rosemond Tuve's *Elizabethan and Metaphysical Imagery* (1947) argues that the metaphysical 'reaction' against Elizabethan conventions has been both exaggerated and inaccurately defined. While some revision of the terms in which the contrast has been stated may be desirable, it seems idle to attempt to minimize the actual difference. An early answer to Rosemond Tuve's arguments was made by William Empson in the *Kenyon Review* for autumn 1949 in an article entitled 'Donne and the Rhetorical Tradition'. My own further discussion of these problems appeared under the title 'The New Scholarship?' in *Scrutiny*, XIX, no. 2 (1952–3, later reprinted in *Selections from Scrutiny* I, 1968).
3. From his *Life of Cowley*, which discusses metaphysical poetry from an eighteenth-century point of view.
4. Helen Gardner's edition of the *Divine Poems* (1952) argues for a date between 1609 and 1611 for most of these sonnets.
5. A higher opinion of Vaughan than that suggested here may be found in M. M. Mahood's *Poetry and Humanism* (1950), ch. 8; E. C. Pettet's *Of Paradise and Light* (1960) and R. A. Durr's *On the Mystical Poetry of Henry Vaughan* (1962).
6. Particularly Grierson in *Cross-Currents in English Literature of the Seventeenth Century* and *Criticism and Creation*, 18–22.
7. See J. Middleton Murry: *The Problem of Style*, 108–21 and note; T. S. Eliot: 'A Note on the Verse of John Milton' in *E.S.M.E.A.* XXI, and 'Milton' in *Proc. Brit. Acad.* XXXIII (reprinted with some omissions in T. S. Eliot:

Selected Prose, Penguin Books, and in *On Poetry and Poets*); F. R. Leavis: *Revaluation*, ch. 2, and 'Mr Eliot and Milton' in *The Common Pursuit*. A different point of view is represented by E. M. W. Tillyard: *Milton*, and *The Miltonic Setting*; C. S. Lewis: *A Preface to Paradise Lost*; Douglas Bush: *Paradise Lost in Our Time; Some Comments*. Attempts to sum up the argument have been made by A. J. A. Waldock: *Paradise Lost and its Critics*; John Peter: 'Reflections on the Milton Controversy', in *Scrutiny* XIX, no. 1 (1952), and *A Critique of 'Paradise Lost'* (1960); C. Ricks, *Milton's Grand Style* (1963), R. M. Adams, *Milton and the Modern Critics* (earlier title *Ikon*, 1955); and G. A. Wilkes, *The Thesis of 'Paradise Lost'* (1961) – to mention only a few.

8. By William Rawley, Bacon's chaplain, in his life of Bacon, 1657.

9. The point is made by Grierson in *Cross-Currents in English Literature of the Seventeenth Century*, 203.

PART III

THE EUROPEAN BACKGROUND TO
BAROQUE SENSIBILITY

ODETTE DE MOURGUES

It is always a temptation to think of England as being, metaphorically as well as geographically, an island; the more so perhaps when we consider the impressive bulk of Elizabethan and Jacobean literature. Scholars may trace the influence of Italian and French sonneteers on English Court poets; they may count up the number of translations of du Bartas and Montaigne; it hardly alters the general picture of an age when strong national characteristics were emphatically stamped on drama, prose, and poetry. But an attempt to connect English literature of the period with the Continent through the study of direct literary influences is bound to be a short-sighted process.

On the other hand, a bird's-eye view of the late Renaissance in Western Europe, in a prize-giving spirit, might be misleading and unprofitable: England stands out with a baffling grandeur which reminds us of the summit of Greek literature in the fifth century B.C.; so does Spain with the splendour of its Golden Age; whereas Italian culture shows signs of decadence, and France and Germany display a confused pattern of uncertain literary values. Yet, whatever the ultimate aesthetic judgement passed on the artistic output of these countries during this period, we have come to think of the late Renaissance as a sort of *'crise de la conscience européenne'*. Recent criticism on French, Spanish, and German literatures has not only been concerned with the revaluation of individual writers of the late sixteenth and early seventeenth centuries; it has been more and more attracted by this age of transition as a time when something of portentous importance was happening to the mind of Europe. We all know the rough outlines of that crisis which originated in the impact of Renaissance and Reformation on the medieval universe of Christendom: the clash between the pagan and the Christian worlds, and inside Christianity between Protestants and Catholics; political unrest and religious wars; the absence of a systematized philosophy which could have suggested some coherent answer to these new problems. We are used to thinking of the period as an era of pessimism, chaos, and violence succeeding the optimism of the Renaissance when Man, having asserted his birthright as the centre of the universe, felt the world was his, and himself and the world were one harmonious whole.

The conflicts, political, religious, or economic, assumed different forms in the different countries, but there was a certain mood which was common to all, a mood which is elusive when we come to defining it. Some would call it 'baroque' – a dangerously fashionable word in the terminology of literary criticism – but this term may be helpful if we use it in order to characterize certain manifestations of the sensibility of the late Renaissance. This sensibility reacted so violently to the problems of the age that intelligence was not always able to control it, and we may perhaps call baroque the artistic outcome of this destruction of the balance between feeling and intellect, this distortion of reality through the cravings of unruly emotions and the desperate vagaries of imagination. The word sensibility must be taken as meaning the senses as well as sentiments (and, in fact, the two connotations are more than once confused in baroque consciousness).

The conflict between the spirit and the senses was not a new one. But if we compare an Italian sacred opera published in the early seventeenth century, *Rappresentazione di anima e di corpo*,[1] with the old morality plays or even with Petrarchan ratiocination on the respective importance of the body and the soul, we realize that the intensified claim of bodily pleasures now made any kind of balance a very precarious one. Renaissance humanism had proposed the *mens sana in corpore sano*, but that was too obviously an enticing pagan tag. The solution of the Jesuits and of devout humanism was to enlist the senses in the service of God. This was one of the most impressive attempts towards preserving at least part of the unity of a threatened universe. It gave birth to the stern *Spiritual Exercises* of Ignatius Loyola, the art of the Counter-Reformation, the Emblem-books of the Jesuits, and an enormous bulk of religious poetry (poetry like that of Crashaw). In its excesses this appeal to the senses *ad majorem Dei gloriam* leads to a distorted vision of life in which religious themes, such as the repentant Magdalene, the ecstatic Teresa, the Sacred Heart, the crucified Saviour, the Holy Innocents, are translated into undulating marble raptures in sculpture or pictorial symbolic metaphors in poetry. They compose a decorative pageant based on an emotion which is of doubtful quality: a strange mixture of crude pathos and sensuous pleasure. It leaves us with the impression that senses and imagination have been indulged out of all proportion to the needs of religion. This carnal mysticism leads us to suspect that something has gone wrong in this interpenetration of spirituality and materiality, and that one thing has been substituted for another: the roses, pearls, flaming hearts, and doves for some kind of escapism into fairy-land; the voluptuous tears of sinners for the bitter-sweet delights of masochism, and the raptures and swoons of saints for erotic experiences. Baroque sensibility has subtle, contorted by-paths and oblique vistas. If we leave aside the questionable expressions of sacred love, we find even in novels, epics, or pastorals dealing with profane love a perverted preference for ambiguous situations: Honoré d'Urfé's shepherds disguised as girls spend days and nights with chaste heroines; Tasso's amazons fight in lascivious tussles with warriors, under the tantalizing protection of golden armour.

But sometimes the balance between the body and the spirit was destroyed in favour of the spirit. Spanish mysticism was still soaring on those supreme heights which St John of the Cross had reached, where, all material life annihilated, the soul rejoices in a luminous void. In France the early seventeenth century is marked by a conflict between abstract mysticism and the last champions of devout humanism; before coming down to the rational and psychological standpoint of Bossuet, French spirituality struggles towards a direct union with pure Divine Essence.

These contrasts and contradictions show that Renaissance man had lost his self-confidence. The hero of Jacobean drama is often torn between a horror of life and a terror of death. So is perhaps the Picaro, the hero of the Spanish novel at the end of the sixteenth century. Renaissance humanism had relied on Nature and Reason to make Man a harmonious whole. But the age of geographical discoveries had become an age of more upsetting explorations: explorations of the mind by itself. St Teresa's autobiographies and Montaigne's essays had found disturbing recesses in human personality; they had passed the frontier which separates the conscious from the subconscious mind. Montaigne especially had shown our psychic life as a threateningly elusive, ever-moving, ever-changing flow, and baroque sensibility vacillated at times over dark rivers. Montaigne was eminently sane, but doubt and uncertainty were not for his contemporaries or followers the *'mol oreiller'* they were for him: they had bad dreams. Uncertainty became distrust: the dry, stiff distrust of the politician and the courtier, which stands out in Bacon's essays or in the works of the Spaniard Gracian. Bad dreams invaded day-life, and in the heated brains of some men recurrent nightmares started to draw odd and terrifying pictures. Melancholy was to be anatomized by Burton. It had indeed many shapes and many faces during the late Renaissance.

These faces became more clearly outlined as they dropped the fragile mask of Stoicism so carefully put on by the sixteenth century, and one of the faces was the flat face of Death. A second Dance of Death passed over Europe. A taste for the macabre permeated French drama of the period as well as the Jacobean drama. The skeleton became a decorative element of Italian mortuary monuments and the grim companion of the poet's love. Yorick's skull, Donne's shroud, Tourneur's horrors are paralleled on the Continent. In French lyrical poetry, Agrippa d'Aubigné decorated his bedroom with bones, and we owe to dark meditations on physical decay the superb sonnets on death by Jean de Sponde.[2] From the Dance of Death we pass to the dance of worms and the dance of evil spirits. The natural disintegration of the human body is not enough to satisfy an imagination which is doggedly determined to go on to the bitter end. In contrast with the rosy paradises of mystical writers like Crashaw or Fletcher, we find the harrowing obsession with 'hell'. The epic, solemnly terrifying hell into which d'Aubigné's enemies are hurled in a blast of heavenly vengeance; the phantasmagoric, grotesque, crude visions of the Spanish writer Quevedo; the picturesque, Bosch-like description of Davies of Hereford's *House of Time* with frozen hearts floating on sulphured streams and a 'goblin, grisly grim, fishing for a Soule'. The horrifying supernatural element crept into the life of the living, taking the form of magic and witchcraft. It is hardly surprising that some of the writings of the time reveal a divided personality in the writer or even a disjunction in his vision of reality which may go as far as the absurd. In Italy, the poet-philosopher Bruno (put to death in 1600) expressed in sibylline incoherence the boldest theories, and the visionary Campanella dabbled in occultism and wrote violent and dark poetry, involved and abrupt. In France a puzzling ode by Théophile de Viau presents us with a mad universe where everything is upside down.

Reality is thus viewed in distorted and grinning mirrors. For the Renaissance the solid wholeness was implicitly given by the complementary union of the Macrocosmos, the totality of things, with the Microcosmos, the 'little world', Man. The Renaissance poets, like Ronsard, had with patience and love tried to build up the cosmos into a harmonious whole, where Nature's eternal laws ruled in magnificent hierarchy the rose, Man, and the stars. But now the sense of proportion vanished. The giddy imagination is attracted by the colossal, the limitless: continental poets, like d'Aubigné, wander like roaring giants in interplanetary spaces, hurling down stars and suns. The sense of disaster pervading the period had to take apocalyptic proportions, and one of the favourite themes of late Renaissance poetry is that of the Last Judgement:

> At the round earth's imagin'd corners, blow
> Your trumpets, angels ...

Donne is concerned with his own relationship with God and for him the theme is just a starting-point, but many continental poets seem to take an almost malignant delight in describing this colossal disorder in Nature. Fragments of the cosmos, magnified by anxiety and made more terrifying by their isolation, haunted the poets of the late Renaissance and provided them with a rich store of poetic images. Such are the moons and suns which Shakespeare placed on the face of Antony.

But, on the other hand, baroque sensibility delights in the diminutive. Devout humanism spent endless hours contemplating a dewdrop on the petal of a carnation; the French Libertin poets, Théophile and St Amant, reduced seascapes to the dimensions of a goldfish bowl and landscapes to that of a Chinese garden. In Italy, Marini was conspicuous for his myopic vision of the universe.

Not only were the proportions of the world so strangely altered, but, as if under the effect of some invisible crack, reality split apart and fell into separate pieces. The trumpets of Doom were not even necessary. The poets mentioned above, Théophile and St Amant, offer us pictures which are disconnected as well as diminutive. They pass from one object to another without supplying any logical link. Their technique is a kind of *pointillisme*, which reminds us of impressionist pictures. The disorderly enumeration of various objects which appeal to their fancy is furthermore stressed by the jerkiness of the rhythm. Perhaps, as Professor Forster remarks in his study *The Temper of Seventeenth Century German Literature*,[3] the fragmentation of subject is linked with the fragmentation of time: 'Time is felt to be split up into a series of moments, of *occasiones* . . . The poet sees one thing at a time, in its momentary, changing aspect, and the change is an abrupt one.'

This juxtaposition of images or moments which fail to fuse into unity may well recall to our mind Coleridge's well-known distinctions between Imagination and Fancy, in which Fancy is 'a mode of Memory emancipated from the order of Time and Space' receiving 'all its material ready-made from the law of association'. In fact, the word *fantaisie* is a key-word when judging the works of some baroque writers; the Libertin poets mentioned it all the time and asserted their right to follow the capricious meanderings of their *rêverie*, and the English metaphysical poets have been grouped in an unusual anthology under the title of the Fantasticks.[4] Coleridge's definition would perhaps account for the impression of extreme artificiality and, at times, extreme monotony we have when reading some of the late Renaissance poets. Crashaw, Théophile, St Amant, Gongora, Marini replaced the living universe by a world of correspondences. A network of recurrent motifs is constantly being interposed between reality and ourselves: tears, wounds, flaming hearts, the turtle-dove, and the phoenix, the grave and the nest in the mystical baroque poets; tritons, shells, water-fowl, and rushes, grottoes, the Naiad, and the poppy in the French Libertin poets. The shimmering quality of this network is made even more artificial by a riot of colours and a profusion of jewels. In Crashaw's poetry blood-drops are like rubies and tears like pearls. In the universe of Marini and the Libertin poets, the sea is green enamel and cut jasper with diamonds at the crest of the waves. In the extremely elaborate texture of Gongora's *Solitudes*, Nature is in the same way made tame and ornate, infinitely artificial, sparkling with gold and silver, an object of supreme luxury. In spite of the endless flow of metaphors and metamorphoses, this baroque poetic universe retains a hard, glittering solidity even though things appear as if they were melting away – this was not romantic escapism into a kind of Shelleyan ecstasy. But it is difficult to assess whether such poets were satisfied with gliding over the surface of things with dazzling brilliance or whether they wanted to convey a particular experience of the world. Some of Gongora's most common adjectives – *confuso, incierto, inconstante, inquieto*[5] – are disquieting, as if imagination was desperately trying to seize some ultimate reality beyond clouds of uncertainty.

Thus life appeared as a series of *fantasques tableaux*, to use St Amant's own words. Life as a picture, life as a stage, life as a dream. We come to the fundamental uneasiness which underlay this deliberate artificiality, these shifting visions, this playing up to a sort of super-reality. The senses and the spirit are usurping each other's vested interests; time has split into unconnected moments; the cosmos, magnified into prodigious infinity or reduced to derisive minuteness, has dissolved into fragments; the irregular beats of the human heart swing from paradise to hell; what is reality? Baroque sensibility was bound to question the intrinsic value of its wild flights of fancy. Hence this theme of the confusion of reality and illusion, which is one of the most important themes of the first half of the seventeenth century. In Germany the themes of the 'Theatre of the World', of 'Life as a Dream', the interplay of *Sein* and *Schein*, are characteristic of the literature of the period. They are also to be found in Shakespeare, in the French dramatist Rotrou, and in the famous play of Calderon, *La vida es sueño*. The puzzling qualities of Corneille's comedies *L'Illusion comique* or *Le Menteur* may be partly due to the impact of illusion on reality. Misunderstandings, lies, or magic are not merely dramatic devices – they illustrate and stress the repeated assertion that human beings are not what they seem to be, that night is very dark and love uncertain. The fashionable Pastoral, French, Italian, or English, and later the Opera, open the gates of a paradise of fallacies and disguises, an earthly compensation for frustration and failure. And of illusion and reality, which is the more valuable? On the threshold of the baroque era, Cervantes's *Don Quixote* seems to stand like a warning that man loses his life when he loses his illusions.

This simplified study has emphasized the most violent reactions of European sensibility to the spiritual crisis of the late Renaissance. It has been more concerned with what men of that age felt than with what they thought. I have mentioned what they feared or were attracted by rather than what they were endeavouring to do in order to solve their contradictions. The tortured, restless, tense sensibility which led writers to a distorted vision of the universe – mystical or macabre, morbid or absurd, colossal or diminutive – could be and was checked, transcended, or otherwise made harmless. We know that the English metaphysical poets, controlling their imagination and sensibility, achieved a perfect balance in a blend of passion and intellectual subtlety. Men like Herbert certainly escaped the dark vistas of the baroque. In most continental countries the seventeenth century is marked by a quest for certainty and absolute values, for order and safety. Wild passions were curbed by Court life and drawing-room standards. It is interesting to see how the most disturbing baroque themes, the end of the world and churchyards, were turned into the frivolous hyperboles of gallant poetry. Dangerous moods were tidily classified by Court poets and *précieuses*; the Libertin poets' landscape neatly trimmed into landscape gardening. It is significant also that the formidable baroque sun which, either black or dripping with blood, had presided over many an apocalyptic catastrophe, was reassuringly transformed into a mere adjunct to human glory and, carved in homely timber, became with Louis XIV the symbol of solid royalty whose task it was to provide order and hierarchy. Men of the seventeenth century were responsible for the rise of the absolute power of kings. In France and in Germany, this absolute power with which the readers of the English seventeenth-century theorist Hobbes are familiar, was strongly built on a well-ruled, tidily stratified, courtly world.

French classicism was the first and the most spectacular reward of that quest for order within the boundaries of Reason and Nature. But even before the time when the sobered humanist, overcoming the metaphysical crisis of the late Renaissance, had become the 'moralist' for whom 'The proper study of mankind is man', we see the early-seventeenth-century man opposing the threatening nightmares and the deceptive appearances of a confused reality with forces from within. A haughty *culte du moi* developed during the first half of the seventeenth century, based on will-power. Man challenged the world and stiffened into an uncompromising code of honour, himself sought to be superior to his own nature. 'I can rise higher than myself', says a character in one of Calderon's plays, and is echoed by Corneille: '*Je suis maître de moi comme de l'univers.*' Quietly but confidently Descartes states that even if everything is a deceitful dream, '*Cogito, ergo sum*'.

We may now come back to our starting-point: England as an island. Keeping in mind the European traits of this crisis of sensibility and the baroque themes which swept over England as well as over Spain, Italy, France, or Germany, we may realize better the essential Englishness of a Donne, a Thomas Browne, a Milton. This rapid survey may also help us to understand better some of the reasons for that 'dissociation of sensibility' which, according to T. S. Eliot, is a characteristic feature of the latter part of the seventeenth century.

NOTES

1. Emilio de' Cavalieri's *Rappresentazione di anima e di corpo*, produced in 1600 at San Filippo Neri's Oratory in Rome.
2. Sponde: an early-seventeenth-century French poet whose works have been discovered and edited by Professor A. Boase.
3. Inaugural Lecture delivered at University College, London (published London, 1951).
4. *The Fantasticks*, by W. S. Scott (London, 1945).
5. See *The Literature of the Spanish People*, by Gerald Brenan (London, 1951).

THE POEMS OF JOHN DONNE

R. G. COX

If we generally think of Donne as a seventeenth-century poet, that is because most of his work was not published until after his death, in the collection of 1633. Yet he was born only ten years later than Shakespeare; and by no means all of what we now consider to be typically Elizabethan poetry was in existence when he began to write. It is only too easy to over-simplify the pattern of literary change into a neat succession of 'movements' and 'reactions' and to forget that in periods of heightened vitality developments in different directions often take place side by side.[1] It remains true, nevertheless, that Donne chose to do something different from his predecessors and from those of his contemporaries who were still exploiting and developing the existing modes; and younger followers like Carew looked back on this choice as revolt or reform:

> The Muses garden with Pedantique weedes
> O'rspred, was purg'd by thee; The lazie seeds
> Of servile imitation throwne away
> And fresh invention planted ...
> (*An Elegie upon the death of the Deane of
> Paul's, Dr John Donne*)

Modern students of rhetoric have argued that Donne's innovations did not run counter to contemporary rules,[2] but even if he is to be regarded as implementing existing theoretical possibilities, his practice remains the kind of new departure which marks a decisive alteration in the course of literary history.

In considering the nature of Donne's poetic originality, it is common to begin with his development of the metaphysical conceit. Yet there is a great deal to say on the subject of his verse style before broaching the topic of imagery at all. The first point likely to strike the reader who comes to Donne from the smooth fluency of the average Elizabethan lyric or sonnet is the surprising directness of the speaking voice conveyed by his rhythms and diction:

> For Godsake hold your tongue, and let me love,
>   Or chide my palsie, or my gout,
> My five gray haires, or ruin'd fortune flout,
>   With wealth your state, your minde with Arts improve,
>   Take you a course, get you a place,
>   Observe his honour, or his grace,
>   Or the King's reall, or his stamped face
>   Contemplate, what you will, approve,
>   So you will let me love.

(The Canonization)

Here the occasional inversions of normal speech-order and the fact that line 4 by itself might come from an eighteenth-century couplet hardly affect our general impression that technique and conception are essentially dramatic; the colloquial outburst of line 1, the heavy stresses on 'palsie' and 'gout', the contemptuous alliteration of line 3, above all the play of an exasperated splutter of short phrases across the intricate stanza form, all impose on the reader the desired emphasis, tone, and mood. Plainly the aim here is not sweetness, grace, or verbal melody, either for its own sake or to accommodate any possible musician who, as Donne complains in *The Triple Foole*,

> his art and voice to show
> Doth Set and sing my paine.

It is rather a realistic expressiveness of the kind developed in the 1590s by the dramatists, above all by Shakespeare, and nothing quite like it had previously appeared in lyric poetry,[3] in spite of certain foreshadowings in Wyatt. As in dramatic verse, the aim of realism is, of course, not absolute; whatever metrical licences are taken, the pattern of line and stanza remains, to reinforce, modify, or generally play against the rhythms of speech with the effects of heightened intensity and concentration proper to poetry. When we speak of realistic expressiveness we use a shorthand term for the maximum of realistic expressiveness compatible with a sense of artistic form. Donne's lyrics have a music of their own, though the immediate effect is of vivid speech rather than song:

Deare love, for nothing lesse than thee
Would I have broke this happy dreame,
    It was a theame
For reason, much too strong for phantasie,
Therefore thou wakd'st me wisely; yet
My Dreame thou brok'st not, but continued'st it,
Thou art so truth, that thoughts of thee suffice,
To make dreams truths; and fables histories;
Enter these armes, for since thou thoughtst it best,
Not to dreame all my dreame, let's act the rest.
                        (*The Dreame*)

That Donne could write with a simple lyrical sweetness when he
chose is shown by one or two songs to existing airs, especially
'Sweetest love, I do not goe,/For weariness of thee',[4] though even
here his originality comes out in the careful subtlety of the poem's
argument. He was a conscious artist, and his avoidance of conventional fluency of movement and courtliness of diction must be assumed to be deliberate.

As with the lyric stanza, so in his satires and elegies with the couplet,
Donne makes use of licences similar to those of dramatic blank verse.
Always the formal devices of poetry – metre, rhyme, alliteration, and
other effects of sound – are made to serve an expressive purpose; a
constant control of pause, stress, and tempo works to the same end.
It is interesting to compare the formal dignity of Spenser's last two
stanzas on mutability at the end of *The Faerie Queene* with Donne's
tone of passionate argument on the same theme in *The Second
Anniversarie*:

And what essential joy can'st thou expect
Here upon earth? What permanent effect
Of transitory causes? Dost thou love
Beauty? (And beauty worthy'st is to move)
Poore cousened cousenor, *that* she, and *that* thou,
Which did begin to love, are neither now;
You are both fluid, chang'd since yesterday;
Next day repaires, (but ill) last dayes decay.
Nor are, (although the river keepe the name)
Yesterdaies waters, and todaies the same.

Here the play of the sense across the couplet pattern produces what is
essentially a dramatic emphasis, setting 'permanent effect' against
'transitory causes' with a feeling of scornful *reductio ad absurdum*,

contrasting 'yesterdaies waters' and 'todaies' in a strong argumentative climax, and making colloquial concessions and qualifications in the rapid parentheses. There is a characteristic use of the slight pause at the end of a line in the question

> > Dost thou love
>
> Beauty?

to produce the conversational effect of an implied 'for example' or 'shall we say?' before coming down with special stress on the important word. Examples may be multiplied; in the much-quoted passage on truth in *Satyre III*:

> > On a huge hill,
> Cragged, and steep, Truth stands, and hee that will
> Reach her, about must, and about must goe;
> And what the hills suddennes resists, winne so;

critics have noted that the verse-movement imposes on the reader incipient muscular movements which seem to enact the meaning, and that this way of using language is remarkably close to Shakespeare's in directness and concreteness of suggestion.[5] It is for reasons of this kind that we are not so ready as earlier readers to blame Donne for harshness and ruggedness or a 'defective ear'.

Another aspect of this dramatic quality of Donne's rhythms and diction is his controlled variety of tone. If it is a speaking voice that strikes us in the *Songs and Sonets*, it is a voice with many inflexions and intonations, from the assertive forthrightness of *The Broken Heart*:

> He is starke mad, who ever says,
>   That he hath beene in love an houre,

to the meditative musing of *Loves growth*:

> Me thinkes I lyed all winter, when I swore
>   My love was infinite, if spring make it more ...

or from the coarse cynicism of *Loves Alchymie*:

> Hope not for minde in women; at their best
> Sweetnesse and wit, they are but Mummy, possest ...

to the enigmatic irony of *The Funerall*:

Who ever comes to shroud me, do not harme
  Nor question much
That subtile wreath of hair, which crowns my arme;
The mystery, the signe you must not touch,
  For 'tis my outward Soule ...

Even more remarkable are the transitions of tone in a few lines of the same poem: *Lovers infinitenesse*, for example, begins on a note of simple tenderness, passes through a bewildering series of doubts and suspicions, worked out in riddling casuistry, and returns at the end to more wholehearted expressions of love. The effect is always that of hearing a particular tone of voice rather than of merely following words on a page.

Donne's imagery has always impressed readers by its range and variety and its avoidance of the conventionally ornamental. *The Good-morrow* refers to the familiar processes of suckling and weaning, snoring, dreaming, and waking, but also to voyages, maps, and hemispheres, scholastic theories of the nature of pure substance and general philosophical speculations about our experience of space. *The Extasie* draws on theories of the nature of souls and the way heavenly influence may work on man, on physiological notions of animal spirits, on medieval cosmology, on alchemy and chemistry, but also on negotiations between armies during a truce, imprisoned princes, sepulchral monuments, the transplanting of flowers, and threading beads on a string. Some of Donne's most powerful images are learned and scientific, as when in *A Valediction: forbidding mourning* the idea that the higher nature of the lovers' relationship will lead them to avoid outward demonstrations of grief is enforced through an analogous contrast between the dangers of earthquakes and the harmlessness of the more important irregularities of movement among the heavenly bodies:

Moving of th' earth brings harmes and feares,
  Men reckon what it did and meant,
But trepidation of the spheares,
  Though greater farre, is innocent.

'Trepidation', or trembling, of the spheres was the explanation in medieval astronomy of phenomena actually caused by the slight wobble of the earth on its axis. A poem which particularly depends upon learned references is *A Nocturnall upon S. Lucies day, Being the shortest day.* It begins with a solemn setting of the scene – midnight, the shortest day, the winter solstice, tempered by the wit of St Lucy's 'unmasking' for only seven hours and the ironical comparison of the sun to a flask of spent gunpowder. The short line

> The world's whole sap is sunke

states with particular emphasis the deadness of the season, which is further driven home in the medical metaphor ascribing the fall of the sap to the earth's dropsy and in the assertion that life has shrunk back to earth 'as to the beds feet'. The conceit that the lover is the 'epitaph' of the dead world warns us of the refinements upon the concepts of nothingness and death which are to follow. The second stanza depends on the reader's knowledge of the meaning, in alchemy, of 'quintessence' – the pure essence of any substance, containing its fundamental qualities. Love has 'pressed out'

> A quintessence even from nothingnesse,
> From dull privations, and leane emptinesse:

'privation' being used in its strict philosophical sense of 'absence' of a quality. In a further hyperbole the lover is said to have been 're-begotten' by all 'things which are not' – absence, darkness, death. In the third stanza the alchemical metaphor continues as the lover says that he has been transformed in Love's 'Limbecke' (or chemical retort) into a grave comprehending everything negative, whereas other people can take from all things the positive principles which constitute their nature and being. Then follows a series of references to the previous occasions in the relationship of the lovers when grief, distractions, or absence have reduced them to states comparable to world destruction, or the primitive chaos before the Creation, or death. But by the death of his mistress the lover has sunk much further in nothingness, becoming (again in alchemical terms) the 'Elixir' (or quintessence) of original chaos; he no longer has the self-consciousness which is the mark of man, nor the more elementary powers of response that belong to the animal, the vegetable, or even the mineral kingdoms. He has less existence than is implied by such an 'ordinary nothing' as a shadow; he lacks the solidity of a body, and the light of his sun is withdrawn. An adroit twist of the figure brings him back to the 'lesser sun' (that is, inferior, and at the same time of a wintry weakness), which at this season is in the zodiacal sign of the Goat (Capricorn); it will return in spring bringing for other lovers 'new lust' (the goat's proverbial quality), but he must prepare to join his dead mistress, who now is identified with, or replaces, St Lucy as patron of this time of midnight and mid-winter, and so the poem returns to the statement of the opening line:

> Since shee enjoyes her long nights festivall,
> Let mee prepare towards her, and let mee call
> This houre her Vigill, and her Eve, since this
> Both the yeares, and the dayes deep midnight is.

These hints are intended to bring out the primary sense; it is not suggested that they exhaust the poem's full meaning. It is essentially the work of a mind trained in the handling of abstractions and the multiplying of subtle distinctions; it draws upon current beliefs in metaphysics, cosmology, natural science, medicine, and alchemy – yet the learning and the argument are controlled to generate a profound and intense emotion. In the total effect of the poem a great part is played by the grave and sombre movement of the verse with its weighty stresses on key-words, and by the stanza form with its emphatic short line at the centre and its effect of accumulation in the three consecutive rhymes of lines 5–7.

Even in the *Nocturnall* there are 'squibs' and 'beds-feet' besides quintessences and investing properties, and many of Donne's images derive their force from everyday and commonplace experience. For the lover in *The Sunne Rising* 'houres, dayes, moneths' are 'the rags of time'; death, in *The Second Anniversarie*, becomes

> ... a Groome,
> Which brings a Taper to the outward roome,
> Whençe thou spiest first a little glimmering light ...

and every now and then, as in the letter *To Mr T. W.*, we have a vivid glimpse of the contemporary scene:

> As in our streets sly beggers narrowly
> Watch motions of the givers hand and eye,
> And evermore conceive some hope thereby.

In the past the learned element in Donne's imagery has perhaps received more stress than the familiar, and particularly his use of medieval theology and contemporary science.[6] Drummond seems to have had Donne in mind when in 1630 he objected to the modern attempt to 'abstract poetry to metaphysical ideas and scholastic quiddities', and Dryden later complained that 'Donne affects the metaphysics not only in his satires but in his amorous verses', and 'perplexes the minds of the fair sex with nice speculations of philosophy'. Dr Johnson spoke of Donne and his followers as 'the metaphysical poets' in his *Life of Cowley*, referring particularly to their exhibition of their learning, and 'metaphysical poets' they have remained ever since. The term may be regarded simply as a label, of no precise significance, and it is often convenient to leave it at that. On the other hand, it may be justified in a general sense: the best-known and the most satisfactory attempt of this kind is Grierson's.[7] The word does not apply to Donne, he admits, as to Dante or Lucretius, poets inspired by a whole philosophical conception of the universe. Yet it lays stress, he says, on the right things: the reaccentuation in the work of the seventeenth-century poets of the metaphysical strain in medieval Italian poetry,

the more intellectual, less verbal character of their wit compared with the conceits of the Elizabethans; the finer psychology of which their conceits are often the expression; their learned imagery; the argumentative, subtle evolution of their lyrics; above all, the peculiar blend of passion and thought, feeling and ratiocination, which is their greatest achievement.

A more precise justification may be found in James Smith's essay 'On Metaphysical Poetry'.[8] This isolates an element in the poetry of Donne and his followers where the poets seem to come up against fundamental problems and oppositions of a strictly metaphysical nature and to express them by a special kind of paradoxical metaphor, of which Marvell's 'green thought in a green shade' and Donne's

> ... her pure and eloquent blood
> Spoke in her cheekes, and so distinctly wrought,
> That one might almost say, her body thought

are typical examples. This definition of the term 'metaphysical' involves, of course, a careful restriction of its use, which has not been generally accepted.

The points made by Grierson have been taken up in various forms by many other critics. He recognizes that conceits and wit were common in Elizabethan poetry, but stresses the learning and the greater play of mind brought in by Donne. To the range of subject-matter drawn upon we must add the remarkable power of perceiving relations between different levels of experience, the sense of a mind always aware of various points of view, the continual effects of surprise and intensity. T. S. Eliot has remarked[9] that these sometimes depend upon the extreme elaboration of a comparison, as with the famous compasses of *A Valediction: forbidding mourning*, sometimes on a development by rapid association calling for great agility of mind in the reader, as in the second stanza of *A Valediction: of weeping*, sometimes on sudden contrasts of associations concentrated in brief phrases.

When, in *The Will*, we come upon the lines

> And all your graces no more use shall have
> Then a Sun dyall in a grave ...

the effect depends on the shock of passing at once from associations of summer and sunlight to those of darkness and death: when *Loves Exchange* begins

> *Love*, any devill else but you,
> Would for a given Soule give something too

we are startled into attention by the unexpected term 'devill' as applied to Love. Even more arresting are the complex juxtapositions of *Twicknam Garden*:

> The spider love, which transubstantiates all
> And can convert Manna to gall ...

Here, long before we have recovered from the surprise of considering love as a spider, with its various possibilites of irony, we come to all the metaphysical and scriptural reverberations of 'transubstantiate', 'Manna', and 'gall'. This is again a device associated with the dramatists, though Shakespeare uses it already in the *Sonnets* with his 'Lilies that fester'. Those who would argue that Donne's imagery depends chiefly on rational analogy and that little part is played by sensuous and emotional connotations might be asked to consider whether the first of the above examples would be equally effective if he had written 'Than a Sun dyall in a *cave*'.

Dr Johnson's objection to metaphysical wit was that, as he said, 'the most heterogeneous ideas are yoked by violence together'. Most modern critics would admit the heterogeneity, but deny that 'yoked by violence' was a fair description of the general effect. At its best the metaphysical conceit communicates a unified experience; what matters is the sense of imaginative pressure and intensity; it is only where this is absent that the ingenuity seems obtrusive and we feel impelled to speak of 'frigidity' and 'fantastic hyperbole'. The extreme cases are easy enough to pick out; against the successes already quoted we may set the extravagance represented by the following:

> Pregnant again with th' old twins Hope and Feare ...
> (To Mr T. W.)

> Or as sometimes in a beheaded man,
> Though at those two Red seas, which freely ranne,
> One from the Trunke, another from the Head,
> His soule be sail'd, to her eternall bed ...
> (The Second Anniversarie)

but there must necessarily be an indeterminate region where the degree of success is a matter of opinion. The chief advantage of the conceit as Donne uses it is the quality of inclusiveness it makes possible. It is a way of bringing effectively into poetry all his interests, activities, and speculations. No part of his experience is regarded as intrinsically unpoetical; all is equally available to him in the act of composition. Here again the parallel is with the dramatists, especially the mature Shakespeare, Ben Jonson, and the Jacobean tragedians.

It was with both the dramatists and the metaphysical poets in mind that Eliot made his famous remark about 'a mechanism of sensibility which could devour any kind of experience', and suggested that in the later seventeenth century 'a dissociation of sensibility set in, from which we have never recovered'. These phrases have often been taken from their context and made to bear more weight than they were designed for: treated as philosophical definitions and solemn historical generalizations they constituted for many years something of a critical battleground, and often tend to be regarded now as quaint period aberrations. But, as F. R. Leavis insisted in a late lecture,[10] they embody essential insights concerning the changes in language and sensibility between Donne and Dryden, and they point to qualities in Donne and the metaphysicals that all critics must find some way of defining even if they reject Eliot's formulations. Grierson, as we have seen, spoke of the blend of passion and ratiocination as the metaphysical poets' greatest achievement. It is certainly characteristic of

Donne that profound emotion generally stimulates his powers of intellectual analysis and argument, and that for him the process of logical reasoning can be in itself an emotional experience. As he brings to the lyric poem a new realism and urgency and a new penetration of psychological analysis, so he carries further than any previous poet the use of dialectic for a poem's whole structure and development. And as reasoning and analysis are not incompatible with feeling and sensuous immediacy, so there is no antithesis between wit and seriousness; seriousness, for Donne, never becomes simple solemnity.

There are, of course, in Donne as in all other poets, passages where the vitality lapses – where the rhythmical irregularities seem a tiresome mannerism, the conceits mere displays of ingenuity, and the argumentation tedious casuistry. But these are not nearly so numerous or characteristic as the general opinion assumed up to about 1920, and it seems unlikely that any readjustment of critical values will lead to a return to all the old objections of harshness, perverse obscurity, frigid intellectualism, and the rest. The criticism that Donne shows little feeling for beauty, and particularly for natural beauty, deserves a somewhat closer examination. It is not always easy to know how serious a charge is intended: if it is meant that certain attractions in the poetry of Spenser, Keats (before the revised *Hyperion*), or Tennyson are not to be found in Donne, it may be argued that his verse offers other, and equally (if not more), important qualities: if the comparison is with Dante or Shakespeare his inferiority may be readily conceded; if with Marvell, then it must be admitted that Marvell shows the possibility of combining many of the merits of Donne's style with others not characteristic of him. But it is as well to remind ourselves that just as there are exceptions which show that Donne could write smooth lyrics if he chose, so there are passages which suggest that the comparative rarity of natural beauty as a theme in his poetry was not due to complete insensibility; there is the unexpected simile in *Elegy XIX*:

> Your gown going off, such beautious state reveals,
> As when from flowry meads th' hills shadow steales;

the stanza on the birds in the Palatine Epithalamion, and, perhaps more significantly, the feeling for natural growth in one or two of the *Songs and Sonnets:*[11]

Gentle love deeds, as blossomes on a bough,
From loves awakened root do bud out now.
(*Loves Growth*)

Any attempt to trace Donne's poetic development or to relate his
work to the events of his life is made extremely difficult by the uncertain dating of the poems, very few of which were published before
his death. Broadly speaking, his adult career falls into three main
periods: from his arrival in London to his marriage, from his marriage to his ordination, and from his ordination to his death. Born
in 1571 or 1572, he was educated as a Catholic and remained one
until about 1598. In 1592 he entered Lincoln's Inn, and before this he
may already have travelled abroad. During the nineties he appears
as a student and man of fashion about London, and as an adven-
turer in Essex's expeditions to Cadiz (1596) and the Azores (1597).
To this period belong most of the *Satyres* and *Elegies* and probably
a good many of the *Songs and Sonets*. In 1598 Donne became private
secretary to Lord Keeper Egerton, but in 1601 his hasty marriage to
Anne More, the niece of Egerton's second wife, led to his dismissal
and ruined a promising career. For the next ten years or so he lived
in poverty and melancholy, dependent on the charity of friends and
with no constant occupation. The poems of this time include many
verse-letters and occasional poems of compliment and condolence,
as well as the rest of the *Elegies* and *Songs and Sonets* and the first of the
religious poems. In 1611 and 1612 there appeared the two *Anniversaries: An Anatomie of the World* and *Of the Progress of the Soule* commemorating Sir Robert Drury's daughter, whom Donne had never
seen. (The second of these should not be confused with the earlier
unfinished satire, *The Progresse of the Soule*, also known as *Metem-
psychosis*.) In the same period he wrote certain prose works of controversy and meditation, including *Biathanatos*, a discussion of suicide.
In 1615, after years of persuasion and postponement, Donne was
finally ordained, becoming Reader in Divinity at Lincoln's Inn the
following year, and Dean of St Paul's in 1621. His wife died in 1617.
To this last period may belong some of the *Holy Sonnets*[12] and the rest
of the *Divine Poems*, as well as the sermons and other religious writings. The first collection of his verse was published in 1633, two years
after his death.

Donne's poems, then, may be considered in three main groups:

the love poetry, the miscellaneous and occasional poems and verse-letters, and the religious poems – corresponding roughly, but not exactly, to the early, middle, and late periods of his career. The first contains the work by which he is probably best known. It is remarkable for realism, psychological penetration, and above all for the range and variety of mood, corresponding to the variety of tone and style already discussed. This extends from ecstatic and passionate poems, like *The Sunne Rising*, *The Dreame*, or *The Good-morrow*:

> And now good morrow to our waking soules,
> Which watch not one another out of feare;
> For love, all love of other sights controules,
> And makes one little roome, an every where.

to the deliberately cynical flippancy of *The Indifferent* or *The Flea*; from poems of fulfilment and happiness in love like *The Anniversarie* to *A Nocturnall upon S. Lucies day* with its intensity of privation and desolation; from the convincing affirmation of constancy in absence in *A Valediction: forbidding mourning*, or in a different way in *Elegy V*, to the savage bitterness of *The Apparition*. The poet who writes 'Goe, and catch a falling starre', or *Communitie*:

> Chang'd loves are but chang'd sorts of meat,
> And when hee hath the kernell eate,
>   Who doth not fling away the shell?

also gives us the profound sense of spiritual union in love in *The Extasie*:

> A single violet transplant,
>   The strength, the colour, and the size,
> (All which before was poore, and scant,)
>   Redoubles still, and multiplies,
> When love with one another so
>   Interinanimates two soules,
> That abler soule, which thence doth flow
>   Defects of lonelinesse controules.

In between these contrasting extremes are many poems difficult to classify, of mixed mood and shifting tone, or qualified by subtle ambiguities. In poems like *Aire and Angels* the total attitude can be defined only through a complete analysis of the whole poem. Even so apparently simple an expression of feelings as *A Valediction: of weeping* may be shown to carry overtones of a number of other possible responses to the situation, even if these are not perhaps so many or so complex as Empson's analysis in *Seven Types of Ambiguity* would suggest. Further, there remains a group of poems in which Donne returns for special purposes to a modified and highly personal use of the Petrarchan convention to express platonic love and friendship, possibly to his patronesses Lucy, Countess of Bedford, and Mrs Herbert, but such conjectures remain doubtful. In these poems genuine personal feeling, the playing of a conventional game, irony, and a certain imaginative fire in elaborating a dramatic situation, all contribute something to the total effect; there is no simple way of summing up *The Funerall*, *The Relique*, or *Twicknam Garden*.

Classification of this kind must always remain very tentative: many poems cannot be made to fit simply into any scheme. There is a natural temptation to try to find biographical explanations; but this opens the door to conjecture of all kinds, and except in the most general and provisional form it is not likely to further disinterested appreciation. The only safe procedure is to treat each poem on its merits, and analyse carefully what it communicates, remembering that the relation between art and the raw material of experience may vary almost infinitely. In answering the criticisms of C. S. Lewis and J. E. V. Crofts on Donne's love poetry, J. B. Leishman and Joan Bennett are right to insist on the need for a sensitive discrimination of tone. But they are both inclined to move a little too easily to deductions about Donne's personal experience; in this connection 'sincere' and even 'serious' are slippery terms to handle, and considerable vigilance is needed to see when the interest shifts from the literary to the biographical side. What is always constant throughout the changing moods of Donne's love poetry is the habit of introspection and analysis, the heart 'which love[s] to be Subtile to plague [it]selfe', the turn for realistic and dramatic presentation and for making connections between the given situation and many other aspects of experience.

The miscellaneous poems form perhaps the least successful group of the three, though there are interesting exceptions. For the most part the *Satyres* are the adaptations to contemporary life of stock Latin themes. The third stands out for its penetrating and serious discussion of the problem of choosing between rival religious beliefs, the alternative possibilities being embodied in short satirical portraits. The vogue for satire declined somewhat after the ban of 1599, and the satirical spirit found an outlet elsewhere, but Donne's fragment of 1601, *The Progresse of the Soule*, belongs, with its bitter and sceptical quality, to this division of his work. Of the *Elegies*, some go with the love poems and invite similar comments; others are linked to the *Satyres* in their use of classical models and their witty and dramatic tone. No. IX, *The Autumnall*, seems connected with the poems of platonic love and the complimentary epistles to great ladies. These form one section of the group of verse-letters; it includes also the brilliant descriptions *The Storme* and *The Calme*, which won Ben Jonson's praise, and such urbane intercourse with friends as the letters to Sir Henry Goodyere and to Sir Henry Wotton 'at his going Ambassador to Venice'. The *Epigrams* are mere displays of ingenuity; the *Epicedes and Obsequies*, with their involved and elaborate hyperbole, are very little to modern taste. It is easy to believe Jonson's story that the elegy on Prince Henry was written 'to match Sir Ed. Herbert in obscurenesse'. The *Epithalamions*, on the other hand, have their rewarding moments: they show Donne for once celebrating courtly pleasures – 'warmth and light and good desire'. Two are dated 1613 and one much earlier, but all three show some approach to the melodious strophes of Spenser with a recurring refrain-line – further proof, as Leishman has said, that Donne wrote as he usually did from choice and not incapacity.

The religious poems form the second in general interest of the three main groups. The earliest, which include the *La Corona* sonnets and several meditations[13] in couplets, hardly show Donne's characteristic power, though *The Litanie* is notable for the balanced psychological insight of some of its petitions asking for deliverance

> From being anxious, or secure,
> Dead clods of sadnesse, or light squibs of mirth,
> From thinking that great courts immure
> All, or no happinesse, or that this earth
> Is only for our prison frame'd,

and

> From needing danger, to bee good.

The *Anniversaries* belong to this group in that they are in essence less about Elizabeth Drury than life and death in general, meditations on the corruptions of this world and the glories of the next. They show Donne at his most extravagantly fantastic, and also at his most powerfully imaginative. Within twelve lines of the notorious invocation to the 'immortall maid' to be a father to his muse, he can rise to the sublimity of

> These Hymnes thy issue, may encrease so long
> As till God's great *Venite* change the song.

The two poems are in accord with many aspects of contemporary thought and sensibility, besides constituting a remarkable expression of Donne's own speculation, scepticism, and melancholy. But Donne's chief power as a religious poet is shown in the *Holy Sonnets* and the last hymns. Only in a few late hymns do we find an assured faith; elsewhere there is always an element of conflict and doubt or fear. The best of the *Holy Sonnets* express these struggles with unparalleled force. There is no essential change of style: Donne can stop to remember that the round world's corners are 'imagin'd' without destroying the power of his vision of Judgement Day; he treats God as a conqueror or a ravisher, or employs the kind of wooing used to his 'profane mistresses'. As in the love poetry, too, there is a considerable variety of tone and method, ranging from mere casuistry and debating tricks to a profound urgency and conviction, and sometimes both may be found in the same poem. The best show the characteristic wit reinforcing the emotional intensity:

> Onely thou art above, and when towards thee
> By thy leave I can looke, I rise againe;
> But our old subtle foe so tempteth me,
> That not one houre my selfe I can sustaine;
> Thy Grace may wing me to prevent his art,
> And thou like Adamant draw mine iron heart.

Donne's poetic fame remained high up to the Restoration, but sank to a low level in the eighteenth century. Nineteenth-century taste was hardly more favourable to him, in spite of some discriminating praise from Coleridge and the enthusiasm of Browning. During the early years of this century critical opinion turned in his favour to an extent that raised him by the twenties to unprecedented heights. This was of course closely connected with a general reaction against the decadent remains of the Romantic tradition and the rise of a new poetry which found a special stimulus in the work of the seventeenth-century poets and the Jacobean dramatists, and it is not surprising that Eliot should have contributed considerably to the change of opinion. Donne's vogue in the twenties, however, was to some extent a matter of fashion, as Eliot himself suggested in an essay of 1931,[14] though he thought that whatever reaction might supervene, Donne would never sink back to his earlier obscurity, and would always remain as 'a great reformer of the English language, of English verse'. If this seems disappointingly over-cautious we should remember that in Eliot's critical idiom it would be by no means faint praise. Fifty years later it certainly does not look as if the rehabilitation of Donne was a temporary phenomenon. In the period since 1945 new editions and critical studies have appeared in steady succession, and the four-hundredth anniversary of his birth produced a crop of essays written from many different angles. Indeed, the danger today is rather that having become academically respectable Donne's work may be buried beneath the weight of scholarly commentary and the force of its impact dulled.[15] The most helpful criticism is that which, while giving its due weight to historical scholarship, keeps us sensitively responsive to the vitality and authority of Donne's individual voice – 'the voice', as Wilbur Sanders[16] has put it, 'of a man who knows the precise cost of his words' and who 'is never content with feeling which has been separated from understanding'.

NOTES

1. A point well brought out by Esther Cloudman Dunn in *The Literature of Shakespeare's England* (1936), and by J. B. Leishman in *The Monarch of Wit* (1931; 6th edn 1962), among others.

2. See particularly Rosemond Tuve: *Elizabethan and Metaphysical Imagery* (1947), and the answer by W. Empson: 'Donne and the Rhetorical Tradition' in *The Kenyon Review* for autumn 1949.

3. The point is made by T. S. Eliot in his essay on 'Donne in Our Time', in *A Garland for John Donne*, ed. Theodore Spencer (1931).

4. Certain MSS carry the note that this and one or two other poems were 'made to certain ayres which were made before'. See Grierson's edition of the poems, Vol I. note to p. 18.

5. See especially F. R. Leavis in an essay 'Imagery and Movement' in *Scrutiny*, XIII (1945), reprinted in *The Living Principle* (1975).

6. The special significance that certain images seem to have possessed for Donne is discussed interestingly in M. M. Mahood, *Poetry and Humanism*, ch. IV.

7. See the introduction to *Metaphysical Poems and Lyrics of the Seventeenth Century*.

8. In *Determinations*, ed. F. R. Leavis.

9. See his essay on 'The Metaphysical Poets' in *Selected Essays*.

10. See *Nor Shall My Sword* (1972), 115–18.

11. L. C. Knights has some illuminating discussion of this point in his essay 'The Social Background of Metaphysical Poetry', reprinted in *Further Explorations* (1965).

12. Dame Helen Gardner, in her edition of the divine poems, argues that most of the Holy Sonnets were written between 1609 and 1611.

13. It has been suggested by several scholars that Donne in many of his religious poems adopted the special techniques for meditation recommended in various Catholic writings of the sixteenth and seventeenth centuries, such as the *Spiritual Exercises* of St Ignatius Loyola. See especially Louis L. Martz: *The Poetry of Meditation* (1954, rev. edn 1962).

14. The essay 'Donne in Our Time' in *A Garland for John Donne*, ed. Spencer.

15. A forceful warning to this effect was made by Patrick Cruttwell in an essay, 'The Love Poetry of John Donne: Pedantique Weedes or Fresh Invention?', in *Metaphysical Poetry* (Stratford-upon-Avon Studies 11, 1970).

16. In *John Donne's Poetry* (1971), 13.

THE PROSE OF DONNE AND BROWNE

GILBERT PHELPS

The word 'metaphysical' as used by literary historians usually refers to the group of seventeenth-century poets who explored their experience by way of the intellectual excitements and preoccupations of their day. The label, however, can equally well be applied to many of the prose writers of the period. In a famous passage from his 'Life of Cowley', Dr Johnson declared that in the work of the metaphysical poets 'the most heterogeneous ideas are yoked by violence together', and in his *Life of Sir Thomas Browne* he described Browne's prose in very similar terms:

> His style is a tissue of many languages; a mixture of heterogeneous words, brought together from distant regions, with terms originally appropriated to one art, and drawn by violence into the service of another.

There is no violence involved, therefore, in yoking the prose of John Donne (1572–1631) and Sir Thomas Browne (1605–82). But even if we start at a level where the superficial resemblances are most likely to appear, important differences at once emerge. Take, for example, the way in which each writer, according to the metaphysical fashion, 'played' with an idea. *The Garden of Cyrus* (1658), by Sir Thomas Browne, is a fanciful dissertation on quincunxes (that is, the arrangement of objects in sets of five – like the five spots on a die), which leads him into an elaborate investigation of the possibilities and implications of the theme, artistic, historical, botanical, magical, and so on. He observes, for example, that:

> In the Laureat draughts of sculpture and picture, the leaves and foliate works are commonly thus contrived, which is but an imitation of the *Pulvinaria*,[a] and ancient pillow-work, observable in *Ionick* peeces, about columns, temples, and altars. To omit many other analogies, in Architectonicall draughts, which art itself is founded upon fives, as having its subject, and most graceful peeces divided by this number.

> a couches used for the images of gods in Roman antiquity.

Donne could fasten upon a fanciful idea just as doggedly. In *Paradoxes and Problemes*, his earliest prose writings, which are contemporary in date with his early poems (and in many respects similar in mood and temper), he will take some conventional theme and then conduct elaborate, and paradoxical, five-finger exercises upon it. In the first of these, for example, he begins:

> That Women are *Inconstant*, I with any man confess, but that *Inconstancy* is a bad quality, I against any man will maintain: For every thing as it is one better than another, so it is fuller of change; The *Heavens* themselves continually turn, the *Stars* move, the *Moon* changeth; *Fire* whirleth, *Aire* flyeth, *Water* ebbs and flowes, the face of the *Earth* altereth her looks, *time* staies not; the Colour that is most light, will take most dyes: so in Men, they that have most reason are the most alterable in their designes, and the darkest and most ignorant, do seldomest change; therefore Women changing more than Men, have also more *Reason*. They cannot be immutable like stocks, like stones, like the earth's dull Center; Gold that lyeth still, rusteth; Water, corrupteth; Aire that moveth not, poysoneth; then why should that which is the perfection of other things, be imputed to Women as greatest imperfection? . . .
> (*A Defence of Women's Inconstancy*)

Neither of these passages represents its author at anything like his best, but they serve to bring out some of the basic contrasts in the texture and tempo of the prose, and in the attitudes, in general, of the two men towards their medium.

It is useful, perhaps, to begin with what may be called a purely subjective reader's response, ignoring for the time being the historical and literary provenance of the two passages. At this rather superficial level the striking difference is one of energy. In the extract from *The Garden of Cyrus* the balance of the words and clauses, the leisurely spacing and punctuation, induce a slow, relaxed rhythm. The effect is to make the reader curious as to what might follow – but not excited. There is no pressure or urgency: the connection between the separate ideas is casual and it is possible to break off at the end of almost any sentence without loss of continuity.

In the Donne passage, on the other hand, it is very difficult to cut across the jet of thought: clause springs from clause and sentence from sentence (in spite of a strong Euphuistic element) as it takes fresh impetus; there is a complex criss-cross and overlay of ideas, a continual reference back and catching up with the sense. The punctuation itself is part of this progression: there are few real rests, for the thought hardly ever comes to a definite stop, and the punctuation marks for the most part serve as a momentary slowing down, preparatory to a fresh spurt.

This is really another way of saying that the movement of the prose gives the impression that Donne is more immediately engaged with his material than Browne with his. This is in spite of the fact that the modern reader cannot himself be much engaged with the actual content of the passage, which must strike him as a typical example of Donne at his most cynical and flippant, playing with a proposition he doesn't believe in simply in order to show off his mental and verbal agility. The earliest of the paradoxes and 'problemes' in the collection, indeed, like the earlier poems, many of which play with the same themes (including the 'inconstancy of women') belong to the period when Donne was most subject to what he himself called (in another of his 'paradoxical' writings) 'itchy outbreaks of far-fetched wit'.

Yet somehow the impression of intellectual urgency remains. As Frank Kermode has said, in a discussion of Donne's wit: 'we cannot think of Donne without thinking of relentless argument', and this is just as applicable (though of course in a more limited sense) to the juvenile *Paradoxes and Problemes* as it is to the later works.

As a matter of fact *Paradoxes and Problemes* is by no means as flippant and barren as it seems at first sight. For one thing it has a whole tradition behind it. The 'rhetorical paradox', or formal defence and praise of an unexpected, unworthy, or indefensible subject, originated in the ancient world. Classical examples are Gorgias's praise of Helen (traditionally regarded as 'a thing without honour'), Synesius's praise of baldness, Lucian's of the fly, and Ovid's of the nut. The form was revived and extended during the Renaissance, and was practised in one way or another by many European writers, among them the great humanist Erasmus in his *Praise of Folly* (1509).

The main purpose of the rhetorical paradox in its simplest form (apart from sheer intellectual entertainment) was not to reach a conclusion but to stimulate further speculation, qualification, and even contradiction – in other words to stir up the mental processes in order to prevent them from becoming ossified or self-satisfied.

Donne himself says something like this in a letter of about 1600 (itself wittily paradoxical) addressed to a friend to whom he was sending a copy of his *Paradoxes and Problemes*:

> Only in obedience I send you some of my paradoxes; I love you and myself and them too well to send them willingly for they carry with them a confession of their lightness, and your trouble and my shame. But indeed they were made rather to deceave tyme than her daughter truth ... if they make you to find better reasons against them, they do their office: for they are but swaggerers: quiet enough if you resist them ... they are rather alarums to truth to arme her then [i.e., *than*] enemies: and they have only this advantadg to scape from being cald ill things that they are no things: therefore take heed of allowing any of them least you make another.[1]

The use of the terms 'ill things' and 'no things' in that last rather cryptic sentence is a reminder that the rhetorical paradox could impinge upon all kinds of complex philosophical and theological issues, as it had done, for example in the *Parmenides* of Plato and in the speculations of several of the early Christian apologists. As far as the latter were concerned, this aspect of the paradox was related to what was known as 'negative theology': God, that is, is so far beyond the limits of man's understanding and of his linguistic and descriptive capabilities that any attempt to define him must inevitably be paradoxical, so that images of insignificant or even low and sordid objects ('ill things' and 'no things') are the most appropriate for attempting comprehension of the divine essence.[2]

It is this strand of theological thinking that lies behind the fondness of the metaphysicals in their devotional poetry for placing 'low things' side by side with the highest – as when George Herbert likens Christ to a bag, or God to a coconut, and when Donne himself compares the flea's 'triple life' to the Trinity.

It is true that when Donne began writing his *Paradoxes and Problemes* he had already left the Roman Catholic faith in which he had been reared, and at a time when his mood was at its most worldly and cynical, but even during this period religious issues continued to preoccupy him, and when eventually he joined the established Anglican Church it was because he had come to the conclusion that it was now more truly Catholic than any other and he remained a disciple of St Augustine and St Thomas Aquinas, both of whom he quoted frequently in the sermons of his later years. The serious issues behind the paradox, as explored by the medieval theologians, were in his mind when he was writing *Paradoxes and Problemes*, and his awareness of them helps to explain the energy and intellectual drive of the style. There is, in fact, an underlying seriousness in even the most flippant of Donne's writings.

This is not to suggest that Sir Thomas Browne wasn't also thoroughly acquainted with the rhetorical paradox (he practised the form himself) and its varied implications. But these implications were not for him, as they were for Donne, a matter of profound personal significance. There are all kinds of reasons for this, including differences of temperament and the later, somewhat less passionate period in which Browne lived, but the one that concerns us here is the cast of mind revealed even in the short extract quoted above from *The Garden of Cyrus*.

Its most obvious feature, perhaps, is its lack of urgency or commitment. In his dedicatory letter to his friend Nicholas Bacon, Browne apologizes for choosing gardens as his subject, in view of the fact that he is not a gardener himself, explains that he is not attempting a 'Herball', disclaims any intention of adding to botanical knowledge – and admits that he is merely seeking an area of inquiry that hasn't been explored before. He has no consuming interest in it: any other topic would have done just as well. Neither does he pretend that it is of any particular interest in itself: indeed he confesses that he prefers 'barren' subjects: '... such Discourses allow excursions, and venially admit of collateral truths, though at some distance from their principals'. It is the by-ways of the theme that concern him more than the theme itself. These by-ways are full of all kinds of curious and whimsical reflections, backed by an impressive display of erudition. But they, too, are not attended by any real conviction. They are not related to any central argument, let alone a conclusion. Browne couldn't care less, we often feel, about either. What interests him rather is the *process* of inquiry, whether it leads anywhere or not, and in *The Garden of Cyrus*, as Joan Bennett has said, 'there appears to be no division for Browne between useful and useless knowledge'. Dr Johnson was right, in fact, when he described the work as little more than 'a sport of fancy'.

It would not be fair, of course, to apply Johnson's phrase to Browne's more important works. There is intellectual, moral, philosophical, and religious seriousness, at times reaching profundity, in

Religio Medici (1643), *Urne Buriall* (1658), the posthumous *Christian Morals* (1716) – and sometimes even in the distinctly 'sportive' *Pseudodoxia Epidemica* (1646). Awareness of the theological implications often lies behind his own playing with paradoxes, contradictions, and oddities. His animadversions on the intricate patterns of Nature were often informed with a sense of wonder and a conviction that they revealed the controlled design of God, the Great Artificer – to some extent, indeed, this is true even of *The Garden of Cyrus*. Nevertheless, a strong fanciful element is present in all his writings, even in those where 'fancy' has been transcended into 'imagination', and given his easy-going nature, his avid but largely uncritical curiosity, and his discursive frame of mind, it could hardly be otherwise.

These are qualities which make for charm rather than passion or power. The absence of a sustained emotional and imaginative drive tends to produce uneven writing, with marked 'highs' and 'lows' – stretches of low-key ramblings and ruminations, accompanied by occasional passages in which the medium is screwed up to its highest pitch, as the writer suddenly concentrates his whole self and gives of his best. Inevitably such passages tend to have the air of set-pieces or special performances.

Some of these, of course, result in superb prose. One of the most famous examples comes from *Hydriotaphia, Urne Buriall; Or, a Discourse of the Sepulchrall Urnes lately found in Norfolk* (to give it its full title), in which Browne's contemplation of the funeral urns and the human bones they contain launches him into one of his most inspired meditations:

> But the iniquity of oblivion blindely scattereth her poppy, and deals with the memory of men without distinction to merit of perpetuity. Who can but pity the founder of the Pyramids? *Herostratus* lives that burnt the Temple of *Diana*, he is almost lost that built it; Time hath spared the Epitaph of Adrian's horse, confouned that of himself. In vain we compute our felicity by the advantage of our good names, since bad have equal durations; and *Thersites* is like to live as long as *Agamemnon*.* Who know whether the best of men be known? or whether there be not more remarkable persons forgot, then any that stand remembered in the known account of time? Without the favour of the everlasting register, the first man had been as unknown as the last, and Methuselah's long life had been his only Chronicle.

*In Homer's *Iliad* Thersites is the contemptible and foul-mouthed man of low birth who rails at Agamemnon, King of Argos and leader of the Greek host before Troy.

Oblivion is not to be hired: The greater part must be content to be as though they had not been, to be found in the Register of God, not in the record of man. Twenty-seven Names make up the first story before the flood, and the recorded names ever since contain not one living Century. The number of the dead long exceedeth all that shall live. The night of time far surpasseth the day, and who knows when was the Aequinox?* Every hour adds unto that current Arithmetique which scarce stands one moment. And since death must be the *Lucina*† of life, and even Pagans could doubt whether thus to live, were to dye. Since our longest sunne sets at right descensions, and makes but winter arches, and therefore it cannot be long before we lie down in darknesse, and have our light in ashes. Since the brother of death daily haunts us with dying *memento's*, and time that grows old in it self, bids us hope no long duration: Diuturnity is a dream and folly of expectation.

It is interesting to set against this undoubtedly fine and impressive piece of prose, a passage from Donne on a similar theme. It is taken from one of his best-known sermons, preached 'at the Earl of Bridge-water's house in London at the marriage of his daughter, 19 November 1627':

There are so many evidences of the immortality of the soule, even to a naturall man's *reason*, that it required not an article of the Creed, to fix this notion of the Immortality of the soule. But the Resurrection of the *Body* is discernible by no other light, but that of *Faith*, nor could be fixed by any lesse assurance than an *Article* of the *Creed*. Where be all the splinters of that Bone, which a shot hath shivered and scattered in the Ayre? Where be all the Atoms of that flesh, which a *Corrasive* hath breath'd, and exhal'd away from our arms, and other Limbs? In what wrinkle, in what furrow, in what bowel of the earth, ly all the graines of the ashes of a body burnt a thousand years since? In what corner, in what ventricle of the sea, lies all the jelly of a Body drowned in the *generall flood*? What cohaerence, what sympathy, what dependence maintaines any relation, any correspondence, between that arm that was lost in Europe, and that legge that was lost in Afrique or Asia, scores of yeers between? One humour of our dead body produces worms, and those worms suck and exhaust all other humour, and then all dies, and all dries, and molders into dust, and that dust is blowen into the River, and that puddled water tumbled into the sea, and that ebbs and flows in infinite revolutions, and still, still God knows in what *Cabinet* every *seed-Pearle* lies, in what part of the world every graine of every man's dust lies; and *sibilat populum suum*, (as his Prophet speaks in another case) he whispers, he hisses, he beckons for the bodies of his Saints, and in the twinckling of an eye the body that was

---

* This refers to the current seventeenth-century belief (derived from early Christian writers – and indeed from the *New Testament* itself) that the Creation was in the process of 'running down'. It affected the imagery of many contemporary writers (e.g. Donne in his poems *A Nocturnall upon S. Lucies Day* and *The Second Anniversarie*).

† An ancient Italian deity presiding over childbirth.

scattered over all the elements, is sate down at the right hand of God, in a glorious resurrection. A Dropsie hath extended me to an enormous corpulency, and unwieldinesse; a Consumption hath attenuated me to a feeble macilency[a] and leanesse, and God raises me a body, such as it should have been, if these infirmities had not interven'd and deformed it.

(*Fifty Sermons*, 1649: Sermon I)

In the Browne extract there is the same tempo as in the passage we have already quoted from *The Garden of Cyrus* – though now the tread is stately rather than leisurely. The 'spreading out' is again achieved by the firm punctuation, by the rhythmical balance of the clauses, and their slow unfolding ('... and deals with the memory of men without distinction to merit of perpetuity'); and it is heightened by the careful incidence of the latinisms ('... and time that grows old in it self, bids us hope no long duration: Diuturnity is a dream and folly of expectation'). By these means Browne creates a deliberate, architectonic effect, as of a lofty vault filled with reverberating echoes. But this very deliberation produces a certain distancing of the emotion; the funeral urns have somehow been too much in the nature of 'an occasion', and the impact on the reader is in consequence less palpable. We are invited to solemn admiration rather than to emotional participation.

In the Donne extract there is the passionate re-creation of an experience. As in *Paradoxes and Problemes*, clauses and sentences take fire from each other, and there is continual heat and motion. It is interesting, too, to notice that as a quotation it again seems incomplete; we feel that we want to know what goes on before and after. And indeed any quotation from Donne must seem torn from its context, producing an effect of broken tissue and ligaments, for each of his prose works is an organic whole, and the total effect cannot be satisfactorily judged apart from that whole.

He does not merely examine his theme academically and from a safe distance, articulating its various parts at leisure. He *experiences* it, in the mind and 'on the pulses', in all its exact sensuous connotations. Ideas, theories, doctrines, quotations, allusions, imagery are all devoted to this end, they are inherent, all caught up in the intensity of the emotion. The repetition and alliteration, the internal assonance and the rhythms, all drive inwards to its core. For example, the actual

a thinness (i.e. emaciation).

sensation conveyed by the verbs that follow 'corrasive' – 'breath'd, and exhal'd away' – is heightened by the subsequent concrete reference to 'consumption' and the active preposition 'away from' itself adds preciseness to this sensation of the stripping away of flesh. In the same way the repetitive questions – 'In what wrinkle, in what furrow, in what bowel of the earth' and 'In what corner, in what ventricle of the sea', and the unexpected rhyme of 'and then all dies, and all dries', all these communicate a sense of physical exploration. Even the so-called 'morbidity', repugnant to some readers, is symptomatic of the same intensity of contact.

We must distinguish, of course, between the morbidity of decadence, in which the symbols of death and decay are arranged from outside, either in a haphazard fashion (as in some of the later Jacobean dramatists; contrast the way in which they introduce the skull – in order purely to heighten the horror – with its precise implications in Tourneur's *Revenger's Tragedy*) or with deliberate effect in the service of a romantic self-indulgence or sensationalism (as in Shelley's *The Cenci*, or in writers of the Romantic decadence, such as Thomas Lovell Beddoes) – and the morbidity that is a concrete manifestation of a profound inner awareness of mortality. It is in this serious and fundamentally moral sense that Dr Johnson and Swift are morbid. This, too, is the morbidity of the medieval *danse macabre* (or of Hamlet's preoccupation with death and decay – working from inside the agonizing discovery that 'this majestical roof fretted with golden fire' is at the same time 'a foul and pestilent congregation of vapours'), and it is a kind of morbidity that springs not from weakness but from a mature acceptance of life in death. In the extract from Donne we have just quoted, the 'humour of our dead body' that 'produces worms', the worms that 'suck and exhaust all other humour', the 'Dropsie that hath extended me to an enormous corpulency', and the Consumption that 'hath attenuated me to a feeble macilency and leanesse', convey in tangible terms the determination to probe with the mind and the senses along the nerves and into the very marrow of the experience, and is in no way a 'morbid' surrender to it.

This distinction between a prose which translates experience directly and palpably and a prose of the literary occasion is inherent in any examination of Browne and Donne, and is apparent in every aspect of their work. Take, for example, the use that each makes of his learning. In the one case a curious and roving mind delights in illustrating an argument with all kinds of unexpected references, examples, and allusions – and in embellishing the theme with numerous quotations. But generally speaking it *is* 'embellishment' – that is, an extraneous arrangement of objects related to the theme, but not urgent or intrinsic to it. And the attention Browne invites is also of a roving and curious kind: usually he speaks as an amateur and a spectator, rather than as a participant, and much of our pleasure is thus of a detached and bookish nature. When he rises to his great perorations on death and decay he is, of course, more universal – but at the back of them we are still conscious of the museum and the study. In Donne, however, the impulse is altogether different. He is completely caught up in the excitement of the moment – whether spiritual, intellectual, or sensual, and the quotations and allusions are functional, entirely related to that excitement and subjugated to it.

There are in addition considerable differences between the two writers in the nature of their learning, or at any rate in their attitudes towards it. The few years' gap in dates is of some significance here. As Donne was born in 1572 (or possibly a year earlier) and died in 1631 he was, chronologically, more than half an Elizabethan. Browne, on the other hand, was born (in 1605) two years after the death of Queen Elizabeth, lived through the period of the Civil War (supporting the Royalist cause) and into the Restoration, with its changed cultural, social and political emphases, dying in 1682 when it could be said that the Age of Reason had already begun.

To some extent Browne was caught in a kind of cultural no-man's-land. At Oxford he was trained – on the basis, it goes without saying, of a thorough grounding in the Classics – in the traditional disciplines of Logic, Rhetoric, Divinity, and Aristotelian philosophy. But he also studied Anatomy and Botany, which Oxford had recently added to the curriculum in order to supplement the antiquated courses on the ancient Greek physicians Hippocrates and Galen – and there were opportunities too at Oxford for studying clinical cases. Later he attended the School of Medicine at Montpellier in France, where observation, experiment and logic were supplanting traditional medical and religious authority, and then at the medical school at Padua in Italy, celebrated for its teaching of anatomy and clinical observation, and for its early experiments in vivisection. He completed his medical training at Leyden, in the Netherlands.

Like many of his contemporaries, however, Browne was poised between the old world of 'authority', magic and superstition and the new one of free inquiry and experiment, in the spirit of Sir Francis Bacon's 'Great Instauration'. He believed implicitly, for example, (again like many of his contemporaries) in witchcraft, and was often superstitious and credulous. Yet there are plenty of instances in both *Religio Medici* and *Pseudodoxia Epidemica* where, in the exploration of natural phenomena, his allegiance is unequivocally given to experiment rather than to authority, and where he refuses to accept 'marvels' on hearsay evidence alone.

In these respects he was in harmony with the spirit and practice of the Royal Society, which had been founded in 1662, and with which he had close relations. On the other hand he never became a Fellow. One of the reasons may have been that he was too much of an individualist and eccentric, too much a collector of odds and ends of classical and medieval learning, of folk-lore, archaeology, and pseudo-science. Another reason, several literary historians have suggested, may have been that Browne's prose was too far removed from the ideal of plainness and 'shortness' laid down by Thomas Sprat in his *History of the Royal Society* (1665) as essential for the advancement of scientific inquiry. As a prose stylist Browne was certainly no innovator: it seems difficult to believe, for example, that only ten years separated *The Garden of Cyrus* and Dryden's *Essay of Dramatic Poesy* (1668). Browne's prose style was formed about 1630 and shows little development. It is a prose of conscious art, often striking one as archaic in much the same way as Malory's *Morte D'Arthur* (printed by Caxton in 1485) was in its day outside the mainstream of literary development.

And yet at the same time the tone of reasonableness and tolerance (especially in religious matters) in Browne's *Religio Medici* (and some of his other writings) belongs very much to the Restoration period with its search for balance and stability after the violent passions of the preceding age, and from time to time a note of almost Augustan urbanity is sounded.

The fact that Browne displays such a medley of cultural interests and impulses tended perhaps to heighten his natural discursiveness, and to make it difficult to find any firm intellectual centre to his work. By contrast we are always aware, partly because he lived earlier, partly because of his Jesuit upbringing, that Donne *does* have this firm centre. He was, of course, writing at a period of intellectual ferment, when, for example, the 'new Philosophy calls all in doubt' – as he puts it in his poem *The First Anniversarie*. But such recent astronomical discoveries as the elliptical movement of the planets, which overset the old Ptolemaic concept of the heavens, could not (as some critics have suggested) disturb him fundamentally, confident as he was of the other order of reality that belonged to his religious faith. 'If there be any addition to knowledge', he declares in a sermon of 1626, 'it is rather new knowledge, than a greater knowledge.' For, he argues, the accumulation of knowledge is by itself irrelevant beside the only kind of knowledge that is really worth having: if you know as much as Socrates, really you know nothing, and as St Paul discovered 'to know Christ' is 'to be all knowledge'.

In spite of his vivid interest in contemporary currents of thought, the energy and originality of his mind, and his new metaphysical imagery, Donne is closer to the medieval traditions of thought than Browne. He is not even a true humanist – in that he seems to have studied the Greek authors only in Latin translations, and he always quotes the New Testament in the Vulgate. He displays, however, a minute knowledge of the works of the Fathers, the Schoolmen, the medieval jurists, and the Roman and Protestant controversialists. His method of argument, too, was fundamentally medieval, founded on syllogistic reasoning, and with frequent appeals to authority, while his philosophy was a continuation of the ideas of Augustine and Aquinas. And this firm grounding in medieval culture gives his work discipline and coherence, in spite of the passionate, frequently helter-skelter nature of his thought and language.

But Donne is also steeped in the language of the medieval and Tudor preachers, and of the translators of the Prayer Book and the Bible. Browne's grandiloquent style has often been compared to that of the Bible, but a glance at the two passages we have quoted will show how much closer is Donne's language, in spirit and texture, to this tradition than is Browne's. Donne, while never letting go of his theological argument, in all its complexity, uses as his staple style the muscular, sensuous language and imagery of common speech.

Thus the dust of our dissolution becomes 'puddled water tumbled into the sea'; as for the Prophet – 'he whispers, he hisses, he beckons' and 'in the twinckling of an eye, that body that was scattered over all the elements, is sate down at the right hand of God'. Time after time in the sermons the most subtle of scholastic arguments are brought to a climax and driven home, in the manner of the parables or the *exempla* of the medieval and Tudor preachers, by some homely idiom or image, which extracts from the mass of theory and doctrine the human and universal truth it was designed to communicate.

In Sermon LXVI (*Eighty Sermons*, 1640), for example, he concludes an argument on Divine Grace:

> ... yet if God with-draw not his spirituall blessings, his Grace, his Patience, If I can call my suffering his Doing, my passion his Action, All this that is temporall, is but a caterpillar got into one corner of my garden, but a mill-dew fallen upon one acre of my Corne; The body of all, the substance of all is safe, as long as the soule is safe.

And in Sermon IX (*Eighty Sermons*) he urges his congregation:

> Pay this debt to thy selfe of looking into thy debts, of surveying, of severing, of serving thy selfe with that which is truly thine, at thy noone, in the best of thy fortune, and in the strength of thine understanding; that when thou comest to pay thy other, thy last debt to thy self, which is; to open a doore out of this world, by the dissolution of body and soule, thou have not all thy money to tell over when the Sun is ready to set, all the account to make of every bag of money, and of every quillet of land, whose it is, and whether it be his that looks for it from thee, or his from whom it was taken by thee; whether it belong to thine heire, that weepes joyfull tears behinde the curtain, or belong to him that weeps true, and bloody teares, in the hole in a prison.

Even in the most characteristic of his metaphysical images the pre-occupation is serious and entirely human:

> Upon this earth, a man cannot possibly make one step in a straight, and a direct line. The earth it selfe being round, every step wee make upon it, must necessarily bee a segment, an arch of a circle. But yet though no piece of a circle be a straight line, yet if we take any piece, nay if wee take the whole circle, there is no corner, no angle in any piece, in any intire circle. A perfect rectitude we cannot have in any wayes in this world; In every Calling there are some inevitable tentations. But, though wee cannot make up our circle of a straight line, (that is impossible to human frailty) yet wee may passe on, without angles, and corners, that is, without disguises in our Religion, and without the love of craft, and falsehood, and circumvention in our civill actions.

> (*Eighty Sermons*: Sermon LXVII)

By comparison with the variety and richness of Donne's language and imagery – subtle, witty, intellectually tough, at the same time that it is vivid, sensuous, and dramatic – Browne's stylistic resources often seem limited and contrived. The range of feeling and human observation in Donne's language is symptomatic of a mind in touch with experience at every point, while even the finest of Browne's 'fine passages' are by comparison academic and even at times second-hand (the sentiments expressed in them are, after all, the commonplaces of Elizabethan and Jacobean literature). They have charm and even grandeur, but they are fundamentally 'safe'.

There is certainly nothing safe about Donne's prose. It forces the reader, not to the solemn ruminations of the detached observer, but to a struggle, intellectual, sensuous, and spiritual. There is nothing fixed or static in his prose. In the sermons he may adopt a medieval structure – analysing in minute detail the several parts of his text, illustrating each step in the analysis with arguments drawn from the Fathers and the Schoolmen, and then reconstructing it from these elements (this process can perhaps be seen at its most typical in the moving sermon on the text 'Remember now thy Creator, in the days of thy Youth' – *Twenty-six Sermons*, 1660: Sermon XIX). But the combination of formal structure and molten fluidity of style serves to heighten the intellectual and emotional tension which is the product of a profound sensibility of mind and senses in direct contact with the issues of human destiny. With Donne it really *is* a matter of life and death.

The personality that emerges, in consequence, is itself fluid and restless – always changing, expanding, struggling, developing – exploring new channels, sometimes tortuous, always original, into which to pour its restless energy. It is impossible, therefore, ever to say that we have isolated Donne's personality – not, of course, because he is not present in his work, but because the term has no real meaning apart from the organization of words into which it has been absorbed. He is too deeply committed to his experience: as an artist he remains in control – but as a man he surrenders to it. Indeed, to speak of the personality of a writer as if it were a separate element in his work is, as a general rule, beside the point. It is not irrelevant here because in reading Sir Thomas Browne we *do* come away with a definite picture of character. He means that we should – for to him personality is an important part of his stock-in-trade.[3] He is one of the first English prose writers to set out deliberately to cultivate 'the gentle reader'. He takes him into his confidence, inviting admiration for his learning, indulgence for his foibles and eccentricities, and awe in the face of his perorations. But it is not only in these obvious ways that Browne parades his individuality – the whole of his writings are devoted to the careful distillation of a distinctive personal aroma.

This deliberate exploitation of personality, with the self-conscious attitude towards literature that it involved, was one of the symptoms of the changes that were taking place in English culture in the seventeenth century. The reasons for these changes are examined elsewhere in this volume; briefly they relate to the gradual break-up of the Elizabethan 'world-picture' and of the medieval traditions of learning and belief that lay beyond it, and to the consequent irruption of new and revolutionary ideas and theories. In a period when everything was in a state of flux, many writers turned in a more deliberate way than they had previously to the exploration of the quirks and oddities of personality. There was, for example, the vogue of eccentricity, practised with varying degrees of self-consciousness, by such writers as Thomas Coryate (1577?–1617), Robert Burton (1577–1640) and Sir Thomas Urquhart (1611–60). The pedantic nature of Urquhart's eccentricity is apparent in such titles as *The Trissotetras*, *Pantochronocanon* and *Logopandecteision*, though of course there was more to it than that, and the tendency stood him in good stead in his translation of Rabelais. The cultivation of eccentricity might perhaps be considered as a form of escape from the perplexities of a period of instability, a kind of frantic thrusting upwards of the personality at a time when the roots were in danger of becoming parched through lack of nourishment.

The shift in perspective in the attitude towards the writer's self reveals itself in other contemporary developments – in the growth of autobiography and memoirs (for example, Lord Herbert of Cherbury, 1583–1648 and Kenelm Digby, 1603–65); in the appearance of intimate 'table talk' (notably, of course, with John Selden, 1584–1654); and in the gossip and self-revelation of the famous diarists Samuel Pepys (1633–1703) and John Evelyn (1620–1706). In the essay, too, moral analysis as practised by Francis Bacon (1561–1626) and Abraham Cowley (1618–67) was accompanied by a degree of personal analysis, which was to become gradually more pronounced – growing worldly and urbane in Lord Halifax (1633–95), Sir William Temple (1628–99) and Lord Shaftesbury (1671–1713), but at the same time pointing forward to the more intimate confessions of the Romantic Revival. A similar heightening of the personal element can be seen, too, in such writers as Izaak Walton (1593–1683), Thomas Fuller (1608–61), and John Aubrey (1626–97) in whom charm, whimsicality, quaintness and temperament are dispensed with a certain air of self-conscious artifice which was comparatively rare among the earlier writers.

This increase in the awareness of personality as part of a writer's stock-in-trade was attended by a more detached approach to the observation of the elements of character, and a tendency to isolate them for curious examination, notably, of course, in character-writers like Sir Thomas Overbury (1581–1613) and John Earle (1601–65). A similar shift in the point of view, with an emphasis on the external traits of personality in place of the old unity of character, theme and background, is also apparent in much seventeenth-century drama. There are, for example, the rapid thumbnail sketches thrown off by Famineo in John Webster's *The White Devil* (produced about 1608) and by Bosola in his *The Duchess of Malfi* (about 1614) which have obvious affinities to the character-writers and which, though woven into the fabric of the play, really detract from the total dramatic impact. At the same time in the actual 'persons of the play' there is, in much later Jacobean drama, a sense of wavering perspective, of incompleteness and scrappiness that reflects the increasing uncertainty about values. They are closer to 'characters' in an actor's sense – prolific of grimaces, gestures, witticisms and 'dark sayings', but often with little organic relationship one with another or with an over-all pattern and theme.

These tendencies must be set side by side with the gradual emergence of the new kind of prose, designed to further scientific speculation and investigation, of which Sir Francis Bacon must be acknowledged as one of the pioneers. Most of the philosophical works, in which he argued the need for a new system to replace that of Aristotle and to be based on a right interpretation of Nature, were in Latin, but *The Advancement of Learning* (1605) was written in English. Although Bacon's prose style in many of his other English writings was close to that of the Elizabethans, in *The Advancement of Learning* it is subordinated to his overriding purpose: and the images and various figures of speech are deployed not in order to express the whole range of his feelings about the case he is arguing but in order to gain a dialectical victory.

In Tudor prose, however, the imagery was used primarily to increase the emotional effect and to heighten the muscular sensation rather than to enforce a strictly logical meaning, because it was exactly here – in expressing the whole texture of an idea or a situation – that the writer's chief interest lay, and not so much in the desire to analyse, argue, and prove.

There had, in fact, been little specialization or differentiation of function in Tudor prose – because there had been no overriding necessity for it. It had been at the same time the prose of narrative, description, theology, controversy, and the senses. It appealed, as L. C. Knights has said, not only to the eye that measures and calculates, but also to the hand that feels and weighs. The muscular content was part of the meaning. The relationship between word and sensation, word and action, was more intimate than it is today – and the thought (as in Donne) was itself 'felt'. This was true not only of writers such as Greene and Nashe, who were particularly close to contemporary idiom, but in a sense also of the theologians such as Hooker and even of the Euphuists. Lyly and Sidney, for example, were more elaborate than Sir Thomas Browne in their stylistic devices, but these sprang more directly from their emotional commitment and were not picked up and laid down like objects in a collection. Their use of literary convention, moreover, was bound up with a powerfully nostalgic feeling for the past, and in addition there was the energy and excitement of experimentation in a comparatively new medium. In reading Hooker's great perorations on Order and the Light of Reason, too, one has the sense of absorption in the material in a passionate, unequivocal way, so that the eloquence rises naturally out of an amalgam of the theology, the thought, and the feeling.

This account of Tudor prose and of the changes that followed in the seventeenth century is, of course, very much simplified and compressed. It does not give sufficient weight to the survivors of the Elizabethan tradition, and notably Milton, or to the vitality and resilience of the Tudor tradition in prose, and its resurgence in Bunyan, the religious controversialists, and the Puritan pamphleteers. It does not examine the ways in which the new self-consciousness on the one hand and the new Baconian objectivity on the other enriched our culture, for example, in the development of the novel. Above all, it leaves out of account the creation of another kind of cultural unity and 'world-picture' (narrower, perhaps, but with its own toughness and energy – and with its roots, moreover, in the past) in the Restoration and Augustan periods. Nevertheless, its main contention would seem to be a valid one: that in the seventeenth century a split in the functions of English prose begins to make itself felt, between, at the two extremes, the Baconian prose of inductive reasoning and the whimsical over-literary prose of Sir Thomas Browne (and in this connection it is interesting to note Browne's popularity with the most whimsical of the essayists of the Romantic Revival) – and that this carried the possible implication that the prose of the new instauration of learning was the really serious vehicle for contemporary thought and endeavour, while that of literature might, in consequence, be regarded as fanciful and remote. ·

This is perhaps related to T. S. Eliot's famous theory of a 'dissociation of sensibility' which, he argued in his essay on 'The Metaphysical Poets' (1921), began to take place in the seventeenth century, and from which English culture has suffered ever since, although a number of later critics have poured scorn on the concept for a variety of reasons.

At any rate there can surely be little doubt that there has been a growing fissure between the two kinds of language. It had not gone very far in the seventeenth century, but the prose of Sir Thomas Browne is already symptomatic of it. As we have seen, he is not unequivocally absorbed in his experience: he is not so passionately caught up in it that it speaks powerfully through his medium in spite of himself; on the contrary, he can stand back and calculate his effects. His great passages in consequence do not grow inevitably out of his material – they are externalized and their connection with it is not organic. At the same time there is a new element of self-consciousness in his relation to his audience. He has no passionate concern to communicate with his fellow men from the deepest level of his being – to share his experience and *live* it side by side with them – as Donne does; he is concerned rather in showing off his learning, skill, charm, and whimsicality in front of a select audience composed of people of similar tastes and interests. His attitude, in other words, is already to some extent that of the dilettante or the belle-lettrist – who treats literature as something separate from the mainstream of contemporary life.

Hitherto prose had been a medium for the whole range of human experience; Browne demonstrates how its pitch can be screwed up or down, not according to the emotional demands of the situation, but at the whim of the curious and experimental manipulator. Donne's prose, on the other hand, shows no sign of that kind of self-consciousness or literary artifice: he still belongs to a tradition in which the 'whole man' is used up in writing, and when he rises to the heights of eloquence, he is driven to them by the cumulative force and energy of his intellectual, sensuous, and spiritual explorations.

Thus the comparison between Browne and Donne is particularly fruitful because it throws into relief the changes that were taking place in English sensibility in the seventeenth century, and is therefore valuable for an understanding of the period; and because in doing so it emphasizes the distinction between two quite different literary modes or approaches. Donne emerges from the comparison as the greater writer because as a man and an artist he was in complete organic relationship with his material. When the whole man is thus engaged, the language is both sensuous *and* functional, and the 'fine passages', if indeed they can be isolated from the total effect, grow out of the greatness of the theme and the degree of passion and sincerity with which it is envisaged.

NOTES

1. The letter is quoted in *A Study of the Prose Works of John Donne*, by Evelyn M. Simpson (2nd edn 1962) – the most helpful book on the subject. The standard biography is *John Donne: A Life* by R. C. Bald (1970).

2. There is a thorough and fascinating discussion of the whole subject in *Paradoxia Epidemica: The Renaissance Tradition of Paradox*, by Rosalie L. Colie (1966).

3. For a good evocation of the personality of Sir Thomas Browne see the essay on him by Leslie Stephen in *Hours in a Library*, 2nd series, 1874–9.

BACON AND THE ADVANCEMENT
OF LEARNING

THEODORE REDPATH

The contribution by Bacon (1561–1626) to the advancement of learning was made almost entirely in Latin.[1] He certainly had no faith in the future of English as the language for English learning. 'These modern languages,' he wrote, 'will at one time or other play the bankrupts with books.' Fortunately the chief part of the Latin works have now been available in an authoritative translation (by Ellis and Spedding, in their edition of Bacon's works) for over a century. (Translations of the Latin works should, however, be more widely published.)[2]

Apart from occasional pieces, Bacon's works fall roughly into four groups: legal works, historical works, political and moral works, and works concerning the philosophy of science.

The legal works are of some interest to the historian of English law, but not to the general reader.

Of the historical works only the *History of the Reign of Henry VII*, a late work published in 1622, is complete. It deserves to be read more widely than it is. Grotius and Locke praised it understandably as a model of philosophical history. Bacon shows a penetrating sense of the trends of the reign, and the significance of particular events. He writes, as one would expect, with a ready understanding of affairs of state, and has a clear view of the implications of specific Acts and Orders. Moreover, Bacon's speculations on motive are most acute. He presents living figures in living scenes, and his highly discerning portrait of Henry VII affords a striking contrast to the laudatory or insipid sketches of the earlier histories. The writing, furthermore, is always to the point, and the narrative is animated by touches of shrewd wit. The style is neither tortuous nor bare, but pithy and enlivened with vivid and apt imagery. This is typical of Bacon's prose style at all periods.

The *History* was certainly a contribution to 'the advancement of learning'. The political fragments, *Of the True Greatness of the*

Kingdom of Britain (1607) and *An Advertisement touching an Holy War* (written 1622; published posthumously 1629), though both of interest, have, on the other hand, no relevance to our theme. On the other hand, the celebrated *Essays or Counsels, Civil and Moral*, published in ever-increasing collections from 1597 (ten essays) till 1625 (fifty-eight essays), not only themselves show 'learning', but also further 'the advancement of learning' within their specific fields. Their style, moreover, and especially their vivid imagery, is calculated to persuade their readers of the attractiveness of knowledge and wisdom in moral and civil affairs, and so, probably, to cause an appetite for knowledge in other areas. They are also often concerned to train the minds of readers, and enable them to exercise their intelligence in fruitful intellectual and practical pursuits.

Very early in life Bacon had become impressed with such fertile inventions as printing, gunpowder and the magnet and mariner's compass; and he cherished the great dream of increasing to a vast extent human power over physical objects, so as to relieve humanity from wretchedness and inconveniences, and to expand and enrich human experience. He devoted much of his energy to an attempt to stimulate people to try to realize this dream. The vast increase of human power, as he fully understood, could only be achieved through a commensurately vast increase in human knowledge. Experts on Bacon have differed on how far he valued knowledge independently of its contribution to power over nature.[3] This is a difficult question; but what seems certain is that he did value knowledge whose application to increasing power was neither immediate nor immediately obvious. Moreover, he does in several places state that he is primarily concerned with the acquisition of knowledge.[4] On the other hand, he was exceedingly keen that knowledge should issue sooner or later in discoveries which might bring practical results contributing to material welfare.[5] The main substance of his dissatisfaction with ancient and medieval philosophy was that it had largely concentrated on matters which not only had no tendency to promote important practical achievements, but diverted attention from fields of thought which had practical promise. He was, however, also mistrustful of more recent activities of a different kind, such as uncontrolled experiments, the retailing of old wives' tales about the physical world, and the impostures of quacks. His attitude to alchemy was somewhat ambivalent. He approved of such aims as the transmutation of metals, but had nothing but loathing and contempt for the pretentious jargon of some of the alchemists, and their hoodwinking of ignorant dupes.

Bacon was not, on the other hand, himself a distinguished scientist. He did conduct some scientific experiments; but these are not his claim to fame. He was, in addition, as Spedding long ago indicated, apparently ignorant, not only of some of the scientific advances of his own time, but also of certain discoveries of long standing. He seems, for instance, to have been ignorant of Kepler's astronomical discoveries, of Napierian logarithms, of the geometry of Archimedes and Apollonius, and of the methods of determining specific gravity used by Archimedes, Ghetaldus, and Porta. In writing of the progress of mechanics he does not mention Archimedes, Stevinus, or Galileo, interestingly showing no acquaintance with Galileo's theory of the acceleration of falling bodies (though we must remember that Galileo did not *publish* his discoveries till 1632). Bacon appears also to have been ignorant of the theory of the lever, and of the precession of the equinoxes. The list is imposing, but it does not really derogate from Bacon's real achievement, which is both as a powerful propagandist for science, and as a bold and fertile philosopher of science, offering a grand plan for *future* discoveries, clearing away noisome obstructions of various kinds, and making seminal suggestions about the basic logic of discovery.

One obstruction from which Bacon was concerned to free science was hostility from those theologians and their followers who considered science to be actually or potentially dangerous to religion, either by contradicting theological dogma or biblical teaching, or by diverting men's attention from the salvation of their souls to the aspiration to worldly power, riches and comfort. Bacon firmly separates revealed and natural theology on the one hand from natural science on the other, holding that there is no contradiction between them. It is interesting that Bacon was to receive support in this view from the fair number of distinguished clerics who joined ultimately in the early work of The Royal Society. Besides holding this view, however, Bacon positively regarded it as a religious duty to investigate nature and increase man's power over it. He seems, moreover, to have taken very seriously the statement in the first chapter of the

Book of Genesis that God gave man dominion over all creatures, and to have believed that this dominion had been, for one cause and another, lost, and had to be renewed. This is evidently the significance of his choice of *Instauratio Magna* (*The Great Renewal*) as the title of his unfinished work setting out his monumental programme for science. As for personal salvation, Bacon believed that Christianity required the fulfilment of duties to other people and to the public at large, and favoured the active against the purely contemplative life; and the most important element in active life was, for him, discovery and the works resulting from it.

Another sort of obstruction consisted of philosophical malpractices, such as hasty generalizations, trivial controversies, and scepticism.[6] Bacon was to contend against these and other forms of philosophical impediment throughout his philosophical work. Indeed, this polemic, which involved Bacon in a steady attack on the university curricula of his day, as well as on traditional philosophies, constitutes one important part of Bacon's philosophical achievement. His cautions against error, however, ran even deeper, and in his doctrine of the Idols, to which I shall come in due course, he strikes at some more widespread sources of scientific mistake.

Besides his attempt to remove obstacles, Bacon also made constructive contributions to the philosophy of science: his classification and review of the state of the sciences, his indication of an inductive method, and last but not least, his plan for a total natural philosophy. I must presently say something about each of these achievements. They all lie within the bounds of the *Instauratio Magna* (incomplete, but published partially in instalments 1620–26, and partially only posthumously). There is considerable difference of opinion as to precisely which of Bacon's works should be counted as falling within these bounds. The most reasonable view seems to me to be that of F. H. Anderson, that the only philosophical works which we can assign with any confidence to the *Instauratio* are all those which Bacon prepared between 1620 and his death in 1626, except the *De principiis atque originibus* (*On Principles and Origins*), and *The New Atlantis*. The works within the *Instauratio*, on that view, are only half in number (though more than half in bulk) of the thirty-odd philosophical works. I shall return to the *Instauratio* presently.

Meanwhile, what of the other philosphical works? Are any of them worth the general reader's attention today, and, if so, why? Philosophically speaking, there is little of importance in the works written before 1620 that is not to be found in the *Instauratio*. For anyone concerned to understand the *development* of Bacon's thought, however, many of the earlier works would be useful, and they are often written in a very lively style. One of the most vigorously written of them, the *Temporis partus masculus* (*The Fertilizing Birth of Time*, probably written before 1605), is also philosophically the most irresponsible. Bacon lays about him in violently abusive language, pouring scorn on, among others, Plato, Aristotle, and Galen (whom he calls *canicula*, which we might perhaps translate as 'a wretched little dog'). This scornful work should probably be regarded as springing from Bacon's sense of frustration at the uncritical reverence for ancient philosophical authority shown by many of his contemporaries in positions of influence, and seen by him as standing in the way of philosophical and scientific advance. He was certainly not so foolish as to fail to recognize Plato and Aristotle as 'among the greatest minds of humanity'. In the *Cogitata et visa* (*Thoughts and Conclusions*, probably started about 1607, and perfected over an unknown period of years: published posthumously by Gruter, 1653) and the *Redargutio philosophiarum* (*The Refutation of Philosophies*, written 1608) Bacon traces the limitations of ancient and medieval philosophy not to lack of individual geniuses but to its historical context, including geographical ignorance, religious narrowness, the diversion by Socrates of philosophy from scientific investigation to ethical analysis, and later, the concentration on political and military affairs, and eventually, in the Christian era, on theological problems, which commanded 'the most handsome rewards and generous aids'. Bacon shows himself disposed to draw favourable attention to pre-Socratic natural philosophy. He decided, for strategic reasons, not to publish these polemical works; but he took up the attack again more than ten years later in the *Instauratio*. The *Cogitata et visa* is, in my view, also especially worth reading as a finely finished and compact account of some of Bacon's main philosophical positions. Before either the *Cogitata et visa* or the *Redargutio* Bacon had written the English work for which, together with the *Essays*, he is now best known, *The Advancement of Learning* (written 1603–5, published 1605). Even this work, however, though it fully deserves to be read today for its superb Baconian English, has no strong philosophical claims on the modern reader, since its revision and Latin translation, the *De dignitate et augmentis scientiarum* (*On the dignity and extensions of the sciences*, published 1623), must be regarded as Bacon's definitive pronouncement.

The *De augmentis*, however, forms part of the *Instauratio*, which was the work that Bacon himself 'most esteemed'. To this work we must now turn. Its six-fold division had been thought out by Bacon at least as early as 1607, and the plan as announced by him in 1620 comprises six parts:

    I. A classification and review of the state of the sciences;

    II. A new logical method for discovery;

    III. A natural and experimental history, on the basis of which inductions could be made;

    IV. Examples of discoveries and inventions achieved by the new method, set out in tables;

    V. A temporary list of discoveries and inventions already made in the course of scientific inquiry, but not according to the new method (the contents of this list to be tested eventually by proper scientific method);

    VI. A scientific synthesis of the inductive conclusions.

The general outline of this plan is clear enough, and the plan is nobly conceived and, moreover, nobly explained by Bacon in a powerful Preface addressed to the general reading public. Yet, though Bacon worked hard (perhaps too hard) during the last few years of his life to complete the work, the result is highly fragmentary, even taking account of those parts of it published posthumously.

    Part I is represented by the *De augmentis*.

    Part II is represented by the *Novum organum sive indicia de interpretatione naturae* (*A new instrument, or directions for the interpretation of nature*, under preparation for at least ten years, published 1620).

    Part III is represented by (a) an introduction to natural and experimental history, the *Parasceve ad historiam naturalem et experimentalem* (*A Preparation for a Natural and Experimental History*), and a catalogue of particular histories, the *Catalogus historiarum particularium* (*A Catalogue of Particular Histories*, published 1620); (b) some half-dozen histories, only about half of which were completed by

Bacon, in particular the *Historia ventorum* (*History of the Winds*, published 1622), and the *Historia vitae et mortis* (*History of Life and Death*, published 1623); and (c) some miscellaneous works including the *Sylva sylvarum* (*A Forest of Growths*, the last of Bacon's works, published by Rawley 1627).

Parts IV and V are only represented by Prefaces, whose date of composition is uncertain. They were published by Gruter in 1653. Part VI is not represented by any extant work.

There is only space to write (and very briefly at that) on the *De augmentis*, the *Novum organum* and the *Parasceve*.

The *De augmentis* is a compendious survey of knowledge existing in Bacon's time and of what Bacon thought to be the gaps in it. He classifies knowledge as revealed and natural, each comprising three kinds deriving from one of three human 'faculties', Memory furnishing History, Imagination Poetry, and Reason Philosophy. Revelation always has to be accepted, but, according to Bacon's bold position, as we have seen, it can never contradict a scientific truth arrived at by Reason. He was not, of course, confronted, as nineteenth-century theologians and scientists were to be, by Lyell's geological or Darwin's biological researches. He was, in any case, more concerned to free science from theological impediments than to defend in detail biblical pronouncements apparently at odds with scientific knowledge.

'Natural knowledge' was, indeed, his main concern. History he divides into Natural and Civil. Natural History was especially important for him and he sketches a plan of a natural history in the *Parasceve*, including in its scope normal natural phenomena, abnormal natural phenomena, and experimental phenomena. Poetry he treats very cursorily, regarding it as 'feigned history'. Contrary to his reputation, however, Bacon evidently holds what he calls 'Poetry' (which probably includes all forms of literary fiction) in high regard, especially Parabolical Poetry, in which ideas are represented in sensory form. Indeed, he himself, as I shall later mention, uses 'poetical' devices both in his *Essays* and in his philosophical works, to further 'the advancement of learning'. Philosophy he divides into Natural Theology, the Science of Non-human Nature, and the Science of Man. At the basis of all three branches he holds that there is a science, 'First Philosophy', consisting of two parts. The first part comprises axioms common to all three branches, e.g. 'if equals be added to unequals the whole will be unequal'. The examples he gives, however, form rather a hotch-potch. The second part deals with such concepts as quantity, similarity, possibility, being and not-being, raising such questions as 'Why is there more iron than gold?' 'Why is there more grass than roses?', 'Why are there often intermediate forms between two species, e.g. bats?'. Such examples are just one instance of the range in character of Bacon's intellectual curiosity. Natural Theology consists of knowledge of God (and of Angels and Spirits) obtainable by human reason. Bacon is very cautious about accepting claims to such knowledge. The Science of Non-human Nature divides into Speculative Doctrine and Operative Doctrine. Speculative Doctrine consists of Physics, which investigates efficient and material causes, and Metaphysics, which investigates final causes and 'forms'. Bacon believed that such philosophers as Aristotle and some of his followers had fallen into error by imagining final causes (purposes) and introducing them prematurely into explanations of physical phenomena. The investigation of 'forms', on the other hand, is one of the central goals of Baconian natural philosophy, and I shall say something of it when I come to the *Novum organum*. Operative Doctrine also has two parts, Mechanics, corresponding to Physics, and concerned with producing macroscopic changes, and Magic, corresponding to Metaphysics, and aiming at producing microscopic changes. Mathematics is a handmaid to both Speculative and Operative Doctrine. The Science of Man consists of the Philosophy of Humanity and Civil Philosophy. The Philosophy of Humanity consists of Doctrine concerning the Soul of Man, and Doctrine concerning the Body of Man. Interestingly, Doctrine concerning the Soul of Man includes Logic and Ethics. 'Logic' is used by Bacon in a wide sense, as including 'the Arts of Discovery, Judging, Retaining and Transmitting'. Ethics includes the description of ethical standards and the means to attain them. Bacon does, however, believe that the supreme guide to conduct lies in revelation. As to Civil Philosophy, that includes politics and diplomacy.

That is a brief outline of the *De augmentis*. The survey is a masterly one. Indeed, as Macaulay thought, Bacon excelled in 'knowledge of the mutual relations of all the departments of knowledge'. This is true, despite the gaps already mentioned in his specific acquaintance with both recent and long-standing scientific advances. There is evidence, in any case, that Bacon did not regard even the *De augmentis* as a perfect fulfilment of Part I of his plan.

Having pointed out gaps in human knowledge Bacon's next move was naturally to indicate how they could be filled. His first steps are to show how ignorance and error have sprung from various human weaknesses, and then to remedy this by introducing a proper scientific method. The *Novum organum* (which Bacon apparently rewrote more than a dozen times) was intended to do both. In showing how various human weaknesses have impeded science Bacon is brilliantly successful, especially in his famous doctrine of the Idols (Book I). The choice of the term 'Idols', with its natural reminder of Moses and the priests of Baal, is an outstanding instance of Bacon's skill in metaphorical rhetoric. The Idols are of four kinds: Idols of the Tribe, Idols of the Cave, Idols of the Market-place, and Idols of the Theatre. Idols of the Tribe are sources of error common to all humanity, such as preoccupation, narrow-mindedness, interference by emotion and desire, limitations of the senses, and a tendency to believe in the reality of mere abstractions. Idols of the Cave are sources of error peculiar to individuals from birth or through training, habit or accident. As instances Bacon mentions the tendency of scientists and philosophers to construct complete systems in accordance with their favourite subjects, and he also instances bias towards antiquity or novelty. Idols of the Market-place, which Bacon thinks the most troublesome of all, are sources of error lying in language. These Idols are of two kinds, one arising from names of things which do not exist, and the other from names attached to abstractions faultily made. Bacon thinks the second class the more dangerous. He instances the word 'humid', which might appear to have a clear meaning, but which, when its use is investigated, can be seen to be far from clear. Idols of the Theatre arise from false principles of philosophy and mistaken rules of demonstration. These are the only Idols that can, in his view, be completely eradicated. He tries to do this by indicating the radical defects of the main systems based on them, namely excessive Rationalism, excessive Empiricism, and superstitious Spiritualism. All the Idols could, however, be controlled, and Bacon attempts to do so by recommending and describing an adequate natural and experimental history, and by outlining a new scientific method.

The refutation of the defective systems is the subject of part of Book I of the *Novum organum*. The description of the natural and experimental history is, as I have said, the object of the *Parasceve*. The third task, the outlining of a new scientific method, Bacon undertakes in Book II of the *Novum organum*. Before describing the method in detail he states clearly what he considers the object of natural science, speculative and operative. The ultimate object of *speculative* natural science is to discover the 'forms' of all things; but the immediate object is to discover the 'forms' of 'simple natures'. The object of *operative* natural science is to generate and superinduce new 'natures' on bodies; and this can only be fully accomplished if the 'forms' have been discovered. 'From the discovery of Forms, therefore, results truth in speculation and freedom in operation.' All this requires explanation. Bacon considers in detail the case of heat. 'Heat' (that is *physical* heat, as contrasted with *sensible* heat) is what Bacon would call a 'simple nature'.[7] He considers, moreover, that the whole physical world consists of an immense variety of patterns and compounds of comparatively few such 'simple natures', which thus form the 'alphabet' of nature. Each of these 'natures', according to Bacon, has a 'form', which is really simply a specific modification of a more general 'nature' than the 'simple nature' under analysis. Thus the 'form' of 'heat', in Bacon's view, is violent, irregular, molecular motion. Motion is a more general 'nature' than 'heat', and violence, irregularity, and molecular character are specific modifications of this more general 'nature'.

Having stated the problem as the discovery of these 'forms', Bacon goes on to suggest a method of discovery. Whenever a given 'simple nature' is present, its 'form' will be present; whenever a given 'simple nature' is absent, its 'form' will be absent, and the greater the degree in which the 'simple nature' is present, the greater the degree in which its 'form' will be present. In determining the 'forms', therefore, negative instances and comparisons will be most important: mere collections of affirmative instances, and, even more, premature generalizations of too great scope will be dangerous. The understanding must proceed slowly. It should use both affirmative and negative instances, in addition to instances in which the nature is present in varying degrees, in order to establish axioms of kindred scope. Then from these axioms it may be possible to proceed by the aid of further instances to axioms of greater generality, and then from these to still more general axioms, and so on. There are a number of types of instance, both affirmative and negative, which Bacon considers particularly useful in helping to establish axioms. Bacon calls these instances Prerogative Instances. His description of them is most acute and stimulating. (He also intended to expound a number of other inductive aids.) At each stage when an axiom was arrived at, Bacon thought, it should be noted whether it was claimed to apply only to the particular instances from which it had been inducted or to apply to other particular instances. If the latter, then it should be verified whether it applied to these other instances in actual fact or not. If it did, then the axiom might be regarded as established.

Eliminative induction (i.e. induction making use of negative instances) was old enough in practice, though probably seldom duly emphasized or systematically applied, and pretty certainly never correctly described in logical terms, before Bacon. Bacon claimed for it that it could, as contrasted with enumerative induction, arrive at 'absolute certainty', in a sense that excludes the occurrence of a contradictory instance to the proposition purportedly established by induction. I think it has been clearly shown that this claim of his was excessive.[8]

For the purposes of proof, short of strict certainty, even the detail of Bacon's inductive method, supplemented by such information as an exhaustive list of 'simple natures' (which he never supplies), might have its uses. As a method of discovery in natural science, however, it would almost certainly, even with other aids, be unbearably cumbersome. Bacon was so afraid of hasty conclusions, and so concerned to provide a method which would enable great progress to be made by opening the possibility of effecting at least some discoveries even to men of most ordinary intelligence (a dream which he may have culled from Ramon Lull or Telesius), that he failed to respect sufficiently the possibilities of discovery by means of induction by simple enumeration on the one hand, or by means of the use of bold hypotheses on the other. It is a somewhat ironical fact that the great scientific progress of the next two centuries was to be achieved largely by men who did not follow the cumbersome Baconian methods, because they were superior in intelligence to the men of more ordinary abilities for whom those methods were in fair measure designed. On the other hand, it is equally to be remembered that these great discoverers might well never have applied their minds even in their disobedient fashion, with such vigour, had it not been for the general directions, inspiration, and propaganda for science for which Bacon was responsible.

Bacon hurriedly left the *Novum organum* incomplete, and turned his attention to Part III of his *Instauratio*, the provision of a natural and experimental history. The tremendous plan of this history is sketched in the *Parasceve* and the *Catalogus*. These fully deserve the hour of the modern general reader's time required for reading them, and that hour can give quite a clear idea of the vastness of Bacon's design. There is, moreover, no doubt that this plan was fruitful. It was an inspiration to investigators in the late seventeenth century and in the eighteenth century, both in Britain and on the Continent. It is worth noting that in the *Parasceve* (as also in the *De augmentis*), Bacon, though no mathematician himself (a fault of his early Cambridge training, so different from the Trinity training today!), sees in an immense development of mathematical physics one of the chief keys to scientific advance as a whole.

There has been much controversy as to which part of Bacon's philosophy made the greatest contribution to the advancement of learning. Bacon's distinguished editors, Spedding and Ellis, were themselves divided over this – Spedding laying stress on the classification and review of the sciences, and the plan for a total natural history and philosophy, and Ellis emphasizing the new inductive method. Critics of Bacon's inductive method, and historians of scientific method in general, seem to have shown that Bacon's inductive method, in its detail and in the fragmentary form in which he left it, neither did make, nor could have made, a really substantial contribution to the advance of science along the lines which it followed through Newton and the eighteenth-century scientists, and that even among Bacon's immediate disciples it was seldom used. It has also been amply demonstrated[9] that Bacon's inductive method was quite unfitted for the solution of what Bacon conceived to be the fundamental problem of science, the discovery of the 'forms' of things. At most it could have led to the discovery of empirical laws connecting 'simple natures'. Nevertheless, the general principles of Baconian induction, and some of its detail, did have their influence on natural science and on British mental, moral and political philosophy, and, refurbished by Mill in his 'Joint Method of Agreement and Difference', may perhaps be said to have proved fruitful in nineteenth-century biology, sociology and economics. Furthermore, Bacon's *account* of induction was, in any case, an outstanding contribution to the *logic* of scientific method. With these qualifications it seems that Spedding's emphasis is nearer the truth. Yet this is not the end of the matter, for certainly one of Bacon's greatest contributions to the advancement of learning lay in his clear and eloquent expression of the philosophy of controlled empiricism, of the view that the future of science lay in systematic observation and scrupulously controlled experiment. The present writer has been acquainted with two Nobel prizewinners, both past Presidents of The Royal Society, who have recognized Bacon as 'the father of modern science', and it is a fair recognition of the generative force of his philosophical work. This generative force owes a great deal to Bacon's skill in persuasive writing.

Bacon was naturally gifted as a compelling speaker and writer. Ben Jonson testified that 'no man ever spake more neatly, more pressly, more weightily, or suffered less emptiness, less idleness, in what he uttered'; and his further remark that 'his hearers could not cough, or look aside from him, without loss' indicates the pithy density of Bacon's spoken prose. The importance of persuasion in the courts and in parliament necessarily made Bacon concerned with the nature and methods of rhetoric, and he was keen to develop the most effective ways of convincing the King and other personages of influence of the value and urgency of scientific advance, and of encouraging scientists themselves to proceed with determination. Considerable attention has been given in recent years to Bacon's own forms of rhetoric, and to their evolution during his career as a writer; and also to his theoretical observations on rhetoric.[10] It seems evident that whatever reservations Bacon may have had about Aristotle's logic, physics and metaphysics, and about the cramping philosophical influence of some Aristotelians, he had much recourse to Aristotle's thinking on rhetoric, and, in particular, to its emphasis on solidity of matter, and on the importance of adapting style to the audience in view, and also to its inclusion of reasoning, moral stance, and emotional working in the total scope of persuasion. Bacon is especially close to Aristotle when he writes on human emotions. There are passages in the *Essays* and in the philosophical works for which Aristotle's *Rhetoric* affords striking parallels. Over the years from about 1605 till the early 1620s Bacon developed his style both for popular consumption and also for intellectual audiences. In the end he came to use many resources besides plain argumentation: similes, metaphors, emblems, maxims, aphorisms, fables, allegories, myths, exposure of sophisms; and he seemed also to have gained an ever-increasing grasp of what he took to be the central function of rhetoric in writing. In the *De augmentis* he finally sums this up as being 'to apply and recommend the dictates of reason to imagination, in order to excite the appetite and will' (IV, 455). Imagination left uncontrolled could well lead to fantastic errors; subjected to reason through rhetoric it could breed not only true learning but also fruitful discovery.

An ultimate question has arisen in many twentieth-century minds: whether humanity is really better off for the astonishing scientific advances of the last four centuries, for much of which Bacon can be held in considerable measure philosophically responsible. The possible destruction in the near future of what civilized living there is on this planet, and even of life itself, is a nightmare haunting many contemporaries. Others are repelled by the fierce competition for material benefits which seems to them to characterize many modern societies, and some among those so repelled believe that we should concentrate on other-worldly values, and set less store not only by worldly luxury but even by worldly welfare. Bacon himself was undoubtedly worldly; but he was also beneficent, and further, though worldly, he was not, as the French Encyclopedists thought him, a disguised atheist. This emerges from many of Bacon's writings, and not least from *New Atlantis* (probably written in its present form in 1624; published by Rawley 1627), which may reasonably be taken to embody Bacon's final attitudes to the whole matter of scientific advance. As many readers will know, Bacon there describes the institutions and customs of a mythical island, on which there is established what Bacon clearly implies to be his conception of an ideal state. The state is Christian and monarchical, with the family as its unit. The crowning glory of the state is its college of scientific knowledge and invention, Salomon's House, doubtless intended by Bacon as a marked contrast to contemporary universities in England. The

Father of Salomon's House states its aims as follows: 'The end of our foundation is the knowledge of causes, and secret motions of things; and the enlarging of the bounds of human empire, to the effecting of all things possible.' No aims could be more clearly earthly than that. Bacon, in a spirit of wonder and admiration, gives many details of the vast activity of the institution, which includes experiments in physics, chemistry, physiology, mechanics and other sciences, in laboratories appropriately constructed, some in deep caves, and some on towers half a mile high. The activity also includes invention in all spheres, including such outlying projects as the construction of 'Sound-houses' for the discovery of new musical harmonies. Again: 'We imitate also flights of birds; we have some degrees of flying in the air. We have ships and boats for going under water, and brooking of seas.' E. D. Blodgett has pointed out[11] that it is not impossible that Bacon may have read the Utopian work of the Italian Dominican monk Campanella, published in Latin at Frankfurt in 1623. That work, *Civitas solis* (*The City of the Sun*), suggests similar though far more elementary projects for the advancement of science. The religious, political and social tendencies of *Civitas solis*, however, are utterly different from those of *New Atlantis*. They are monastic and communistic; and it is possible that if Bacon read Campanella's book he was partly concerned in *New Atlantis* to emphasize that revolutionary advances in science need not be associated with radicalism in politics and sociology; and, furthermore, that advances in material comfort and riches were neither to be despised in themselves, nor to be thought incompatible with Christianity. The Christianity of *New Atlantis*, in any case, is plainly of a highly tolerant nature; and what is more, the scientific knowledge, skill and invention are directed entirely to peaceful ends. The spirit of the work is magically pacific. Since early days, indeed, Bacon had placed mastery over nature for the sake of humanity at large above its use for any narrowly patriotic and, still more, any individually egoistic aims. He cannot be blamed for any misuses which this or any other century may have made of science or may make of it in the future.

NOTES

1. The only *philosophical* work he published in English was *The Advancement of Learning* (probably begun immediately after the accession of James I

in 1603; published 1605). The reason he wrote this work in English was not a desire to reach the masses. As Spedding pointed out, it was obviously written for readers familiar with Latin. Bacon's main reason was probably a wish to further the advancement of learning by appealing through Englishry to a King of England, conscious of his Protestantism, and to the English Court, Church, and universities. On this point I accept Professor F. H. Anderson's interpretation (*The Philosophy of Francis Bacon*, Chicago, 1948, 17).

2. This deficiency has been to some degree remedied by the translations of *Cogitata et visa*, *Redargutio philosophiarum* and *Temporis partus masculus* by Benjamin Farrington in *The Philosophy of Francis Bacon* (Liverpool, 1964).

3. See F. H. Anderson, above, P. Rossi, *Francis Bacon* (London, 1968), B. Farrington, *Francis Bacon* (London, 1951), and Lisa Jardine, *Francis Bacon* (Cambridge, 1974).

4. e.g. 'The contemplation of truth is a thing worthier and loftier than all utility and magnitude of works' (*Works*, ed. Spedding, Ellis and Heath, IV, 110) and 'I care little about the mechanical arts themselves: only about those things which they contribute to the equipment of philosophy.' (*Works*, IV, 271.)

5. e.g. *Novum Organum*, Aphorism 81: 'The true and lawful goal of the sciences is simply this, that human life be enriched by new discoveries and powers'; and, from the description of Salomon's House in *New Atlantis*: 'The End of our Foundation is the knowledge of Causes, and secret motions of things; and the enlarging of the bounds of Human Empire, to the effecting of all things possible.' (Bacon's *Works*, III, 510–12.)

6. It is important to realize that Bacon differentiates his cautious theory of knowledge sharply from scepticism: e.g. 'I do not take away authority from the senses, but supply them with helps; I do not slight the understanding, but govern it.' (*Works*, IV. 112.)

7. I have followed Professor Broad's interpretation here (see Broad, *The Philosophy of Francis Bacon*, Cambridge, 1926, 30–33).

8. e.g. by Professor G. H. von Wright, in *The Logical Problem of Induction* (Helsinki, 1941). See also the same author's *A Treatise on Induction and Probability* (London, 1951).

9. e.g. in Professor A. E. Taylor's 'Francis Bacon', *Proceedings of the British Academy*, XII, (1926).

10. See notably P. Rossi, *Francis Bacon: From Magic to Science*, tr. S. Rabinovitch, London, 1968, especially chs III–VI; B. W. Vickers, *Francis Bacon and Renaissance Prose* (Cambridge, 1968); and his 'Bacon's Use of Theatrical Imagery', *Studies in the Literary Imagination*, 4 (1971), 189–226; James Stephens, 'The Origins and Influence of Bacon's Rhetorical Theory' (Univ. of Wisconsin Dissn, 1968); and his *Francis Bacon and the Style of Science* (Chicago and London, 1975); and Lisa Jardine, *Francis Bacon: Discovery and the Art of Discourse* (Cambridge, 1974) chs 9–13.

11. In 'Bacon's *New Atlantis* and Campanella's *Civitas Solis*, a Study in Relationships', P.M.L.A. (1931), 763–80.

BEN JONSON'S POETRY

FRANK W. BRADBROOK

In many ways Jonson occupies an unusual position in English literature. This is partly owing to the length of time that he was a dominant
force in drama and poetry. 'Like Bacon, Jonson mediates between the
age of Shakespeare and the age of Milton.'[1] By 1598 Francis Meres,
who wrote a survey of English literature from Chaucer to his own
day called *Palladis Tamia*, had come to the opinion that Jonson was
one of 'our best for tragedy'. In 1616 the poet received official recognition in the form of a pension from James I, and this was continued
and enlarged by Charles I. Jonson collected his poems, plays, and
masques for publication in a folio volume in the same year that he
received this royal favour. Until his death in 1637 he held a commanding influence over his fellow poets, and after his death his
memory was celebrated with affectionate esteem by his admirers in a
volume of elegies entitled *Jonsonus Virbius*. A further collection of his
poems was published in 1640.

Jonson's poetry is notable for its range and variety, and this is reflected in the breadth of his social contacts. From the beginning of
the century Jonson had presided at the famous meetings of writers
held at the Mermaid Tavern, and it was here that Shakespeare re-
putedly engaged in the famous wit combats with him described later
by the chronicler Fuller. Jonson was 'like a Spanish great galleon . . .
built far higher in learning, solid but slow in his performances'; while
Shakespeare, like 'an English man-of-war, lesser in bulk but lighter
in sailing, could turn with all tides, tack about, and take advantage
of all winds, by the quickness of his wit and invention'.[2] Perhaps this
account has rather prejudiced later views of Ben Jonson. He was certainly a much more learned poet than Shakespeare, but the general
view of his contemporaries, as suggested, for example, in the poem
addressed to him about 1606 by Francis Beaumont, is that there was
nothing clumsy or heavy about the conversations at the Mermaid.

On the contrary, it is the wit, the nimbleness, and subtlety that are stressed, and Ben Jonson himself is praised as one who makes smooth and plain the way of knowledge for others. Jonson, however, did not rely solely on the Mermaid for his company. With John Donne (whom he considered 'the first poet in the world in some things'), Drayton, and several other poets, he shared the inspiring friendship of Lucy, Countess of Bedford. Others who entertained the poet informally at their houses were Sidney's daughter Elizabeth, the Countess of Rutland, and his niece Mary, wife of Sir Robert Wroth, themselves both poets. Sir Robert Sidney and the Earl of Pembroke, son of Sir Philip's sister, were also friends, and from the latter Jonson received £20 every New Year's day to buy new books.[3] Jonson describes in one of his poems the lavish hospitality he enjoyed at the ancestral home at Penshurst.

The theatre, the tavern, and the country house each played their part in shaping Ben Jonson's genius, and it is hardly surprising that his poetry ranges from some of the crudest to some of the most refined and urbane in the English language. In literature the most important influence, apart from Donne, was exerted by the classical poets on whom Jonson deliberately modelled himself, but the vitality that characterizes all his writing and gives the most derivative of poems its special timbre is his own.

Like Sidney, Jonson was a critic as well as a poet. His views on poetry are given in the notes which Drummond of Hawthornden took in 1619 when the poet visited Scotland, and in Ben Jonson's own commonplace-book called *Discoveries*. From these two sources, knowledge of both Jonson's theories and practice in poetry can be gained. In *Conversations with William Drummond* there are brief remarks on many of Jonson's predecessors and contemporaries, and even those whom he admired are commented on with typical pungency. Never reluctant to talk about himself, he reveals his own method of writing poetry: 'That he wrote all his first in prose, for so his master Camden had learned him'; while the robust assertiveness of his views about his position in English literature is characteristic: 'He was better versed and knew more in Greek and Latin, than all the poets in England.'

Timber, or Discoveries made upon men and matter, as they flowed out of his daily readings is not, in any sense, an original work. In his critical ideas, as in his poetry, Jonson drew heavily on classical models.[4] 'I know nothing can conduce more to letters than to examine the writings of the ancients', he says. But he adds a recommendation 'not to rest in their sole authority, or take all upon trust from them ... for to all the observations of the ancients we have our own experience, which if we will use and apply, we have better means to pronounce'. The ancients are, for Jonson, guides not commanders. 'Spenser, in affecting the ancients, writ no language.' To write well, a man must read the best authors, observe the best speakers, and exercise his own style. Jonson himself cultivates style deliberately: 'No matter how slow the style be at first, so it be laboured and accurate.' He is no enemy of inspiration, provided it is genuine, but he is an enemy of facility. Care and industry are needed in the writer as in any other craftsman; it is his duty to revise and polish his work. The best writers 'did nothing rashly; they obtained first to write well, and then custom made it easy and a habit'. Jonson's ideal in style is a modest one: 'Pure and neat language I love, yet plain and customary.' His abomination is a barbarous phrase.

Jonson is both independent and a believer in tradition which he calls 'Custom' ('that I call custom of speech which is the consent of the learned'). But he is opposed to any dictatorship of ancient models ('as the schools have done Aristotle'), and he will not confine a poet's liberty 'within the narrow limits of laws which either the grammarians or philosophers prescribe'. At the same time, Aristotle 'understood the causes of things; and what other men did by chance or custom he doth by reason; and not only found out the way not to err, but the short way that we should take not to err ...'

This combination of respect for tradition and a sturdy independence is what gives Ben Jonson's poetry its variety and flexibility. He can range from the most formal classical style to the racy idiomatic utterance befitting a popular dramatist and the leading spirit of the meetings at the Mermaid. It is, in fact, not at all easy to separate these two sides of his genius. His most classical poems have a racy idiomatic quality, while his most colloquial poems frequently follow classical models. Jonson made no attempt to impose the idiom and syntax of the classical writers on the English language. The spirit in which he uses the classics is very different from that of Milton.

A typical example of the Jonsonian lyric is his *Song to Celia* modelled on the familiar theme of Catullus ('*Vivamus, mea Lesbia, atque amemus*').

> Come my CELIA let us prove,
> While wee may, the sports of love;
> Time will not be ours for ever:
> He, at length, our good will sever.
> Spend not then his gifts in vaine.
> Sunnes that set, may rise againe:
> But, if once wee lose this light,
> 'Tis, with us, perpetuall night.
> Why should we deferre our joyes?
> Fame, and rumor are but toyes.
> Cannot we delude the eyes
> Of a few poore household spyes?
> Or his easier eares beguile,
> So removed by our wile?
> 'Tis no sinne, loves fruit to steale,
> But the sweet theft to reveale:
> To bee taken, to be seene,
> These have crimes accounted beene.

This has been described as 'mediocre' by his Oxford editors, 'merely smooth and insignificant', and is compared unfavourably with 'the superb Elizabethan romanticism' of the poet Campion's treatment of the same theme. F. R. Leavis has referred to the poem in very different terms:

> Jonson's effort was to feel Catullus, and the others he cultivated, as contemporary with himself; or rather; to achieve an English mode that should express a sense of contemporaneity with them ... This mode ... may be described as consciously urbane, mature, and civilized.[5]

Obviously a poet who is able to arouse such difference of opinion among those qualified to judge is still very much alive. Perhaps the point that should be stressed is that Jonson was not alone in this use of the classics, though despite earlier examples, such as the poem of Campion, it was he who was largely responsible for transposing the spirit of the classical *lyric* into English. Jonson's combination of a classical sense of form and restraint with a native English vigour gave the seventeenth-century lyric its distinctive quality. Andrew Marvell, in such a poem as *To His Coy Mistress*, as in many of his other poems, is writing in the tradition initiated by Ben Jonson, modified by the more colloquial manner and the imagery typical of the lyrics of Donne.

Jonson's *Song to Celia* is, in a special sense, dramatic. It is sung by Volpone in the third Act of the play. To be fully appreciated it must be read in its dramatic context. However closely related they are, there is an ironic contrast between Catullus's poem in praise of Lesbia and the song of Volpone the Fox, who is attempting to seduce Celia, the wife of the merchant Corvino. Volpone immediately follows up the song with the offer to his lady of diamonds and jewels:

> ... a carbuncle,
> May put out both the eyes of our St Mark.

A typical satirical flavour is added to the apparently simple lyric. The idea, expressed at the end of the poem, that it is no sin to steal but only to be found out, was a belief held by the Spartans that Jonson may have absorbed directly or indirectly from the classics. But it comes with superb irony from the mouth of Volpone the Magnifico, who has just been described by the misguided husband (who had willingly prostituted his wife) as 'an old decrepit wretch, That has no sense, no sinew'. Such a satirical undertone is quite lacking in Campion's charming lyric.

There is a similar treatment of Catullus in Jonson's other poem to Celia ('Kiss me sweet'), which perfectly catches the tone and accent of its original in the opening lines. Then, in the enumeration of the kisses, the lyric deviates ironically, and contrasts Catullus with the Cockney background of the contemporary lover:

> Adde a thousand, and so more;
> Till you equall with the store,
> All the grasse that *Rumney* yeelds,
> Or the sands in *Chelsey* fields,
> Or the drops in silver *Thames*,
> Or the starres, that guild his streames,
> In the silent sommer-nights,
> When youths ply their stolne delights.

In the last four lines of the lyric Jonson returns to the urbane and poised accent of the opening. Such flexible and controlled transitions from an ideal classical world to the actualities of seventeenth-century London, with the accompanying sense of ironical contrast, distinguish Jonson from a poet such as Campion, and are a proof of his greatness. Because of the restraint imposed by Jonson's sense of form, these transitions are always easy and graceful. There is none of that deliberate shock of contrast such as T. S. Eliot exploits in his early poetry. But for the general method, the ironical opposition of the actual and the classical which is one of the characteristic effects in *The Waste Land*, Mr Eliot could find numerous models and examples in Jonson's poetry.

The edition of Jonson's poems printed in 1616 contains his epigrams and a collection called *The Forest*. In some of the epigrams there would appear to be some justification for adverse comment. When Jonson is not at his best, his poems are too elaborate, lacking in spontaneity and flexibility, clumsy and harsh. Yet there are also to be found in this collection some of the most sensitive and delicate of his lyrics. In poems such as *On My First Daughter*, *On His First Sonne*, together with the epitaphs on Solomon Pavy and Elizabeth L. H., Jonson writes in a style of limpid clarity that conveys by its simplicity and restraint the deepest of human feelings. *The Epigrams* also include the fine tribute, written in an unusual tone of humility, to Jonson's master William Camden, and poems to his friends John Donne, Francis Beaumont, Lucy, Countess of Bedford, and Mary, Lady Wroth. Such poems are the natural product of that intellectual, courtly, and refined society where intimacy and friendship naturally express themselves in formal written compliment. 'Rare poems aske rare friends', as Jonson writes to the Countess of Bedford when sending her Donne's satires. In such a world only the best is good enough: the standard set implies selection. Jonson and his circle were consciously writing for the few. Moreover, there was for Jonson a complete harmony between this actual world and the ideal one of classical literature. In the witty and learned lines *Inviting a Friend to Supper*, Jonson describes at length the food and wine to be offered to his friend. He also dwells on the talk that is to follow, about Virgil, Horace, and Anacreon. This natural association of the ideal with ordinary everyday things looks forward to the eighteenth-century poets, particularly to Pope. Penshurst itself is the home of the Dryads, Pan, Bacchus, the Muses, and Satyrs, but it is also a very real place:

> The lower land, that to the river bends,
> Thy sheepe, thy bullocks, kine, and calves doe feed:
> The middle grounds thy mares, and horses breed.
> Each banke doth yeeld thee coneyes ...

The attitude to the great house and its surroundings, the feeling for nature, together with the style of formal, dignified compliment, are echoed in Pope's lines at the end of Epistle IV (*Of the use of Riches, to Richard Boyle, Earl of Burlington*):

> Whose cheerful Tenants bless their yearly toil,
> Yet to their Lord owe more than to the soil;
> Whose ample lawns are not ashamed to feed
> The milky heifer and deserving steed.

Later, in describing 'thy orchard fruit', 'thy garden flowers', 'the blushing apricot and woolly peach', there is a direct sensuous appreciation of nature that brings to mind *The Garden* and *Bermudas* of Andrew Marvell. The same combination of interests is to be found in the poem *To Sir Robert Wroth*.

Some of Jonson's finest lyrics appear in the masques that he wrote for the Court. The plays also contain numerous songs, some of which were set to music by Jonson's friend, Alfonso Ferrabosco. Generally, under the influence of Jonson and Donne the lyric extended its range, expressing more profound thought and deeper feeling. But in the masques and plays the tradition of the Elizabethan song was continued, and a number of Jonson's finest lyrics are in the earlier, simpler manner. 'Queen and huntress, chaste and fair', 'Still to be neat, still to be dressed', 'Slow, slow, fresh fount', and 'If I freely may discover' are perhaps the best-known examples. Here Jonson casts his learning aside and writes with ease and grace some of the most sensitive and delicate of English songs. If one compares them with a song of Donne's such as 'Sweetest love, I do not goe', it will be seen how much more ingrained in Donne's poetry is the intellectual conceit. The rhythm of Donne's songs is much nearer to colloquial speech, and even the simplest ones would not appear to lend themselves very easily to musical accompaniment.[6]

The series of poems addressed *To Charis* are Jonson's main contribution to the love lyric. They are playful in tone rather than passionate, with the exception of the finest of the pieces, *Her Triumph*. Here, and particularly in the final stanza, 'Have you seene but a bright Lillie grow?', there is a strong direct expression of feeling rare in Ben Jonson's love poetry, though there is another passage in the seventh poem of the series with an echo of the scene with Helen in Marlowe's play *Dr Faustus* and a reminiscence of Donne's *Extasie*:

> Joyne lip to lip, and try:
> Each suck the others breath.
> And whilst our tongues perplexed lie,
> Let who will thinke us dead, or wish our death.

Such passages are unusual. Generally speaking, emotion is suggested and implied rather than directly presented. The neatness of form is what appeals to the reader, and this involves restraint and control. The concern with form and style hardly allows for the intensity that Donne gains in such a poem as *The Canonization*:

> For Godsake hold your tongue and let me love ...

Typical of the Jonsonian lyric is the courtly expression of platonic love beginning:

> Faire Friend, 'tis true, your beauties move
> My heart to a respect:
> Too little to bee paid with love,
> Too great for your neglect.

The poem has been attributed to Sidney Godolphin, one of Jonson's admirers, and resembles the Cavalier poets in manner and style though it has a weight and dignity characteristically Jonsonian. Jonson too combines depth of feeling with a graceful lightness of touch. Though emotion does not directly appear in the poem, the very moderation and modesty of his claims emphasizes the sincerity. The poet is calmly and impersonally recognizing both the reality and the limitations of his love:

> 'T is not a passions first accesse
> Readie to multiply,
> But like Loves calmest State it is
> Possest with victorie.
>
> It is like Love to Truth reduc'd,
> All the false values gone,
> Which were created, and induc'd
> By fond imagination.

'Access' includes the sense of 'attack' (reflected in the image of the victorious man-of-war at the end of the stanza), 'approach', 'advance', and an 'outburst' of feeling. In 'multiply' there is a similar pun on the sexual and mathematical implications, carrying on the suggestions implied in the 'first access' (there is also an echo of Genesis i, 28,

'Be fruitful and multiply'). The verse flows evenly until there is a sudden stress on the word 'possessed'. The poet indicates at one and the same time that he has gained a victory over his passions and that he has all the pleasure of 'possession' in the obvious sexual sense. Like the beauty of Keats's *Grecian Urn*, love has been disciplined until it is 'reduced' to truth. Though this love does not involve physical separation like that described in Andrew Marvell's *The Definition of Love*, it is still primarily 'a conjunction of the mind'. The style, the sophisticated recognition of physical desire at the same time that it is transcended, and the tone and accent combine to make this a particularly 'modern' poem.

The two powerful odes *To Himself* are written in Jonson's more robust and assertive style. When scorn, contempt, or satire are required, Jonson is at his most vigorous best, and here he bitterly attacks the theatre-going public that he fundamentally despised, and the playwrights, including Shakespeare, who pleased them. In the ode beginning:

> Where do'st thou carelesse lie,
> Buried in ease and sloth?

there is again a use of imagery and the intellectual conceit reminiscent of Donne. The taste of the public is contrasted with and 'placed' by Jonson's own classical tastes. The final lines:

> But sing high and aloofe,
> Safe from the wolves black jaw, and the dull Asses hoofe

were remembered by W. B. Yeats in the closing rhyme at the end of *Responsibilities*. Yeats with his concern for 'ancient ceremony' and seeking

> ... under that ancient roof
> A sterner conscience and a friendlier home

is perhaps of all modern poets the nearest in spirit to Jonson. In the second ode ('Come leave the lothed Stage'), written in a superb mood of contemptuous indignation, Jonson again turns to the classics as a relief from the crudities of the groundlings. That in the final stanza he should associate Alcaeus, Horace, Anacreon, and Pindar with King Charles and 'the acts of his sweet raigne' is one of the finest testimonies to the civilization of that age given by a poet who was no servile flatterer. As F. R. Leavis has pointed out, the form and style of the poem recall Marvell's *Horatian Ode*.

Jonson's religious lyrics show the same virtues of surface simplicity, clarity, intellectual discipline, and depth of feeling that are revealed in the best of his other lyrics. The attitude of the poet in *To the World* is stoical rather than Christian, but elsewhere, as in *To Heaven*, he writes in a passionate mood of self-examination and self-reproach. The resemblance here is to Herbert rather than to Donne. Such a poem as Jonson's *A Hymne to God the Father* is closer technically and in every other way to Herbert's *Discipline* ('Throw away thy rod') than to Donne's *A Hymne to God the Father*. The mingling of the doctrinal and the personal in *The Sinners Sacrifice: To the Holy Trinitie* again recalls Herbert. *A Hymne on the Nativitie of my Saviour* contrasts with Milton's longer hymn, though there are certain resemblances in detail. In the religious lyric, as in his other poetry, it is to the line of wit that Jonson belongs. He provided with Donne the foundation on which later poets were to build.

Jonson himself summarizes his character and achievement, and gives a characteristically long negative list of the people and things that he disliked in *An Epistle answering to one that asked to be Sealed of the Tribe of Ben*. His final claim for himself is the classical virtue of self-knowledge:

> First give me faith, who know
> My selfe a little; I will take you so,
> As you have writ your selfe. Now stand, and then,
> Sir, you are Sealed of the Tribe of *Ben*.

Though Ben Jonson has been accused of being 'too personal and self-regarding' and Thomas Carew's reference to his 'immodest rage' quoted in support of such a view,[7] the general conclusion to be drawn from the poems in *Jonsonus Virbius* is that 'dear Ben' was loved as well as admired and feared. The elegies written on Jonson's death included a poem by John Taylor, the Water-Poet ('In Memory of the Rare, Famous, and Admired Poet'), in addition to those of the more celebrated contributors, Henry King, Waller, John Ford, and Herrick. Other admirers included Suckling and Dryden, the poet of the Restoration and of the new Augustan age in poetry. The 'tribe of Ben' were practitioners of pre-Augustan classical verse, who wrote eulogies, epitaphs, epistles, satires, odes, hymns, songs, sonnets, monologues, discourses, moral and topographical poems. But they also wrote in celebration of civilized friendship, and Ben Jonson's influence combined with that of Donne in the gallantry of Cavalier poetry as well as in the wit of the Puritan, Andrew Marvell. Though Milton's *Comus* was described by T. S. Eliot as 'the death of the masque', which Ben Jonson had initiated, one can also see Milton practising in the poetic modes of his great classical predecessor both in his own masque and in such poems as *An Epitaph on the Marchioness of Winchester* and *At a Solemn Musick*.

Perhaps the poem of Ben Jonson that most clearly illuminates his intelligence, sensitiveness and character is the famous tribute to Shakespeare in the First Folio. It is a fine piece of craftsmanship, a formal tribute in the grand manner, a magnificent exercise of rhetorical skill, and a triumph of tone and tact in a poet who was to refer six years later in the *Ode to Himself* to 'a mouldy tale, Like Pericles'. The poem in memory of Ben Jonson's friend and greatest rival is a sincere labour of love, free from envy but not blind to faults, a search for truth which is also warm and affectionate. The *Soule of the Age* is also called *My Shakespeare*. Though he was not buried in Westminster Abbey, as Jonson himself was to be, his works are seen as a living monument, supreme in English drama. It is the ultimate compliment that Shakespeare's tragedies are considered worthy to be heard by the spirits of the dramatists of Greece and Rome, and that the comedies are compared favourably with

> all, that insolent *Greece* or haughtie *Rome*
> Sent forth, or since did from their ashes come.

Despite the recognition of Shakespeare's 'small *Latine*, and lesse *Greeke*', his works are saluted as a triumph of British genius, transcending time, and it is as Apollo and Mercury that Shakespeare is personified. *My gentle Shakespeare* reconciles nature and art, but he does so through discipline and a fierce integrity. It is as a supreme celebration and festive occasion that Ben Jonson recalls the plays and justifies the elevation of Shakespeare to become the 'Starre of Poets'. The inspiration which is the poet's gift is injected into the society which produces him. It is this that Jonson so passionately evokes at the conclusion of his poem to the memory of 'my beloved, the author Mr William Shakespeare: and what he hath left us'; and in the generous praise so magisterially expressed, Ben Jonson set an example that was to be loyally followed by his tribe and his sons when their turn came to express their admiration and affection for their master, 'revived by the friends of the muses'.

NOTES

1. *Ben Jonson*, ed. C. H. Hereford and Percy Simpson, Vol. I, 127.
2. Fuller's *Worthies* (1662), 'Warwickshire', 126.
3. For details, see C. H. Hereford and Percy Simpson, Vol. I.
4. For Jonson's indebtedness in his criticism, see the edition of *Discoveries*, by M. Castelain. Hardin Craig has some sensible remarks on 'imitation' and borrowing in *The Enchanted Glass*, 254–5.
5. F. R. Leavis: *Revaluation*, 19.
6. But see p. 108 and note 4, p. 122.
7. cf. Geoffrey Walton, 'The Tone of Ben Jonson's Poetry', in *Seventeenth-Century English Poetry*, ed. William R. Keast, 154, quoting from Thomas Carew's 'To Ben Jonson upon occasion of his ode of defiance annexed to his play of The New Inn'.

INIGO JONES,
VITRUVIUS BRITANNICUS

ROY STRONG

In 1606, three years after the accession of James I, Edmund Bolton presented a book to Inigo Jones (1573–1652) with an inscription stating that through this one man 'there is hope that sculpture, modelling, architecture, painting, acting and all that is praiseworthy in the arts of the ancients, may one day find their way across the Alps into England'.[1] Jones was thirty-three when his eulogy was written and had not actually erected a single building. All that the public would have known about him was that he was a young man taken up by the Queen, Anne of Denmark, for whom he had designed a court masque for Twelfth Night 1605 and a second for an aristocratic marriage one year later. Revolutionary though we may regard these in terms of the history of the theatre, the first at the time was not viewed as a particular success. In this context Bolton's tribute becomes all the more perceptive for he saw in this man everything that he was to achieve in the next forty years, for without doubt Inigo Jones was to emerge as the most important single figure dominating every aspect of the visual arts during the first half of the seventeenth century in England. His mission is already defined in 1606: to revive the lost arts of classical antiquity, something which had already been achieved in Italy from which the fruits had now to be imported to this remote island kingdom on the fringes of northern Europe.

Bolton's list of the areas that this programme of reform was to embrace reinforces the view that the relatively recent compartmentalization of Jones's work amongst various fields of academic study has detracted from the astounding comprehensiveness of his genius. Even if he was not directly responsible, we are coming to realize more and more that every visual advance made by the Stuart Court almost invariably owed its initial impulse to Jones, whether it was the recruitment of a painter in the new baroque manner such as Van Dyck, the formation of collections of old master paintings and classical statuary or the introduction of the principles of Renaissance gardening. The recent recognition that he not only designed the masques but actually composed them after 1631 and that all through he directed them on stage again has enlarged our vision of his omnipresence. That this was possible reflects not only his quite exceptional abilities and zeal but also could only have occurred within the context of the accepted range of activity of the Renaissance Vitruvian architect-engineer and the quite central position such a figure occupied at courts in an age of emergent absolutism.

Everything that Jones was to achieve as arbiter of taste at the Jacobean and Caroline courts stemmed from his intellectual assumptions, ones which were known to the England of Elizabeth but never applied systematically to the world of visual arts. Jones was not an original intellect but one whose principles came second-hand from the mainstream of Renaissance platonism as it descended from Ficino and the Florentine Academy, in his case as it was incorporated into the great Renaissance architectural treatises by Alberti, Serlio and Scamozzi. The Vitruvian architect's range of knowledge was to embrace, amongst other things, mathematics, astronomy, hydraulics, mechanics, a whole range of subjects that meant that his activities could stretch from designing a palace to arranging the seating in a public theatre. Jones shared the commonplaces of neoplatonic and hermetic thought, which focused on man the microcosm, who could either rise to the stars or sink to the brute beasts, who could, through the forces of natural magic, set himself attune to the occult influences governing a geocentric universe structured according to mathematical ratios. Ben Jonson, after their final quarrel, burlesques Jones the architect on this point: 'Well done, my Musicall, Arithmeticall, Geometricall Gamesters! ... It is carried, in number, weight, and measure, as if the Aires were all Harmonie and the Figures a well-timed Proportion.' This is the touchstone for all Jones stood for in the flowering of the arts in Stuart England, a fact to which the marginal annotations in his books amply bear testimony: 'the same numbers that please the eare please the eie' or 'the bodi of a man well proporsioned is the patern for proporsion in buildings'.[2] And this, of course, explains why Jones and Jonson in the end were incompatible, for the architect's position was actually philosophically superior to that of the poet, *ut pictura poesis*.

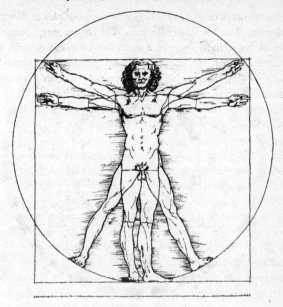

Leonardo da Vinci, 'Vitruvian Figure', Drawing, Academia, Venice

As Jones wrote no formal treatise on architecture our approach to his work must come in a peculiar way, through his study of Stonehenge, a work that was written at the command of James I, although not published until after Jones's death. No other work gives us such a direct notion as to how he approached the problem of designing a building. Often ignoring the reality of the actual remains, in addition to making some astounding leaps of the imagination, Jones proceeds to demonstrate that Stonehenge was in fact built by the Romans in the most primitive of the classical orders described by Vitruvius so as to instruct the Ancient Britons in the principles of harmonic architecture. Upon a tidied up ground-plan he arranges all the stones into a perfect cosmic circle upon which he then superimposes a series of equilateral triangles such as Vitruvius applies to the planning of an amphitheatre. Moving from this demonstration of Stonehenge as being a temple built according to the principles of macrocosm

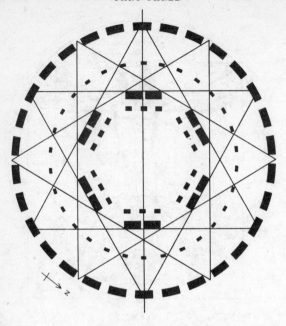

Ground-plan of Stonehenge according to Inigo Jones

and microcosm he argues, through the symbolism of the geometry as explained in a standard Renaissance manual, Piero Valeriano's *Hieroglyphica*, that it was a temple to Coelus, the antique prototype of God the Father. Being a Protestant and, in addition, writing this for a King renowned for his defence of the Anglican theological position, such a conclusion must have been more than gratifying. The Ancient Britons were seen to be already worshipping One God.

Although Elizabethan surveyors had dabbled in geometrical conceits nothing of this kind of total, stylistic control bound to a theoretical stance had been applied before in England. In the case of an actual building we might take the projected new royal palace of Whitehall of which only the Banqueting House (1619–22) was ever constructed. This was conceived on a vast scale that would have

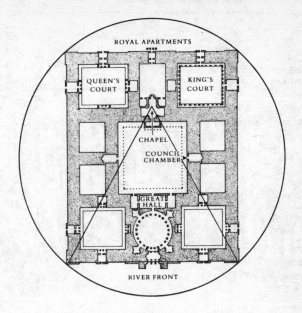

Ground-plan of the projected palace of Whitehall by Inigo Jones, c. 1638

exceeded in size the Louvre and the Escorial. As in the case of Stonehenge Jones's designs stem from a central *idea*, which was the glorification of James I as Solomon.[3] The ground-plan of the palace owes its form to the reconstruction of the Temple of Solomon as described by the Jesuit Juan Bautista Villalpando who argued that the temple (like Stonehenge) had been built according to harmonic Vitruvian principles. The palace ground-plan was a square which could be embraced within a circle that found its centre in the inner courtyard. In addition, an equilateral triangle based on the entrance façade finds its meeting point in the chancel of the Chapel Royal. As in the case of Stonehenge posterity would have been meant to read the symbolic design of the palace. Even the fragment that was built and still survives, the Banqueting House, a perfect double cube, carries on its ceiling Rubens's canvases based almost beyond doubt

St George's Portico: perspective set for the 'Barriers' (1610) in which he super-
imposes Vitruvian classical order onto traditions of chivalrous Gothic (after Inigo
Jones)

upon a programme drawn up by Jones, glorifying James as the British
Solomon whose acts exceeded in achievement even those of his Old
Testament prototype.

It is important to grasp that this architectural revolution was seen
as Protestant and British and that any reading of it by way of
Italianate crypto-Catholicism is wholly wrong. That it was sometimes cast into this sinister light was due entirely to Jones having
to design Catholic chapels for Stuart brides and his work for Henrietta Maria. Thomas Carew's masque *Coelum Britannicum* (1634)
gives invaluable insight into Jones's attitudes and mission. It opens
with a scene of ruins in the classical style 'of some great city of the
Romans or civilized Britons'. So classical architecture is Ancient

British architecture revived and therefore especially appropriate to the revived Empire of Great Britain recreated by the Stuarts. The Ancient British were also Christian, and the Ancient British Church, which had flourished until the arrival of the popish Augustine and his monks, was what the post-Reformation Anglican Church claimed to be. Within Jones's mind all these things interconnected and therefore his constant mission was to educate taste away from the centuries of Gothic corruption and recreate once more the glories of Ancient Britain. This he does over the years in two ways, firstly by means of actual buildings and secondly by way of the masques. He begins by overlaying the new architecture onto the old. Thus, in his setting for Prince Henry's knightly exercise of the *Barriers* (1610) he places the heir to the throne and his companions in a Gothic temple as medieval chivalry required, but fills the scene with structures as varied as Trajan's column, a classical triumphal arch and a sarcophagus based on one by Michaelangelo for the Medici tombs. Jonson in the text articulates Jones's creed:

> More truth of architecture there was blazed
> Than lived in all the ignorant Goths have razed.
> There porticos were built, and seats for knights
> That watched for all adventures, days and nights;
> The niches filled with statues to invite
> Young valours forth by their old forms to fight,
> With arcs triumphal for their actions done ...[4]

A year later in the *Masque of Oberon* (1611) he overlays a Gothic fairy palace with Serlian classical details. In the 1630s he still uses the stage to educate his audience. *Coelum Britannicum* (1634) closes with the vision of a princely villa in the classical style surrounded by a garden with fountains and grottos in the new manner, such as was actually being built at Wilton simultaneously with the performance of the masque.

This was not only a revolution in style but in visual perception. All Jones's work was concerned with the deliberate introduction of what we now conveniently refer to as the Renaissance rediscovery of pictorial space, again stemming from a mathematical basis, that converging lines meant distance, that objects got smaller the further away they were from the eye of the viewer and that colour paled

The masque scene as educator. Inigo Jones presents the ideals of a classical villa and gardens in the masque 'Coelum Britannicum', 1634 (after Inigo Jones)

in intensity towards the horizon. These rudimentary facts, first discovered and applied in fifteenth-century Italy, had to wait until the first decade of the seventeenth century to reach England in any comprehensive form. An Elizabethan portrait depicts a figure stiff within a kiosk, a confined area with looped curtain and chair. There is no sense of infinite space created by applying the lines of perspective or by the tonality of the paint. Mottoes, emblems, inscriptions and inset scenes cover the picture's surface that bear no conceivable relation to each other and break every rule. By the 1630s a portrait by Daniel Mytens or Van Dyck, both artists attracted to royal service from abroad, works from the premise that the picture frame is a proscenium arch through which the viewer passes into a world whose confines are bounded by these scientific principles. Nothing is arbitrarily inserted to destroy the picture's illusion and the sitters now move through their own space turning their eyes momentarily towards us the viewer.

And this first happened not in painting but in Jones's abolition of the theatre-in-the-round in favour of a visual system based on these optical principles. As in the case of style in the arts there was here too a strong educational factor, for the audience proved long in learning the art of how to read stage pictures in this way. This process began in 1605 when Jones designed the *Masque of Blackness* in which a curtain fell revealing a seascape 'drawn, by the lines of perspective, the whole work shooting downwards from the eye' before which floated Anne of Denmark and her ladies on a marine chariot. All that a Jacobean courtier saw at the time was 'a great Engine' with 'all Fish and no water'. Thirty-one years later, in 1636, Jones designed scenery for plays at Oxford for the visit of Charles I and Henrietta Maria. A Cambridge spectator writes a bemused letter clearly not at all comprehending Jones's scenic wonders or appreciating the art of perspective, seeing instead of side wings 'the desks or studies in a Library'. This was only six years before the outbreak of the Civil War. Any examination of the continued vitality of the two dimensional flat hieratic Elizabethan tradition can be corroborated by a study of Caroline provincial painting. England was slow to accept the invention of pictorial space.

The reason for the reluctant reception of these new optical principles may be purely the slowness of an educational process but it could also be due to something else. Jones's insistent use of perspective in the masque was not only to demonstrate a principle of Renaissance optics; it also had an emblematic function. It re-ordered the room in terms of optical hierarchy, for the lines of perspective met only in the eyes of the King. The lower a person was in rank, the further away he was from the monarch and, therefore, the more distorted his view. Truth of vision came significantly with proximity to a monarch who claimed Divine Right. The king as the embodiment on earth of the godhead was central to the whole of Jones's thought. Jonson again articulates this well for his rival:

> Read him as you would do the book
> Of all perfection, and but look
> What his proportions be;

The emblematic scene. Opposition to Royalist policies symbolized in Inigo Jones's Hell scene opening the masque 'Britannia Triumphans', 1638 (after Inigo Jones)

> No measure that is thence contrived,
> Or any motion thence derived
> But is pure harmony.[5]

And that was the motivating force behind Jones's other great pre-occupation in life, the court masques.

Stretching from *The Masque of Blackness* (1605) down to *Salmacida Spoila* (1640), these set out to present their audiences with successive Platonic visions reinforcing the divinity of Stuart rule, vindicating its policies by lifting politics and power onto an ideal level by means of the language of allegory. For Jones and his patrons the masque was the *reality* as they gazed at these profound annual epiphanies of the monarch. The masques express by means of a set of symbolic visions, like those in an emblem book dissolving one into another, a progression from chaos to harmony, from hell to heaven, based on a victory of King and Court over their opponents. Jones's scenic displays are elaborate symbols expressing arcane meanings to which Jonson's texts provide the key. Renaissance spectacle was designed to evoke wonder as an initial response because after wonder came understanding. The stage designs, therefore, fall quickly into two contrasting repertoires: a storm scene is transformed to a garden or a fiery hell to an ordered piazza. Even the practicalities of unfolding the plot by means of the use of professional actors for the anti-masque giving way to the balletic vision of silent aristocratic masquers become the vehicle for a metaphysical conceit.

The masque never really changes over forty years except in emphasis and allusion. The Jacobean ones, in the main by Jonson, are both poetically and scenically superior. *Blackness* in 1605 is a neoplatonic allegory concerning the power of kingship in which the black nymphs of Niger are bleached by the 'sciental' light of the monarch of the white realm of Albion. *Pleasure Reconciled to Virtue* (1618) is about the education of an heir, the future Charles I. Comus, the god of sensuality and revelry, is banished by Hercules, the epitome to the Renaissance of aristocratic virtue. Although these Jacobean masques are absolutist in their assumptions, they never assume the overt stridency of their successors during the years of the Personal Rule of Charles I in the 1630s. After Jonson and Jones quarrelled, from 1632 onwards the latter actually devised the allegories of all the masques in consultation with the King. In them Charles is initially cast as an heroic lover in the classical vein, a role which is overlaid with strong autocratic and imperial overtones as the decade moves towards its disastrous close. In *Albion's Triumph* (1632) Charles is presented as an Emperor enthroned before a temple flanked by consuls and priests swinging censers. By 1640, in the final masque, he is cast as the monarch whose fate it is to rule in adverse times but whose people fail to respond to this manifestation of the good, whose virtues now include those usually attributed to Christ – Innocency and Forgetfulness of Injuries. The Queen in contrast is exalted as a neoplatonic love goddess whose virtue tames a lascivious court. So integral was the masque to the Charles's and Jones's way of thinking as an instrument of royalist policy that, when the judges pronounced in favour of the King in the famous Ship Money case, a masque was rushed together in six weeks. *Luminalia* celebrated the triumph of the Court over its enemies in the purest of neoplatonic terms, of light vanquishing darkness.

Jones's part as the genius behind the masques, with his beliefs that seeing was believing and that one only had to reveal these visions of the good and people would tamely follow the royal will, sprang from his role as a Vitruvian architect-engineer whose tasks included the provision of seating and machinery for public spectacles. The masque stage as it was developed and perfected over four decades was a triumph of engineering, establishing principles which were to be taken into the public theatre in the Restoration period. Although Jones's solution was idiosyncratic it drew both on Vitruvius's description of the use of scenery in the ancient theatre and knowledge of the mechanics developed by Bernardo Buontalenti for the Florentine *intermezzi*. Jones begins in 1605 in *Blackness* with a curtain falling to reveal one set scene. The same year at Oxford he experimented with changing the scene by the use of *periaktoi*, and he followed this in his masques by adopting the *machina versatilis*, a revolving stage, to effect one change of scene subsequent to the removal of a front curtain. It was in *Oberon* in 1611 that he finally hit upon the formula that he adhered to and developed for the remainder of his career, the *scena ductalis*, the use of a series of side wings and backshutters which allowed him any number of scene changes and variations on a production. The backshutter had both an upper and lower section to it, thus allowing scenes of 'relieve' at stage level and celestial visions above. The *prescenia* up until 1630 were square in the main but after 1630 he adopted a rectangular proscenium arch, thus allowing for the development of the fly gallery. This heralded a rapid development in ascents and descents so that by 1638 he was able to stage an entire aerial ballet.

When we turn to the field of actual building Jones was unlucky. Not only did he succeed as Surveyor in 1615, when Stuart finances were taking a disastrous nosedive, but posterity has robbed us of most of his work. Arundel House, Somerset House and Wimbledon House, which he refurbished for the Earl of Arundel and Henrietta

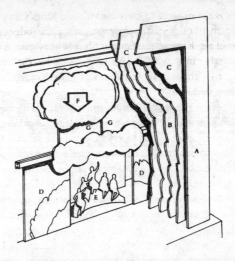

Diagram of Inigo Jones's stage and its machinery for the last of the masques,
'Salmacida Spolia', 1640
Key: A Proscenium arch. B Side shutters. C Cloud borders. D Back shutter
withdrawn. E The King and masquers in tableau. F The cloud bearing the
Queen and her ladies. G. The upper back shutters closed.

Maria respectively, were demolished. The screen he built at
Winchester Cathedral (*c.* 1636) was dismantled in the last century and
the portico he designed for St Paul's (1633–42), the greatest in
northern Europe, vanished after the Great Fire. Even Temple Bar
(1636), which was conceived as a triumphal royal frontispiece to Fleet
Street, is in sad exile in the grounds of Theobalds. The approach
through what actually remains is also dogged by later alterations, such
as the insensitive re-casing of the Whitehall Banqueting House in the
eighteenth century. No interior at all survives in an unaltered form.
Nonetheless from what does exist and from the abundance of architectural drawings for projects and vanished buildings Jones emerges as
the nodal point for the propagation of Palladianism in England both
during his own lifetime and, through his drawings, in the next
century when he was seminal for the Palladianism of the Burlington
circle. The truth of the matter is that Jones was architect to a poor
monarch and the majority of his work was confined to very minor

The palladian ideal. Inigo Jones's Queen's House, Greenwich, begun 1616, finished 1635

buildings or refurbishing and updating existing structures. No large-scale building by him was ever undertaken and one would have been doubtful of its success because he was essentially the master of perfection on a small scale. The Whitehall Banqueting House is a perfect combination of palace reception room and *salle des fêtes*, but as part of a palace stretching over several acres its effect may have been monotonous. Jones is perhaps best appreciated today by looking at the Queen's House, Greenwich (begun 1616). Even in its present bereft state we can still respond and sense the originality of its concept as a Palladian villa lifted from the banks of the Brenta to those of the River Thames, elegant and compact, rich yet restrained, the epitome of Caroline ideals.

Those ideals were, however, linked to a fatal political philosophy. During the Civil War the aged architect, now into his seventies, lived out a final Vitruvian role as a military engineer. After the siege of Basing House he was ignominiously stripped by the soldiery and carried away in a blanket. Darkness enfolds his final years and he died on 21 June 1652, two years after the execution of his royal master. In 1650 Milton set out to demolish divine kingship and its arts, in particular by an attack on the 'conceited portraiture' of Charles I in the *Eikon Basilike* 'drawn out to the full measure of a masking scene, and set there to catch fools and silly gazers' (Fig. 9).

Charles I beatified: after the frontispiece to the 'Eikon Basilike', 1649

'But quaint emblems,' the poet writes, 'begged from the old pageantry of some Twelfth night's entertainment at Whitehall, will do but ill to make a saint or martyr.'[6] In these taunts the central ideas that motivated the art of Inigo Jones received a blow from which they were ultimately never to recover. Seeing had ceased to be believing.

NOTES

1. Quoted by John Harris, Stephen Orgel and Roy Strong, *The King's Arcadia. Inigo Jones and the Stuart Court*, Arts Council Exhibition Catalogue (1973), 28.

2. Quoted by G. Toplis, *The King's Arcadia*, Arts Council Exhibition Catalogue (1973), 62.

3. See Roy Strong, *Britannia Triumphans. Inigo Jones, Rubens and Whitehall Palace* (London, 1980).

4. Stephen Orgel and Roy Strong, *Inigo Jones. The Theatre of the Stuart Court* (London, 1973), I, 160, ll. 52–8.

5. Orgel and Strong, *Inigo Jones. The Theatre of the Stuart Court*, 311, ll. 334–9.

6. Ikonoklastes, in *Complete Poems and Selected Prose*, ed. M. Y. Hughes (New York, 1957), 784.

GEORGE HERBERT AND THE
DEVOTIONAL POETS

D. J. ENRIGHT

George Herbert (1593–1633)

Together with his 'realism' in metaphor, what Coleridge described as his 'neutral style' has served to recommend George Herbert's verse to us during at least the larger part of the present century.

'Neutral' though Herbert's style may be (and gentle as his nature customarily is) he has one of the strongest poetic personalities in English. Devotional though his poetry is – and he certainly considered devotion the better part of poetry – it is in a different class from the tepid, characterless verse which we call, by way of apology, 'devotional'. The Herbertian note is pervasive, but it is not easy to define. First of all there is the quietness of tone, so far removed from ecstatic exaltation, which yet allows him so incisive and exalted a climax as 'You taught the Book of Life my name'. Elsewhere he describes man as the 'Secretary of [God's] praise': a secretary has little to do with ecstasy, his concern is to be exact, methodical, honest, and modest.

Yet Herbert will argue with God, and the peculiar effect of rebellion and reconciliation, of complaint and resolution, is often achieved by the alternation of long sweeping lines with short pointed ones. The latter frequently owe their pointedness to their proverbial form and to Herbert's metaphysical wit, which is generally less brilliant than Donne's and more homely and more immediately apprehended:

> Love is that liquor sweete and most divine,
> Which my God feels as blood; but I, as wine.

That is superb; there is not the slightest 'quaintness'. But elsewhere – and we can afford to admit it – the 'conceits' are sometimes a little self-conscious and laboured; in *Prayer* (I)[1] – where among other comparisons prayer is described as 'reversed thunder' – we are aware of a *tour de force* rather than of a forcefully created experience.

In imagery, Herbert is especially fond of church furniture, flowers, trees, herbs, stars, music, and the law (particularly regarding debt, for man's great debt to Christ). In this connection, the rough obvious difference between Donne and Herbert is that while the former arrives by strange means at an unorthodox end –

> Kill, and dissect me, Love; for this
> Torture against thine own end is,
> Rack'd carcases make ill Anatomies

– the latter arrives by simple means, put to unorthodox uses, at orthodox ends; the one explores, the other reveals. Thus Herbert's *The Bag* centres on the linking of Christ's wounded side with the diplomatic bag, a comparison whose immediate oddity is redeemed by the blend of the common, the apt, and the poignant in the closing line:

> If ye have any thing to send or write,
> (I have no bag, but here is room)
> Unto my fathers hands and sight
> (Beleeve me) it shall safely come,
> That I shall minde what you impart;
> Look, you may put it very neare my heart.

Arguing with himself, or with God, Herbert makes effective use of the rhetorical question followed by the telling answer or second thought; of the 'King of grief' he demands, 'how shall I grieve for thee?':

> Shall I weep blood? Why, thou hast wept such store
> That all thy bodie was one doore ...

Paradox, too, is one of his metaphysical habits, and *Repentance* ends with the aphoristic line, 'Fractures well cur'd make us more strong'. But a more interesting and personal characteristic is the poet's use of personification. This often occurs so quietly that we are not conscious of it as such –

> I scarce believed,
> Till grief did tell me roundly, that I lived

– and it is found, of course, in the 'play-poem' so common in Herbert, or the dramatic parable, of which *Love* (III) is one of the most perfect examples: a volume of theological commentary lies behind each short phrase:

> Love bade me welcome: yet my soul drew back,
>   Guiltie of dust and sinne.
> But quick-ey'd Love, observing me grow slack
>   From my first entrance in,
> Drew nearer to me, sweetly questioning,
>   If I lack'd any thing.
>
> A guest, I answer'd, worthy to be here:
>   Love said, you shall be he.
> I the unkinde, ungratefull? Ah my deare,
>   I cannot look on thee.
> Love took my hand, and smiling did reply,
>   Who made the eyes but I?
>
> Truth Lord, but I have marr'd them: let my shame
>   Go where it doth deserve.
> And know you not, sayes Love, who bore the blame?
>   My deare, then I will serve.
> You must sit down, sayes Love, and taste my meat:
>   So I did sit and eat.

Thus *Humility* (with the Virtues and the Animals) is a mixture of masque and beast-fable, while *The World*, *Redemption*, and *The Quip* bear a certain resemblance to the morality play. *The Pilgrimage* and *Love Unknown* look forward as well as backward – to Bunyan's *The Pilgrim's Progress* – and remind us that Herbert combines in his work both courtly and popular elements:

> I travell'd on, seeing the hill, where lay
>   My expectation.
>   A long it was and weary way.
>   The gloomy cave of Desperation
> I left on th' one, and on the other side
>   The rock of Pride.
>
> And so I came to Fancy's meadow strow'd
>   With many a flower:
>   Fain would I here have made abode,
>   But I was quicken'd by my houre.
> So to Care's copse I came, and there got through
>   With much ado . . .
>   (*The Pilgrimage*)

Yet we have not defined that sense of drama which is everywhere in this poetry, and is independent of personification or dialogue-form; it is identical with the freshness and vividness of his best passages, the feeling that we are now seeing, for the first time, something we had previously heard about from others. The note is struck by the gentle intimacy of an opening like 'Deare Friend, sit down ...' or in the Elizabethan accent of:

> Ladies, look here; this is the thankfull glasse,
> That mends the lookers eyes: this is the well
>   That washes what it shows ...
>   (*The Holy Scriptures*)

It sounds, more humorously, in this description of an astronomer observing the stars:

> He views their stations, walks from doore to doore,
>   Surveys, as if he had design'd
> To make a purchase there ...

and, with a most 'un-devotional' force, in 'My friend may spit upon my curious floor', though still in a most devout context.

That he sometimes betrays a weakness in his use of dramatic imagery must be allowed, and it may be felt that too much strain is placed on the favourite image of the box in the second section of *Good Friday*, where the heart is likened to a writing-case containing at the same time ink and sin. The breakdown in the relation between thought and metaphor is more serious in the final lines of *The Dawning*:

> Christ left his grave-clothes, that we might, when grief
> Draws tears, or bloud, not want an handkerchief.

It is a tribute to the persistence of Herbert's artistic taste that in a poet so consciously concerned with the teaching of central Christian truths, and with their conveyance through everyday imagery, such lapses should not occur more commonly.

Herbert's main themes are what one would expect of an Anglican minister, and foremost among them are the Incarnation, the Passion, and the Redemption. Against this debt is placed man's behaviour, both the unseemliness of his disobedience and the inadequacy of his obedience. In a similar spirit he looks quite simply (not in the sophisticated manner of Marvell's *A Dialogue between the Soul and the Body*) at the dichotomy of body and soul: 'The growth of flesh is but a blister'; and considers at more length the balance between man's greatness and his lowliness. *Man* relates the former –

> Man is one world, and hath
> Another to attend him

– while *Misery* describes the reverse of the medal:

> Man is a foolish thing, a foolish thing,
> Folly and Sinne play all his game.

And, at his most cheerful, Herbert sums up in *The Church-floore*:

> Blest be the *Architect*, whose art
> Could build so strong in a weak heart.

This brings us to what is, I think, the most serious criticism Herbert's work is open to: the rather clumsy way in which the scales are occasionally weighed against earthly pleasures as opposed to heavenly bliss. There is much more of the Renaissance in Donne, even in his most fervent religious poetry, than in Herbert. 'There is no pleasure here', Herbert announces in *The Rose*, and attempts to enforce his judgement by a feeble verbal trick:

> Or if such deceits there be,
> Such delights I meant to say ...

Humane as is his austerity in his best work – where we are not tempted to compare it with Donne's wider emotional range – 'the world, the flesh, the devil' is elsewhere set up too easily and knocked down too easily. The couplet

> Then silly soul take heed; for earthly joye
> Is but a bubble, and makes thee a boy

betrays, by its inept rhyme, the lack of personal feeling – a formula is being repeated; and parts of *Home* impress us as mechanical, pietistic repudiation of a 'weary world' with which (the verse would here suggest) he never profoundly battled. There is an unthinking heaviness about such outbursts: Herbert's 'sighes and groans' sometimes fall too copiously to move us. And this is not simply a question of the reader's personal views, for we cannot but admire those poems which turn on a tactfully contrived collapse of the human before the divine, in which we experience that collapse and are not merely referred to some generalization concerning 'this world of sugared lies' which we accept or reject according to our tastes. *The Thanks-giving* is a witty poem that reaches its climax in a final relinquishment of wit, an evaporation of self, in front of the Passion:

> Then for thy passion – I will do for that –
> Alas, my God, I know not what,

and we cannot but be convinced by the *volte-face* which concludes *The Collar* (a poem in which the typical Herbertian pattern is shown to perfection):

> But as I rav'd and grew more fierce and wilde
> At every word,
> Me thought I heard one calling, *Childe*:
> And I reply'd, *My Lord*.

Herbert came of a noble family, apt in the arts of war, the Court, and the mind, and Izaak Walton remarks that, while at Cambridge, 'his clothes seemed to prove that he put too great a value on his parts and parentage'. His 'parts' as a scholar were impressive, and he became University Orator, an accepted stepping-stone to high civil office. 'My birth and spirit rather took/The way that takes the town', he says in a poem, but he was ordained deacon in 1625–6 and priest in 1630. It has been held that Herbert's vacillation between Court and Church was resolved by the death, around 1625, of King James and of other patrons of his, but F. E. Hutchinson points out that for a man of his qualities all hopes of preferment would hardly have ended for this reason. Probably too much has been made of the struggle between his worldly ambitions and his impulse towards a life of religious duties. In a letter to his mother written in his sixteenth year, he stated that 'my poor abilities in Poetry shall be all, and ever consecrated to God's glory'. We are not to imagine in Herbert any such division as between Jack Donne the gallant and John Donne the Dean of St Paul's, 'Apollo's first, at last, the true God's Priest'. We are told that Nicholas Ferrar (Herbert's friend and literary executor, and the founder of the religious community at Little Gidding) suffered the early temptation of 'whether there was a God, and how to be served'; Herbert's problem was the second, and never the first. L. C. Knights speaks of Herbert's 'feeling of uselessness and self-distrust' and suggests that 'behind the more obvious temptation of "success" was one more deeply rooted – a dejection of spirit that tended to make him regard his own life, the life he was actually leading, as worthless and unprofitable'.

And it is true that the theme of worldly ambition and the imagery of rebellion that run through his work are linked with his sense of inadequacy as an active Christian: he chastises his feebleness by reference to the 'glory and gay weeds' of the courtier, and the implication is that so weak a servant of God might have done better as a servant of the King. In *Affliction* (I) he writes:

> I took thy sweeten'd pill, till I came neare;
> I could not go away, nor persevere.

And we must allow due weight to the words, 'nor persevere': this is the shame of insufficiency in one's profession, not of nostalgia for a different one. Barnabas Oley, writing in the mid seventeenth century, quotes Herbert as saying, 'God has broken into my study, and taken off my chariot wheels, I have nothing worthy of God'. And this discontent – hardly a selfish discontent – is silenced in the end, for 'there is no articling with thee'. His complaints of inadequacy –

> All things are busie; only I
> Neither bring honey with the bees ...

or

> I read, and sighe, and wish I were a tree;
> For sure then I should grow
> To fruit or shade: at least some bird would trust
> Her household to me, and I should be just

– remind us strongly of passages in the poetry of Gerard Manley Hopkins, a Jesuit priest and teacher who also suffered from ill health:

> ... birds build – but not I build; no, but strain,
> Time's eunuch, and not breed one work that wakes.

But the ultimate reconciliation is there, too; Hopkins wrote, in a letter, 'Nothing comes: I am a eunuch – but it is for the kingdom of heaven's sake'. It remains to add that Herbert's dissatisfaction is not merely personal, although it is personally felt; the final recognition is that man is by nature unable to requite his debt – even though the heart is pure, Herbert says:

> Yet one pure heart is nothing to bestow:
> In Christ two natures met to be thy cure.

Those who are sensitive enough to feel this as a personal deficiency are not always best equipped to ward off a persistent if limited melancholy which, in poetry, is merely melancholy.

But perhaps a more illuminating link between his life and his poetry may be perceived in his aspect as a parish vicar, a practical clergyman. His first task on taking orders was to rebuild the church of Leighton Bromswold and, on his induction into Fulston with Bemerton four years later, he undertook extensive repairs to both churches and to his rectory. His concern was at once with public worship – 'Down with thy knees, up with thy voice' – rather than private adoration. Further experience of practical Christianity came to him through his contact with Little Gidding, while his short country ministry reinforced both the teacher in him and, by implication, the popular elements in his style. Respecting the former, we can adduce the little book which he wrote at Bemerton, *A Priest to the Temple, or The Country Parson*, a practical guide for the practising country parson, founded on the definition that 'A Pastor is the Deputy of Christ for the reducing of Man to the Obedience of God', and purposing, through a detailed treatment of every aspect of the parson's vocation, 'to keep the middle way between superstition and slovenliness'. For his rather conscious attitude, in these last years, to the popular in his writing, we can cite a passage in which Walton says that the first sermon Herbert delivered to his parishioners was of a 'florid manner ... with great learning and eloquence', but that Herbert then told them that 'that should not be his constant way of Preaching, for, since Almighty God does not intend to lead men to heaven by hard Questions ... his language and his expressions should be more plain and practical in his future Sermons'.

It has already been suggested that for Herbert the justification of his poetic work was that

> A verse may find him, who a sermon flies,
> And turn delight into a sacrifice.

But didacticism, implying the urge towards clarity and immediate impact, is a less dangerous preoccupation, in a poet of his nature, than it usually is. It is part and parcel of his straightforwardness and of his rejection of conventional poetic devices: *Jordan* (I) is his manifesto here, 'I envy no man's nightingale or spring'; while his concern above all to be understood and useful probably served as a safeguard against eccentricity – for

> The fineness which a hymn or psalm affords,
> Is, when the soul unto the lines accords.

Hopkins surmised that what he himself needed, to be 'more intelligible, smoother, and less singular', was an audience. Herbert had an audience. There is no need to suppose that this concern of Herbert's did not exist before he became a country rector, and we see how it agrees with the homely imagery, the recurrent box, for instance, in which either sweets or sins are kept. His attitude towards flowers is eminently practical and down-to-earth:

> Farewell, dear flowers, sweetly your time ye spent,
> Fit, while ye liv'd, for smell or ornament,
>   And after death for cures.

Despite the naïvety that has sometimes been ascribed to Herbert, his collection of poems, *The Temple*, – with its individual titles, *The Church-porch*, *The Altar*, *Church-monuments*, *Church-music*, *The Windows*, and so on – partakes of that orderly, deliberate, and business-like nature which rebuilt churches, and which, together with what Walton calls 'an almost incredible story, of the great sanctity of the short remainder of his holy life', caused his ministry of three years soon to become a classic example for the English Church. We take leave of him with a short extract from *Providence*, full of his characteristic tenderness and finely uniting his practicality with his courtesy, the country gardener with the true gentleman of the university and the town:

> Rain, do not hurt my flowers; but gently spend
> Your hony drops; presse not to smell them here:
> When they are ripe, their odour will ascend,
> And at your lodging with their thanks appeare.

Henry Vaughan (c. 1622–95)

Unlike Herbert, Henry Vaughan began by writing secular verse, either discursive or amatory. His first volume, *Poems*, contains such titles as *Les Amours* and *To Amoret: The Sigh*, and phrases like 'a woman's easy faith' and 'That face hath many servants slain'. Donne was his master here; *An Elegy* has the striking opening we associate with him – "'Tis true, I am undone' – but the poem has none of Donne's preciseness and bite, and we are more aware of a playful fancy than of the peculiar seventeenth-century imagination. *To Amoret, of the difference 'twixt him, and other Lovers* ('Just so base, sublunary lovers' hearts ...') is modelled on Donne's *A Valediction: forbidding mourning* ('Dull sublunary lovers' love ...'), but where the latter is compact, the former is dispersed and repetitive.

Perhaps another influence is to be detected there: that of Herbert – the line in *To Amoret Weeping*, 'I envy no man's purse, or mines', echoes Herbert's customary forthrightness and 'I envy no man's nightingale or spring'. But despite its derivativeness, the collection hints at the kind of poetry Vaughan was later to write. *Upon the Priory Grove, his usual Retirement* anticipates that individual effect of calm and stillness which he achieves in his most famous lines, while his gift for the macrocosmic evocation is seen, if dimly, in a passage where he compares Amoret's eyes with the sun and speaks of

> . .'. the vast Ring
> Amidst these golden glories,
> And fiery stories ...

The religious conversion which Vaughan experienced about the year 1648 has been attributed to the national unrest (he was a Royalist), to prolonged illness, to the death of his youngest brother. Vaughan himself, in the preface to the second edition of *Silex Scintillans* (1655), seems to ascribe it to Herbert: 'The first, that with any effectual success attempted a diversion of this foul and overflowing stream [i.e. of 'witty' amatory verse], was the blessed man, Mr George Herbert, whose holy life and verse gained many pious Converts (of whom I, am the least) and gave the first check to a most flourishing wit of his time.'

From *Silex Scintillans*, the volume that contains his essential contribution to English poetry, we should quickly deduce that, in poetry at least, he was a 'convert' of George Herbert. The borrowings are abundant and unashamed. Thus,

> I have deserv'd a thick, Egyptian damp,
> Dark as my deeds,
> Should *mist* within me, and put out that lamp
> Thy spirit feeds
>
> (*The Relapse*)

obviously derives from this passage in *The Temple*:

> I have deserv'd that an Egyptian night
> Should thicken all my powers; because my lust,
> Hath still sow'd fig-leaves to exclude thy light
> *(Sighs and Groans)*

and even the volume's subtitle is taken from Herbert's title-page. Correspondences of this kind, both to *The Temple* and to Owen Felltham's prose *Resolves* (first edition *c.* 1620), are listed in the notes to L. C. Martin's edition of Vaughan, and F. E. Hutchinson remarks that 'there is no example in English literature of one poet borrowing so extensively from another'.

An examination of several passages in which Vaughan is clearly remembering something of Herbert's is useful in bringing out both the former's weaknesses and his originality. Our general impression is that Vaughan's advantage over Herbert lies in his longer breath, his greater fluency, and in what at first seems a more positive vitality. On the other hand, Vaughan is sadly lacking in Herbert's sense of climax – his poems generally go on a little too long – and his imagery (on the whole more intellectual and 'elevated' than the elder poet's: the recurrent image is no longer 'box' but 'star') lacks the dramatic liveliness whereby Herbert's justifies itself. *Regeneration*, the opening poem of *Silex Scintillans*, is Vaughan's equivalent of Herbert's *The Pilgrimage*; it has the same parable-form and the same theme – the necessity of struggling on in spite of hardship and disappointment. We see that Herbert is more 'primitive', nearer to the morality (to Bunyan, too), simple and dramatic. Vaughan is noticeably less simple and less dramatic, in a sense more 'personal' because less traditional. He gives the impression of going further, perhaps because he shows us fewer landmarks. And it may be felt that the parable-form is not altogether suitable for this more personal, more esoteric utterance; we are not always sure of how to interpret something that calls for interpretation:

> I wonder'd much, but tir'd
> At last with thought . . .

Vaughan is more suggestive, mysterious, than Herbert, and the poem contains some striking natural description; but he leaves us 'wondering' where Herbert leaves us *knowing*.

Didacticism enters into Vaughan's work – notably in *Rules and Lessons*, which reminds us of *The Church-porch*, though its instructions are less directly practical and down-to-earth – but it is much less pervasive than in *The Temple*. Vaughan has not the same compulsion to be understood. Here, as elsewhere, we find him, in comparison with Herbert, moving towards nineteenth-century romanticism, where the individual is the great theme rather than the social or religious community.

Vaughan, too, is concerned with the dichotomy of body and soul – especially in relation to the Resurrection – and, more important, with the Incarnation and the Passion, though he displays a less personal anguish than Herbert at man's ingratitude and lack of merit. In his inconstancy, man is contrasted with the natural creation – with birds, bees, and flowers:

> I would (said I) my God would give
> The staidness of these things to man!

And the 'fair, order'd lights' of *The Constellation* make him think of the 'Obedience, Order, Light' which man has not achieved. The injunction, 'Observe God in his works', suggests an aspect of Vaughan's originality: parts of 'And do they so?' call Wordsworth to mind:

> Go go; Seal up thy looks,
> And burn thy books –

though the lesson which Nature will teach is rather more precise. The similarities between Wordsworth's *Intimations of Immortality* and the attitude towards childhood of Vaughan and of his contemporary, Thomas Traherne, are too well known to need much comment here. Vaughan associates childhood with 'whiteness', the symbol of purity; 'dear, harmless age', it is also 'an age of mysteries'. Thus *The Retreat* runs parallel with *Intimations of Immortality* for a part of the way:

> When yet I had not walkt above
> A mile, or two, from my first love,
> And looking back (at that short space)
> Could see a glimpse of his bright-face ...
> > (*The Retreat*)

> ... the growing Boy
> ... beholds the light, and whence it flows ...
> The Youth, who daily farther from the east
> Must travel, still is Nature's Priest,
> And by the vision splendid
> Is on his way attended ...
> (*Intimations of Immortality*)

But their paths soon divide: Wordsworth declares himself an early-nineteenth-century thinker, while Vaughan emerges as a seventeenth-century religious 'metaphysical' – for *The Retreat*, one of his finest poems, one of the few that are exactly the right length, is not far from Donne in its 'wit', its compactness, and the physical reality of phrases like (the borrowed) 'bright shoots of everlastingness'.

Before leaving this point it should be remarked that there is a relation between the state of childhood and that of man in those other 'early days', after the expulsion from Eden. In *Corruption* he writes:

> Man in those early days
> Was not all stone, and Earth ...
> He saw Heaven o'er his head, and knew from whence
> He came (condemned), hither ...
> still *Paradise* lay
> In some green shade, or fountain.

Both poets lament the loss of 'a white, Celestial thought' or 'celestial light' (in Traherne, 'my pure primitive virgin light'), but Vaughan, whose desiderations are more clearly defined than Wordsworth's – the God whose nearness he describes in these nostalgic poems is more 'present' than the later poet's – finds less consolation here and now. Wordsworth was readier, in Herbert's words, to 'rest in Nature, not the God of Nature'.

Vaughan, then, is more interested in natural creation, in the nature of the country, than Herbert; it conducts him to the creator – 'rural shades are the sweet fence / Of piety and innocence' – but he delights in it on the way. Yet *The Search* indicates how he is, by comparison, 'unworldly'. This poem has the final turnabout which we met in *The Temple*, the short answer to a lengthy question. 'Me thought I heard one singing thus' – and it is perhaps indicative of Vaughan's greater elaborateness that the voice should be 'singing' instead of 'calling' (cf. Herbert's *The Collar*):

Search well another world; who studies this
Travels in Clouds, seeks *Manna*, where none is.

Herbert at least found manna through the imagery of this world; his 'convert' is more abstract in his language, more declamatory, and more leisurely.

This being so, it says much for the strength of the metaphysical wit tradition that it should so often save his work from shapelessness. We may instance the poem which begins 'Joy of my life!'; it moves freely from stars to the saints, who are 'shining lights', 'candles', 'our Pillar-fires', or indeed the 'shining spires' of the City 'we travel to'. The poem seems about to disintegrate, but the final, forthright image, evoking the flaming sword in Eden, succeeds in pulling it together:

A swordlike gleame
Kept man for sin
First *Out*; This beame
Will guide him *In*.

On Herbert's ground, Vaughan is no match for him. 'He has more glow and freedom than Herbert but less fragrant sweetness,' Hopkins wrote in a letter to R. W. Dixon, 'Still I do not think him Herbert's equal.' But there is a handful of poems in which Vaughan appears as a distinctive figure both in the seventeenth century and in English poetry as a whole. These poems – and notable among them are *The Retreat*, *Peace*, *Ascension Hymn*, *Quickness*, *Regeneration* (in parts), and *The World* – turn on images of peace, majesty, security, and controlled power, 'an illuminated vision', in Hutchinson's words, 'of the universe, newly apprehended':

I saw Eternity the other night
Like a great *Ring* of pure and endless light,
    All calm, as it was bright,
And round beneath it, Time in hours, days, years
    Driv'n by the spheres
Like a vast shadow mov'd, In which the world
    And all her train were hurl'd ...

They might seem to have been written, in T. S. Eliot's phrase, 'at the still point of the turning world'; but perhaps their peculiar quality is hinted at by Vaughan himself:

But life is, what none can express,
A quickness, which my God hath kissed.

Richard Crashaw (1612/13–49)

Richard Crashaw is a very different kind of poet. His relation to Herbert is much slighter than might be supposed from the title of his first volume of English verse, *Steps to the Temple*, for his temple is Catholic, baroque, and Italian. The son of a Puritan rector for whom the Pope was Antichrist, Crashaw came under the Laudian High Church influence at Cambridge – he was a frequent visitor at Little Gidding – and turned to Roman Catholicism, probably in 1645, when it seemed that the 'middle way' of Anglicanism could not survive. (For the religious background to this essay, readers are referred to Part I of the present volume.) At his death Crashaw held a minor position at the Cathedral of the Holy House in Loreto, Italy. He is pre-eminently the English poet of the Counter-Reformation.

If Herbert can be related to the popular sermon and the morality play, then Crashaw must be related to Catholic ritual and the masque. Thus *Epiphany*, 'A Hymn, sung as by the Three Kings', with three solo parts and chorus, is quite operatic in form, while *The Mother of Sorrows* opens in the Handelian manner:

> In shade of death's sad TREE
> Stood Doleful SHE.
> Ah SHE! now by none other
> Name to be known, alas, but SORROW'S MOTHER.

The Sorrows are rendered remote and impersonal by their rhetorical, repetitive, and ornate presentation. We understand why the reader should not be invited to identify too closely with the 'Sancta Maria Dolorum': there are to be no unseemly grovellings in the aisles; on the other hand, there is the danger that the reader will experience nothing – or, at any rate, nothing that could not have been prompted by some accepted and more modest aid to devotion.

Examining *The Weeper*, a series of variations on the theme of the Magdalene's tears, we realize that, though Crashaw's poems are often longer than Herbert's or Vaughan's, his poetic breath is really shorter, for his poetry is continually stopping and restarting. Some of the variations betray a humourlessness – a 'brisk cherub' sips the tears 'And his song / Tastes of this Breakfast all day long' – but others have the true dignity of the seventh stanza.* Crashaw's first publication

---

* Numbering of the version published in 1648 and 1652.

was a collection of 'sacred epigrams', and it is the epigrammatic aspect of his work that most nearly approaches the metaphysical school; it emerges here in

> O wit of love! that thus could place
> Fountain and Garden in one face,

and it endows the poem with an occasional and welcome neatness and intellectual force:

> Others by moments, months, and years
> Measure their ages; thou, by TEARS,

and, indeed, in its last lines *The Weeper* achieves a climax rare in Crashaw: the tears themselves take over the burden:

> We go to meet
> A worthy object, our lord's FEET

Notorious in Crashaw's work is his sensuousness, and in particular his use, in picturing sacred love, of the metaphors – indeed, the evoked atmosphere – of human love, both of mother for child and of man for woman. This sensuousness is rather ambiguously present in his handling of spiritual and physical torture: 'blood' and 'milk' are his characteristic references:

> To see both blended in one flood,
> The Mothers' Milk, the Children's blood,
> Makes me doubt if Heaven will gather,
> *Roses* hence, or *Lilies* rather.
> (*Upon the Infant Martyrs*)

The reader may feel faintly repelled, but not shocked, for the verse has no immediacy; the experience reaches us at second hand, as if the poet is describing the picture of something and not the thing itself.[2]

The ornate, decorative image – the 'baroque conceit'[3] – is the very basis of Crashaw's poetry; it is lovingly handled, but sometimes too lovingly fondled. An English taste is unlikely to find any poem of his entirely successful, for the locks between one level of imagery and another do not always function smoothly; but Crashaw's finest poem, as an *English* poet, is the *Hymn to Saint Teresa*. One welcomes the direct and firm opening – 'Love, thou art Absolute sole lord/ OF LIFE & DEATH' and the passage which follows.

> Those thy old Souldiers, Great and tall,
> Ripe Men of Martyrdom, that could reach down
> With strong armes, their triumphant crown;
> Such as could with lusty breath
> Speak loud into the face of death
> Their Great LORD's glorious name ...

is dramatic and unusually masculine for Crashaw. Teresa's childhood is related with that sweet tenderness, both akin to and distinct from Herbert's or Vaughan's, for which this poet must be prized:

> She'll to the Moores; And trade with them,
> For this unvalued Diadem.
> She'll offer them her dearest Breath,
> With CHRIST's Name in't, in change for death.

And though the hymn is weakened by a cloud of abstractions ('WORKS ... SUFFERINGS ... TEARES ... WRONGS ...'), from time to time 'large draughts of intellectual day' shine out in phrases like

> 'Tis LOVE, not YEARES or LIMBS that can
> Make the Martyr, or the man.

In the previous paragraph I stressed the word *English* by way of suggesting that, though Crashaw's work is in a tradition, that tradition is not exactly English. It is an Italian school, the 'conceited' school of Marino, to which he properly belongs, and what one misses in him is the Saxon contribution to our tradition, the unadorned, robust and earthy elements of our literature. It is not an adequate defence of his use of English to describe him as 'primarily a European'. And one does not, finally, complain of over-excitement, 'ecstaticness', but rather the opposite; the individual beads are highly coloured, yet the fingers that thread them are cold and even mechanical. The prevailing mood, as Basil Willey has remarked, is 'at once inflamed and relaxed'. The artist who creates is, here, too separate from the martyr who suffers, and often the ecstasy is left outside, outside the language and outside our response; a formal, public act of worship which tastes simultaneously of the cathedral, the stage, and the study.

In moving from Herbert through Vaughan to Crashaw, we have noticed an increasing 'romanticism' in their work — it is not merely because of similarities in belief that Vaughan has been likened to Wordsworth and Crashaw to Francis Thompson. While this implies a certain liberation, an increased lyricism, a greater evocativeness, it also means a certain loss in intellectual impact and conviction. A comparative evaluation of 'romantic' and 'metaphysical' lies, happily, outside the scope of this essay, but it may be remarked in concluding that what we value in seventeenth-century metaphysical poetry is, in its simplest terms, the union of hard thinking with deep feeling.

NOTES

1. Reference is to *The Works of George Herbert*, ed. F. E. Hutchinson, where numbering is adopted if two or more poems have the same title.

2. Reference may be made to *English Emblem Books* (1948), by Rosemary Freeman. Miss Freeman tends to overstress emblematic qualities in Herbert, but what she says is certainly relevant to Crashaw. Whereas Crashaw describes the emblem, Herbert makes it unnecessary.

3. See James Smith, 'On Metaphysical Poetry', in *Scrutiny*, II.

THE CAVALIER POETS

GEOFFREY WALTON

To appreciate the poetry associated in varying degrees of intimacy with the Court of Charles I requires, I believe, certain important mental and emotional readjustments. One is not dealing with major poetry – though there are several major poems – and therefore it is necessary to feel an especially close sympathy with the social and cultural attitudes and interests of a particular group of men and women in particular surroundings. Perhaps we know a little more about the surroundings as a result of the opening of more and more stately homes of all periods to an increasingly numerous public. But in other respects there may be difficulties for many readers. The communications media harp continually on the simple human phenomenon of social class and its injustices actual and potential, while on the other hand the permissiveness of our affluent society encompasses a cult of dreariness, not to say squalor. Personal elegance and courteous behaviour seem not to be conspicuously fashionable. Cavalier poetry embodies very fully the life and culture of upper-class pre-Commonwealth England where the ideals, if not perhaps always the practice, were just these qualities. Furthermore it is learned – mainly in the classics – and theologically minded. It is at once eminently English and strongly influenced by the cosmopolitan interests and affectations of its writers and public. The Court was, needless to say, not puritanical, but the tone of most of its lyric poetry suggests that it was addressed to social equals though we do not usually know their names. The reader who is prepared to accept such a social situation and such attitudes and interests as a conceivable and not entirely reprehensible way of life can, one hopes, find the poetry a lively and pleasurable experience.

Cavalier poetry presents a surprising mixture of elegance and sophistication with naïvety and schoolboy obscenity, but it is rarely vulgar or sneering. One senses these qualities in reading. Further knowledge of the way of life that produced it helps to explain the paradoxical qualities. One comes to realize that in submitting oneself, with the efforts involved, to the effect of the poetry, one is submitting oneself to the influence of a phase of English civilization.[1] Our relationship with these knights and squires is a fairly close one. Their way and manner of speaking comes out directly in

> I tell thee, fellow, who'er thou be,
> That made this fine sing-song of me,
>   Thou art a rhyming sot.
>
> > (Suckling)
>
> Now you have freely given me leave to love
>   What will you doe?
>
> > (Carew)

or again in:

> Hearke, reader! wilt be learn'd i' th' wars?
> > (Lovelace)

The idiom is the conversation of the Court circle in all its variety, cultivated and colloquial, with that tendency to the racy and the slipshod which has been characteristic of English aristocratic speech ever since the speech of the educated became formalized, and which has produced so remarkable a succession of literary achievements from this time to Byron's.[2]

The body of Cavalier poetry is remarkably homogeneous, as perhaps the foregoing generalities have suggested. The four or five principal talents have certain individually distinctive qualities, but the lesser figures can be more easily classified as being better or worse poets or as being nearer to, or farther from, their masters than by personal characteristics. As the poetic masters of these poets, Donne and Jonson formed an almost ideal partnership, at once stimulating and disciplining, arousing exuberant feeling and ingenious elaboration of the fancy and exerting a dignified restraint and a sensitive literary tact.[3] The influence of Donne is the most obvious. One has cases of the direct imitation of his conceits, such as Carew's *Upon a Ribband*:

> This silken wreath, which circles in mine arme,
> Is but an Emblem of that mystique charme,
> Wherewith the magique of your beauties birds
> My captive soul . . .

which is clearly based on *The Funerall*. One also finds the wider influence of themes and attitudes. Donne's *The Extasie* and *A Valediction, forbidding Mourning* are behind a long series of poems, including Lord Herbert's *Ode upon a Question moved, Whether Love should continue for ever?*, Lovelace's *To Lucasta, going beyond the Seas*, and Suckling's *To Mistress Cicely Crofts*, which characteristically reverses the theme:

> There rests but this, that whilst we sorrow here,
>   Our bodies may draw near;
> And when no more their joys they can extend,
> Then let our Souls begin where they did end.

Beyond this again is, of course, the spirit of Metaphysical wit, that source of imaginative strength which enabled more or less irresponsible young men about Court to analyse their feelings and build up sustained poetic arguments, and to bring into their poetry their miscellaneous dabblings in theology, philosophy, natural science, and whatever else caught their interest. The Cavalier elegies on Donne make their debts to him explicit and, if one allows for the customary obituary hyperbole, show in at least one case remarkable critical insight and power of definition; while their couplets clearly derive from his *Satyres* and the *Anniversaries*. From the work of Lord Herbert, Falkland, Carew, Mayne, Cartwright, Godolphin, and Porter — the last almost neo-classically elegant — one must select Carew's (1595?–1640?) for examination. He presents a very full account of Donne as a 'reformer and preserver of the English tongue' in poetry, e.g.:

> The Muses garden with Pedantique weedes
> O'rspred, was purg'd by thee; The lazie seeds
> Of servile imitation throwne away,
> And fresh invention planted, Thou didst pay
> The debts of our penurious bankrupt age;
> Licentious thefts, that make poetique rage
> A Mimique fury, when our soules must bee
> Possest, or with Anacreons Extasie,
> Or Pindars, not their owne; The subtle cheat
> Of slie Exchanges, and the jugling feat
> Of two-edg'd words, or whatsoever wrong
> By ours was done the Greeke, or Latine tongue,
> Thou hast redeem'd, and open'd Us a Mine

> Of Rich and pregnant phansie, drawne a line
> Of masculine expression ...

One only wonders why he instances Pindar and Anacreon rather than Petrarch.

Jonsonus Virbius and other complimentary verses establish Jonson in a corresponding position. The majority of the Cavaliers had been admitted to the 'Tribe of Ben', and liked to call themselves his 'Sons'; Suckling celebrates rather disrespectfully a *Session of the Poets*. In their poems the tribe naturally take his work as a whole, or his dramatic work in particular and, as he had taught them, stress its moral value. Once more, out of poems by Falkland, May, Habington, Waller, Cleveland, Mayne, Cartwright, Carew, Lord Herbert, Suckling, and Randolph one selects Carew's for his fine verse, his tact in dealing with an embarrassing situation – Jonson's *Ode to Himself*, which Carew feels to be a tragic lapse of taste – and his exact reference to the lyrics and their classical ancestry:

> Repine not at the Tapers thriftie waste,
> That sleekes thy terser Poems, nor in haste
> Prayse, but excuse; and if thou overcome
> A knottie writer, bring the bootie home ...

The Cavaliers were following Jonson when they naturalized the themes of Catullus and other Latin lyrists. His influence on them was an example of careful art – 'no matter how slow the style be at first, so it be laboured and accurate; seek the best, and be not glad of ... first words ...' (*Timber*) – urbanity of tone and control of emotion, rather than as a source of images and phrases. Rough as he was in himself, he taught them how to put the tone of the gentleman into poetry:

> Aske me no more where *Jove* bestowes,
> When *June* is past, the fading rose:
> For in your beauties orient deepe,
> These flowers as in their causes, sleepe

shows Carew combining both metaphysical and classical material with courtly elegance. On the other hand, Lovelace's

> Strive not, vain Lover, to be fine,
> Thy silk's the Silkworms, and not thine;

> You lessen to a Fly your Mistris Thought,
> To think it may be in a Cobweb caught ...

restates 'Still to be neat ...' from the opposite side, and also gives it a more solemn moral note.

Lord Herbert of Cherbury (1583–1648)

If one takes the principal 'Sons of Ben' in approximate order of seniority, one obtains a fairly clear picture of how Cavalier poetry developed as the years went on. Lord Herbert scarcely qualifies for the rather vague title of 'Son of Ben' or, on account of his seniority, as a Cavalier, but his lyrics, such as 'Come hither, womankind', 'I am the first that ever lov'd' and

> If you refuse me once, and think again
> I will complain,
> You are deceiv'd: love is no work of Art,
> It must be got and born,
> Not made and worn,
> Or such wherein you have no part

decidedly have the tone and accent of the group, and he was associated with his 'witty Carew' in that his *A description* was apparently the occasion for the latter's *Complement*, and in the disputed authorship of 'Now you have freely given me leave to love'.

Robert Herrick (1591–1674)

Herrick belongs much less to the tradition, though he was a member of the tribe and celebrate its meetings in verse.[4] He also wrote a fine portrait of *His Cavalier*:

> Give me that man that dares bestride
> The active sea-horse, and with pride,
> Through the huge field of waters ride:
> Who, with his looks too, can appease
> The ruffling winds and raging seas,
> In mid'st of all their outrages.
> This, this a virtuous man can doe,
> Saile against rocks, and split them too;
> I! and a world of pikes passe through.

But the metaphysical manner is beyond Herrick's powers of imagination and he lacks Jonson's polished technique and emotional discipline. *Upon Julia's Clothes*:

> When as in silks my Julia goes,
> Then, then (me thinks) how sweetly flowes
> The liquefaction of her clothes

has some of their strength and elegance. 'Gather ye rosebuds' is a pleasant version of the '*Carpe diem*' theme, but it lacks complexity. His epitaphs and poems on children are, if placed beside Jonson's, sentimental. Herrick is a poet of a charmingly fanciful but simple sensibility. *Corinna's going a-Maying* is in the sixteenth-century convention, with its mass of flowery imagery and naïve medley of classical allusions and colloquial phrases. Its virtue is in its very lack of discipline:

> Get up, get up for shame, the Blooming Morne
> Upon her wings presents the god unshorne.
>> See how *Aurora* throwes her faire
>> Fresh-quilted colours through the aire.
>> Get-up, sweet-Slug-a-bed, and see
>> The Dew bespangling Herbe and Tree.
> Each Flower has wept, and bow'd towards the East
> Above an houre since; yet you are not drest,
>> Nay! not so much as out of bed?
>> When all the Birds have Mattens seyd,
>> And sung their thankfull Hymnes: 'tis sin,
>> Nay, profanation to keep in,
> When as a thousand Virgins on this day
> Spring, sooner than the Lark, to fetch in May.

Herrick undoubtedly had a real feeling for flowers and trees and for country customs and beliefs, as one sees them in *Night-piece to Julia*, *Fairies*, *A Country Life*, and *The Hock Cart*, despite his complaints at 'banishment' from London.

Thomas Carew (1595?–1639?)

One finds the great house and the idealized patriarchal community again in Carew's *To Saxham* and *To my friend, G.N.* Both these poems are heavily dependent on Jonson's *Penshurst*, but the fact that a man like Carew could write them at all shows, I think, that Charles I's courtiers – Carew is one of the most urban as well as urbane – had not entirely forgotten their social responsibilities and the quality of life outside London. *In Answer of an Elegiacall Letter upon the death of the King of Sweden* puts the Court before us – and a pastoral masque. If Carew is perhaps not a major poet, he has certainly been under- as much as Herrick has been over-rated. He has, as Sir Herbert Grierson says, a deeper vein of thought than one might expect from a gay and frivolous Court official; the two influences of Donne and Jonson are fused in him by a considerable native talent. Borrowings from Donne are comparatively rare in his work, but imitations of Marino and other continental poets show the width of his culture. His poems on Donne and Jonson show not only his immense admiration for them but also his critical intelligence and power of sustained thinking in verse. This intelligence is the controlling force in his lyrics.

Let us examine his *To my Inconstant Mistris*:

> When thou, poore excommunicate
>   From all the joyes of love, shalt see
> The full reward, and glorious fate,
>   Which my strong faith shall purchase me,
>   Then curse thine owne inconstancie.
>
> A fayrer hand than thine, shall cure
>   That heart, which thy false oathes did wound;
> And to my soule, a soule more pure
>   Than thine, shall by Loves hand be bound,
>   And both with equall glory crown'd.
>
> Then shalt thou weepe, entreat, complaine
>   To Love, as I did once to thee;
> When all thy teares shall be as vaine
>   As mine were then, for thou shalt be
>   Damn'd for thy false Apostasie.

We begin with a characteristic religious conceit to express with suitable force his rejection of his mistress for her infidelity; it is worth noting that Roman Catholic practices were respected at the Court of Henrietta Maria. Faith, in fact, connotes both his religion of love and his own constancy in it which contrasts with the lady's lack of that quality. But the blasphemous exaggeration together with the sarcastic note of line 1, and the angry off-hand last line of the stanza, give an undertone of mockery to the whole. Carew has a critical anti-Petrarchan attitude, but he is not writing a solemn denunciation. He continues his attack in the next stanza with a closely argued state-ment, in firm sinuous rhythms, of his relationship to his new mistress;

he is polite but delicately ironical ('a soule more pure Than thine'). The new mistress is canonized in glory along with him, and the old is 'damn'd', both according to the convention of worship and also by Carew's real anger. The first three and a half lines of the last stanza have the accent and manner of the man speaking his mind. Though the poem's solemnity may be mock solemnity, a deeper seriousness seems to emerge at this point. Such complexity is typical of Carew at his best. His lyrics are conventional verse in the best sense; that is, the convention really corresponded to an actual way of thinking and feeling, and the lyrics had their accepted and recognized place in the relationship between men and women. 'Give me more love, or more disdaine ...' loses nothing from the fact that Godolphin and Lovelace, and no doubt others, followed out its argument exactly or that Petrarch or Jonson ('Or scorne or pittie on me take ...') may have given the hint. *To a Lady that desired I would love her*, if it be his, is both more conversational and slangy and more serious:

> Then give me leave to love, and love me too,
> Not with designe
> To rayse, as Loves curst Rebells doe,
> When puling Poets whine,
> Fame to their beautie, from their blubbr'd eyne.
>
> Griefe is a puddle, and reflects not cleare
> Your beauties rayes,
> Joyes are pure streames, your eyes appeare
> Sullen in sadder layes,
> In chearfull numbers they shine bright with prayse.

It is a highly individual lyric, using, later, 'Wounds, flames and darts' with an air of freshness and almost of originality.

The wit of Carew includes, besides his metaphysical scope of imagery and intellectually critical discipline, this urbanity or sense of social fitness. His attitude is related to chivalry, but is more sophisticated and more egalitarian as between the sexes. Though he is often critical and even angry with Celia, whoever, or however many, the name represents, he is not cynical or coarse – *A Rapture* is frankly luxurious and sensual – or familiar; there is always present something of the respect with which he regards the Countess of Anglesey, while there is at the same time a certain freedom in his attitude to her:

> You, whose whole life
> In every act crown'd you a constant Wife,
> May spare the practice of that vulgar trade,
> Which superstitious custome onely made;
> Rather a Widow now of wisedome prove
> The patterne, as a Wife you were of love:
> Yet since you surfet on your griefe, 'tis fit
> I tell the world, upon what cares you sit
> Glutting your sorrowes; and at once include
> His story, your excuse, my gratitude.

Carew looks forward to the manners of the Augustans, but he is not so formal as they tend to be and he has a more intimate personal delicacy. His elegies have this poise and balance of phrase and emotion. *Maria Wentworth* is in the great tradition of seventeenth-century elegies and exemplifies particularly a well-known feature of wit not yet dwelt on, the blending of the light and even humorous with the solemn:

> And here the precious dust is layd;
> Whose purely-tempered Clay was made
> So fine, that it the guest betray'd.
>
> Else the soule grew so fast within,
> It broke the outward shell of sinne,
> And so was hatch'd a Cherubin.

Finally, *To my worthy friend Master Geo. Sand* must be mentioned to show the full range of Carew's poetic achievement. Written near the end of his life and the end of an epoch, it has an urbane reverence:

> I presse not to the Quire, nor dare I greet
> The holy place with my unhallowed feet;
> My unwasht Muse . . .

and 'a holy mirth' and a profound sense of sin and penitence are realized in magnificent metaphysical imagery and solemn, emphatic Donnean rhythms:

> Though nor in tune, nor wing, she reach thy Larke,
> Her Lyrick feet may dance before the Arke.
> Who knowes, but that her wandering eyes that run,
> Now hunting Glow-wormes, may adore the Sun,
> A pure flame may, shot by Almighty power
> Into her brest, the earthy flame devoure.

> My eyes, in penitentiall dew may steepe
> That brine, which they for sensuall love did weepe.
> So (though 'gainst Natures course) fire may be quencht
> With fire, and water be with water drencht.

The biographical background of this does not concern us here. It is enough that Carew has a sense of values and has written a great poem. Something that one may risk calling the poetic spirit of the age, its richly imaginative sensibility, has inspired him to write above his usual self without, at the same time, borrowing from his masters.

Sir John Suckling (1609–42)

The double influence shows itself again with Suckling, but he is far less urbane and civilized than Carew and, though he wrote a prose work on religion, far less serious as a poet. His delicacy of imagination, such as it is, his fluency – he criticized Carew as laboured – and his uninhibited and boisterous cynicism come out in:

> Hast thou seen the down in the air,
>   When the wanton blasts have toss'd it?
> Or the ship on the sea,
>   When the ruder waves have cross'd it?
> Hast thou mark'd the crocodile's weeping,
>   Or the fox's sleeping?
> Or hast view'd the peacock in his pride,
>   Or the dove by his bride,
>   When he courts for his lechery?
> O, so fickle, O, so vain, O, so false, so false is she?

'Out upon it, I have lov'd ...' turns the attitude on himself. His language is racier and more careless than Carew's.

> 'Tis not the meat, but 'tis the appetite
>   Makes eating a delight,
>   And if I like one dish
> More than another, that a Pheasant is ...

shows how thoughtlessly he can throw off a conceit to express his feeling about a woman. In Dryden's *Essay of Dramatic Poesy* Lord Buckhurst as Eugenius is made to say that none of his contemporaries in drama 'expresses so much the conversation of a gentleman, as Sir John Suckling'. The spirit of his poetry, the controlling wit, is a good sense or horse sense, and the social tone belongs to a masculine company – his most urbane poem is probably 'My dearest rival ...' *A Ballad upon a Wedding* is a charming dramatic achievement. Suckling knows just how to assume the manner of the 'awe-struck' yeoman without being patronizing, and he gives an ironic glance at good society at the end. Perhaps the poem implies the kind of underlying sympathy with the rural community that caused Carew to write *To Saxham*.

Richard Lovelace (1618–58)

Suckling's forthright Royalist *Answer*, quoted at the beginning of this chapter, reminds us of the Cavalier exemplar, Lovelace. He is a very uneven poet and often seems both careless and amateurish. His finer sensibility, however, redeems the clumsiness of his syntax, and he is a poet of very varied interest. His famous lyrics to Lucasta and Althea, *A Mock Song* and, with them, Montrose's 'My dear and only love ...' voice the Cavalier attitude at its best to life and to the war. We find here the surviving code of chivalry and the public values of the seventeenth-century country gentleman expressed with great clarity and with intellectual ingenuity and sophistication of tone. Lovelace is not on Marvell's level of intelligence, but he is not a simpleton – he is a courtier and a soldier of European culture; beside his work, the revolutionary and nationalist ardours of the Romantics of his class seem crude. One sees the more private interests of the Kentish squire, and once again the rural roots of the Cavaliers, in another interesting group of poems, *The Ant, The Snail, The Toad and the Spider, The Falcon* and *The Grasshopper*. These combine first-hand observations of nature with superstition, and traditional knowledge of field sports with literary allusion and inoffensive moralizing in a manner very characteristic of the early seventeenth century. The following examples must suffice:

> Look up, then, miserable Ant, and spie
> > Thy fatal foes, for breaking of her law,
> Hov'ring above thee, Madam, *Margaret Pie*,
> > And her fierce servant, Meagre – Sir *John Daw*;
> Thy Self and Storehouse now they do store up,
> > And thy whole Harvest too within their Crop.

> Thus we unthrifty thrive within Earths Tomb
>   For some more rav'nous and ambitious Jaw:
> The *Grain* in th' *Ants*, the *Ants* in the *Pie's* womb,
>   The *Pie* in th' *Hawk's*, the *Hawk's* i' th' *Eagle's* maw:
> So scattering to hord 'gainst a long Day,
> Thinking to save all, we cast all away.

and the deservedly famous

> O thou that swing'st upon the waving haire
>   Of some well-filled Oaten Beard,
> Drunke ev'ry night on a delicious teare,
>   Dropt thee from Heav'n where now thou art rear'd ...

It must not, incidentally, be forgotten that *The Grasshopper* is an
invitation to conviviality of which the insect is supposed to set an
example. *A Loose Saraband* is even more bacchanalian:

> Lord! What is man and sober?

Poetry of this quality on themes of all these kinds would seem to
end with Lovelace and his friends, such as Charles Cotton. Charles
II's 'mob of gentlemen' are inferior even in drinking songs.

Lovelace's love poetry has similar qualities – freshness and exuberance, a delicacy and strength of fancy, and a courtly tone. He is
not often vulgar like Suckling, but sometimes has a deeper cynicism
that surprises one. *The Scrutinie* is tough and detached in the manner
of Donne's *Communitie*. He has some brilliant contracted conceits,
such as:

> Like the Sun in's early ray,
> But shake your head and scatter day.
>   (*To Amarantha*)

or:

> Not yet look back, not yet; must we
> Run then like spoakes in wheeles eternally,
> And never overtake?

from *A Forsaken Lady to her False Servant*, a fine dramatic monologue
in couplets. *Ellinda's Glove* is equally brilliant at greater length:

> Thou snowy Farm with thy five Tenements!
>   Tell thy white Mistris here was one
>   That call'd to pay his dayly rents;

> But she a-gathering Flowers and Hearts is gone,
> And thou left void to rude Possession . . .

Gratiana Dancing and Singing, another large-scale conceit, is at once ingenious, rhythmically subtle, and also a little clumsy:

> See! with what constant Motion,
> Even and glorious as the Sun,
>   *Gratiana* steers that Noble Frame,
> Soft as her breast, sweet as her voyce
> That gave each winding law and poiz,
>   And swifter than the wings of Fame.
>
> She beat the happy Pavement
> By such a Starre made Firmament,
>   Which now no more the Roofe envies,
> But swells up high with *Atlas* ev'n,
> Bearing the brighter, nobler Heav'n,
>   And, in her, all the Deities . . .

Lovelace was never a 'Son of Ben', and there seems to be a lack of his disciplining influence over the suns and flowers that burst forth a little too brightly in this poetry. The gentle, courtly tone is Lovelace's own contribution, and owes nothing directly to others. But this sometimes lapses badly; the vital elements of irony and humour fall into abeyance and exaggeration effects get out of control. I think that this is the defect, rather than mere indecency as Dr Johnson and the nineteenth-century critics thought, of such things as:

> Heere wee'll strippe and cool our fire
> In Creame below, in milke-baths higher;
>   And when all Wells are drawne dry,
> I'll drink a teare out of thine eye.

or *Lucasta taking the Waters at Tunbridge* or *Love made in the First Age*; there is also the 'reverend lady cow' in *Amarantha*. If Suckling foreshadows the tone of Charles II's Court, Lovelace by these flaws in the quality of his wit gives an indication that the Donne–Jonson aristocratic synthesis was breaking up with the Court that had cherished it.

217

NOTES

1. See Part I, especially pp. 18–31, and also L. C. Knights' 'Social Background of Metaphysical Poetry' in *Scrutiny*, XIII for further information and reflections on this theme. There is also an extremely interesting essay, 'The Social Situation of Seventeenth-Century Poetry' by J. W. Saunders in *Metaphysical Poetry*, ed. M. Bradbury and D. Palmer, Stratford-upon-Avon Studies, II, which is concerned more with the status of the poet, and of poetry, and with publishing. Chapters 3 and 4 of Mark Girouard's *Life in the English Country House* (1978) present the physical setting.

2. There is an interesting and controversial article by Marius Bewley, 'The Colloquial Mode of Byron', in *Scrutiny*, XVI; he writes on Lovelace and more minor Cavaliers.

3. See ch. 1 of F. R. Leavis's *Revaluation* (1936) for a further discussion of this, and Sir Herbert Grierson's introduction to *Metaphysical Poetry* (1921) for a different point of view. George Williamson, in *The Donne Tradition* (1930), handles the subject in more detail, and his *The Proper Wit of Poetry* (1961), especially chs. I and III, gives his mature conception of that quality.

4. In *English Literature in the Earlier Seventeenth Century* (1945), ch. IV, Douglas Bush describes Herrick's work in similar terms to mine, but places him in a relatively higher position – in fact the older, traditional one.

MILTON'S RELIGIOUS VERSE

L. A. CORMICAN

Of all the great figures in English literature, Milton (1608–74) is in several ways the most controversial. No writer, except Shakespeare, has been so continuously admired; no teacher, except perhaps Bunyan, has been so revered by so many generations. Yet since Addison's famous remark in 1712 that our language 'sunk under him', there have been many derogatory criticisms not merely of details but of whole aspects of his work. It is impossible to read Milton without feeling that we are in the presence of a great mind; yet even critics who have praised him most highly have felt it was necessary to come devoutly and staunchly to his defence.

The reasons for this long-standing diversity of opinion form a useful introduction to his work. To both the general reader and the professional critic, Milton presents special difficulties which, if they cannot be overcome, must at least be recognized. In the first place, he has built lengthy works out of religious convictions which are widely discarded or despised today. Without a fair understanding of these convictions and a certain amount of (at least temporary) sympathy towards them, we are likely to misread him; in few poets in any language can we make less distinction between the doctrinal content and the literary art, or concentrate on the purely 'aesthetic' side of his poetry.

In the second place, his greatness and the nature of his topics invite comparisons with Shakespeare and Dante. As T. S. Eliot pointed out, the basic tools of criticism are analysis and comparison. The critical judgements we arrive at will depend on what we compare with what, and there is no doubt that Milton suffers by comparison not only with Shakespeare and Dante, but also with Donne and Hopkins; he has little of the latter poets' capacity for startling phrase and packed emotion, and neither Dante's vivid intimacy nor Shakespeare's profound psychological insight. Our effort must then be to see what special qualities he possesses and what special difficulties he faced.

Thirdly, the very nature of his themes and the great purpose he had in mind remove his poetry to a much greater extent than that of others, even the biblical poets, from the ordinary concerns and common experience of men. For his material he chose the fall of man,[1] the tempting of Christ by Satan, and the Lord's vengeance on His enemies through Samson. The existence of angels, the fall of a whole race in Adam, the restoration of that race in Christ, the deliberate destruction of God's enemies – these are ideas which, whether accepted or rejected, have little affinity with the mentality of the twentieth century, and are remote from the common experience even of the devout believer. Milton, then, presented himself with a particularly difficult task, a task faced neither by the Hebrew poets (who concentrate on the experience of the Israelites); nor by the Greeks (who, even in dealing with the gods, are constantly concerned with the human situation); nor by Dante (who expresses his theological material in terms of a human pilgrim progressing towards Heaven through a series of vivid encounters with human beings); nor by Shakespeare (who, in presenting a profound study of human character, abstains from personal moral judgements). Even the great bulk of medieval religious poetry (the anonymous hymns and lyrics, *Piers Plowman* and the medieval plays) does not attempt to elaborate the story of the early parts of Creation; it keeps religious beliefs and moral principles constantly in touch with the world we know. We might perhaps conclude that Milton's artistic judgement was at fault, that what he attempted was beyond the reach of human language, that he should, as he had first intended, have dealt with some more 'human' story such as the legend of Arthur. But that conclusion could reasonably be based only on great critical ability, on a precise estimate of his difficulties, and on a very wide and exact grasp of the theology which exerts so deep and so pervasive a pressure on his verse. Milton was guilty of some hyperbole in describing his 'adventrous Song' as pursuing 'things unattempted yet in Prose or Rhime'; but the hyperbole may stand as a reminder of the great difficulties he entered into with such deliberate choice and after so long and so careful a preparation. Unless we see his difficulties, we cannot fairly estimate his success or his failure.

The difficulties are further aggravated by Milton's intense conviction that his poetry must teach. And the influence of the Old Testament is seen in his conception of teaching; he wishes not merely to instruct the mind but to purify and elevate the heart, and in this one word, 'heart', he is supposing in the reader some knowledge of the Books of Wisdom in the Old, and the Epistles of the New, Testament. His great object, he says, is to

> .. assert Eternal Providence
> And justify the ways of God to men.
>
> (I. 25)

The whole of *Paradise Lost* (1667) must be understood in the light of the exordium (lines 1–26), and the exordium in the light of the whole poem; we misunderstand the poem from the outset if we think of it as another seventeenth-century controversial tract. The criticism that Milton does not succeed in justifying God's ways is based on a misconception of what Milton meant by God and what he meant by justification. It should be clear from the whole poem that, to Milton, God always remains the Great Mystery whose inscrutable ways can be comprehended only in the 'light' which is as yet inaccessible to men.

By justification Milton did not mean a merely logical demonstration which would prove an intellectual conclusion and bring God within the framework of the rational universe. He uses the word with the overtones it acquired from New Testament usage, where it implies a divine, not a human or logical, understanding, a supernal illumination from the Holy Spirit whom he invokes for special guidance in his difficult task.[2] Milton aspires to higher things than were possible through the Greek Muses or even through the inspiration of the Old Testament. If the ways of God can be justified, it must be through a purification of the heart rather than by the reasonings of the intellect.[3]

The poem is, among other things, a prayer addressed to the Deity from all mankind, a prayer in which he perseveres even though he concludes, from his biblical sources and his personal experience, that many would reject the divine revelation; hence the later form of his prayer (VII. 31) that his Muse, 'heavenly-born Urania' who 'with Eternal Wisdom didst converse', might 'fit audience find though few'. (The whole passage, VII. 1–39, should be closely connected with the opening of Book I.) We should then understand Milton as aspiring through his poem to prepare the hearts of men for the coming of the

Spirit whose great office is to lead men into the truth about God and themselves.

The main question for the reader of Milton's poetry is not, indeed, the nature of his theological doctrine or his value as a moral teacher, but the extent to which theology and morality are transmuted into poetry. But no estimate of his poetry can be arrived at in complete abstraction from the discussion of his doctrinal content; the way in which his words 'work' – the definable effect they have on our minds – depends so largely on the religious connotations and suggestions they have for an individual reader. Different interpretations of the words 'Father' and 'sin' do not necessarily result in different estimates of Donne's *Hymn to God the Father* because the experience within the poem does not depend on the technical meaning we assign to them. But disagreement on 'justify', 'Victor', and 'Mightiest' (*P.L.*, I. 26, 95, 99) will deeply affect our understanding of Satan and our literary judgement of the poem. The two *Paradises* draw constantly on a doctrine no one point of which can be fully understood through the poems alone. Yet a certain amount of Milton can be enjoyed immediately with no reference to doctrine (e.g. II. 51–105, XII. 624–49, or – a good introduction to Milton – the passages in any good dictionary of quotations). Such passages, like Shakespeare's 'Friends, Romans, countrymen', should encourage the reader to go further in the endeavour to understand the presuppositions and qualities of the writer's art.

We can assist ourselves by noting a parallel between the opening of *Paradise Lost* and that of *Antony and Cleopatra*. However concerned both writers are with exposition, they are already, at the opening, supposing a great deal in the reader. To catch the many hints and overtones of Philo's speech, we need a knowledge of love, war, and politics; Shakespeare is drawing on forms of knowledge which have no necessary connection with poetry. In somewhat the same way, to perceive Milton's meaning in the generalized 'Man', the implication of 'first' and of 'fruit' supposes our ability to bring what we know of Christianity to bear on the opening sentence.

> Of Man's First Disobedience, and the Fruit
> Of that Forbidden Tree, whose mortal taste
> Brought Death into the World, and all our woe,
> With loss of *Eden*, till one greater Man

Restore us, and regain the blissful Seat,
Sing Heav'nly Muse, that on the secret top
Of *Oreb* or of Sinai, didst inspire
That Shepherd, who first taught the chosen Seed,
In the Beginning how the Heav'ns and Earth
Rose out of *Chaos*: or if *Sion* Hill
Delight thee more, and Siloa's Brook that flow'd
Fast by the Oracle of God; I thence
Invoke thy aid to my adventrous Song,
That with no middle flight intends to soar
Above th' *Aonian* Mount, while it pursues
Things unattempted yet in Prose or Rhime.
And chiefly Thou O Spirit, that dost prefer
Before all Temples th' upright heart and pure,
Instruct me, for Thou know'st; Thou from the first
Wast present, and with mighty wings outspread
Dove-like satst brooding on the vast Abyss
And mad'st it pregnant: What in me is dark
Illumine, what is low raise and support:
That to the highth of this great Argument
I may assert Eternal Providence,
And justifie the wayes of God to men.

'Man', the second word of the poem, introduces us to one of the main themes – the unity of the human race whose sinfulness, woe, and hope of restoration are summed up in Adam. The *first* disobedience is thus not only the first in time; it is in a general manner (whose mysteriousness Milton does not claim to be able to clarify) the source of all other disobedience. All he can say about the disobedience for the moment is condensed in the word 'fruit', which is both the edible fruit itself and fruit in the biblical sense (i.e. the results which grow as naturally from decisions as fruit from a tree). In Milton's idiom (since he frequently uses a participle with a noun force), the 'Forbidden Tree' is equivalent to 'the divine command which forbade man to eat of the tree', the transgression of which had such vast results. He thus connects the 'Disobedience' with the whole plan of Divine Providence, and indicates that it was not the temporary trespass of an arbitrary command but a violation of that divine order which the Spirit drew from the 'vast Abyss'. The second half of the sentence suggests how, in spite of men's sins, divine inspiration followed the chosen race from Egypt to Jerusalem, from ancient to apostolic times. The key terms thus reinforce and clarify one another in a manner very similar to the theological shorthand so often employed by Dante. Milton draws on a different kind of knowledge from Shakespeare; but in either case, if the knowledge is not there, the verse will not 'work' properly.

Even the least experienced reader can easily see the marked difference between the jerky, flat language of the 'arguments' and the evocative language of the poem. An analysis of the differences between the two would elicit many points on Milton's verse style, but particularly the accumulative quality by which, though no one phrase is immediately felt as striking, the large scope of the poem, and the multiple interrelation of its parts, gradually become evident. While this method carries with it a sometimes disconcerting shifting of focus and a lack of sensuous contact with reality, it is still fit for Milton's purpose, if we see how the verse is constantly reaching out in different directions – to Heaven, Hell, and earth; to sin, redemption, and Providence – and is thereby assimilating the human to the divine mind which sees all time and space at once. Some readers feel an hypnotic or incantatory quality in such sentences as this, and obviously it has not the brisk, curt quality of Philo's speech; but the endeavour to respond fully to the implications of the terms and see the ways in which they clarify each other should sharpen rather than dull the mind.

The second sentence (which concludes the introductory section) draws a parallel between the divine and the human work of creation, between producing the world and creating great poetry, a parallel which is intended to suggest the poet's scope and his (and the reader's) need for divine help. The idea of an analogy between art and divine creation was not, of course, original to Milton, but he gives it a particular relevance by speaking of the creative power as Spirit and Dove, that is, as combining in himself divine power, wisdom, and gentleness; it is because God has these qualities that Milton confidently addresses to him a prayer for help in his 'adventrous Song'. God is thought of not merely as a gentle dove, but as having wings wide enough to brood over the 'vast Abyss', and as having wisdom and power enough to draw order out of chaos; this God, gentle, wise, and powerful, is now besought to establish intellectual and moral order in the poet by cleansing, strengthening, and elevating his heart, by enlightening and making pregnant his mind. All the items in the exordium have an exact relevance to what Milton is doing at the moment and hopes to do in the poem as a whole. This degree of poetic condensation is not indeed maintained throughout the work; yet the opening gives some suggestions of the literary excellence we are to look for in the poem, particularly the power to keep central themes steadily, if loosely, in control of a multiplicity of details, the power to achieve a great sweep of meaning in a single sentence, and the occasional power to fuse apparent contradictories without incongruity. The passage on the Dove recalls the metaphysicals; the Dove is both gentle and mighty; while remaining motionless ('satst brooding'), it became the source of all creation and movement by turning the 'vast' (i.e. 'waste' or 'lifeless') abyss into the womb of the whole universe. Every detail carries the parallel between creation and poetic inspiration a step further.

At the same time, Milton is not concerned with any mere theory of aesthetics; he appeals to the Dove-like Spirit because, to achieve his moral aspiration in poetry, he must have some share in the peace and width of the divine mind, in the divine wisdom and strength. The notion of the 'pregnant Abyss', with its suggestion of the analogy between the darkness of the abyss and that of the womb, and the contrast between the formless desert of the one and the organized life of the other, is a good example of Milton's occasional power to fuse disparate ideas without incongruity while fitting the language to the illustration of his main themes. If he turned from the metaphysical style which he attempted in *The Passion* (1630), he did not discard all that could be learnt from the metaphysicals. That he moulded rather than copied the metaphysical style is evident from the fact that the 'pregnant Abyss' has none of the startling effect which we find (and rightly enjoy) in Donne's 'Busie old foole, unruly Sunne', or in Hopkins's *May-mess*. Milton is not arousing us out of our ordinariness to see the human world through the eyes of a startlingly original mind, but is endeavouring to lift us to the peace of the divine vision. In such ways as these, Milton adapts his language to his moral purpose and his theological doctrine.

There is a minor point in Milton's treatment of religion which gives a disproportionate amount of trouble to many readers. All the important forms of religion and culture in seventeenth-century England were derived from the continent, but were profoundly modified by the English mind. Thus Milton's mysticism is not merely Christian but English and Miltonic; it is coloured by the strongly controversial spirit of the times and by the exploratory and argumentative bent of Milton's mind. *Paradise Lost* was probably written while he was exploring Christian doctrine to decide what he should believe. The poem is not, consequently, based on a finally settled creed such as we find in Dante or Bunyan, and incidental blows are directed in it against such things as medieval beliefs about angels, the Roman doctrine of indulgences, and the Anglican hierarchy. Controversial asides and doctrinal discrepancies within the poem need not be given serious consideration by the critic, and can be completely overlooked by the general reader.[4] Once we are aware that we may find controversial asides and doctrinal discrepancies, we can afford to treat them with the passing interest they deserve, and concentrate on the main purpose, which is not to expound a theological thesis but to reinforce a mystical mood and habit of mind.

The poem is a survey of the whole scheme of Providence by which Milton hopes to attune the human to the Divine Mind, and thus purify the human heart and elevate it to God. Milton wishes to present the Fall of Adam as a key incident that would lead men to a divine understanding of the larger story of the Creation and of the Fall and restoration of man. Theological doctrine he does suppose but, as in the poetry of the Old Testament (from which Milton drew so much inspiration), the emphasis falls not on speculative doctrine but on the practical task of inducing the right attitudes in both writer and reader. Unless we read the invocations (at the beginning of Books I, III and VII) as Milton meant them – as prayers – we mis-read them. Every poet must produce the moods and attitudes by which his work is understood and enjoyed; the bulk of serious adverse criticism of Milton argues that he lacks this very important element of poetic ability. We should remember, however, that such failure may be due to the reading public as much as to the writer (the slow recognition of Wordsworth or Eliot is a case in point). Milton's failure has been due largely to two things: his deliberate choice of topics which preclude recurrence to common experience, and the unwillingness of the modern mind to have any precise demands made on its credence or its morals (and neither Wordsworth nor Eliot makes such demands). It is rather vain to hope (as Douglas Bush hopes in various places in '*Paradise Lost*' *in Our Day*) that the reading of Milton will help to restore high moral standards; for unless we are already willing to accept Milton's moral mysticism, either permanently or temporarily, we are unlikely to understand him. Poetry written in an age very different or distant from our own requires us to do what we can to recapture the mind and mood of those to whom it was addressed.

Here again the comparison with Shakespeare can be very misleading. For besides his own unique excellence in disentangling human situations from merely local conditions, and thereby giving them a universal appeal, Shakespeare has one advantage which Milton deliberately discarded, the advantage of confining himself to the temporal as contrasted with the eternal point of view. What Shakespeare aimed at in his audience is what any audience has in common with ourselves. But when we think of Milton's audience, with its definite religious convictions, its intense moral fervour, its willingness to apply religious principles to every phase of the national and individual life, we find a world which is mentally much farther from our own than Shakespeare's or even Homer's. From this point of view, the understanding of Milton is discouragingly difficult; but from another it is relatively easy, and consists in taking his prayers and mysticism with complete seriousness. It may be suggested that the best 'preface' to Milton is not a piece of scholarship or literary criticism, but the intense reading of the Psalms, which Milton could take for granted in his 'fit audience'. Hebrew poetry can, more effectively than scholarship or criticism, habituate the reader's mind to Milton's mood and purpose. To endeavour to read him without any close acquaintance with the Bible is to evade the kind of preparation which he assumed.

It will follow from the above that neither structure nor style in Milton can be discussed apart from his central preoccupation with a mystical vision. It is almost entirely irrelevant to adduce Greek or Latin epics, or Aristotelean principles, in order to examine the structure of *Paradise Lost* or *Paradise Regained* (1671), though Greek tragedy supplies useful hints for *Samson Agonistes* (1671). Since what he created is so specially Miltonic in both poetic excellence and religious purpose, parallels with other writers can mislead as well as guide. We may, however, find a useful approach through Hebrew and Shakespearian poetry, where the structure consists not so much in the concatenation of events or the logical development of an idea, but rather in the gradual exploration or 'explication' of an opening theme, such as 'the triple pillar of the world transformed into a strumpet's fool' (*Antony and Cleopatra*), or 'The Lord is my shepherd' (Psalm 23).

The arrangement of the incidents in Milton is determined, not by the desire to tell a good story (as in the *Iliad*) nor by the narrative exposition of a theological system (as in *The Divine Comedy*), but by the gradual reinforcing and intertwining of four central themes – the universality of Divine Providence, the reality of evil, the hope of redemption from evil, and the unity of the human race.* It is the repetition and mutual clarification of these four themes, far more than any manipulation of the incidents, that gives the poem whatever structural unity it possesses. They are kept alive sometimes by explicit statement, but more often by reference and allusion. They are not dealt with separately in different parts of the poem because Milton is constantly aware of their close inter-connection; his language is turned to the task of keeping them pervasively present and at times (e.g. III. 1–21, IV. 32–112) intensely felt. There is, for example, a nice adjustment of emphasis in Book I. The obvious emphasis falls on the vigour, independence, and resoluteness of Satan; but there is a subtler emphasis on the dedication of these powers to evil. Both emphases are expressed in a way which helps us to see the range of Satan's pride (the source of the first violation of divine order) and to see in Satan and his plans a parody (completely humourless but effective) of God and Divine Providence. If we avoid the mistake of understanding Milton's God through Satan's mind (as we should wish to avoid understanding King Claudius merely through Hamlet's mind), we can see Milton's purpose in Satan's reference to the 'Realms of Light' (line 96); the darkness of Hell is not merely exclusion from glory and happiness, but the darkness of uncertainty and error in which Satan must plot to defeat the designs of God. The reference to light comes not merely from the desire to present a portrait of Satan, but from the desire to keep the whole scheme of the poem in mind. Milton offers the exclusion from light as his own comment on the ultimate futility of Satan's plan:

> If then his Providence
> Out of our evil seek to bring forth good,
> Our labour must be to pervert that end,
> And out of good still to find means of evil;
> Which oft times may succeed, so as perhaps

---

* It is probable that no poet would accept anyone else's summary of his themes; the four given above are offered merely as handy terms of reference.

Shall grieve him, if I fail not, and disturb
His inmost counsels from their destined aim.
(162–8)

In many other places do we find a similar inter-weaving of the main themes by which Milton explores the antecedents and the consequences of 'Man's first disobedience'. To knit so many large issues (each of them a complexity in itself) into one large pattern, to make them clarify and reinforce each other in so long a poetic work, is a major achievement in poetic structure.

The events are thus means to an end, not the main interest; similarly, the various shifts of attention (from the exordium to Hell, to Heaven, to Eden) are not the dramatist's or novelist's devices for keeping the various parts of the story abreast of each other, but rather a circular tour through the whole scheme of Divine Providence. Thus by the beginning of Book III, the Fall of Man (described in detail in Book IX) is yet a further event for Satan and Adam, but is spoken of (III. 86–131) as already present in God's manner of cognition and as already incorporated into the divine plan. The 'discussion' which follows on the method of redemption is not a heavenly council of deliberation, but Milton's way of affirming the ancient Christian teaching that God fulfils His design by the co-operation of free agents.[5] The problem of reconciling divine foreknowledge with human freedom is not a poetic but a religious one; Milton assumed (and expected his audience to assume) that it was one of the divine mysteries, discussible but not soluble. Similarly, the end of the poem is not (as it is with the multiple deaths of an Elizabethan tragedy) the end of the story; it does not conclude Milton's survey, but is rather the beginning of that long life of woe, the delivery from which is an integral part of the main poetic theme. The Redemption has already been presented in considerable detail in Books III, X, XI, and the early part of Book XII. Such telescoping of events is not, of course, peculiar to Milton; but it is used by him for a special purpose – to present the successive working out of what is eternally present in the Divine Mind. It is probable that Milton derived hints for such a treatment not only from the similar conspectus in Augustine's *City of God*, but also from Hebrew grammar which does not possess the Occidental distinctions of past, present, and future, and frequently speaks of future events in the Hebrew 'imperfect' to which the closest English equivalent is the past.

For much the same reasons, it is rather superfluous to discuss where the crisis or climax of *Paradise Lost* occurs. The poem is much too concentrated in many places, and much too long, for any one incident to carry an emphasis which is readily perceived as greater than that of others. Besides, the story is not a series of incidents but a circular contemplation of God's ways, and contemplation does not lend itself to crisis or climax. The poem contains a series of emphases (alternated with descriptive and reflective material); to decide which of these is the greatest is a highly personal or subjective question.[6] Milton's whole cast of mind (at least by the time he wrote the last three works) rather closely resembles Wordsworth's; both present incidents, but incidents 'recollected in tranquillity', not portrayed in dramatic evolution. It is not only the close of the stories, but the poems as a whole that we are to read in 'calm of mind, all passion spent' (*Samson*, 1758). The reader is expected to survey the actions of Satan, Adam, and Eve from the calm beatitude of Heaven, that is, with as close an approximation to God's own view as human nature, elevated by grace, permits. Miltonic structure must then be discussed, not in terms of 'plot' or arrangement of incidents, but through the careful reading of key passages which recall and reinforce the divine point of view. This will imply (among other things) the effort to understand such key words as 'Providence' (I. 25), 'Reason' (III. 108), and 'incensed Deity' (III. 187) as they were understood by the Puritan mind.

If the structure depends on individual passages, the latter also depend on the structure, and depend in a way which has been little discussed. Milton's style, like Shakespeare's, has various levels of meaning, the understanding of which comes, not so much from further literary training as from deepening and widening our experience. To increase our grasp of Hamlet's soliloquies or of the political situation in *Antony and Cleopatra* is a matter of becoming not more scholarly but more adult. In much the same way, no increase in critical ability or scholarship will by itself take us very far into Milton's meaning; while it may clarify individual points, it will leave the total effect or appeal of the poems very much where it stood before. But the re-reading of Milton presents another and special difficulty, the difficulty of deepening religious beliefs and stabilizing religious moods. Without this deepening and stabilizing, scholarship fastens more and more on details, and critical ability may turn earlier pleasure into later distaste. Milton's complexity rather resembles that of the great passages in the Psalms or the New Testament; he cannot be read merely as literature since he is not re-living or re-enacting personal religious experiences in the manner of Herbert or Hopkins, but is inculcating a particular attitude towards God. The parallel between Milton and the Bible is true to this extent that it is only by an intensification of the religious spirit, as well as by expanding experience, that we can come to grasp the complexity of the great Psalm 22, the Lord's Prayer, or *Paradise Lost*; can come to see explicitly what was before only implicit to our less developed religious sensibility. It is probably only a man who has passed through what John of the Cross calls 'the dark night of the soul', or some analogous experience like that of Milton after the Restoration of the Stuarts to the throne, who could seize the full meaning of:

> Man therefore shall find grace;
> The other [Satan], none. In mercy and justice both,
> Through Heaven and Earth, so shall my glory excel;
> But mercy, first and last, shall brightest shine.
>
> (III. 131)

If the reader considers the distinction made here between Satan and Adam to be the result of mere arbitrariness on God's part, if he does not find in the phrase, 'mercy, first and last', a summary of Divine Providence and of the whole poem, it is because he is unaware of the commonplaces of theology in Milton's time and probably because he has had little religious experience. Without that experience, the last three poems will have as superficial a meaning as *Romeo and Juliet* to the youngster who has never been in love.

There is a good reason why Milton's peculiar complexity has been little discussed. In so far as religious growth occurs, it is a growth which almost defies formulation in words unless they be the words of the rare hymnographer like the author of the *Stabat Mater*, or the rare Dante or Milton, who possess the power of carrying the contemplation of Divine Providence a step further – a power which no critic of Milton has possessed, which cannot perhaps be expressed in criticism at all, and which has never yet been expressed but in great creative writing.

The conclusion can hardly be drawn that it is only the convinced Christian who can perceive the complexity of Milton, any more than it is only the Thomist who can perceive the complexity of Dante. The atheist or agnostic who is willing to re-create in himself something at least of the religious mentality Milton supposed, who is humble enough to keep his own pre-judgements out of the way, can do for Milton what he must, on a smaller scale, do for Donne or Hopkins. It is because Milton's verse so constantly demands our acceptance of his religious mood, because he is habitually so far from common experience, because he affords us so little opportunity to look at things from the merely human point of view (as he does in the felicitous description of Mulciber's fall, I. 738–46), because he so seldom allows us to enjoy beauty in a merely human manner (as he does in the description of Paradise, IV. 213–87), that we tend to refuse to Milton the 'willing suspension of disbelief' – the condition on which alone most people today can enjoy religious poetry. Even in such passages as those just cited, Milton is still mindful of his general scheme to which he quickly returns the reader's attention. When he adds a line of comment like 'Thus they relate erring', he is not tacking an extraneous ornament on to his main theme or apologizing for indulgence in luxurious poetry inappropriate to a Puritan. Having afforded a resting-place for the reader, he is contrasting the merely human or the pagan with the Christian conception of the universe; he is reinforcing the central interest. These resting-places (corresponding roughly in poetic function to the deliberately quieter passages in Shakespeare, e.g. the welcome to Duncan in *Macbeth*, I. vi) become rarer towards the end of the poem; a larger number of them, organically built into the structure, would have made it a better poem, or at least one better accommodated to the limitations of the ordinary reader. If Johnson voices a common impression in feeling that 'none ever wished the poem longer', it is because no other poem imposes so constant a strain, except perhaps *King Lear*, which is Shakespeare's greatest endeavour to lift the popular audience above its habitual self. The perusal of *Paradise Lost*, says Johnson, 'is a duty rather than a pleasure. We read Milton for instruction, retire harassed and over-burdened, and look elsewhere for recreation.' But before deciding whether this is a judgement on the weakness of the poem or on the limitations of the reader, we should remember that intense religious feeling (as in Psalm 91 or in the poetry of John of the Cross) is little concerned about the reader's convenience; and (since the poem is a prayer) we should recognize the common weakness of men who seldom desire their prayers to be longer or consider prayer as a form of recreation.

Johnson was nearer the mark when he quoted a Milton encomiast as saying that 'in reading *Paradise Lost* we read a book of universal knowledge'. For the poem is not, as Johnson hints, an encyclopaedia of natural history, ancient fable, and modern science; it is the last of the medieval attempts to write the history of Everyman, to survey the whole course of events from the Creation to man's final ascent into Heaven, and to relate this course to the universal plan of Divine Providence. It is the highest achievement of the Protestant mind looking at the whole created cosmos through faith purified and elevated till it coincides with the mind of God. Milton was incurring serious dangers when he made God a spokesman in the poem (though it is worth noting that God is a spokesman rather than a participant in the action); but if we argue (as Sir Herbert Grierson does in *Criticism and Creation*) that it would have been better to omit God, then we are arguing that the poem should have been radically different.

It is with a knowledge of Milton's scope and purpose that we can best discuss the vexed question of his style. Milton himself touches off the controversy (in his prefatory note on *The Verse*) by rejecting rhyme as the 'invention of a barbarous age'; and something of Milton's belligerent spirit of insensitive generalization has entered into the later discussion. Since it is impossible, except in a large book, to examine even the main critical positions on the style, what follows is merely a guide to the discussion.

(*a*) We do not find in Milton either the constant sensuous contact with physical reality, or the frequent alternation of swift intensity with calm slowness, or the profound insight into character and motive which keep most people's interest in Shakespeare alive; and only rarely do we find the short, pregnant phrase which strikes us immediately because of its concrete, aphoristic, or poignant quality. Shakespeare and Pope excel in a kind of condensed poetic vitality, in packing so much meaning into a short passage that the poetic life survives when the phrase is separated from the total work of art to which in Shakespeare and Pope it is usually subordinated. Shakespeare, however, has also a number of phrases (e.g. 'Nothing will come of nothing' in *Lear*) which gather a great deal of meaning from the context, but are rather flat, lacking in rich suggestiveness or connotative power, when taken by themselves.

Much of Milton is like the second kind of Shakespearian language. As is suggested below, Milton was too concerned with an ideal audience, too careless of the reader's ease, approval, or delight. By a combination of indifference to the public and a certain hardening of his mind, he fails to condense his effects, to localize his main interests in short passages. As a result, the analysis of short passages of Milton, unless accompanied by an extensive and rather unwieldy body of exegesis and cross-references, tends to throw the emphasis on what is wrong with the verse – the grandiloquence, the cumbrous involution of phrases, the lack of focus, the remoteness from concrete experience. When we add to this that Milton, in spite of his love of music and in spite of the fact that he dictated the poems orally, had very little feeling for the cadences and emphases of the speaking voice, we find the source of most of the disapproval with which his verse has met. Milton's verse moves with relatively little variety of speed or emphasis. The main point of interest, instead of being precisely localized or standing in sharp relief from the rest, is often lost in the successive surge of clauses. In spite of his close attention to the Psalms and to the Latin periodic sentence, Milton learnt neither pointedness from the one nor strong emphasis from the other. The shifting of focus which enables him to achieve a wide survey in the better sentences leads him into diffusiveness and pointless piling up of effects in the worse. Occasionally, he smothers the main idea by prolonging the sentence too far; by the time we come to line 208 or 355 in *Paradise Lost*, Book I, the point of the comparison has been lost in rather wanton luxuriance. What is true of individual sentences is true of whole passages; it is not, however, so true of the poem as a whole; partly through, and partly in spite of, the accumulative style, the main themes of providence, evil, redemption, and human unity are kept fairly steadily before our eyes. His own kind of preoccupation with God makes the essential themes sufficiently salient, but leads him into a neglect of the human means by which greater appeal and force could be given to them.

(*b*) While Milton had the well-instructed Christian in mind as his reader, the three great poems are not addressed to any particular public in the same sense as, say, Shakespeare's plays. He thought of himself as writing 'general' or 'catholic' works in the manner of the epistles of James and Peter in the New Testament (as contrasted with the 'local' epistles of Paul). It is from this, as well as from the special qualities of his character and genius, that the characteristics of his style derive. For example, he frees himself at once from any need to cater to low taste, to prejudices religious or literary in his readers, and, quite content to alienate the audience which is not 'fit', can treat his topic exactly in the manner which seems right to him. He thus achieves full scope for the use of biblical references (and for a more technical use of them than Shakespeare employed) and for the long-sustained sentence in which he is often at his best. But the fact that he is engaging in so solitary a poetic effort and has no definite group of human beings in mind, encourages him also to indulge his own foibles (as when his love of argument reduces God to a seventeenth-century controversialist – III. 106–28; his views on women make Eve ridiculous and the verse naïve and tumid – VIII. 39–58; or his desire to remain dignified urges him into a pompous parody of his own style – VIII. 4–38).

Of the many penalties Milton paid for his poetic freedom, attention may be directed to one in particular. While he learnt much from earlier writers, he reversed the Renaissance tradition in England. Marlowe, Shakespeare, and Jonson had achieved new effects in drama largely by blending with classical seriousness and profundity the vigour, raciness, and earthiness of the folk mentality. Milton had shown an admiration for the blend in *The Nativity Hymn* (1629) and in *Comus* (1634); but by the time of writing the later poems, his ideas of seriousness, restraint, and religious decorum had narrowed and hardened. His Puritan solemnity eschewed the homely, familiar manner of speaking about divine things which is found in the Psalms and in the medieval plays. Milton marks the point at which reserve and respectability were becoming marked qualities of English life and religion. The arguments of Tillyard, Bush, and many others that the poet must be allowed to 'wear his singing robes' are not very convincing, since the Hebrew and medieval poets wrote of God with much less attention to literary decorum and in a much more conversational idiom than Milton.

In other words, Milton's implied theory of epic is not related to the concrete experience of men in the way in which the theory of epic in Homer or of tragedy in Shakespeare grows out of the way in which men actually feel and speak. Even the best equipped and most sympathetic reader is unable, except at rare moments, to feel himself involved in the story, to be deeply moved, or to find an echo of his own experiences. It is this removal from common experience which makes it so difficult for Milton to do what comes readily to Shakespeare – to create and maintain the mood in which the poetry is enjoyed. Unless we bring the mood to the poem (say, through previous partial readings of it), our impression is like that of an Englishman watching an Oriental ritual – admiring the splendour and the formal patterns of movement, but remaining an external spectator. In *Paradise Regained*, even more than in *Paradise Lost*, Milton's preoccupation with the divine point of view keeps the situations and the speakers at too great a distance from ourselves. And in *Samson Agonistes* it becomes quite apparent that the non-dramatic quality of the language results not only from the calmness of Milton's contemplation, but also from a rigidity of mind which does not accommodate itself sufficiently to the shifting moods of the story. We note, for example, how tenuous is the relation between the speaker and the immediate situation in Dalila's self-defence, and how easily the speech (841–70) could be turned into a messenger's impersonal account of her betrayal. In such respects *Samson* is inferior to the much earlier *Comus*. Milton's independence and artistic solitariness involved him in the loss or decay of powers which a surer critical instinct and a greater need for popular appeal might have led him to cultivate.

(*c*) There are three methods of language (three fusing qualities of the one style) which sustain Milton in the great task he set himself; alternate use of condensation and expansion, structural devices recalling the divine point of view, and a high degree of allusiveness. The three are found in the first eighty lines of *Paradise Lost*. The opening sentence (one of the most condensed in English) contains references to Greek mythology, some dozens of allusions to particular passages in the Old and New Testaments, and is intended to attune the reader's mind to the aspect under which all subsequent considerations are presented. It is not a mere opening flourish of loud trumpets, as C. S. Lewis seems to consider it, but is the first statement of the mood and purpose which Milton wishes to pervade the whole poem. It has a markedly different rhythm from the following section (27–80), which fixes attention on Satan immediately after his fall. The first exchange between Satan and Beelzebub (81–191) is built around clear and varied but subtly appropriate repetitions of the opening theme; he then expands his vision till it includes the whole fallen army, the meaning of

Hell, and the dedication of the devils to evil. After the more detailed description of Book II, he returns to another condensed passage on the central theme in the great address to 'Holy Light' (III. 1–21). Such is Milton's general method: to embrace everything in the opening, concentrate on a particular point, expand it, recall the opening, transfer the scene of the action, and expand again.

(d) The last three poems represent a kind of triumph of language which has no parallel elsewhere in English. Milton lived and worked in three worlds which were in conflict along various fronts: the medieval, the Renaissance, and the Puritan. It was Milton's great achievement to draw on all three, to harmonize the wide range of medieval beliefs with the intense seriousness and sense of responsibility of the Puritan mind and with the Renaissance discussions of the good life and the ideal state. If his psychological insight was weak, he at least shows some of the forces which were at work when modern England was coming into being. His verse is one of the great vehicles by which we come to know the cultural, religious, and political vitality of his times. If it has serious and disconcerting limitations, if it presents no vivid portrait of human beings, it does give a special insight into a religious doctrine and mentality without which we cannot understand what England then was or later became.

NOTES

1. It is worth noting, as one of the points of doctrine necessary to understand Milton, that the whole human race suffers from the Fall of one, while the angels fall individually – they are merely led by Satan who cannot involve others in his sin except by their free consent. This is one of the subtler points which complicates Milton's theology but which helps to shape his verse. It enables him, for example, to reinforce one of his main themes, the unity of the human race (united in one way by its fall in Adam and in another by its elevation in Christ), and to establish a strong contrast between human and angelic guilt, between the bitterness and recrimination in which Adam indulges, and the calmer, more intellectual fixation on evil which he makes so forceful in the devils (e.g. I. 105–9). Milton succeeds unobtrusively in making us feel that fixation, and thus reinforces another theme – the reality of evil.

2. *Paradise Lost* contains many echoes of St Paul's doctrine of the Spirit which Paul himself sums up in 1 Cor. ii. 6–16. It was a commonplace of biblical theology that the Spirit was richer in gifts to the Christians of the New Testament than to the Israelites of the Old.

3. Cf. *Samson*, 322–5.

4. Milton's pneumatology hardly deserves all the space C. S. Lewis gives it in ch. XV of *A Preface to 'Paradise Lost'*. His impressive array of theological authorities does not begin to answer the questions: How good is the poetry of Book VI? Is the humour successful? Is the invention of angelic artillery great epic or is it ludicrous?

5. The point would present little difficulty to Milton's contemporary reader; he would recall, for example, the passage in John's Gospel (vi. 5–6) where Jesus asks Philip, 'Whence are we to buy bread?' ... 'and this he said to prove him; for he himself knew what he would do'.

6. See, however, E. M. W. Tillyard's lengthy discussion of the question in 'The Crisis of *Paradise Lost*' in *Studies in Milton*.

PARADISE LOST: CHANGING
INTERPRETATIONS AND CONTROVERSY

W. W. ROBSON

Milton is such a towering figure in English literature that it is surprising to learn how little impression he seems to have made, as a poet, in
his lifetime. The volume of 1645, which includes such famous poems
as *Comus* and *Lycidas*, did not go into a second edition till 1673. And
the three later poems on which Milton's international reputation rests
– *Paradise Lost* (ten-book version 1667), *Paradise Regained* and *Samson
Agonistes* (both 1671) – appear to have caused, at first, no great stir in
the literary world. But before Milton's death in 1674 the mysterious
forces by which poetic fame is created were already at work, and by
the end of the century his main work, *Paradise Lost*, had already reached
the position it was to occupy, virtually unchallenged, till the 1920s, as
an established classic of English poetry, seeming to have been always
'there', part of the literary environment of every educated person.

Just how this momentous change in the status of Milton came about
is hard to discover, and must remain largely a matter of guesswork.
Scholars have suggested that political opinions played a part in it.
During Milton's life his reputation as an inveterate pamphleteer and
controversialist – in part, probably, a somewhat unsavoury reputation
– may well have stood in the way of his recognition as a poet. The
Roundhead ideologue that he had become eclipsed the scholar-
aesthete and man of taste that he had been in his younger days (and
indeed always remained). But in the years after the Restoration of
Charles II in 1660, Milton's political views may have actually helped
to strengthen his reputation among younger writers and intellectuals,
growing more and more disillusioned about the Stuart monarchy and
full of nostalgia for the days of Cromwell and the Good Old Cause.
From the first Milton's fame as a poet was bound up with his symbolic
status as a defender of 'English liberty'.

However that may be, it is clear as a fact of literary history that the
establishment of Milton's poetry at the centre of the canon of English

literature was due to the 'wits' rather than the 'Puritans'. Paradoxically, it was in the 'age of Dryden' that Milton's greatness as a poet was acclaimed and his poetry became the potent influence on other English verse that it was to be until quite recent times. For by 1667 the poetic revolution inaugurated by Denham and Waller, and brought to consummation and consolidation by John Dryden, had been effected. An atmosphere of wordly wisdom, epigrammatic couplets and metropolitan urbanity now pervaded poetry, suggesting standards of taste and judgement very remote from the solitary, unworldly, unaccommodating visionary. Yet Dryden, the chief poet of the age and most active and influential of its men of letters, Dryden, most generous and catholic in taste of all the great English critics, admired Milton immensely. His mature verse bears splendid witness to the impact of Milton, in his Odes and in *Absalom and Achitophel* and elsewhere. Dryden was on friendly personal terms with Milton, who civilly gave him leave to 'tag' his verses – that is, to produce a rhymed dramatic version of *Paradise Lost* called *The State of Innocence*. And after Milton's death Dryden was to commemorate him in an epigram of 1688 which declares him to have combined the powers of Homer and Virgil. Dryden, then, takes his place in literary history as the first and not the least gifted member of the School of Milton which, with only slight exaggeration, may be said to dominate English poetry for two centuries.

So it is tempting to see this meeting of the minds of Milton and Dryden, partial though it must have been, given the very different temperaments and poetic capacities of the two men, as a crucial factor in the establishment of *Paradise Lost* as the chief monument of the 'Augustan', post-Civil War culture. But some other, more general, considerations are also relevant. First, there was the contemporary concentration on *literary* works and interests, as shown by the flourishing of literary criticism, partly under French influence: no doubt a reaction against the political and religious obsessions of the Civil War and Commonwealth period. The richness of phrasing and verse-music of *Paradise Lost* provided an ample banquet for the scholarly wits and cultivated courtiers of Restoration days. Then there was the still active longing, which goes back as far as the Renaissance, for 'Christian epic': something which the poets of England, like the poets of continental Europe, had dreamed of for centuries. We might think of the Great American Novel as a comparable dream of later times. But while the Great American Novel has never appeared, the judgement of the generations following Milton's was that he actually had created a Christian epic. He alone had the combination of qualifications that were necessary, as the critics of the time saw it, for such a poem: the religious zeal and high spirituality, the command of all the arts and sciences, the reading in literatures ancient and modern, the capacity to make large-scale structures in verse while investing all the local details of the poem with poetic skill and feeling. Finally, and surely not least in importance, we must bear in mind the long-felt need for a great work of English literature, something that would be the equal, at least, of the great Greco-Roman classics. There had been some fine scholars in England since the Renaissance, and some major poets. But in Milton alone the new age saw the unique and happy fusion of the great scholar with the great poet.

Yet even in the early days of Milton's poetic ascendancy doubts and uncertainties began to emerge, which were to break loose in the great twentieth-century questioning of his status, one day to be known as 'the Milton Controversy'. Had *Paradise Lost* after all really performed the miracle, which had defeated all other Christian poets, of harmoniously uniting the two norms of the culture which gave birth to it – the 'Christian' and the 'classical'? Some, at least, of the difficulties that have been found in the poem certainly arise from Milton's decision to treat the theme of the Fall of Man in a form based on the models of ancient epic. And this consideration suggests something deeply paradoxical and problematic about Milton's whole undertaking. He was the most learned of English poets, and perhaps the only one whose work is truly 'classical' in spirit. Yet for him much of what the pagan writers said was not only false, but pernicious. And in recent years scholars have come to see *Paradise Lost* as not so much an 'epic' as a radical *questioning*, a *criticism* (and at times an adverse criticism) of 'epic': in its treatment of norms of the Heroic, not so much a neoclassical homage to them, as almost a parody or an anti-epic. The early critics of Milton did not see the poem quite in this way. But even in the first published appreciation of *Paradise Lost*, Andrew Marvell's verses prefixed to the second edition of 1674, we seem to catch a note of misgiving about the congruity between its matter and its form. Having noted the vast scale of Milton's undertaking (Marvell sees the poem as not merely concerned with the incident of the Fall but with the whole of the fundamentals of Christianity):

> Messiah Crown'd, God's Reconcil'd Decree,
> Rebelling Angels, the Forbidden Tree,
> Heav'n, Hell, Earth, Chaos, All: . . .

Marvell says

> . . . the Argument
> Held me a while misdoubting his Intent,
> That he would ruin (for I saw him strong)
> The sacred Truths to Fable and old Song.

Marvell of course goes on to say gracefully how, as he read, his doubts were overcome by Milton's mighty genius. But the impression still remains, amid all the admiration and respect (Marvell knew Milton personally), of a certain caution and reserve. Similarly we may see an anticipation of much later controversy in Dryden's remark in 1697 that *Paradise Lost* would have been more satisfactory as an epic 'if the Devil had not been his hero instead of Adam'. Dryden's casual tone suggests that it was already a commonplace that Satan was the hero. Addison disagreed (*Spectator*, No. 297): '. . . it is certainly the Messiah who is the hero, both in the principal action, and the chief episodes'. Other critics were to suggest that Adam was the hero, or Adam and Eve together; or the seraph Abdiel, or Milton himself. In our own time the great scholar Sir Herbert Grierson was to rebuke a French writer for raising the question again; in this country, Grierson told him, it has been settled long ago. But has it been settled? Perhaps it has, more strictly speaking, been shelved.

Some of the other questions which early critics and editors brought up, most notably the question of the blank verse of *Paradise Lost*, Milton's innovation in using it for a narrative poem, its various peculiarities – is it a 'sport', or part of the mainstream of English versification? – were to recur later. But on the whole the eighteenth century was the time when the complete *success* of *Paradise Lost*, its total *adequacy* to the needs of the civilization it adorned, were the things that were most emphasized. Its standing as a work comparable in importance to the Classics and the Bible was reinforced by the enormously detailed commentary of Patrick Hume (1695).

But an established classic is not the same thing as a popular favourite. It was Steele in the *Tatler* (1709) and Addison in his *Spectator* papers of 1712 who seem to have brought Milton's poem home to the business and bosoms of ordinary English readers. In the twentieth century, when it is rarely read except by scholars and literary specialists, we are likely to forget how popular *Paradise Lost* once was. It stood on the shelves of every respectable household, beside the Bible and *The Pilgrim's Progress*. The whole literate community, with all shades of opinion from that of the pious John Wesley to that of the sceptical David Hume, paid homage to it. It is a safe guess that in the transmission of *Paradise Lost* to the general eighteenth-century culture the part played by the great educators, the *Tatler* and *Spectator*, was important.

Some continental European scholars have even maintained that Addison's *Spectator* papers really 'made' *Paradise Lost*. But this is probably not true. What Addison does seem to have done is to foster interest in the poem and widen its reading public. Addison's critique of *Paradise Lost* is not today much esteemed. Many would agree with Matthew Arnold that 'it is all based on convention'. And like much else in Addison's writings it may be more distinguished for felicity of expression than for profundity of thought. Nevertheless Addison's critical achievement should not be minimized. It is true that he was very much a man of his time, and respected conventional opinion. He venerated Homer and Virgil, and deferred to 'the rules of Aristotle' as his age understood them. He opposed critics such as John Dennis, who tended to see Milton as an 'irregular' genius, like Shakespeare. He adopted a critical method of his time when he treated his subject under the four headings laid down by the French critic Bossu: fable, character, thought and expression. Addison, then, is 'dated'. But he was less the slave of classical precedents and authorities than most other critics of the day. He showed real independence of mind in judging that Milton at certain times is actually superior to Homer or Virgil, not merely a skilful follower. And he made a sustained attempt, as perhaps some other famous critics of *Paradise Lost* have not done, to capture the spirit of Milton's undertaking, to see the poem as the unique thing Milton meant it to be.

But the importance of Addison's criticism is today mainly historical. It is part of the evidence for the cult of Milton that began to pervade English literature. Milton's influence was now so vast and pervasive that it cannot be summarized. He was parodied, travestied, imitated, like an ancient. Eighteenth-century 'Miltonics' constitute a large proportion of the verse of the time – Thomson, Young, Akenside and the rest. Nor is it only the blank verse poets who are in his debt. The couplet poets draw on him as well. Pope, the chief poet of the age, carried out his own distinctive mutation of *Paradise Lost* in *The Rape of the Lock* and the *Dunciad*. In a single witty line he sums up what many readers have felt about certain speeches in Book III and elsewhere:

> And God the Father turns a School Divine.

Besides the intense and intelligent interest in Milton which Pope showed in his own verse, he made some valuable critical observations in prose. One of these is still very relevant, at a time when Milton has been much condemned as a bad influence on later poets. Pope points out the very *special* purpose of some of Milton's peculiarities of style, as ancillaries to the making of a world that had to be 'created', not 'copied'. He distinguishes Milton from his imitators, who, says Pope,

like most other imitators, are not copies but caricatures of their original; they are a hundred times more obsolete and cramp than he, and equally so in all places; whereas it should have been observed of Milton, that he is not lavish of his exotic words and phrases every where alike, but employs them much more when the subject is marvellous, vast, and strange, as in the scenes of Heaven, Hell, Chaos, etc.[1]

Here Pope has put his finger on what was wrong with much in eighteenth-century Miltonics.

It should not be assumed that the admirers of Milton were so taken with the 'sublime' or 'tremendous' aspect of his genius that they neglected everything else. It is very notable how much Steele and Addison emphasize the 'tender' and the 'pathetic' elements in *Paradise Lost*. They see the treatment of Adam and Eve as contributing to the softening of manners and sentiment after the brutalities of the Restoration – 'melting passions of Humanity and Commiseration'. Milton is thus an important presence in eighteenth-century sentimentalism, as well as in the ambitions of the age to achieve epic grandeur.

The best evidence that *Paradise Lost* was read carefully in the eighteenth century, that the experience of it was not merely a matter of intoxicated self-indulgence in Milton's verbal orotundities and organ-like sonorities, is to be found in the editors and commentators whose work Christopher Ricks has skilfully used in his *Milton's Grand Style* (1963). Much clarification of Milton's way of writing, and illumination on points of detail, resulted from the controversy that arose over the notorious edition of *Paradise Lost* by the great classical scholar Richard Bentley (1732). (This controversy is amusingly discussed, if not with minute accuracy, by William Empson in *Some Versions of Pastoral*, 1935.) Zachary Pearce in 1733, and Thomas Newton in 1749, supply many detailed insights on which a modern scholar is glad to draw. But of these early eighteenth-century Miltonists it is Jonathan Richardson, 'Father and Son', whose 'Explanatory Notes' (1734) are most quoted today, especially the striking assertion that 'a reader of Milton must be always on duty; he is surrounded by sense, it rises in every line, every word is to the purpose; there are no lazy intervals, all has been considered, and demands and merits observation'. This stress on 'sense' is characteristic of the best eighteenth-century criticism of Milton. The prosaicism and literal-mindedness of Bentley are firmly resisted, but without the Romantics' tendency to resort to vague gestures about the 'beauty of sound' or 'magical effect' of this or that reading.

But as the century went on Romantic trends, in criticism as well as in poetry, become more and more evident. They are to be found, in relation to a Miltonic context, in Thomas Warton's edition of the minor poems (1785). It is against the background of this growing Romanticism, and anti-Augustanism, that we must view the most celebrated eighteenth-century critique of *Paradise Lost*, that of Samuel Johnson in his life of Milton (1779). This is one of the most remarkable critical essays ever written, and it has been very influential, probably more so in the twentieth century than in its own time. Johnson's attitude to Milton and his poetry is curious, and not easy to make out fully. It is not clear whether his critique, though memorably phrased, and locally always incisive, is coherent as a whole. In some ways Johnson's treatment of *Paradise Lost* represents the consolidation of the eighteenth-century position. No admirer of Milton could find anything wanting in Johnson's closing tribute, for it is plain that Johnson sees Milton as a great man as well as a great poet.

He was naturally a thinker for himself ... From his contemporaries he neither courted nor received support; there is in his writings nothing by which the pride of other authors might be gratified, or favour gained; no exchange of praise, or solicitation of support. His great works were performed under discountenance, and in blindness, but difficulties vanished at his touch; he was born for whatever is arduous; and his work is not the greatest of heroick poems, only because it is not the first.

It would be easy to arrange quotations from the *Life* so as to make it appear the definitive 'classical' tribute to a great 'classical' work. Johnson calls *Paradise Lost* 'a book of universal knowledge'. He has no fault to find with it on the score of religion or morals. 'Every line breathes sanctity of thought, and purity of manners.' As for the versification, Johnson's tribute to it is all the more impressive because he so strongly disapproves of blank verse outside the drama. He gives a long denigratory account of this verse-form, but then returns upon himself: '. . . whatever the advantages of rhyme, I cannot prevail on myself to wish that Milton had been a rhymer; for I cannot wish his work to be other than it is'. Nothing could better convey the sheer power of Milton's writing than this admission.

Yet most readers of the *Life* have felt, and surely rightly, that Johnson's endorsement of *Paradise Lost* is considerably less than total, and that it is not easy to make his remarks on it 'add up'. It is to be noted that where Milton's other poems are concerned Johnson is not enthusiastic. Perhaps he had in mind the Romantic trend soon exemplified in Warton's edition of the minor poems. At any rate, his castigation of *Lycidas*, a poem that has always been dear to Romantics, is notorious. 'The diction is harsh, the rhymes uncertain, and the numbers unpleasing. Its form is that of a pastoral, easy, vulgar, and therefore disgusting.' Even when this is decoded, as it has to be, the effect is of a severely adverse judgement. Johnson approves of *Comus*, but finds it 'inelegantly splendid, and tediously instructive'. The Sonnets 'deserve not any particular criticism; for of the best it can only be said, that they are not bad'. He thinks *Samson Agonistes* has been too much admired. Johnson, like other eighteenth-century critics, was interested in Milton's poetry, and wrote several studies of it outside the *Life*.[2] But his sympathy with it was clearly imperfect. And where Milton the man was concerned, Johnson's antipathy is hardly disguised. T. S. Eliot, who shared it, is probably right to put it down to political and ideological grounds. The English Civil War had not really ended in Johnson's mind and heart, and Milton had been on the wrong side. Johnson writes as a Tory and a High Churchman. The most unfortunate aspect of this prejudice is that it affected Johnson's approach as a biographer. Passing over the lives of Milton by people who knew him, and who presented him as pleasant and likeable, Johnson preferred inferior traditions which he found more in keeping with the 'acrimonious and surly republican' he believed Milton to have been.

Literary criticism is supposed to rise above personal prejudices. But it is difficult to write fairly about the work of a man you loathe. Perhaps this is the reason why Johnson's reservations about *Paradise Lost* have stuck in the minds of readers more than what he says in praise of it. Many of his criticisms, limiting, qualifying, or adverse, were to be taken up and developed in the nineteenth and twentieth centuries; a good deal of what, for instance, Eliot, Leavis or Waldock were to say is already anticipated in Johnson's remarks about Milton's 'faults'. Some of the points he makes are relatively minor in importance. He objects to the 'unskilful allegory' of Sin and Death. He finds the Paradise of Fools 'a fiction . . . too ludicrous for its place'. He queries the conduct of the action here and there; for instance, 'Satan is with great expectation brought before Gabriel in Paradise, and is suffered to go away unmolested'. Other criticisms are more radical. 'Milton's design,' he says, 'requires the description of what cannot be described, the agency of spirits', and he finds a 'confusion of spirit and matter' in the war in Heaven. C. S. Lewis in his *Preface to Paradise Lost* (1942) opposed Johnson on this point, referring to contemporary speculations about the possible materiality of angels; but A. J. A. Waldock's *Paradise Lost and its Critics* (1947) has plausibly argued that some of Johnson's objections still remain unanswered – and wonders if they can be. But Johnson's main criticisms of the poem strike deeper. They involve radical questioning both of subject and style. The plan of *Paradise Lost*, he says, 'comprises neither human actions nor human manners. The man and woman who act and suffer, are in a state which no other man or woman can ever know.' Granting Milton's soundness as a moral and religious teacher, Johnson observes that

these truths are too important to be new; they have been taught to our infancy. They have mingled with our solitary thoughts and familiar conversation, and are habitually interwoven with the whole texture of life . . . the want of human interest is always felt . . . Its perusal is a duty rather than a pleasure.

Given the importance of 'human interest' and 'pleasure' among Johnson's literary criteria, it is difficult to reconcile these pronouncements with his general judgement:

> Such are the faults of that wonderful performance *Paradise Lost*, which he who can put in balance with its beauties must be considered not as nice but as dull, less to be censured for want of candour, than pitied for want of sensibility.

As for style, it is here that Johnson has been most influential; and it is here that he is most equivocal. Some of his censures had been anticipated by earlier critics: Addison had said that 'our language sunk under him'. But Johnson stated what was to become the Eliot–Leavis 'case' against Milton's handling of the English language in the most incisive and (seemingly) the most condemnatory way. Speaking of the 'uniform peculiarity of *Diction*' in Milton, he says: 'Both in prose and verse, he had formed his style by a perverse and pedantick principle. He was desirous to use English words with a foreign idiom.' Twentieth-century anti-Miltonists have been happy to enlist Johnson's support on this point, a central one for them. F. R. Leavis speaks of Milton's rejection of English idiom, and ascribes this to his addiction, over so many years, to polemics in Latin. Johnson, however, was inclined to ascribe the exoticism of Milton's style to Italian influence, anticipating the argument of F. T. Prince in our own day (*The Italian Element in Milton's Verse*, 1954). But the most important difference between Leavis and Johnson here is that for Leavis the supposedly unidiomatic quality of Milton's style is a matter for condemnation. Johnson is more equivocal. Having said that Milton 'was desirous to use English words with a foreign idiom', he goes on:

> This in all his prose is discovered and condemned; for three judgment operates freely, neither softened by the beauty, nor awed by the dignity of his thoughts; but such is the power of his poetry, that his call is obeyed without resistance, the reader feels himself in captivity to a higher and nobler mind, and criticism sinks in admiration.

On the face of it Johnson has made a big concession to the Romantics here. But how deep does it go? Is there not an oblique suggestion that the suitable reader of Milton's verse is under a sort of hypnotic spell?

It is easy to see, then, why Johnson's life of Milton was widely resented at the time. The poet Cowper, to whom Milton meant so much both as a poet and as a man, wrote that he would like to thrash Johnson's old jacket till his pension jingled in his pockets. Milton was already, as Leslie Stephen says, a taboo figure for criticism. In some ways Johnson can be taken to represent the typical eighteenth-century attitude to Milton, but in other ways he is more in tune with influential critics of the twentieth century.

For the moment literary opinion was not with him. A strong tide of Romanticism was running. And it is noteworthy that the Romantic movement, which attacked much that the eighteenth century admired, did not turn against Milton. On the contrary: Milton's fame was revived and refreshed by the poets of the new century. Wordsworth assailed the 'poetic diction' of the eighteenth century, much of which seems to the literary historian to derive from *Paradise Lost*. But as Wordsworth and Coleridge saw it, Pope was to blame for that, especially in his translations of Homer. Like Shakespeare, the other English idol of the eighteenth century, Milton was acclaimed by the Romantics as representing the true English poetry, in contrast with the artificiality and pseudo-poetry of the Augustans. The Romantics, both of the Wordsworth generation, and of the Keats / Shelley / Byron generation, were much more enthusiastic about Milton than the traditionalist critics, such as Jeffrey or Lockhard or Gifford.

The Romantic poets, of course, were very much individuals, and Milton meant different things to them. To Wordsworth, Milton was a kind of spiritual father and forerunner. He admired Milton's personality: 'Thy soul was like a Star, and dwelt apart'. He saw Milton as patriotic, noble and responsible in a time, like Wordsworth's own, of conflict and national danger: 'England hath need of thee'. It was the reading of Milton's sonnets that inspired him to write his own. *The Prelude* is full of echoes of *Paradise Lost*, and indeed Wordsworth's whole undertaking in this long autobiographical poem can be regarded as a sort of Romantic 'answer' to Milton. The mode of *The Prelude* may be seen as a development of those beautiful personal passages with which Milton opens Books III, VII and IX of his poem. And Wordsworth, like Milton, admired Spenser and was influenced by his work, so that the 'line' Spenser–Milton–Wordsworth is established for the history of poetry. Coleridge too greatly admired both Milton's poetry and his character. He had been a Miltonist before he became, under German influence, a Shakespearean; his earlier verse shows much Miltonic colour, both direct and through Gray and other 'Miltonic' poets of the eighteenth century.

The appreciation of Milton by Wordsworth and Coleridge may have been more intense than the Augustans'. But on the moral and religious side their attitude to *Paradise Lost* does not seem greatly different. Neither of them questions Milton's orthodoxy, any more than Johnson does. Johnson is typical of the eighteenth century in his untroubled assumption that the theology of *Paradise Lost* is in complete conformity with the mainstream of Christian tradition. But for the younger Romantics, who were themselves in revolt against Christianity, the possibility of an antinomian Milton, secretly subverting the official orthodoxy, was attractive. In this notion they may have been anticipated, though they did not know it, by an eighteenth-century thinker, William Blake. Blake wrote in his cryptic *Marriage of Heaven and Hell* (1793) that 'the reason Milton wrote in fetters when he wrote of Angels & God, and at liberty when of Devils & Hell, is because he was a true Poet and of the Devil's party without knowing it'. What exactly Blake meant by this can only be discovered by studying his own system of thought: Blake was, in his way, as complex and enigmatic a poet-mystic as Milton, and Denis Saurat is not the only modern scholar to draw attention to the affinities between them. If his remark is taken straightforwardly, the use of the phrase 'without knowing it' suggests that Blake's position was nearer to that of modern critics like E. M. W. Tillyard or A. J. A. Waldock, who argue that Milton made Satan a more attractive figure than he consciously meant to, than to the 'Satanists' of the Romantic period.

'Satanism' came to mean various things in the nineteenth century. But one thing all 'Satanists' have in common is the treatment of Satan as a character important in his own right, and the real centre of interest in the poem. It may be wondered whether they read much further than Book II of *Paradise Lost*: but of course it is open to a Satanist to reply that the first two Books are the only ones that really matter. At any rate, some of the Romantics saw the God of *Paradise Lost* as a tyrant and believed Satan's revolt against him to be justified. Shelley wrote in the *Defence of Poetry* (1821): 'Nothing can exceed the energy and magnificence of the character of Satan in *Paradise Lost*. It is a mistake to suppose that he could ever have been intended for the popular personification of evil.' Shelley described the wrongs of Satan as 'beyond measure'. His view of the poem has been developed fully in an extraordinarily brilliant and provocative book of our own time, William Empson's *Milton's God* (1961): 'The poem is so good,' says Empson, 'because it makes God so bad ... The poem is wonderful because it is an awful warning not against eating the apple but against worshipping that God.' This is, in essentials, the Shelleyan position. Byron agreed that Satan was the hero of the poem. And the 'Byronic hero' which was, for a time, to fascinate Europe, though of course largely based on elements of Byron's own personality, derives in part from the Satan of Romanticism, the villain-hero whose 'baleful' eyes have inspired a whole literary tradition from *Jane Eyre* to *Light in August*. It would seem that from the historical point of view this ambivalent symbol is the greatest of Milton's creations.

Coleridge did not see Milton's Satan as Byron and Shelley did. In his lecture of 1818 he holds a persuasive balance between moral condemnation and a positive imaginative response to the great figure of the fallen Archangel. 'The character of Satan is pride and sensual indulgence, finding in self the sole motive of action.' 'Sensual indulgence' is not very obvious in the poem, but perhaps Coleridge attached a special meaning to this expression. More persuasive is his account of Satan's 'restlessness, temerity and cunning which have marked the mighty hunters of mankind from Nimrod to Napoleon'. He speaks of Satan's 'intense selfishness, the alcohol of egotism'. But around this character Milton 'has thrown a singularity of daring, a grandeur of sufferance, and a ruined splendour'. This is 'the very height of poetic sublimity'. Coleridge's remarks suggest a more balanced view of Satan than Byron's or Shelley's, one based on a more complete induction, which takes into account the self-revelatory soliloquy in Book IV, and later stages of the story.

It is curious that while renewed attention was being given to the meaning of the poem, which the Augustans had tended to take for granted, little or no use was made by literary critics in this period of that astonishing treatise *De Doctrina Christiana*, which was discovered in 1823 and first published in translation, from Milton's Latin, in 1825. This is the most thorough and systematic exposition of Milton's theological views, and reveals him as a very original and in some ways very unorthodox religious thinker. Twentieth-century scholars have made much use of it in discussing the question whether or not *Paradise*

Lost expresses Milton's private heresies. We may speculate whether the *De Doctrina* would have made more impact if it had been discovered earlier – perhaps for its advocacy of polygamy, if not for its views on the Trinity. But it does not seem to have influenced nineteenth-century ideas about Milton very greatly. It was discussed: the young Macaulay wrote his famous essay on Milton under the pretext of reviewing it. But we have the impression that the nineteenth century had really ceased to care much about Milton's thought, one way or another. His aim to 'justify the ways of God to men' received merely formal notice. Attention was more and more concentrated on the fictional and dramatic aspect of his work, together with his style (that 'magnificent invention', as Leavis calls it).

In some ways the attitude of Keats was to foreshadow much Victorian, Edwardian and modern criticism of Milton. Keats's view of *Paradise Lost* has different facets, and it is closely connected with his own problems as a poet. He wrote the beautiful, if puzzling, fragment *Hyperion* with the deliberate aim, it would seem, of cultivating a 'Miltonic' kind of art, but abandoned it in dissatisfaction. He found too many 'Miltonic inversions' in *Hyperion*, a want of 'the true voice of feeling'. It may have been unwise of twentieth-century critics like Middleton Murry and Herbert Read to generalize Keats's rejection of Milton ('Life to him would be death to me') into a wholesale condemnation of Milton's influence on any poetry. But in the same letter (of 21 September 1819) Keats describes *Paradise Lost* in terms which might have been accepted by many nineteenth-century readers, when he calls it 'a corruption of our language'. 'It should be kept as it is – unique – a curiosity – a beautiful and grand curiosity.' We may couple this with an earlier reference to Milton in a letter of 3 May 1818, in which Keats says: 'Wordsworth is deeper than Milton'. Milton 'did not think into the human heart, as Wordsworth has done'. (We must remember that Wordsworth 'spoke' to the nineteenth century as he does not speak to the twentieth.) For many in the Victorian age Milton remained on his pedestal as a master of language, a word-musician. But *Paradise Lost* was a kind of 'sport', a curiosity, essentially inimitable. Apart from his peculiar linguistic genius Milton was not interesting. His thought was a mere paraphrase of orthodox commonplaces; and his personality was unpleasant.

Such, at any rate, seems to have been the view of the leading

Victorian critic, Matthew Arnold. Arnold did not question the traditional position of Milton, as second only to Shakespeare. But like Landor, De Quincey, and other nineteenth-century eulogists of Milton, he tended to base it mainly on stylistic grounds. For Arnold, Milton embodies in many ways the ideal of classicism which Arnold saw as a needed corrective in his own time: dignity, sanity, just subordination of detail, due adaptation of means to ends, the high respect of the craftsman for his craft and for himself. 'Milton,' he wrote in 1888, 'from one end of *Paradise Lost* to the other, is in his diction and rhythm constantly a great artist in the great style.' But this is very much the official Arnold, the champion of the Grand Style, the high decorum which he most decidedly did not find in England's supreme writer, Shakespeare. In another mood, discussing the iconoclastic views of the French critic Scherer, Arnold candidly admits that he finds the characters in *Paradise Lost* lacking in interest and coherence, and the theological speeches of God the Father repellent.[3] As Charles Williams was to say in 1940, late Victorian academic orthodoxy had established the notion of 'an august, solemn, proud, and (on the whole) unintelligent and uninteresting Milton'.[4]

The liveliest Victorian critic of Milton, Walter Bagehot, writing in 1859, was much more concerned than Arnold with what *Paradise Lost* actually *said*. Bagehot sees it as essentially a *political* poem; the whole action starts from a political 'job', God the Father's sudden exaltation of the Son, which touches off the revolt of the angels. Bagehot's witty, cynical tone is refreshing after the solemn moralizing of so many Victorian Miltonists, and his essay anticipates modern views. Thus like Tillyard he sees the balance of the poem as disturbed by the presentation of Satan, and like Waldock he notices Milton's habit of, so to speak, getting his poem back on course by authorial comments designed to rebuff or tone down what Satan says. Bagehot makes the poem seem challenging and enjoyable, but he does not consider it successful. 'So far from Milton having justified the ways of God to man, he has loaded the common theology with a new encumbrance' – Satan's heroism.

The more reverential Victorian Miltonists were ready to grant Milton, officially, more success in the handling of his theological theme. But it must be remembered that this was a time when the impact of Darwinism and Higher Criticism of the Bible, and the prestige of Victorian science, were doing much to empty it of substance. We get the impression from David Masson's monumental life of Milton (1858–81) that what really matters in *Paradise Lost* is not the argument but Milton's personality, the austere noble Puritan and champion of the Good Old Cause, a Great Man in the Carlylean mould.

The various trends of nineteenth-century thinking about *Paradise Lost* were assembled and consolidated in Walter Raleigh's witty handbook of 1900. It is clear from this critique that by the end of the century the poem still retained its high traditional standing, but that this standing was now very precarious. Raleigh treats Milton with great respect. He quotes Johnson on the poet's 'gigantick loftiness', and Landor's comparison of his verse with the music of Handel. But it is plain that *Paradise Lost* does not appeal deeply to his head or his heart. It is a wonderful *tour de force* of pure style; just trembling on the edge of absurdity, but saved by Milton's unfailing mastery of words. 'We find ourselves in a remote atmosphere ... All is power, and vagueness, and grandeur.' *Paradise Lost* retains its immortality, not because of any profound thought or rich humanity, but through sheer power of style. Otherwise, it is 'a monument to dead ideas'.

Perhaps a whole-hearted supporter of the aestheticism of that time would have had no difficulty in reconciling this view with the traditional acceptance of *Paradise Lost* as a great classic. But for Raleigh, a disciple of Johnson, this cannot have been so. In his book nineteenth-century academic orthodoxy is on the verge of collapse. It is only a short step from Raleigh's 'all is power, and vagueness, and grandeur' to Leavis's 'after the first two books ... *Paradise Lost* ... becomes dull and empty'. No one can sustain interest in so long a poem if it has, essentially, nothing to say.

But in the twentieth century scholars began to question the assumption, so prevalent in the eighteenth and nineteenth centuries, that the meaning of *Paradise Lost* was simple and obvious. Until quite recent times few would have dissented from Addison's view: 'The great Moral ... which reigns in Milton is the most universal and most useful than can be imagined: it is in short this, *that Obedience to the Will of God makes Men happy, and that Disobedience makes them miserable.*' But in our times book after book, essay after essay, has appeared to show that the thought of the poem is nothing like so straightforward as it looks. American scholarship led the way: Edwin Greenlaw's 1917 article in *Studies in Philology* is usually credited with launching the new Miltonism or, as it came to be called, Christian Humanism. Greenlaw argued that the sin which led to the Fall was 'intemperance', and his investigation of what this meant to Milton led him back to Spenser and Book II of *The Faerie Queene*. Other Miltonists like Tillyard and C. S. Lewis disagreed with this interpretation; but they all concurred with other scholars, British, American, and continental European, in their preoccupation with Milton's handling of the Fall, and its moral and psychological subtleties. For Tillyard (1930), everything in *Paradise Lost* is subordinate to the human theme. Satan and the angels, God and his Son, are only of background interest: the real centre of the poem is the struggle in the minds of Adam and Eve. In contradiction of the vulgar belief about Milton's 'Puritanism', these scholars emphasized Milton's fearless treatment of unfallen sexuality, his insistence that Adam and Eve had physical relations before the Fall, his rapturous picture of naked beauty unashamed. Indeed the upshot of the whole Christian Humanist movement was the denial that Milton was a 'Puritan' in any limiting sense. He should be seen as a Renaissance artist, essentially a humane writer, and one whose underlying thought and world outlook had less in common with the sectaries than with authors like Spenser or Shakespeare, Hooker or Bacon.

It is fair to say that twentieth-century Milton scholarship has been dominated by Christian Humanism, though there are still some, like Haller, who stress the older concept of Milton as a Puritan, and others, like Saurat, who insist on the more unorthodox and antinomian aspects of his thinking. But a full account of all this flood of publication is impossible. What has to be said is that while Milton's thought, and the culture that underlies his work, his manifold sources, theological, scientific, and literary, were being studied as never before, the presence of Milton as a great poet and human force, a living part of English literature, was becoming more and more doubtful and ambiguous. We have now come to the 'Milton Controversy', the very influential movement, led by a number of twentieth-century poets and critics, to marginalize Milton's poetry, and in particular *Paradise Lost* (it was on that poem that the fire of the anti-Miltonists was concentrated).

Credit, or responsibility, for this questioning of Milton is usually assigned to the leading poet of the age, T. S. Eliot, together with the most provocative and controversial literary critic, F. R. Leavis. But there are many signs of indifference to or dislike of Milton in other circles which had no particular sympathy with twentieth-century trends in poetry. The decline of interest in verse generally, and in long poems in particular, and their supersession as the main literary form by the novel, have to be taken into account. Whatever the Christian Humanists might urge, there was a lack of interest in the Fall and Original Sin as providing, even in a symbolic way, any true interpretation of humanity's problems. There was a widespread assumption that Milton had been a gloomy, narrow-minded 'Puritan'. Above all, we must remember the virtual disappearance of the Classics and the Bible as effective parts of literary culture. Shakespeare, and most English authors before the twentieth century, are of course deeply in debt to the Classics in all sorts of ways. But Milton is in a unique position of disadvantage here, because he is the only English poet who even arguably succeeded with the classical forms of epic and drama. And Biblicism pervades his three last poems in every detail. Like the Racine of *Athalie* and *Esther*, he was steeped in the Scriptures. But what was once a link between his work and ordinary readers has now become a barrier.

The Eliot / Leavis critique, then, came when the time for it was propitious. Other modern writers had already come out against Milton. Ezra Pound in 1914 called him 'the worst sort of poison'. In *Notes on Elizabethan Classicists* (1917) Pound denounced him for 'his asinine bigotry, his beastly hebraism, the coarseness of his mentality', Ford Madox Ford, Middleton Murry, Herbert Read, all expressed dislike of Milton's stiff, unnatural, pompous style. Today none of these attacks seems particularly impressive or interesting. Only Eliot's two essays, of 1936 and 1947,[5] and Leavis's chapter in *Revaluation* (1936)[6] and his discussion of Eliot's second essay in *The Common Pursuit* (1952), are likely to be remembered, of all that was written in Great Britain and the United States in the course of the controversy.

To the reader who comes to Eliot and Leavis with some knowledge of previous Milton criticism there does not appear to be much that is new in what they say; both of them, indeed, cite Johnson in support of it. Both critics work within 'formalistic' assumptions; that is, they profess to be concerned solely with Milton's poetry 'as poetry'. The discussion, then, turns on style, on the handling of words, although both critics do not conceal their distaste for Milton's subject-matter and attitude: Eliot has 'a glimpse of a theology that I find in large part repellent, expressed through a mythology which would have been better left in the Book of Genesis, upon which Milton has not improved'; Leavis considers that the 'myth' of *Paradise Lost* 'suffers from deficiencies related to those of the verse'. But the main point of the attack is Milton's style. Eliot writes as a practising poet, concerned to explain why Milton had been a bad influence on poetry, and could only be a bad influence. He thinks that Milton's sensuousness was withered by his book-learning, and that his blindness led to an over-development of aural effects in his verse to the exclusion of all others. For Eliot there is little to visualize in *Paradise Lost*. There is nothing much but 'mazes of sound', which Milton delights in for their own sake, at the expense of any concern for conveying his meaning. Leavis's remarkable depreciation begins by calling in Eliot for support, since he thought that Milton's 'dislodgment' was really due to Eliot's 'creative achievement' as a poet, which had placed the history of English poetry in a new perspective.

The essence of Leavis's case is that the 'pattern' of Milton's verse, 'the stylized gesture and movement', 'has no particular expressive work to do, but functions by rote, of its own momentum, in the manner of a ritual'. Unusually good passages, like that on Mulciber (I. 740–46), where the verse-movement really is expressive, only show how external and mechanical it is elsewhere; such exceptions prove the rule. Leavis sees Milton's Grand Style as having 'renounced the English language'. He finds a 'sensuous poverty' in the description of the Garden of Eden in Book IV, a lack of 'sharp, concrete realization'. Though Leavis refers to the poetry of Donne as a standard for expressiveness, it is clear that the main contrast is with Shakespeare. 'Even in the most lively books of *Paradise Lost* the verse, brilliant as it is, has to the ear that appreciates Shakespeare a wearying deadness about it.'

There have been many attempts to rebut Leavis's account, some rejecting the criteria he works with, others accepting them but trying to show that Milton's verse does actually comply with them. Probably the most dubious aspect of Leavis's argument is its conception of a Miltonic 'average' or norm of style; many readers of *Paradise Lost* are doubtful whether it has *one* style that can be adequately represented, and dealt with critically, on the basis of a few selected passages. But the chapter of *Revaluation* raises so many issues of literary criticism, literary history and literary theory, not to speak of more fundamental educational and moral questions, that it cannot be discussed briefly. Eliot's second essay, which some have seen as an attempt to dissociate his position from Leavis's, does not advance the question much further. It would seem that at present attention has shifted away from the argument about style to the broader questions of Milton's handling of his story, his 'myth'.

It is here that A. J. A. Waldock's *Paradise Lost and its Critics* (1947), hailed by Leavis as bringing support to his own case, has been the critical storm-centre. Waldock, like Bagehot before him, finds all sorts of inconsistencies, emotional disharmonies in the poem. He considers that, at what he calls the 'crisis' of the poem when Adam decides to disobey God and defy death because of his passionate love for Eve, *Paradise Lost* 'breaks': the reader is being asked to react in incompatible ways, to feel with the full force of his mind that Adam acted rightly, and that he acted wrongly. Waldock considers that Milton got into this dilemma because he had not sufficiently pondered the problems he was bound to encounter in enlarging the cryptic story in *Genesis* to the proportions of a vast epic.

These debates go on. At present Ricks's *Milton's Grand Style* (1963) is widely regarded as the most effective treatment of the problems raised by Leavis and Eliot; while of the many attempts to show that, contrary to Waldock's opinion, Milton did indeed succeed in writing the poem he meant to write, D. H. Burden's *The Logical Epic* (1967) seems the best. Meanwhile, as Bernard Wright says in his book on Milton (1962), *Paradise Lost* 'is not nowadays widely read or highly regarded'. W. R. Parker, whose life of Milton (1968) has superseded Masson's, says sadly that 'after having disliked Milton's ideas for three centuries, while admiring his poetry, the English have finally decided ... that the poetry too is bad'.

It is possible that a new stimulus may come from the growing interest of contemporary radicals in their great predecessor. The historian Christopher Hill, in his 1977 study of Milton, declares that it is 'quite wrong to see Milton in relation to anything so vague and generalized as "the Christian tradition". He was a radical Protestant heretic.' He 'rejected the Trinity, infant baptism and most of the

traditional ceremonies, including church marriage; he queried mono-
gamy and believed that the soul died with the body'. Hill thinks that
Milton's poetic reputation stands today as high as ever. But he has
become 'the poet of scholars and academic critics' – no longer either a
people's poet or a poet's poet. Whether we agree with Hill's point of
view or not, it seems clear that nothing but good can come from the
rejection of a restricting formalism and the return of Milton's poetry,
and the analysis and appreciation of it, to the real historical world and
the intellectual, moral and spiritual concerns of actual men and
women.

NOTES

1. A. Pope, *Postscript to the Odyssey* (1723).
2. See his *Rambler* articles 86, 88 and 94 on Milton's versification, and 139
and 140 on *Samson Agonistes*.
3. M. Arnold, *Mixed Essays* (1879).
4. C. Williams, introduction to *The English Poems of Milton* (World's
Classics, 1940).
5. T. S. Eliot, 'Milton I' and 'Milton II', in *On Poetry and Poets* (1957).
6. Originally an article in *Scrutiny*, II (1933).

PROSE AND THE DISSOCIATION
OF SENSIBILITY

IAN ROBINSON

The age of 'prose and reason' was Matthew Arnold's characterizing phrase for the English eighteenth century, and the collocation is useful. Prose and reason went together before our Augustan age, though. When Malvolio is shut up in horrible darkness he addresses a letter, in prose, to Olivia, to prove his sanity. Feste tries to read the letter in a mad voice befitting the supposed state of its writer; but when the letter is read as its style demands it has its desired effect:

By the Lord, madam, you wrong me, and the world shall know it. Though you have put me into darkness and given your drunken cousin rule over me, yet have I the benefit of my senses as well as your ladyship. I have your own letter that induced me to the semblance I put on, with the which I doubt not but to do myself much right or you much shame. Think of me as you please. I leave my duty a little unthought of, and speak out of my injury.

THE MADLY-US'D MALVOLIO
(*Twelfth Night* v. i)

What establishes Malvolio's sanity is not so much what he says as that he can say it like this. So too if Hamlet's letter to Horatio had been intercepted he could no longer have been thought mad. The prose is the reason. But our idea of reason may change, with rather important consequences, along with our prose.

Shakespeare was rare in his age in writing ordinary competent English prose, as well as in his better-known achievements. The Renaissance brought with it a demand for a new style of scholarly English prose for biographies, histories, philosophy, criticism . . .; at first there was no effective way of meeting the demand. Naturally the aim was to do in English what had been done in the Latin of the classical age, particularly by Cicero. English periodic sentences were to be written like his Latin ones. The true Ciceronian movement where the structure of the subordinate clauses is clamped together by a main verb held back to the end was never really an English possibility, but learned writers did what they could. Latinized diction is a well-known characteristic of many Renaissance writers including Shakespeare; this attempt to impose Latin syntax on English was a much more important vote of no confidence in the language to hand. The results bear out T. S. Eliot's remark about the absence from the English sixteenth century of a 'mature prose'. Here, for example, is a bit of Roper's life of More:[1]

There tarrying for his coming, as soon as she saw him, after his blessing upon her knees reverently received, she hasting towards him, and without consideration or care of herself, pressing in among the midst of the throng and company of the guard, that with halberds and bills went round about him, hastily ran to him, and there openly in the sight of them all, embraced him, took him about the neck and kissed him. Who well liking her most natural and dear daughterly affection towards him, gave her his fatherly blessing, and many godly words of comfort besides. From whom after she was departed, she not satisfied with her former sight of him, and like one that had forgotten herself, being all ravished with the entire love of her dear father, having respect neither to herself, nor to the press of the people and multitude that were about him, suddenly turned back again ... [and so on for five lines before the next full stop].

Strange to relate, if this passage were put word for word into Latin it would not be at all bad and would have the ordinary prose virtues of ease, fluency and clarity, so conspicuously lacking from the English.

Much English prose of the sixteenth and seventeenth centuries needs several readings and close attention before its sense can be grasped. It strikes one as inordinately laborious, and anything but ordinary. One of Sir Thomas Wyatt's editors remarked that verse came to him as naturally as leaves to a tree: oddly enough prose did not. Read this aloud quickly and see whether you have any idea at the end what has been said:

And what is more uncomely, than that in suche plays we syt with suche pertynax scylence doing nothing els (as they say) (for there is no man that lamenteth or wepeth, when he seeth Pythia begyn, no more than he is hungry after the feest) and those good ly[ke]nesses whereof god hym selfe is auctor unto us, and in maner player, with lamentying, and sowernesse of mynde, ledyng a dolorous lyfe, we defile and make sorowfull.[2]

The oddity of easy verse and tortuous prose persists right down to Milton's day. Though so decidedly of the Puritan party, Milton himself wrote prose as unprosaic as anything from the King's side, and deliberately scorned short sentences. The result, in my experience, is that his prose is now unreadable. Yet, like Wyatt's, his verse is perfectly controlled – too much so, some have thought. One very rarely gets lost in the long sentences of *Paradise Lost*: the poet's masterfulness allows no stress out of place. Deprived of metre and of modern syntactic control, Milton's prose sprawls. The reader launches off hopefully from one full point towards the next, which may be three pages away, much like Satan flapping through Chaos in the direction of Paradise.

The wandering or Latinate prose had already in the sixteenth century inspired a reaction, from the Ciceronian to the Senecan as they thought at the time,[3] but really from a lengthy style into one of artificially pointed antitheses just as far from anything we could recognize as ordinary prose, but perhaps closer to English idiom as found in the law courts, the pulpits and the tradition of alliterative verse descending from Middle English. The two styles coexisted. Both are found in the work of Bacon, the 'Senecan' most obviously in the essays:

READ not to contradict and confute, nor to believe and take for granted, nor to find talk and discourse, but to weigh and consider. Some *Books* are to be tasted, others to be swallowed, and some few to be chewed and digested; That is, some *Books* are to be read only in parts; others to be read but not curiously, and some few to be read wholly, and with diligence and attention ... Reading maketh a full man; Conference a ready man; and Writing an exact man; and therefore, if a man write little he had need have a great memory; if he confer little he had need have a present wit; and if he read little he had need have much cunning, to seem to know that he doth not.[4]

Euphuism, a style that would survive only in histories of the literature were it not that Falstaff's parody preserves a little life to it, is another development of this obviously artificial antithetical manner:

I, but she is bewtiful; yea, but not therefore chast: I, but she is comly in al parts of the body: yea, but she may be crooked in some part of the mind: I, but she is wise, yea, but she is a woman! Bewty is like the black-berry, which seemeth red, when it is not ripe, resembling pretious stones that are polished with honny, which the smother they look, the sooner they breake. It is thought wonderful among the seamen, that Mugil, of all fishes the swiftest, is found in the belly of the Bret, of al the slowest: And shall it not seeme monstrous to wisemen, that the hearte of the greatest con-querour of the worlde, should be found in the handes of the weakest creature of nature? of a woman? of a captiue? Hermyns haue faire skinnes, but fowle

liuers; Sepulchres fresh colours, but rotten bones; women faire faces, but false
heartes.   (John Lyly, *Campaspe*[5])

The latinate and artificial prose of the sixteenth century constituted
a distinct break with English tradition.[6] There was a mature English
prose long before any of these tortuous or frothy writers; English
prose has a continuity from the Anglo-Saxon period and did not suffer
at the Conquest the same deep interruption as courtly English verse.
This old prose of the native tradition is quite unlike Renaissance
latinizings; it works on a different principle and does not aspire
towards the periodic sentence.

In fact Middle English prose is not written in sentences at all. This
may seem an extravagant contention and no doubt it would be
possible to conduct a syntactic analysis of selected words from, say, the
Ancrene Riwle and declare them to form sentences, though the gram-
marian who approached fifteenth-century proseworks with the intention of analysing their syntactic structures would be frequently
confronted with the Chomskyan spectre of the million-word sentence. Or rather, the decisions about where sentences began or ended
would be quite arbitrary.

The old prose did not work like the modern written paragraphs:
like the old verse, from which it is not so sharply distinct as modern
prose is from modern metrical verse, it is built of two-beat phrases held
together by the stress-patterns within and between phrases.[7] Rhythm
is more important than syntax, even when there is syntax. Characteristically the old prose will not have much syntactic subordination but
will consist of strings of shortish main clauses connected by 'and' or
'but'. If it is not monotonous (as of course it can be) that can only be
because of the way the rhythm instructs us to read. If this sounds vague
one can produce a huge well-known example, for the old prose
reached its final flowering, contemporary with the wanderings I have
quoted and in the lifetime of Shakespeare.

I refer, of course, to the English Bible. The *Authorized Version* of
1611, a conservative reworking of the Reformation versions which
themselves descend from the Middle Ages, is the consummation of the
old prose. Its rhythmic units are basically similar to the two-beat
phrases of alliterative verse. By a happy coincidence the Psalms go
very easily into English because the stress habits of English permit an

effective poetic style imitating the quite different Hebrew metre. This is nevertheless prose not verse, and, in all its distinction, an ordinary prose, capable of being written in large quantities by people without individual genius and in a manner developed from a tradition well established for nearly a thousand years:

God be merciful unto us, and bless us: and cause his face to shine upon us.
  That thy way may be known upon earth, thy saving health among all nations.
  Let the people praise thee, O God; let all the people praise thee.
  O let the nations be glad and sing for joy: for thou shalt judge the people righteously, and govern the nations upon earth.
  Let the people praise thee, O God; let all the people praise thee,
  Then shall the earth yield her increase; and God, even our own God shall bless us.
  God shall bless us, and all the ends of the earth shall fear him.

(Psalm lxvii)

Here the individual phrases are built into the larger unit of the verse by various relations of similarity and contrast between them, and so on upwards to the larger units which in turn, as wholes, control the basic phrase-rhythms. Modern reprintings of the Bible in verseless paragraphs are the perverse imposition upon it of modern prose practice, for the verse is the essential intermediate unit between phrase and paragraph. Here we have an instance of the old necessary paradox about rhythm: the parts derive from a whole which is, however, only made by the relation of the parts. The unity of thought of this psalm controls the phrasing and verse-pauses of which it is made.

Since T. S. Eliot coined the phrase 'dissociation of sensibility' for what happened to English after the Civil War, much ink has flowed through the scholarly periodicals, and his idea (which is, I think, essential for the understanding of English history) is not now in favour. But it surely could be agreed that if we put together Shakespeare's tragedies and the Bible, belonging to the same decade and the same language, we have an *association* of sensibility which generations of readers have found to be the characterizing expression of the genius of the English language.

Only fifty years after the Bible and the Folio Shakespeare sensibility, or the language, had changed so drastically that both were of the old, vanished, unreproducible world, though both were kept in use in the new present. The name commonly associated with the new state of affairs is that of John Dryden, though it is one of the marks of the new age that, unlike Shakespeare's, it can have no one predominant genius.

Dryden's prose is as far from the paratactic prose of the Bible as it is from the Latinate learned prose contemporary with it. Dryden achieved his mastery of English prose even before his mastery of the heroic couplet. The Preface to *Annus Mirabilis* is modern, the heavy quatrains of the poem itself are archaic.

Dryden's great achievement was the development and perfect naturalization in English prose of the periodic sentence. We have seen what happened when a son-in-law of More tried to write English with the Latin periodic sentence in mind. The true Augustan English prose inaugurated by Dryden, the true imitation of Latin, is English through and through, but when in his first considerable prose work, the *Essay of Dramatic Poesy*, Dryden quotes 'Tully', the Latin runs with the English like an elder brother. To call Dryden's prose periodic is not to deny Johnson's observation about its informality, and I do not mean by the term the sonority of Johnson himself. I mean that in Dryden's prose the spoken rhythms of the sentence – 'the sentence' being a concept we now need – follow from the syntactic shape of the sentence. In much of the older prose the clauses or phrases may be individually pungent and pithy but are not really part of any larger whole, so that the reader gets bogged down trying to connect them. With Dryden the movement of the sentence through its main and subordinate clauses draws, with great ease and confidence, the speech phrases after it. This shaping, like the idiomatic phrasing, is English and not Latin. Nevertheless Dryden is doing for English something much like what Cicero did for Latin:

> After they had attentively listned till such time as the sound by little and little went from them, *Eugenius*, lifting up his head, and taking notice of it, was the first who congratulated to the rest that happy Omen of our Nation's Victory: adding, we had but this to desire in confirmation of it, that we might hear no more of that noise which was now leaving the English Coast.[8]

Here the opening temporal clause is not haphazard but the right articulation of sense, and the two participial clauses immediately following the subject of the sentence are not a bit clumsy. The real mark of mastery here, though, is what follows 'adding'. This word in the older writers would have been the licence for an indefinite pro-liferation of wandering phrases. In Dryden it introduces something which beautifully rounds off, in a perfectly natural speaking voice, what is truly a sentence. The length is the opposite of the old wanderings; a whole is made which is clear, logical, articulate – and which also insinuates, I think, that we are all, all the time and nothing else, beings fully accountable for in this brisk, robust style of social common sense. There are no more things in Dryden's Heaven and earth than can be brought into this beautiful natural prose of 'reason, truth and nature': beyond it is mere madness.

Punctuation is one mark of the new prose: here we meet punctuation that is syntactic, not rhetorical or metrical. For the first time a semi-colon is a clause-division not a longish pause, and a mark of admiration (!) a note that what grammar views as an exclamation has been uttered, not necessarily that we must read with emphasis. Modern punctuation took some time to become universal in the printing trade. The loyalist historian Sir Thomas Dugdale frequently has full points between major clauses where we would have colons or semi-colons, or even commas, for he will sometimes start a new sentence with what we should regard as a relative clause of the previous sentence. Bishop Berkeley, as late as *The Principles of Human Knowledge* (1710), does the same. As it was scribbled before being printed, much Augustan prose was punctuated by dashes. (Samuel Richardson, a professional printer before he became a novelist, thinks it worth telling us that his heroine Clarissa's letters are always nicely punctuated.) This is to see prose from the point of view of the speaking voice, still as two-beat phrasal. It remains true that the phrases have a new interrelationship which can be usefully pointed in the modern manner. It was not until Sterne that the long punctuation dash was elevated to the dignity of the printed page.

What Dryden did rapidly became an example of what any gentleman could do, even if not so well. We now take modern prose so much for granted as to make it worth remarking that there was nothing inevitable about the particular style modern prose took, though one may certainly call it fatal. The losing side threw up other possibilities. At the same time as Dryden was attuning himself to the spirit of a new age, Milton, Bunyan and Marvell were all still at work. They had been preceded by the puritan pamphleteers and letter-writers, not least Cromwell himself:

> Sir, God hath taken away your eldest Son by a cannon-shot. It brake his leg. We were necessitated to have it cut off, whereof he died.
>
> Sir, you know my own trials this way: but the Lord supported me with this, That the Lord took him into the happiness we all pant for and live for. There is your precious child full of glory, never to know sin or sorrow any more. He was a gallant young man, exceedingly gracious. God give you His comfort.[9]

This manly plainness is surely that of a true prose, and one out of which we can imagine a modern development: evidently, however, this prose does not make any break with the tradition behind the Bible.

Bunyan is more strongly suggestive of what an un-Drydenesque modern prose might have been like. He too belongs to the new age and writes sentences, but they are not quite the sentences of Arnold's age of prose and reason:

> Then I fell to musing upon this also; and while I was thinking on it, and fearing lest it should be so, I felt my heart sink in despair, concluding it was too late; and therefore I resolved in my mind I would go on in sin: for, I thought, if the case be thus, my state is surely miserable; miserable if I leave my sins; and but miserable if I follow them: I can but be damned; and if I must be so, I had as good be damned for many sins as be damned for few.[10]

This has a wit recognizably belonging to the age of the heroic couplet, though the antitheses are more those of basic English folk wisdom than of the artificial, applause-seeking pointedness of the coffee-houses; Bunyan can include more in prose than Dryden. The orthodox Augustan tone excludes religion.

The other writer I will mention from the losing side who does hint at other possibilities for prose is, I think, not religious. Andrew Marvell (1621–78), the great poet, is plainly at the end of the age of Shakespeare. The depth of the *Horatian Ode* is in its full perception of tragedy in the history of the revolution; the unique Marvell note is the clarity of judgement in which the unreduced tragic events are held, so that, in that characteristic fineness of balance which is the opposite of fence-sitting, the *Horatian Ode* is also a comic poem. The poem allows me to understand these events, as Clarendon or Dugdale do not, as the culmination and political enactment of Shakespeare's great tragic theme, the death of the royal father. The imaginative range of the language also descends from Shakespeare. In Marvell's poems of the 1650s one still sees the Shakespearean association of sensibility. But under Charles II, as an important leader of the Country Party in a determinedly untragic world, Marvell fell in verse into comparative triviality. His Flecknoe poem is funnier even than Dryden's, with a surprise in every line: it is close to speech, lively, anything but polite and decorous. But the life is that of a squib, and there is never any clear line in Marvell's Restoration verse between satire and squib. (Which is that very lively piece *The Character of Holland*?) Some of his best parliamentary effects were practical jokes.

Marvell's prose is more of a bid for the centre, though one that did not succeed. I will take my examples from the first few pages of *The Rehearsal Transpros'd*[11] in the hope of inspiring a few readers to look at the rest:

> *Put up your Trumpery good noble Marquess.* But there was no holding him. Thus it must be, and no better, when a man's Phancy is up, and his Breeches are down; when the Mind and the Body make contrary Assignations, and he hath both a Bookseller at once and a Mistris to satisfie: Like *Archimedes,* into the Street he runs out naked with his Invention.

This is certainly prose of the age of Dryden – fluent though complex, close to the witty speech of the coffee house. But I think there is more life in it than in Dryden in the form, if the word be admissible in literary criticism, of more *fun*. Marvell will sometimes write a long periodic sentence; he will use such frameworks as 'Firstly . . . secondly . . . but chiefly . . . lastly'. But 'having had our Dance', he says, 'let us advance to our more serious Counsels': the prose is as much a dance as the satirical verse and the serious counsels do not prevent its being so. Marvell is not himself to be accused of running out naked into the street with his invention, for he still has his sardonic poise. He can indeed rebuke Bramhall for indecorum. His range includes a kind of grand style and stern rebuke; it is close to the character of one very individual man, but is nevertheless prose, part of a general possession:

> He could never have induc'd himself to praise one man but in order to rail on another. He never oyls his Hone but that he may whet his Razor, and that not to shave, but to cut mens throats. And whoever will take the pains to compare, will find, that it is his only end; so his best, nay his only talent is railing. So that he hath, while he pretends to much for the good Bishop, used him but for a Stalking-horse till he might come within shot of the Forreign Divines and the Nonconformists. The other was only a copy of his countenance: But look to your selves, my Masters; for in so venomous a Malice, Courtesie is always fatal. Under colour of some mens having taxed the Bishop, he flyes out into a furious Debauch, and breaks the Windows, if he could, would raze the foundations of

all the Protestant-Churches beyond Sea: but for all men at home of their perswasion, if he meet them in the dark he runs them thorow.

This is prose of the new age, but not confined to 'prose and reason': it is imaginative, it enacts, it is by a poet who has not turned into something else in order to write prose. Read *Antony and Cleopatra* next to Marvell's prose and see the survival of Enobarbus.

I am anxious not to cast Dryden as the villain of this piece: his prose too has a fluency that is certainly that both of the man himself and of the conversational milieu of Will's Coffee House where he sat pontificating. In its origins modern prose was not mechanical or removed from life. What is more, there is something passionate and committed about it. At the end of the seventeenth century reason, common sense, moderation, was seized upon with passionate intensity. The belief, the philosophical department of the new prose, that all proper discourse is descriptive and propositional, was embraced with emotional fervour. Men abandoned themselves to 'reason' as in a previous age they had fought 'like mad or drunk / For Dame Religion as for punk'.

It is not always fully realized how the development and imitation of a style commits a writer and makes a world. Our world is limited by our styles of making sense, as well as created by them. The individual is the rhythm of his styles. There is a necessary and useful paradox: we make sense individually or not at all; on the other hand the styles in which we make sense are not the creation of any individual. The great common styles are those to which there is a common commitment.

Modern prose is not a fact of nature but one of the styles of the English language. In it we constantly remake and commit ourselves to our own versions of the world it makes possible. We are drilled in English prose at school, unless we are very unlucky; we become easily proficient in it and express, without worrying much about the mode of expression, a wide range of the senses we individually make. A restriction is always a permission: modern prose permits us to express very many senses. There is point here, however, in drawing attention to the fact, of great importance in our history, that from its inception in the days of Dryden modern English prose *has* been restrictive.

Modern prose began as the worship of a peculiarly restricted notion of reason and it committed its writers to that eighteenth-century world of 'reason-truth-and-nature'. That was the *telos* aimed at by the heterogeneous parties to the Restoration coalition: the scientists of the Royal Society, the philosophers, the gentlemen and wits. Their creation was of a world in which, shall we say, Addison was perfectly at home. Their reaction against the religious and imaginative excesses of the preceding age was no doubt, as Matthew Arnold himself finely recognized, necessary, and without it we could not have the modern world. But then, the modern world is sometimes found by its inhabitants to be lacking in some of the qualities we can see in the Shakespeare tragedies or in the English Bible. The new age developed no new language of religion and went on using the old – until (I write in the year of the publication of the Church of England's *Alternative Service Book*) its recent common abandonment and replacement by the frankly and irreligiously prosaic. The eighteenth century, as the legitimate heir of classical civilization, was determined to have its proper quota of verse tragedies, but *couldn't*. Poetry had been taken over by the new prose[12] and Dryden was notoriously indifferent on one occasion as to whether he should write verse or run his sense into the 'other harmony' of prose. His own tragedies are either prosaic, however decorous (as *All for Love*), or, taking deliberate flight beyond prose and reason, straightforwardly raving mad.[13] The freedom from prose and reason really is, for Dryden, the denial of all sense.

The new prose could not encompass the range of imagination of the metaphysical poets, the depth of religious language in 1611, or the passion and adventure of Shakespearean tragedy. It had already found its first nemesis in Book IV of *Gulliver's Travels*, published 1726, where it is the worship of reason – or one might as well say prose – as exemplified in those damned horses, that itself drives Gulliver certifiably insane. The Houyhnhnms have no religion, no politics, no philosophy, no poetry, no love, no quarrels, because they have taken prose and reason as far as it will go. A later nemesis is the nineteenth-century and modern academic prose which seems to be aspiring towards the linguist's dream of language manufactured by computer. This is not what Chaucer or Shakespeare would have understood as reasonable. If our world is that of modern prose it does suffer from a certain impoverishment: we are not, in Lawrence's phrase, so 'vitally conscious' as our forefathers if our ordinary written language is without some of the essential powers of theirs.

Dryden himself had an imagination, however severely he held it in check, and we see in him for the first time a sort of Augustan syndrome. Poetry survived as attack, and not, despite Pope's claims, attack in defence of the prose virtues. Pope and Swift both made poetry out of coprophilia, a fact which, though unmistakable, our academic establishment is naturally anxious to deny. Only by way of the mock-heroic, the mock-tragic, the seamy, could the eighteenth century come close to its heroic, tragic ambitions and give any freedom to the imagination. It was not until William Blake and the wonderful generation of the Romantics that English poets again made a head-on push towards new creation beyond the limits of the Augustan rational; as is well known the romantic outburst was remarkably short-lived, and as is less well known it hardly affected prose at all. Wordsworth, for instance, writes the prose of an eighteenth-century gentleman.

The real, long-enduring effort to reclaim the written language for imagination, religion and passion, has been that of the English novelists from Richardson to D. H. Lawrence, with Jane Austen and Dickens to remind us that imagination, religion and passion may well belong to comedy. It is the English novel which, so far as it has been done, has rescued English from the dissociation of sensibility; and it has done so by subversion, working within the Dryden mode to leaven that lump. But that, of course, is another and very various set of stories.

NOTES

1. *Sir Thomas More: Selections from his English Works and from the Lives by Erasmus and Roper*, eds P. S. and H. M. Allen (Oxford, 1924), 33.

2. Modernized from the quotation in Kenneth Muir, *Life and Letters of Sir Thomas Wyatt* (Liverpool, 1963), 11.

3. cf. Brian Vickers, *Francis Bacon and Renaissance Prose* (Cambridge, 1968).

4. *The Oxford Book of English Prose*, ed. Sir Arthur Quiller-Couch (Oxford, 1925), 141.

5. John Lyly, *Campaspe; The Pelican Book of English Prose* Vol. I, ed. K. Muir (Harmondsworth, 1956), 185.

6. The indispensable work here has been done by R. W. Chambers in an essay originating as the introduction to Harpsfield's life of More and now published separately by the Early English Text Society as *On the Continuity of English Prose from Alfred to More and his School*. It will be seen that I disagree with Chambers – by his own light, I think – about what happened to English prose in the sixteenth century. My own view is necessarily stated here in a much truncated form: I hope one day to unpack it.

7. On the rhythms of the prose and verse of Middle English cf. my *Chaucer's Prosody* (Cambridge, 1971).

8. *An Essay of Dramatic Poesy*; repunctuated from *The Works of John Dryden* Vol. XVII (California, 1971), 9.

9. Thomas Carlyle, *Cromwell's Letters and Speeches* (London, 1845 and reprints), letter xvi.

10. *Grace Abounding to the Chief of Sinners*, ed. R. Sharrock (Oxford, 1966), 12–13.

11. Gregg facsimile edn of *The Rehearsal Transpros'd* (repr. Farnborough, 1971), 10.

12. 'Our literature required a prose which conformed to the true law of prose; and that it might acquire this the more surely, it compelled poetry, as in France, to conform itself to the law of prose likewise.' (Matthew Arnold, Preface to *The Six Chief Lives from Johnson's 'Lives of the Poets'* (1881), xxiii – a work indispensable to this subject.)

13. I am here much indebted to work in progress by Mr C. J. Purvis.

MARVELL AND THE LINE OF WIT

FRANK W. BRADBROOK

During the nineteenth century Andrew Marvell (1621–78) was chiefly remembered as a public figure, a Puritan who was a defender of toleration as well as of individual liberty. The revival of interest in his poetry in this century coincided with the fashionable cult of John Donne and the metaphysical school of poets. But Marvell was also the subject of one of the finest of T. S. Eliot's essays, a piece of criticism that remains the best introduction to the poems. Marvell's reputation depends upon a few lyrics, but within this small compass there is great range and variety. His quality is best seen in such poems as *A Dialogue between the Resolved Soul and Created Pleasure*, *To His Coy Mistress*, *The Definition of Love*, *The Garden*, *An Horatian Ode upon Cromwell's Return from Ireland*, the pastoral dialogues and 'mower' poems, *The Picture of Little T.C. in a Prospect of Flowers*, *The Nymph Complaining for the Death of her Fawn*, some of the stanzas of *Upon Appleton House*, *On a Drop of Dew*, and *Bermudas*.

The exact date of composition of the majority of Marvell's poems is not known. The first collected edition was not published until 1681, and except for two copies this omitted one of the finest of his poems, *An Horatian Ode*, which was not generally printed until 1776. Some of the best-known lyrics, including *The Garden*, were almost certainly written during the two years (1650–52) that Marvell was tutor to the daughter of General Fairfax at Nun Appleton House in Yorkshire. 'It was as the result of those years of uniquely peaceful and agreeable life, in his own country, and in such a setting of learning, piety, and rural privacy, that Marvell seems to have produced his best work'.[1]

A Dialogue between the Resolved Soul, and Created Pleasure is a soliloquy in which two opposing impulses debate with each other. The martial and biblical imagery of the opening, based on Ephesians vi. 16–17, is common in the literature of spiritual struggle. It is to be found, for instance, in Bunyan's *Holy War*. But though there is an atmosphere of siege in Marvell's poem, the attitude of the poet towards his subject is ironical. The almost jaunty rhythm emphasizes the playfulness with which the theme is to be treated:

> Courage my Soul, now learn to wield
> The weight of thine immortal Shield.
> Close on thy Head thy Helmet bright.
> Ballance thy Sword against the Fight.

The sense of the poem appears to be simple and straightforward at first reading, though it depends for its final effect on delicately veiled puns and double-meanings, and on the subtle use of rhythm. The word 'balance' suggests rhythmically its meaning. One can feel the swords crossing and sliding against each other, and the balance of the sword in the hand. With its further suggestion of delicately poised scales it is an image of the debate which is to follow between 'Pleasure' and 'Soul' (emotion and reason). The soul 'holds the balance' or has the power to decide, and its actions and opinions are 'weighed' by the demands of pleasure. Yet behind the antithesis there lies harmony. The replies of the soul are gentle and genial. There is a suggestion of the dance as well as of the debate. The battle is a battle of wits in which pleasure woos the soul and finally surrenders to it. Moreover, the pleasures with which the soul is tempted are the delicately sensuous ones of nature and of art. Its resistance to them is firm without being priggish, the firmness being implied in the terse epigrammatic replies which contrast with the generous expansiveness of the temptations. The detachment of the poet is also underlined by this neatness and by the slight air of exaggeration of the dialogue, the first part of which ends with an image of music and the paradoxical but stern reply of the soul:

> Cease Tempter. None can chain a mind
> Whom this sweet Chordage cannot bind.

'Chain' implies not merely 'fetter' but the chains used on board ship to fasten shrouds, and thus connects with 'thy stay' and the 'fall' referred to in the previous stanza by Pleasure. 'Chordage' re-emphasizes the imagery of music. But it also supports the nautical suggestion of 'chain', and appropriately rounds off the exchange with mathematical neatness. The power of Marvell's poetry is partly owing to this ability to use such an apparently simple word (a sixteenth-century refashion-

ing of 'cord') with such different meanings as the harmonious combination of notes, the straight line joining the extremities of an arc, the
string of a musical instrument (in this sense first used by Milton), a rope
used for hanging, and in the figurative sense used in the Bible ('the
cords of sin' and 'the cords of friendship').[2]

The chorus returns at the end of this section to the imagery of battle:

> *Earth cannot shew so brave a Sight*
> *As when a single Soul does fence*
> *The Batteries of alluring Sense,*
> *And Heaven views it with delight.*

The word '*fence*' refers back to the 'ballance' of the opening of the
poem, but also includes the sense of the noun which meant not only 'a
barrier' but 'a bulwark'. At the beginning of the poem the fight had
been imagined as one between two armies: this first section of the
poem ends with the imagery of a sea-battle.

Pleasure continues the contest with the temptations of sex, wealth,
glory, and knowledge, and the Soul replies to these Mephistophelian
baits with Socratic scepticism. The situation is dramatic, almost that of
a morality play, and the rejection of knowledge in favour of humility
finally clinches the argument. The completeness of the victory of the
Soul is stressed with an almost burlesque exaggeration by the chorus at
the end of the poem. The poet himself remains detached. The attitude
towards the subject is very different from that in the much lengthier
treatment of the theme by Milton in *Comus*.

The Soul is not allowed the same triumph in another poem of
Marvell's entitled *A Dialogue between the Soul and Body*, where, on the
contrary, it is the Body which has the last word. The imagery of chains
and fetters reappears to describe the subjection of the Soul, and there is
a similar use of paradox and exaggeration to create an effect verging
on comedy. But in the second dialogue the Soul and Body reflect
antithetically. Whereas the first reminds one of Milton, the couplets
and personifications of the second look forward to Pope.

The use of paradox and exaggeration to produce an effect of
comedy is one aspect of the wit that Eliot pointed to in his essay as
characteristic of the poetry of Marvell. He describes it as 'an alliance of
levity and seriousness' by which the seriousness is intensified. 'Wit,' he
continues, 'is not erudition; it is sometimes stifled by erudition, as in
much of Milton. It is not cynicism, though it has a kind of toughness

which may be confused with cynicism by the tender-minded. It is confused with erudition because it belongs to an educated mind, rich in generations of experience; and it is confused with cynicism because it implies a constant inspection and criticism of experience. It involves, probably, a recognition, implicit in the expression of every experience, of other kinds of experience that are possible.' This quality of wit, defined elsewhere by Eliot as 'a tough reasonableness beneath the slight lyric grace', was inherited by Marvell from his literary master Ben Jonson. It pervades all of his best poetry, and is found in a particularly concentrated form in his love lyric *To His Coy Mistress*.

The general idea on which this poem is based is classical: the belief in the virtue of enjoying oneself while one is still young ('*Carpe diem*') has been so often made the subject of lyric poetry as to be in some danger of becoming commonplace. Like Ben Jonson's *Song to Celia* ('Come my Celia let us prove'), Marvell's *To His Coy Mistress* derives directly from the well-known theme of the Latin poet Cattulus ('*Vivamus, mea Lesbia, atque amemus*'), though in its details it is original. The treatment of the theme of time is both witty and imaginative, the effect being gained, as so often in Marvell, by the combination of rhythm and ambiguity:

> My vegetable Love should grow
> Vaster than Empires, and more slow.

'Vegetable' means 'having the power of sense-perception' as well as 'like a plant' (the Latin *vegetabilis* actually suggests speed and is equivalent to 'animating', 'enlivening', 'lively', 'quickening').[3] The anti-climax is gained by the contrast between the size of the love and the time it takes to grow, and rhythmically this is given in the verse by the sudden pause in the middle of the second line, and the three dead, heavy monosyllables, emphasized by the long-drawn-out vowels. The reader taking 'vegetable' in its Latin sense would meet a sudden contradiction and reversal of meaning.

The tone and movement of the verse both suddenly change in the second section of the poem, achieving that effect of surprise noted by T. S. Eliot:

> But at my back I alwaies hear
> Times winged Charriot hurrying near ...

Then, pausing again, the poet concentrates the thought of death into a single brief and vivid image:

> Desarts of vast Eternity.

The verse renders perfectly the feeling of desolation and the sense almost of betrayal that comes with death. The epigrammatic force of this line and the reflections on the horrors of the tomb which follow it could be paralleled in many of Donne's lyrics where he contemplates this subject. The description of the opening of his own tomb in *The Relique*, for instance, has the same epigrammatic force:

> And he that digs it, spies
> A bracelet of bright haire about the bone ...

Marvell treats the theme rather more lightly. He is mainly concerned with death as a means of frightening his mistress and as a contrast with the invitation to love contained in the final section of the poem. Vital and dynamic, love is contrasted with the coldness and silence of the tomb where the only movement is that of the worms, and with the dullness and monotony of a humdrum passive life, the iron gates through which love must tear its way. Time and death, the theme of so much Elizabethan and seventeenth-century poetry, are conquered by love as they were conquered by nature in Marvell's other great lyric, *The Garden*. The means by which the poet reaches this climax after the leisurely and apparently digressive opening is a triumph of control and of organization. The verse gradually quickens, until at the end there is again a sudden pause, accentuating by contrast the momentum of the previous lines, giving the last two lines a note of finality:

> *Thus*, though we cannot make our Sun
> *Stand still*, yet we will make him run.

The Definition of Love shows Marvell at his most metaphysical, and even closer to Donne in style and subject than in *To His Coy Mistress*. It consists of eight four-lined stanzas and deals with the subject in the formal manner befitting 'a definition'. Puns, ambiguities, paradoxes, and double-meanings are common to both poems, but whereas the subject of one is desire and fulfilment, the other deals with despair and the impossibility of desire ever being fulfilled. Despair is paradoxically described as 'magnanimous'. The lover is overwhelmed by the excellence of the person loved: to hope would be a sign of superficiality. The excellence of the loved person is matched by the despair of the lover. To complain at the impossibility of fulfilment would be a proof of petty-mindedness. This is a complete statement of platonic love. The soul is described as both 'extended', drawn out to unite itself with the other soul, and 'fixed', kept firm and stable because its attention is constantly directed towards the other. The soul is 'fixed in' the loved person so that they are both one and part. But events (the 'iron wedges' of fate) kept them separate. Their love would not be so perfect if this were not so. Moreover, if they could unite physically, fate, in the sense of death or destruction, would herself be destroyed. So fate separates them with her decrees of steel like the sword placed down the middle of the bed to ensure chastity. Though the whole world of love 'wheels' about them, they can never embrace. They are as distant as the two poles. To unite them the earth itself would have to be flattened as on a map. Here, again, there is a typical paradox. For the verb 'cramped' ('cramp'd into a Planisphere') suggests the noun. The world could be held flat only by a strong iron bar which would still separate the lovers.

This image is continued in the next stanza with the mathematical figure of the oblique and parallel lines. Obtuse lovers, like obtuse angles, can meet anywhere, like 'the dull sublunary lovers' of Donne's *A Valediction: forbidding mourning*, which Marvell's lyric closely resembles. In Donne the communion of the two souls is compared to 'gold to ayery thinnesse beate' and to two arms of a compass, while their separation is like 'a trepidation of the spheares'. Both poems contrast ordinary worldly lovers, who are neither truly one nor separate, with the lovers who can be so united only because they are apart from each other, like the parallels of latitude on the globe. They are parallel, too, in the sense of spiritually corresponding to each other; their relationship is only so perfectly proportioned because they are analogous, two similar or identical spirits. Fate 'debarrs' the union, but by doing so 'unbars' their love (the French *débarrer* has the contrary sense to the English verb). The lovers may be poles apart physically, but mentally they are like two heavenly bodies in proximity to each other.

The great strength of Marvell is his ability to make poetry out of such paradoxical and complex material. He is much less slight and light than many other poets who self-consciously adopt an attitude of profundity. *The Definition of Love* is no mere display of intellectual fireworks, but a graceful and perfectly proportioned lyric. All the resources of rhythm are used, and emotion is generated by the very simplicity of the form. In such a poem of apparently bare statement, the slightest mistake in the choice of words would be disastrous. But there is an inevitability both in the detail and in the development and building up of the argument. The argument is not so much stated as embodied in the verse, as in the lines on hope in the second stanza, with their sensitive use of rhythm, rhyme, imagery, and alliteration.

There is a similar kind of philosophical argument, though with a much more strongly stressed natural background, in *The Garden*. The garden itself is a complex symbol. Marvell has a real garden in mind, the garden of Lord Fairfax at Nun Appleton House, and it is freshly and vividly described. But it is compared with the garden of Eden and hence represents symbolically the state of innocence, as Keats was much later to use autumn as a symbol of fruition and maturity. Philosophically the Garden is associated with the school of Epicurus, and the poet seems partly to share his view that the highest good is pleasure (particularly sensuous enjoyment). Pleasure is synonymous with virtue. From another point of view the garden is an indication of an ideal of human character. (In one of the early biographies of Sir Thomas More his personality is similarly described in terms of a garden, and his various characteristics in terms of flowers.) This use of a symbol with layers of allegorical interpretation ends in poetry with Marvell. It was a literary tradition and a habit of mind that connected the metaphysical poets with the Elizabethan dramatists and with medieval usage. It is to be found still later on in the century in prose in the work of Bunyan.

The Garden is opposed in every way to ambition and to the coarser worldly amusements. The palm, the symbol of victory and the prize for excellence, the oak, which was the civic crown, and the bay leaves, awarded as an honour to poets, are all rejected. That this should be done in a poem celebrating, among other things, the beauty of trees, is a characteristic paradox. The trees mock the human beings who use their leaves for such trivial and ridiculous purposes. Their mockery is prudent in case humanity retaliates by cutting them down. The poet, by implication, chides and reproaches too. As the home of innocence and quiet, the pleasures of the garden and the woods are reserved, as in Milton's *Il Penseroso* (a much lighter treatment of a similar theme) for the solitary and thoughtful man. Human love itself is rejected in the third stanza. The beauties of the garden excel those of any mistress; no woman could give such a constant love as nature. The gods themselves are shown finding solace in nature for frustrated sexual passion, and it is even hinted, in a characteristically witty paradox, that the quiet of nature was what they were really seeking:

> *Apollo* hunted *Daphne* so,
> Only that She might Laurel grow.
> And *Pan* did after *Syrinx* speed,
> Not as a Nymph, but for a Reed.

Then follows an impassioned and voluptuous wooing of the poet by nature. After the rejection of human love all the emotions associated with it are regained in the garden itself. To this extent the poet is like the gods. Nature, as here described, is very different from the rather languorous 'mellow fruitfulness' of Keats's autumn. It is active, almost in a state of revolt:

> What wond'rous Life is this I lead!
> Ripe Apples drop about my head;
> The Luscious Clusters of the Vine
> Upon my Mouth do crush their Wine;
> The Nectaren, and curious Peach,
> Into my hands themselves do reach;
> Stumbling on Melons, as I pass,
> Insnar'd with Flow'rs, I fall on Grass.

Marvell succeeds in conveying the tactile sense of the fleshy ripeness of the apples and the sound of their falling. The adjective 'luscious' gives both the smell and taste of the vine clusters which crush their wine on his mouth. The nectarine, though a kind of peach, naturally suggests by its sound and derivation 'nectar', the drink of the gods in Greek mythology. The peach itself is 'curious' in the Latin sense of 'full of care'. It is considerate, as well as strange, surprising, and odd. The poet may stumble and be ensnared, but his fall is a soft one.

In the sixth stanza the emphasis changes suddenly from the body and the senses to the mind itself. The mind 'withdraws' after all this activity of nature and in self-contemplation reaches a state of peace:

> Annihilating all that's made
> To a green Thought in a green Shade.

This means either 'reducing the whole material world to nothing material', i.e. to a green thought, or 'considering the whole material world as of no value compared to a green thought'.[4] Green was the colour for lovers,[5] so that the 'withdrawal' of the mind is not egoistic or a mere absorption in its own perfections. It 'creates' as well as 'withdraws'. The poet now reaches the highest and most impersonal state of contemplation and of love. He regains the primal state of innocence and purity. Then his attention returns to the outside world and he sees in a floral sundial the symbol of nature's permanent conquest over time that he himself had temporarily attained through nature. By its sweet smells and sounds the sundial measures time more effectively than the sun itself. Time has no power over the flowers, herbs, and industrious bees. On the contrary, without them time would not exist; they indicate and measure the passage of time. The garden and nature are not merely healthy influences in the Wordsworthian sense – they are symbols of the triumph over decay and the other morbid influences of time.

The version of *The Garden* that exists in Latin is a reminder of Marvell's debt to the classical poets. In some of his minor pastoral poems there are resemblances to the Eclogues and Georgics of Virgil, themselves an imitation of the Greek pastoral poems of Theocritus. Marvell's debt here is shared by Spenser in his *The Shepheardes Calender,* Sidney, and many of the Elizabethan lyric poets through whom he assimilated the influence. *To His Coy Mistress*, on the other hand, treats themes common in the poetry of Catullus and Horace, and it is the Horatian influence that is the most important in Marvell's poetry, as it had been in that of Ben Jonson before him. The polished and graceful transitions from one state of mind or feeling to its opposite, the appreciation both of the countryside as a retreat and of the town and Court as providing standards of manners and behaviour, the mixture of gallantry and cynicism, the concern with the problems of death and time with its natural corollary of '*carpe diem*', are to be found in both Horace and Marvell. Of one of the greatest of Marvell's poems, *An Horatian Ode upon Cromwell's Return from Ireland*, Goldwin Smith remarked: 'Better than anything else in our language this poem gives an idea of a grand Horatian measure, as well as of the diction and spirit of an Horatian Ode.'[6] The resemblance to Ben Jonson's *Ode to Himself* ('Come leave the lothed Stage') has also been pointed out, while in parts of the poem, such as the passage praising Cromwell and the description of the death of Charles I, there are numerous verbal echoes from Lucan's *Pharsalia*.

An Horatian Ode also provides a clear indication of the character of the poet himself. Marvell expresses sympathy with the King, but thinks that Cromwell is more efficient as a ruler. Viewing the conflict between them impartially, he is able to see the virtues of both men, and the human and dramatic situation interests him more than the clash between parties and principles. Cromwell is the man of the moment, 'moved by and yet driving [line 12] a power which is above justice [line 37]'. But Charles is the more attractive as a person. The detachment and impersonality are typical both of the poet and the man, and are evident even at the climax of the Civil War. Marvell remains independent, and without being irresponsible is in a sense above the struggle.

The first few lines of the poem call upon the youth of England to reject poetry and take up arms. Marvell himself, however, had not yet given up poetry, and the poems composed at General Fairfax's residence were written during the next two years. The attitude towards Cromwell and the war is, from the beginning, one of tolerant approval rather than of enthusiasm.

Marvell admires Cromwell's past life more than his present triumphs, and the central passage praising him anticipates the mood of *The Garden*:

> Who, from his private Gardens, where
> He liv'd reserved and austere,
>   As if his highest plot
> To plant the Bergamot . . .

The ideal way of life celebrated in *The Garden* is that lived by Cromwell himself in retirement. Just as 'th' industrious Bee' in the garden 'computes its time as well as we', so Cromwell with his 'industrious Valour', rifling the state as the bee rifles the flowers, climbs 'to ruine the great work of Time'. As the poet describes the struggle between Cromwell and Charles, the dramatic tension increases and the language becomes complex with puns:

> Where, twining subtile fears with hope,
> He wove a Net of such a scope,

> That *Charles* himself might chase
> To *Caresbrooks* narrow case.

'Subtile' is used partly in the old sense of 'finely woven', and 'case'
means both 'plight' and 'cage'. Whether the cage in which Charles is
trapped is that of a lion, a mouse, or a butterfly is left characteristically
ambiguous, but there is no doubt of the sympathy expressed for the
King when facing his death. While there is a suggestion of the
flamboyant and theatrical in the picture of 'the Royal Actor' adorning
'the Tragick Scaffold', Charles is still capable of moving the armed
bands of soldiers, and by the picture of them clapping their bloody
hands the reader's sympathy is also drawn to him. At this point Charles
compares favourably with Cromwell himself. His aristocratic poise
and courage emphasize the crudity of 'the forced Pow'r'. His eye is
sharper than the edge of the axe as he examines it ('axe' may recall
Latin *acies* suggesting both sharpness of eyesight and the keenness of
the blade).[8] The hard brutality is transformed by the dignity of
Charles himself:

> *He* nothing common did or mean
> Upon that memorable Scene ...
> Nor call'd the *Gods* with vulgar spight
> To vindicate his helpless Right,
>   But bow'd his comely Head,
>   Down as upon a Bed.

Charles in his death has all the dignity of a martyr. The subtle placing
and stress of the word 'down', the gradual slowing of the rhythm, and
the contrast between the sharp and soft vowels of the last four lines,
help to produce this effect. At the same time, the image of the
handsome monarch dying with the same calm as he would put his
head on a pillow contrasts with the force, power, and energy of his
opponent. Marvell goes on to show, with a mixture of admiration and
scepticism, how

> The same *Arts* that did *gain*
> A *Pow'r* must it *maintain*.

An Horatian Ode upon Cromwell's Return from Ireland relates the grim
realities of contemporary history to the timeless permanence of
nature, which provides the stabilizing background to Marvell's poetry
as a whole. It is the subtle interplay between the actual and the ideal, or
nature and art, which frequently lies behind Marvell's wit and gives his

poetry its characteristic depth. The art with which Cromwell gained power involved a ruthless insensitivity and yet it had the discipline, control, economy and force which are exemplified in Marvell's poetry, so that the concluding lines are both ironic and sympathetic, detached and yet establish a kind of empathy between the poet and his subject.

As a natural contemplative, the poet is utterly opposed to the man of action and to the world of politics, and yet Marvell never indulges in mere escapism, even in his most artful verses. The classical, pastoral dialogue *Clorinda and Damon* transcends its genre by passing from the subject of the sheep and the grass on which they feed to the theme of 'the grass withereth, and the flower fadeth' of *Isaiah*. Pan and the Old Testament God who 'shall feed his flock like a shepherd' are interchangeable, just as Milton in *On the Morning of Christ's Nativity* can pass from describing the New Testament shepherds to mention of 'the mighty Pan', who is Christ. (Spenser had set the precedent in *The Shepheardes Calender*, May, where the source of the association in Plutarch is referred to in the gloss, and the Spenserian influence generally fuses with the metaphysical wit in Marvell's pastoral poems.)

The close association between poetry and music, which was particularly apparent in the masque in the seventeenth century, is also to be seen in the paradoxically harmonious tension of the dialogues of the pastoral poems. They have a crisp cleanness in their sharp interchanges, which is not inconsistent with wit, but which never allows it to become a mere end in itself. A lyric such as *The Fair Singer* shows Marvell writing in the gallant, courtly style of the Cavalier poets, who were indebted to Ben Jonson for their clarity and sense of form and to Donne for the witty expression of their passion, but in the pastoral dialogues the war of the sexes is viewed with the detachment of comedy, though modified by occasional tenderness.

The playfulness of Marvell's tone and attitude in *The Picture of Little T.C. in a Prospect of Flowers* also has a courtly gallantry, but here there is a mock-heroic association of love and war which modifies the charmed sense of the child's beauty, itself seen against the background of nature. The possibility that the child may die, like the flowers that she picks, is a reminder, particularly appropriate at a time of civil war, that inevitable mortality constantly places a limit on human hope and joy.

One of the most widely interpreted of Marvell's poems is *The Nymph Complaining for the Death of her Fawn*, where the fawn has been considered to be a symbol of Christ, the Church of England, and the Holy Ghost. The poem opens just as the fawn has been shot by the 'wanton troopers', but it is not yet dead. The image of the hunted pet reminds one of the relationship between Charles and Cromwell in *An Horatian Ode*, and the imminent death of the fawn seems to be representative of the general destructiveness of war, which is an extreme example of the constant threat of mortality hinted at in *The Picture of Little T.C.* Against that threat, there is only the delicate and vulnerable security offered by the garden, with its lilies and roses, where the nymph celebrates her love for the fawn in words that recall *The Song of Solomon*. The tears of the fawn as it dies are compared to 'the wounded Balsam', a witty paradox, since Balsam was a balm for healing wounds, though it could also flow like tears, being oily. There is no sentimentality in the concluding twenty lines of the poem, which merely elaborate the mourning of the nymph, as she anticipates her own death. An ironical detachment is maintained, and the subtlety is in the deliberate ambiguity about the extent of the irony and detachment. In this way, the effect of such an apparently simple poem is almost as complex as that deliberate and studied exercise in impartiality, *An Horatian Ode*.

Marvell's longest poem, with the exception of the late satire, *The Last Instructions to a Painter*, is *Upon Appleton House*, which has as its subject the civilization of the country house, the background to much of the finest poetry in the seventeenth century.[9] The unusual length of the poem involves greater diffuseness than one generally expects to find in Marvell's poetry, and there are examples of the kind of metaphysical wit of which Dr Johnson complained in his *Life of Cowley* ('The most heterogeneous ideas are yoked by violence together'). But there are also passages in which the intensity and concentration of the shorter lyrics are evident. It is typical of Marvell's sensuous appreciation of nature that gardens should inspire some of his finest lines, but the gardens of General Fairfax's house are martial and well disciplined. The brisk and alert rhythms of the poem culminate in a passage of patriotic exultation that recalls John of Gaunt's dying speech in *Richard II*, where he looks back, nostalgically, to 'This other Eden, demi-paradise'. Marvell, too, evokes the vision of England as another Garden of Eden when he addresses it as

> that dear and happy Isle
> The Garden of the World ere while,
> Thou *Paradise* of four Seas,
> Which *Heaven* planted us to please,
> But, to exclude the World, did guard
> With watry if not flaming Sword; ...

But just as John of Gaunt mourned the corruption of the present state of England, Marvell is reminded by the contemporary scene that it was in a garden that man and woman originally sinned. The only hope is that the pristine innocence of the Garden of Eden will be regained when man rejects force and war, and cultivates the civilized arts of peace. Marvell's poetry is, itself, the product of this cultivation, though the ironic description of himself as the 'easy philosopher' conferring among the birds and trees suggests a critical view of peace at any price, and the poem draws to a conclusion with typically gallant praise of 'the young Maria', General Fairfax's daughter, whose tutor Marvell was.

> This 'tis to have been from the first
> In a *Domestick Heaven* nurst,
> Under the *Discipline* severe
> Of *Fairfax*, and the starry *Vere*; ...

The final vision is a witty one, though it has been questioned whether the wit is successful:

> But now the *Salmon-Fishers* moist
> Their *Leathern Boats* begin to hoist;
> And, like *Antipodes* in Shoes,
> Have shod their *Heads* in their *Canoos*.
> How *Tortoise like*, but not so slow,
> These rational *Amphibii* go!
> Let's in: for the dark *Hemisphere*
> Does now like one of them appear.

This analysis of a few poems reveals that Andrew Marvell had a range and depth out of all proportion to the amount that he wrote. The friend of Lovelace and Milton, he seems to combine in a unique synthesis the virtues of the Puritan and the Cavalier. The kind of reconciliation of opposing thoughts and feelings to be found in his best poetry would hardly have been possible if his style, and the general poetic tradition on which it was based, had not been extremely flexible. Writing in the middle of the seventeenth century his language is still Shakespearean in its complexity. The Restoration involved a radical change, and in many ways a deterioration and a coarsening. Although Marvell continued to write poetry, his best work belongs to the tradition initiated by Donne and Jonson. Dryden, the poet of the new age, was in some ways a greater poet than Marvell, but in Eliot's opinion 'he lacked what his master Jonson possessed, a large and unique view of life: he lacked insight, he lacked profundity'. Marvell was more immediately and intimately the poetic heir of Jonson, and yet he was no mere imitator. What Marvell gained from his master can be seen by comparing his lyrics with those of 'the mob of gentlemen who wrote with ease' after the Restoration. Andrew Marvell was a gentleman but he did not belong to a mob, and from Ben Jonson he learned that one could write too easily. Marvell, with all his variety, was no mere facile versifier. His style is always deliberate and accurate, conforming to the ideal of the best writers mentioned in Ben Jonson's *Discoveries* who 'did nothing rashly; they obtained first to write well, and then custom made it easy and a habit'.

NOTES

1. M. C. Bradbrook and M. G. Lloyd Thomas: *Andrew Marvell*, 25.

2. These examples of the different senses in which the word could be taken in Marvell's time are given in *The Oxford Dictionary*.

3. A further possible meaning is 'characterized only by growth (in accord with the doctrine of the three souls, vegetative, sensitive, and rational)', *Andrew Marvell, The Complete Poems*, ed. Elizabeth S. Donno, 234.

4. H. M. Margoliouth: *The Poems and Letters of Andrew Marvell*, Vol. I, 268.

5. M. C. Bradbrook and M. G. Lloyd Thomas, *Andrew Marvell*, 59n.

6. Quoted from Ward's *English Poets*, II, 383.

7. F. R. Leavis, *Revaluation*, 21.

8. This is pointed out by William Empson in *Seven Types of Ambiguity* (1947), 166.

9. cf. L. C. Knights. 'The Social Background of Metaphysical Poetry', *Further Explorations*, 99–120, and Richard Gill, 'The Poetry of Property', *Happy Rural Seat*, 225–52.

MARVELL: SYMBOL, STRUCTURE
AND SATIRE

JOHN BROADBENT

The most helpful work on Marvell is still Empson's essay on *The Garden* for, being so tentative with his brilliance, and letting the way his mind worked show, Empson allowed us to share his reading.[1] At about the same time, though, T. S. Eliot led readers astray.[2] As part of a campaign against sloppiness, Eliot stressed the irony and wit of the 'metaphysicals' (itself a term no longer of use). He defined Marvell's wit as 'a tough reasonableness beneath the slight lyric grace'. That has made it difficult, ever since, to give voice to the gleaming coral edges of Marvell's verse as we speak it; and, equally, to let ourselves explore the weird under-ocean that lies beneath that shelly surface – utterly unreasonable, sometimes mad. More difficult still, academic critics have sought to explicate many of Marvell's strange images and allusions in terms of contemporary knowledge, and of the traditions he was writing in. That needed to be done; indeed Marvell is not, in a European context, as singular as he may appear in England. Unfortunately some of the results have been over and over re-enshrined in critical anthologies intended for people who are *starting* to read Marvell. This is not the fault of the original scholars but of the paperback editors; but it has given the impression that instead of enjoying their own reaction to Marvell's vivacious utterance – 'Sits on thy skin . . . Into my hands . . . The nun's smooth tongue' – readers new to Marvell ought to be trying to say something like this:

Many poets known to Marvell practised this genre [solitary seclusion poems], among them Fane and Fairfax and the French poets, notably Saint-Amant, whose *Solitude* demonstrates how easily he moved in this, the antithesis of the *Jouissance* mode. This famous poem was translated by Fairfax and by Katharine Phillips. This is the poetry of the meditative garden, whether the meditation be pseudo-Dionysian, or Ciceronian, or merely pleasantly Epicurean, like Cowley's.[3]

In this chapter I suggest ways of reading some of Marvell's poetry which depend less than usual, I hope, on the reader's being compatible

288

with a special literary culture and ethic. They draw either on structure, or on subjectivity, or on performance.[4]

By structure I mean the patterns that we can see and hear in a poem. They will be especially made up of material that recurs, whether it be content or form, and which can then be allocated into categories. The categories declare the pattern. An adjective that often recurs in Marvell's poems is 'green': as soon as it is noticed, other colour words begin to lift off the page to join it and so we arrive at a category, colour, which is 'dominant' in that text. With form, we may notice the part played by verbs and how often they form rhymes. Sometimes, though, it is not the dominant category but the deviant that is interesting – that which belongs to no set and therefore has all the more force. This may seem mechanical but the advantage is that people can usually collaborate about such an investigation, and feel unworried by it; and it keeps attention at work when we are stuck for subtler readings. In other words, it is a good base for further exploration; it avoids the futility of unprepared 'discussion' or compulsory 'response'.

In any case, structural analysis needs to be used alongside 'subjectivity'. By that I mean listening for, and giving value to, what our *own* associations with the poem's materials may be (with green, or garden, or grave). Sometimes they will be learned, sometimes quite personal; but we need to permit the unconscious to proffer its readings; to let ourselves dream the poem, or become a part of it; and that may lead to writing our own extensions of the poem, or our own poems about some image of Marvell's. (So for me, for example, the nymph suckling the fawn with her fingers reminds me of doing this for calves as a child, and leads into all sorts of unwritten interior texts about fatherhood, transmogrification, nurture and death – texts which could be written.) That is part of what I mean by 'performance': when the reader turns into a writer. The other part is agreeing with other people to learn about the poem by repeatedly reading it aloud in different ways, using all the voices actually in the room: exploiting it physically, giving it actual existence in our own historical present (just as I assume that readers of this chapter have their texts of Marvell open in front of them).

The Definition of Love

My love is of a birth as rare
As 'tis for object strange and high:
It was begotten by Despair
Upon Impossibility.

Magnanimous Despair alone
Could show me so divine a thing,
Where feeble Hope could ne'er have flown,
But vainly flapped its tinsel wing.

And yet I quickly might arrive
Where my extended coul is fixed;
But Fate does iron wedges drive,
And always crowds itself betwixt.

And so on. If we read *The Definition* and mark those items of content or of form (e.g. syntax, sound) which are hard or sharp and those which refer to union, oneness, we shall probably have lists that begin like this:

hard, sharp	union, oneness
iron wedges	begotten
crowds … betwixt	arrive
decrees of steel	close (meaning come close)
poles	union
etc.	etc.

I had this pair of categories in mind already; but it came to me only after I had started to look for dominant materials because the poem as a whole was baffling my more sensitive attention. I began to see that separating, slicing, dominates the poem. Having seen that, I can 'go into' the poem more confidently. Now, with my subjectivity, I sense the iron wedges as not merely things elsewhere in reality driven into a tree-trunk to split it, or even things brought into the poem as a metaphor: I sense them driven into me, as poem and its poet-reader, so that I am riven in the centre of my poetic spine. Thus the poem is not just 'about' two people out there being separated: it constitutes an experience of mine of being halved, split, taken to pieces.

Apart from me, though, there is an active dramatic character in the poem: Fate. She is female, with jealous eye, tyrannic power. She is the agent of separating; and so the enemy of the other, unifying category.

That category – begotten, arrive, soul, close and so on – seems to contain the qualities more conventionally projected onto women, including love itself; but here they are defeated by that other kind of femaleness, Fate. I am confused because I suspect that the conflict between these two principles is not straightforward. There may be historical issues – perhaps the poem is a seventeenth-century puzzle about the nature of femininity. To clarify, I try attending to the poem as performance:

> For Fate with jealous eye **does see** ♯
>
> *Two* perfect loves; ♯ nor lets *them* close ♯
>
> *Their* <u>union</u> would her <u>ruin</u> be, ♯
>
> / / / / /
> And her tyrannic pow'r **depose**.

As I try to find ways of reading this aloud with more and more meaning, I notice (or my listener does) that the stanza distinguishes the 'Two perfect loves ... them ... their' quite sharply, in their plurality, from the singleness of Fate and what is hers; but reading aloud the pun on eye / I puts me on Fate's side, against the loves. Then the loves are isolated by the break in line 2, and held apart by the isolating clause 'nor lets them close' (isolated at one end by the break in the line and at the other by the end of the line and the semi-colon, which together are equivalent to a pause of at least two main beats). So the whole line enacts separation. In line 3 'Their union' is phonetically almost the same as 'her ruin': implying that union *is* ruin. And in the last line, although we are being told what *would* happen, in performance we enact in the present a riffle of drums ending with the double beat that signals halt. It is as if the power of Fate had taken over the poem. I begin to think that it is not a poem regretting separation (though that is what it 'says') so much as one celebrating separation, by dominance, by the riving metaphors I experience, and now by the pronouns and rhythms I pronounce and perform.

Using the notion of what is deviant or odd in the text, we may notice that although this is a love poem, actually a definition of love, the only fully sexual materials are 'begotten' and 'birth' in stanza 1; and their father and mother are Despair and Impossibility. The other words of union may have a sexual tinge but if so they are deviant in the sense of being contradictory, oxymoronic – union is ruin, joining is cramp and so on. It is as if the poet were identifying with Despair as male, and identifying the female with Impossibility. This is supported when we look at the formal structure of the poem as a whole: then we see that the begetting and birth in lines 3–4 of the first stanza are balanced in lines 3–4 of the last stanza by conjunction (i.e. conjugation, union) of the mind *versus* opposition of the stars (i.e. astrological incompatibility, a fateful nativity). So what the poem sexually enacts, in the begetting metaphor and in that structural balance, is a pattern of this sort:

Despair as male (and mental?)	kept apart by Fate (also female)	Impossibility as female (and physical? – nativity)

but the separation itself engenders a particular kind of love – defined, rare; and perhaps engenders this poem

To reach for a hypothesis about what 'generates' the poem, it is that – separation. It is not a poem regretting separation but one generated by the poet's need for it. It is a poem *of* separation. Put more mythically, the poet projects onto a female Fate, a dominatrix, his fantasies of pain, and splitting, his inability to join and love. This might then be tested once again on the experience of the poem in performance, with its biting obsessive beats and rhymes, and its final sky-ey collapse into mind and stars.

Marvell's poem *Mourning* has received no entirely satisfactory interpretation so readers are free to try their own methods on it. It stands in the context of many seventeenth-century poems about weeping. Poets often used tears as discrete objects, like snowflakes and pearls and candles and flies, on which to base a moral lesson or a paradox. Examples are Donne's valedictions *Forbidding mourning* and *Of weeping*, Marvell's own *Eyes and Tears*, Herrick's *Tear sent from Staines*, Crashaw's *Weeper*. There were many treatments of Mary Magdalen, the penitent prostitute who washed the feet of Jesus with her tears, from Donatello's sculpture to Titian's painting (Rodin also sculpted Magdalen). It is important to check on Danaë (painted, again, by Titian; and by Klimt): her father imprisoned her in a brass tower but Zeus ravished her by pouring through the window into her lap in a shower of gold. Strephon and Chlora in *Mourning* are conventional names for shepherd and shepherdess. In the suggestions about reading below, numbers refer to stanzas.

1 You, that decipher out the fate
 Of human offsprings from the skies,
 What mean these infants which of late
 Spring from the stars of Chlora's eyes?

 . . . . .

9 I yet my silent judgement keep,
 Disputing not what they believe;
 But sure as oft as women weep
 It is to be supposed they grieve.

(1, 9) The first stanza collars us with 'You' and the last opens with 'I'. So crisp a signal about speaker and audience, identity and pronoun, and about shape, suggests it will be worth looking at the mathematical middle of the poem. But in saying 'You' the poet not only alerts our reason: he also commands us to enter subjectively into a dialogue with him or the poem. So let us become those people who decipher out the fate of human offspring – that is, astrologers who cast nativities; forecasters; critics, perhaps, taunted to decipher a poem which is itself a mysterious offspring? So the poet gives us the experience of being both you and I, objective and subjective.

2 Her eyes confused, and doubled o'er,
 With tears suspended ere they flow,
 Seem bending upwards, to restore
 To heaven, whence it came, their woe:

3 When, moulding off the watery spheres,
 Slow drops untie themselves away;
 As if she, with those precious tears,
 Would strow the ground where Strephon lay.

(2) To go on being subjective, what do we see when he shows us infants springing from the stars which are Chlora's eyes, in these two first stanzas? (3) And we may be able to enter into the experience of the tears themselves as they 'untie themselves away'. Then there is Strephon on the ground: in what condition? Only imagination can tell.

4 Yet some affirm, pretending art,
 Her eyes have so her bosom drowned
 Only to soften near her heart
 A place to fix another wound;

5 And, while vain pomp does her restrain
 Within her solitary bower,
 She courts herself in amorous rain –
 Herself both Danaë and the shower.

6 Nay others, bolder, hence esteem
   Joy now so much her master grown,
   That whatsoever does but seem
   Like grief, is from her windows thrown.

7 Nor that she pays, while she survives,
   To her dead love this tribute due;
   But casts abroad these donatives
   At the installing of a new.

(4) 'Pretending art' means claiming that she is being artificial, insincere. The stanza places eyes and breasts, heart and 'another wound', in a pattern. What is the other wound, and what does the pattern mean?

(5) If 'vain pomp' is false mourning, art, Chlora is like Olivia in *Twelfth Night*, staying indoors for otiose grief. But supposing, as in poetry we must, that the bower is not merely 'real' – her habitation, the place where she is grieving – but also metaphorical: then what may it be in the imagination?

(5, 6) Now her tears turn into the shower of Zeus. Suppose the whole stanza were a dream, how would we interpret it? ('Esteem' means judge that.) In (5) she became a male god, Zeus; in (6) Joy (*jouissance*?) becomes a master; and instead of receiving gold through windows she throws grief out of them. Consider the windows, then, and the patterns of in / out, of contradiction.

(7) Money is often a metaphor for love in seventeenth-century poetry. (Donatives are ritual gifts associated with the installing of popes and emperors.) The stanza continues the series of reversals but seems rather thin; it repays reading aloud to test exact possibilities of inflection: it is a speaking poem and we may need to say, 'What?'

8 How wide they dream! The Indian slaves
   That sink for pearl through seas profound
   Would find her tears yet deeper waves
   And not of one the bottom sound.

(8) We have been tricked into moving away from Chlora and viewing her ironically. Now we are sent back into the depths of the poem, and the depths of Chlora, again. So we sink with the eastern divers, into her tears. Tears were often imaged as pearls; here we seek pearls inside themselves. In a more structured mode, 'the bottom sound' rhymes with 'her bosom drowned': the poem holding tightly together. But is there anything in it that does not hold together, that is

deviant and so might give us a clue? Or we may want, here, noting the emphasis on depth, to trace back through the poem for other dominant categories.

(9) It would be conventional here to discuss Marvell's tone; we could compete with finding words for it. I prefer to wonder why he says 'silent' and what part of the poem that belongs to; and to study the meanings of 'grieve'.

There are various ways of reading *The Nymph complaining for the Death of her Fawn*; this is faintly anthropological. The letters mark distinct patches of reading; they need not be in this order.

(a) The context of the poem is the Civil War; and *The Song of Solomon*:

> My beloved is like a roe or young hart ... My beloved is mine, and I am his ... he feedeth among the lilies ... Thy two breasts are like two young roes that are twins, which feed among the lilies. Until the day break, and the shadows flee away, I will get me to the mountain of myrrh, and to the hill of frankincense ... A garden enclosed is my sister, my spouse.

There is also a tradition of poems on the death of girls' pets: Catullus laments for Lesbia's sparrow (III. 6–10), Ascanius kills Silvia's pet deer (*Aeneid* VII). It is obvious enough from slang in Marvell's time (hart, deer) and in our own (chick, stag-party, pussy) that animals are totems for men and women as sexual prey, and also for their sexual parts. Unfortunately we have lost most of the seventeenth-century sense of these things as being both profane *and* sacred. Even at the secular level a fawn, like any game animal, has taboos attached to it, and reverence. At a higher level, in *The Song of Solomon* and in Donne's sermon, for example, at the funeral of Magdalen Herbert where he quotes from it, the mountain of myrrh is a vulva and simultaneously heaven. It is the co-presence of the sacred with the profane that matters. The spouse is, in allegory, the Church, the bridegroom is Christ; at the same time, as Donne says in that sermon, 'Beloved, every good soul is the spouse of Christ'; and beyond that again every wife is a garden, every husband feeds on her. So this poem exists in a context of transformation, co-presence.

(b) The poem's paragraphs divide into a series of scenes and topics:

     (i) Troopers kill the fawn. Theology, guilt.
    (ii) Sylvio gives the fawn, takes her heart.
(iii–vi) Nymph and fawn play, in the open.

   (vii) Nymph and fawn kiss, and feed, in the garden.
(viii–ix) Fawn dies, and
    (x) goes to heaven; Nymph dies, and
   (xi) prepares their joint monument.

Clearly there is a series of oppositions and parallels such as soldier / hunter *versus* girl / animal; open / enclosed; but some of them are strangely elaborated: the fawn is both the bribe that Sylvio gives to the Nymph, and the virginity he takes from her – the price that each pays, then; a medium of exchange. The garden is cultivated, tame, on the side of civilization against the soldiers and Sylvio (whose name suggests forest); yet it has a wilderness inside it.

(c) More detailed sets and categories can be discovered if we consider such qualities in the poem as colours, parts of the body, liquids. (The brotherless Helíadës were sisters of Phaëton. When he crashed they bewailed his death and turned into poplars dripping resin.)

(d) Transformations: Nymph and fawn keep turning into each other: 'It blessed itself in me ... I it at mine own fingers nursed', and elsewhere.

(e) The Nymph's voice performs this monologue poem. The fawn is with her but the men are absent. At times she is vividly inflective – 'Ungentle men! They cannot thrive to kill thee: thou ne'er didst, alive, them any harm!' Yet this speaking country girl passes in the middle of the poem into an almost animal identification with the speechless fawn; and at the end she turns herself into an alabaster statue. Human, animal, or artefact is she?

(f) In her voice, pronouns predominate: 'Nay, and I know what he said then, I'm sure I dŏ. Said he ...' Can we relate this to the frankincense and the Helíadës?

When we consider a poet's *oeuvre* the best evidence is what carries over, overtly or in some way transformed, from poem to poem. In Marvell's case, even with *Mourning* and *The Nymph*, it is clear that tears, liquids, pronouns, grief, are common concerns: so also are heroines. If we can build up more arcs from one poem to another, the set of arcs may themselves begin to constitute a meta-poem, or metaphor of Marvell's *oeuvre*.

*

Now some points about Marvell as satirist. I suggest that the critical factors of satire have become distorted in literary history, and hence in the canon of literature and in syllabuses, so that it is difficult to see straight. Let me start with Dryden. Dryden's trenchant skill lies, I think, in his more generalized public poems such as *Annus Mirabilis* (about the Second Dutch War and the Fire of London) and his translations of Latin satires. But these have been subordinated to the interest of such works as *Absalom and Achitophel* and *Mac Flecknoe* – satires which are more individualized and more party-political and, to my mind, weaker in imagination. I think this has happened because those latter works, and the scholarship they attract, obscure by their individualizing complexity the vital issues of the time – which in the former works are more available to the imagination. For example, consider the seriousness, and the possibilities offered to our imagination, in Dryden's account of Prince Rupert's battle against the Dutch fleet in *Annus Mirabilis*:

> Plied thick and close as when the fight begun,
>   Their huge unwieldy navy wastes away;
> So sicken waning moons too near the sun
>   And blunt their crescents on the edge of day.

The imagery of wasting, of sickened appetite, of morbid light, is consistent over numerous stanzas. It sets up a complex of ideas about the *experience* of this war for both sides – a war characterized for us by incompetence, corruption, greed. The incident ends with Rupert's ship taking the wind out of the sails of two enemy ships so that 'flagging sails on heartless [disheartened] sailors fall'. Incapacity, the reduction of combatants to helplessness, concludes when a last Dutch shot dismasts Rupert's ship: 'All three now, helpless, by each other lie, And this offends not, and those fear no more'.

It is that kind of skill that Marvell disposes in his *Last Instructions to a Painter* (1667) – a satire which has been subjugated to his more ironic poems on Charles I and Cromwell. This poem's title parodies a panegyric by Waller, *Instructions ... for ... the Drawing of ... His Majesty's Forces at Sea*; but, as with Dryden at his best, Marvell's strength is not in satirical *allusion* but in what he offers here and now to the exploring imagination of the reader and then, perhaps as with Brecht, to the reader's judgement.

'Paint Castlemaine' (Charles II's young mistress), he orders, 'in

colours that will hold – her, not her picture (for she now grows old)'.
The sense of a deliquescent Britain, stopped from running with
cosmetics, recurs with Clarendon, the chief minister. His bankers, like
male prostitutes, 'Lie nuzzling at the sacramental wart': Court, administration, economy all adrip. And so with the navy, neglected by
those rulers:

> There our sick ships unrigged in summer lay
> Like moulting fowl, a weak and easy prey,
> For whose strong bulks earth scarce could timber find ...

The strength available in that last line (the strength of the navy as built
by Cromwell) has been realized and kept up by the Dutch:

> So have I seen in April's bud arise
> A fleet of clouds sailing along the skies;
> The liquid region with their squadrons filled,
> The airy sterns the sun behind does gild ...

The lines remind us of Shakespeare and the Armada's defeat; and of the
ability to work with nature instead of against it. But while the Dutch
use the sky, and look like art, the British paint their faces and look like
sick hens. In the satirical tradition as we have it, irony, sneers at hinted
individuals, moral verdicts, footnotes to *The Dunciad*, all immunize
the reader, set up their own resistances. Presumably it is *because* such
satire blocks its own effect that we have given it pride of place in the
canon; and we have displaced those satires of Dryden and Marvell (and
of Jonson and Donne) which invite the reader to imagine society and,
in imagining, to take back into himself or herself its evil and its good.

In his long poem *Upon Appleton House*, Marvell's imaginatively
satirical view of historical experience, and his structures and symbolism, join in a difficult whole. We can deal with the difficulties properly
only by discussing stanzas in a small group of readers who trust each
other uncompetitively; but here are some signposts. Appleton is an
actual estate near York. It belonged in Marvell's time to the Lord
Fairfax who had a brilliant career in the Parliamentary army but
disapproved of regicide and retired there in 1650: a peaceful general, a
roundhead nobleman. He appointed Marvell tutor to his daughter
Maria (*c.* 1651–3) while she was either side of fifteen. The house had
originally been a nunnery; the Fairfax family acquired it at the
dissolution of the monasteries.

Marvell's poem is firstly a testing to destruction of the country-house poem such as Ben Jonson's *To Penshurst* and Herrick's *Hock-cart*. After the usual asseveration that this house is not built for pride, the house itself begins to break up as Fairfax enters it:

> But where he comes, the swelling hall
> Stirs, and the square grows spherical ...
>
> (51)

Marvell is not concerned to keep an old social ideal in fixity, but to explore the arrival of individualism, perhaps, certainly to explore the mobility of things, their tendency to change – the principles of entropy, transformation, evolution. So later in the poem he treats wood as a fifth element; night, instead of time, is space; and Maria turns into one of her ancestors who was immured by the nuns, and into the Virgin Mary, and a kingfisher.

It was a seventeenth-century habit to test its genres like that: tragedy, masque, epic and here the country-house poem fell to geniuses responding to the enormous pressures on human experience in the years 1610–60. We may compare Yeats's *Meditations in Time of Civil War*. Yet the poem has a sequence of distinct episodes, ordered in terms of space–time (that is, of miniature history), something like this:

(a) The house now.
(b) The nunnery as it was in the past, with Maria's ancestor.
(c) The garden at dawn today.
(d) The meadows at noon today. An 'I' figure enters at line 369.
(e) The wood this afternoon.
(f) Maria this evening. 'We' are implied in the penultimate line.

Some sections have other arenas attached to them: (c) seems to be about history especially, (d) about eternity, (e) about Church and State. The first and last episodes are perhaps partly about the poem itself, or the poet's mind – or our minds – symbolized as a house that can't contain its master, an evening that can't contain Maria, a poem that can't contain a world of disorder. In the famous last stanza we – the writer–readers of the poem, and its inhabitants – end up as a man with a boat on his head or his head in his shoes, the world in the dark.

Looking back over the poem from the end, we can see that Marvell has in each episode revealed, in an orderly way, the disorder latent in things. He does this in many poems but especially in *Appleton House*. It is as if he were defending himself against disorder – civil war, uncertainty, despair, the speed of change? – by turning things upside down and inside out, and jamming incompatibles against each other to form oxymorons. So the nuns (in what I call episode b) are soldierly and lesbian (line 200); in episode (e) a bishop seems to emerge from the forest like an ivy-clad faun. Flowers are a 'sweet militia' (line 330), tears are like musketry and sighs like cannon (line 714). As in many lyrics of the century, undertones of war sound briefly like distant hooves or guns – breaks, cut, sword, scythe, fell, shooting, fetters, overthrown; their warlike significance asserts itself only when they are accumulated. But nature is wrong too: humans are inverted trees (line 567); the water-meadows become an abyss, a Red Sea, with gigantic grasshoppers; eels swim in the bellies of oxen (line 474). Nunnery, Church, nature fail; all have their wrongness. In the afternoon the poet wanders into a wood for sanctuary but, like *The Garden*, the wood is disturbed by ambiguous hints of chaos and pain – an impassioned nightingale, a felled oak which might be an executed king, a snake in Eden, and – in a stanza which I don't fully understand – a cry for 'natural life' which is simultaneously a sexual fantasy and a parody of the crucifixion:

> Bind me, ye woodbines, in your twines!
> Curl me about, ye gadding vines,
> And O so close your circles lace
> That I may never leave this place.
> But, lest your fetters prove too weak,
> Ere I your silken bondage break,
> Do you, O brambles, chain me too,
> And, courteous briars, nail me through.
>
> (609–16)

Critics of *Appleton* argue about the tone, and commentators about the emblematic significance of this or that item – oak, heron, briar, etc. This is to evade the poem's impact on different imaginations. When we read it candidly together, we are likely to find that for some people 'nail', for instance, in that stanza, does evoke the crucifixion; for others it is a fantasy of rape, or of a woman's sharpness. Then again, some of the people who hear a crucifixion allusion may find it falsely clever; for others it will be a sign of integration, of drawing the suffering of God on a tree into the confusion of men in the middle of a wood. When such arguments founder, as they often will, we can appeal to the structure: the dominance of circular binding motifs, and of constraining metal; the addressing of the rampant plants as 'you' and the centrality of the speaking poet; the closing in of the stanza on a few repeating rhymes as if it were a series of cries on the sounds in I! O! You!

When we engage with the text like that, do we create out of it a wry acceptance of the unreliability of things – Church, nature, myth all disordered underneath, and we unable to agree – or is the product more positive and complex? I have no answer to cover every occasion; and the final episode of the poem perhaps makes it only more difficult. As the poem ends, the bird symbolism which has dominated it continues with

> The modest halcyon comes in sight,
> Flying betwixt the day and night.
> (669)

The halcyon is the bird of peace which floated on the sea hatching its eggs at the birth of Christ. It is also the kingfisher, labelled here as bird of the margins – day / night, air / water, coloured / invisible. The implication, I suppose, is that we find rest by living along the boundaries, incorporating the ambivalence of experience instead of trying to make it single. But is that what actually happens as we read this poem? And then the kingfisher dissolves into Maria; and after some complimentary stanzas Marvell focuses peace in her:

> 'Tis not, what once it was, the world,
> But a rude heap together hurled;
> All negligently overthrown,
> Gulfs, deserts, precipices, stone.

That sums up the world he has been discovering, whether of Appleton or on a larger scale. Then:

> Your lesser world contains the same,
> But in more decent order tame.

Appleton, or Maria herself?

> You Heaven's centre, Nature's lap,
> And Paradise's only map.

In seventeenth-century poems, centre, lap, paradise mean not only the focus of the universe but also vagina. We are faced with the difficulty of holding those meanings together. In serious seventeenth-century poetry it is often a girl such as Elizabeth Drury in Donne's

Anniversaries, and perhaps here Maria Fairfax flitting through the twilit margins, who stands for that force which we sometimes feel drives through the universe giving it order and purity: 'A motion and a spirit that impels all thinking things' Wordsworth calls it; Donne, the 'intrinsic balm' (*First Anniversary*) or simply soul – 'True virtue is soul, always in all deeds all' (*Letter to Lady Carey and Mrs Rich*). That is spirit, transcending wit.

NOTES

1. 'Marvell's Garden' in his *Some Versions of Pastoral* (1935, 1966), repr. in various anthologies including the Penguin Critical Anthology on Marvell ed. John Carey (1969) which is the most useful.

2. 'Andrew Marvell' in his *Selected Essays* (1932) repr. from *The Times Literary Supplement* in 1921. Also in Carey.

3. 'The argument of Marvell's *Garden*', *Essays in Criticism*, II (1952), repr. in Carey.

4. For more expansive readings and references see my anthology *Poets of the 17th Century*, Vol I (New American Library, 1974).

POLITICAL DEBATE AND
THOMAS HOBBES

D. H. PENNINGTON

Political thought, in the period covered by this volume, was dominated by a few inescapable questions. Who should hold power in the organized community? When was it justifiable to overthrow by force an established government? And why should the citizen who had disobeyed one government obey the next one? These were no longer matters of abstract theory: they arose repeatedly in urgent practical form. Nothing like it had ever occurred in England before. There had always been learned disputes about the rights and duties of rulers and subjects; there had been turbulent nobles, Court factions, riots and rebellions. But a civil war, an explosion of ideas that questioned the whole order of society, the destruction of the monarchy, the House of Lords, and the Church – all this would have seemed inconceivable until it happened. Twenty years later it had become inconceivable again. The conflicts were fought out not only between armies but in a huge output of printed argument ranging from lurid propaganda to high philosophy. Into it went some of the greatest literary gifts of the age.

Much of the debate was inevitably conducted in religious terms. The easiest and least satisfactory answer to every question was that God had so determined, and had said so in the scriptures. The Authorized Version was a contemporary work in which every writer could find common ground with his readers, and since a still accepted method of conducting a dispute was the competitive piling-up of quotations, even those who had doubts about the universal relevance of every phrase of the Bible constantly cited it. Moreover the religious community – the Church or the independent congregation or sect – was for most people a more real and comprehensible one than the state. But the religious framework in which medieval political thought had largely been confined had by now become less rigid. Human rights could be derived less from God than from Law. Its most practical form was the Common Law of which Sir

Edward Coke had become the acknowledged champion. The Law of Nature, which had always been a familiar and conveniently vague notion, came to be associated with a common 'birthright' and a universal morality to which political institutions ought to conform and which could be demonstrated by reason alone.

Political ideas were of course disseminated in speech at least as much as in writing. Much of the argument took place in churches and conventicles, in Parliament and courts of law, in the armies and in countless outdoor gatherings. There is no firm line between the printed pamphlet and the printed speech; some of the best expositions of political ideas survive in the reports of debates at Westminster and at Putney. But we shall deal here only with material that is primarily literary in origin. Much of this was concerned more with vituperation than with argument. The broadsheet ballads that were sold and sung in the streets of London; the newspapers, legal and illegal, official and unofficial, that exchanged lively abuse and stories of heroism on their own side and atrocity on the other; the scandalous revelations like Clement Walker's exposure of the profits of war for the Independents – such material had usually little literary merit. But occasionally scurrility rose to artistic heights. The dedication to Cromwell of *Killing No Murder*[1] – written to justify assassination of the Protector – is an ironical masterpiece:

And if in the Black Catalogue of High Malefactors, few can be found that have lived more to the affliction and disturbance of mankind, than your Highness hath done, yet your greatest enemies will not deny but there are likewise as few that have expired more to the universal benefit of mankind than your Highness is like to do.

The outstanding best-seller among popular propaganda was unquestionably *Eikon Basilike*, John Gauden's ornate version of the thoughts of the martyr-king, compounded from the unfinished manuscripts which Charles had left and from the author's imagination. It was at once accepted by Royalists as the King's authentic work, and despite attempts to suppress it, it ran through forty English editions and several translations before 1660.

From all this ephemeral controversy there emerge a few works in which the major topics of conflict are seriously discussed. Some were as much a part of the struggle as anything that happened in Parliament or on the battlefield; others had no immediate relevance to it. The two sides in the war were not far removed from each other in their theoretical position. Parliamentarians proclaimed their loyalty to the king whom they were saving from his evil counsellors; Royalists paid tribute to the constitutional importance of Parliament. The divine right which James I had upheld much on paper and little in practice was not in 1640 an urgent issue. The most unqualified defence of royal absolutism, Sir Robert Filmer's *Patriarcha*, was written before the war and circulated in manuscript among his friends, but was not printed until long after the Restoration, when it achieved notoriety through the attack on it by Locke. Even Filmer, though he bases his argument firmly on the Scriptures, offers a natural rather than a supernatural basis for royal absolutism. Obedience to a king is a moral duty because it is identified with obedience to a father. Adam exercised, by God's will, a father's authority over his children; Noah divided that authority among all his sons, from whom it descended to modern rulers.

However fantastic his own arguments, Filmer sometimes scores in exposing the absurdities of those who justified obedience to limited monarchies by hypothetical consents and contracts. Logically, he insisted, the only alternative to absolutism is anarchy. But it was in a constitutional monarchy, however illogical, that the ordinary supporters of Charles I believed; they fought, not for the right of a monarch to do as he pleased, but for stability and against rebellion. Like their opponents, they believed that they were upholding the Rule of Law. The claims of this constitutional royalism were argued by such writers as Sir John Spelman,[2] Henry Ferne[3] and Dudley Digges.[4] All these were involved in controversy with the one outstanding theorist of the moderate Parliamentarians, Henry Parker, a prolific pamphleteer whose *Observations on some of His Majesty's Late Answers ...* (1642) was based on the claim that power was originally 'inherent in the people'. The King held his authority as a limited and revocable trust from the people as represented in Parliament, whose sovereignty, though derivative, was absolute. It was subject to no overriding laws, but was itself the guardian of the law against excesses of radical democracy. The safety of the state must be its guiding principle. Yet since Parliament was in part an elected body, it would never use its absolutism for wrong purposes. Parker's arguments were derived partly from the immediate crisis and partly from the 'charter of Nature'. The weakness of the assumption that Parliament represented the people became even more evident when nearly half the M.P.s left to support the war against it.

The mutual denunciations of Royalist and Parliamentarian during the war could not be expected to contribute much to serious political controversy. Indeed the quarrel that led to the war, since it kept within the bounds set by the existing social structure, was much less far-reaching than those that followed it. The conditions created by the war made possible the brief period, from 1646 to 1649, when a real social revolution seemed possible. The sudden emergence, among ordinary soldiers and the London populace, of the Leveller move-ment, with its demands for an equal share in political power and for a series of radical reforms, is an astonishing phenomenon. John Lil-burne, Cromwell's only rival as a popular leader, had made his sufferings in the Puritan cause well known even before 1640. After the war he turned his two trials into personal triumphs, and became the hero of the mass of Parliamentary supporters who felt cheated of their victory. In 1645 he wrote, in prison, *England's Birthright Justified*, proposing many of the reforms which became the standard Leveller programme – annual Parliamentary elections, free speech, free trade, and publication of the laws in English. Lilburne's vigorous clarity avoids many of the common literary vices of the pamphleteers; but he was neither the best writer nor the most original thinker of the movement. *England's Birthright* shows him already under the influence of the two men from whom Leveller ideas chiefly originated – William Walwyn and Richard Overton. Walwyn had published in 1643 *The Power of Love*, a sermon which set the tone for all his later writing – faith in and love for his fellow men, rational questioning, hatred of 'tyranny, oppression, cruelty, perjury, and deceit', and a gentle unassuming manner which contrasts sharply with Lilburne's self-advertisement.[5] He wanted 'more of the deeds of Christians and fewer of the arguments'. Politically he based his devotion to liberty on 'reason, sense, and the common law of equity and justice'. His brilliance and lack of self-assertion made opponents label him as the secret and sinister influence behind the left-wing sectaries, a serpent whose craft and subtlety were 'seducing the indigent and poorer sort of men'.

Overton's contribution is in some ways the counterpart of Walwyn's – satirical humour, a call to action, and a little bitterness.

Man's Mortality, a highly heretical argument that the body and soul are inseparable, earned him an undeserved reputation for atheism and materialism. *A Remonstrance of Many Thousand Citizens*, written in support of the imprisoned Lilburne, calls on the House of Commons to assert its sole claim to sovereignty: 'Ye only are chosen by Us, the People; and therefore in you only is the power of binding the whole nation by making, altering, or abolishing of laws.' Afterwards, from prison, he developed his angry attacks on the House of Lords and on the unworthy element in the Commons, neatly linking his constitutional theory with denunciations of the grievances of the moment.

In later Leveller pamphlets the work of Lilburne, Walwyn, and Overton cannot always be disentangled with certainty. All three, together with Thomas Prince, were imprisoned for the second part of *England's New Chains Discovered* (March 1649), though Walwyn was no longer closely associated with the others. Directly or indirectly all contributed to the final version of the *Agreement of the People* (May 1649), in which Leveller theory was worked out as a written constitution. They had rejected Ireton's claim that political power was for those with a 'permanent fixed interest in this kingdom'. 'The people in general are the original sole legislators and the true fountain and earthly well-spring of all just power' (*Regal Tyrany Discovered*, 1647). But though Rainsborough at Putney appeared to advocate universal – or universal male – suffrage, most Leveller writings later excluded from it beggars, or all alms-takers, and 'servants'. The meaning of this term has been vigorously disputed: probably only the most cautious stretched it to cover all wage-earners. But it was generally accepted that the original rights of every man could be destroyed by the complete loss of his independence. The elected chamber was to have sole legislative power; but having 'by wofull experience found the prevalence of corrupt interests powerfully inclining most men once entrusted with authority' (*Article IX*), the Levellers bound the assembly by an irrevocable constitution. It could not restrict religious toleration, impose conscription, collect tithes, or levy any tax except 'by an equal rate in the pound upon every real and personal estate' (*Article XIX*). Privilege of every kind was as far as possible to be eliminated, but the Levellers remained the spokesmen not of the destitute but of the lowest classes of property holders and producers.

There is little to justify the accusation that they would reduce all men to economic equality or would have property held in common.

For ideas like this we have to listen to the almost unsupported voice of Gerrard Winstanley, leader of the Digger community that tried to practise its economic creed on the commons of St George's Hill in Surrey. In him the doubts and qualifications of the Levellers are thrown aside. He calls for equality of power and possessions in prose whose passionate directness and moments of lyrical purity are unequalled in any of the other pamphleteers. 'In the beginning of Time the great Creator Reason, made the Earth to be a Common Treasury, to preserve Beasts, Birds, Fishes, and Man, the lord that was to govern this Creation' (*The True Levellers' Standard Advanced*, 1649). But then selfishness and covetousness appeared, 'and the Earth that was made a Common Storehouse for all is bought and sold and kept in the hands of a few'. Private property brought in many other evils – war, the oppression of governments, the wiles of lawyers and clergy. With the abolition of property and the universal recognition of the Reason that Winstanley identifies with God, 'covetousness, pride and oppression' will disappear. Despite his faith in the inherent goodness of man, his Utopia[6] is not an anarchy, but a highly organized agrarian democracy, where 'overseers' planned economic affairs and filled the common storehouses from which all could draw according to their need.

The establishment of the Commonwealth in 1649, and the requirement that every adult male should take the 'engagement' to be loyal to the government without a king, faced the ordinary citizen with formidable problems of expediency or morality, and the politicians with an urgent need to justify their claim to allegiance. They were not short of defenders. A few months after the King's execution Francis Rous in *The Lawfulness of Obeying the Present Government* argued that the scriptural command to submit to 'the powers that be' must apply without regard to the 'lawfulness' of the government. Success was a sign of divine approval, and history was full of instances of regimes that had been established by force and then accepted as legitimate. A more prolific pamphleteer and journalist, Marchamont Nedham, was in a strong position to advocate submission to governments irrespective of their legitimacy, since between 1642 and 1676 he wrote for almost every successive regime. In 1650 his *Case of the Commonwealth of England* avoided the pitfalls of religious arguments for obedience. The existing government was giving protection to its subjects, and that in itself entitled it to claim their support. The successive constitutions were also defended by an official spokesman more eminent, though not in this more successful, than the rest. John Milton did not put aside his poetry to become a mere government hack. Each of his pamphlets is full of personal ideas and experiences – even of personal doubts and spites. His contributions to political debate before 1649 had been mainly his pamphlets against episcopacy and his *Areopagitica* (1644), an impassioned plea for liberty of speech and thought which excluded from its principles advocacy of the popish idolatry and despotism which he claimed would destroy them. In *The Tenure of Kings and Magistrates* (1649) Milton offered a reasoned defence of the slaying of tyrants. 'All men naturally were born free', but when they fell into 'wrong and violence' they agreed to mitigate the evil by setting up a restraining authority.

The power of kings and magistrates is nothing else but what is only derivative, transferred and committed to them in trust from the People, to the common good of them all, in whom the power yet remains fundamentally, and cannot be taken from them without a violation of their natural birthright.

The destruction of tyrants was the way to Christ's kingdom. A few weeks after publishing this, Milton became Secretary of Foreign Tongues to the Council of State; and it was in a semi-official capacity that he produced, for European circulation, the two Latin pamphlets, the *Defence of the People of England* . . . (1651) and the *Second Defence* . . . (1654) justifying successively the Commonwealth and the Protectorate. 'There is nothing in human society,' he says in the second, 'more pleasing to God, or more agreable to reason, nothing in the state more just, nothing more expedient, than the rule of the man most fit to rule.'

The events of the 1650s meant that it was less unrealistic than in normal times for the political theorist to indulge in the pleasing exercise of devising an ideal state. New constitutions were practical politics, and two of them were actually put into effect in the Protectorate. The *Instrument of Government* with its principle that power must be divided between a single person and a wholly elected Parliament made some rather lukewarm concessions to radical ideas. Its successor, the *Humble Petition and Advice*, bringing back an upper house and, it had been intended, the title of king, was for supporters of the republican and democratic cause a horrifying move towards restoring the pre-war constitution. While it was being debated there appeared a Utopia clearly designed to demonstrate the failures of the Protectorate. James Harrington's *Commonwealth of Oceana* (1656) blends together an imaginative history of England with a plan for the future. It was based, like Winstanley's state, on the dependence of political power on economic. But Harrington did not start from an ideal of common ownership. His scheme is an astonishing mixture of ingenious but misinformed economics and classical notions of government. In a stable society, he asserted, power must rest in the holders of land. To distribute land and power more widely, his Agrarian Law set a limit of £2,000 to the annual value of land an individual could hold. This he reckoned (on no good evidence) would mean that at least 5,000 people would be landowners, and that was enough to constitute government by the 'people'. By abolishing primogeniture he would ensure that the number increased. To preserve a 'balance' in the state there would be two assemblies: only a select few would be capable of proposing and debating legislation which the larger body must accept or reject without comment. It was, as his critics pointed out, a ludicrous picture of how assemblies behave. But in trying to combine democracy with the practical necessities of government he was facing a problem that has never been solved. He came near to the tacit assumption that wealth and intelligence, or at least political competence, go together. The real rulers of Oceana would be gentry, even though it was a large and expanding gentry. For the idea to work they would have to be remarkably law-abiding and altruistic. Much of Harrington's scheme seemed far outside the realities of Cromwellian politics. But in 1659, when the Protectorate was on the verge of collapse, he had a brief moment of glory. A spate of Harringtonian pamphlets, and the Rota club in London that brought together a group of his followers, made him appear as the theorist who might do something to rescue the radical cause.

To defend any of the Interregnum regimes needed a good deal of optimism; and some of the most effective advocates of obedience brought little comfort to the existing government because their arguments were pessimistic. Anthony Ascham, who was murdered in Madrid when he arrived in 1650 as representative of the

Commonwealth, had little to say in favour of his masters. He claimed simply that any effective government was better than none. The purpose of the state was to maintain 'public peace and quietness': if this was done it was better to abandon ideas of individual rights than to risk the miseries of war. In November 1649 his pamphlets were expanded into the book *Of the Confusions and Revolutions of Governments*, addressed not to Parliament or the Council but to the people. Scriptural command and indications of divine approval are mentioned, without much prominence; moral scruples and ideals of freedom were liable to lead to war and disorder in which they would destroy themselves. He does not quite deny all need to question the lawfulness of governments: it might sometimes be necessary to fight against an invader. But 'in this confused state of the world' a government that continued to provide the law and security that existed before it took power could be deemed to take over the status of the previous one. Even an oath of loyalty to a ruler was invalidated if he ceased to rule effectively or endangered the lives of his subjects. We should not delude ourselves into supposing that we could improve our condition: amid the 'ambushes and treacheries of fortune' we can only try to avoid worse misfortunes.

Ascham had come very near to the views often ascribed exclusively to the writer whose intellectual stature and defiance of every conventional assumption made him overshadow all the others as a subject of opprobrium, admiration, and dispute. The study of Thomas Hobbes is beset by paradoxes. His conclusions were totally unacceptable to almost every political and religious group; but he was read avidly, in Europe as well as in England. He was a Royalist and, when he wrote *Leviathan*, a refugee in Paris; yet the book was printed in London under the Commonwealth and bitterly attacked by Filmer and Clarendon. His arguments defended the most extreme form of royal absolutism and denounced rebellion as the worst of crimes; but they made consent the basis of government, and were held to justify submission to Cromwell. He was a retainer of a great aristocratic family, and he exploded many of the cherished ideas of the Parliamentarians; but the terms in which he thought were those of the new society, with the interests and behaviour of competitive men mercilessly revealed. Most of the paradoxes are the product of Hobbes's greatest quality – his integrity. Where others tested existing society by imagined ideals, Hobbes, by reasoning from cause to effect, laid bare the realities of political power. He invoked neither moral condemnation nor visions of perfectibility; the most that political devices could do was to mitigate the evil consequences of human nature.

The *Leviathan* is the last of three main statements of Hobbes's political thought, in which, though the essentials remain the same, we can trace an increasingly confident rejection of orthodox ideas. The *Elements of Law*, written in 1640 and printed in 1650, is no more than a pamphlet. *De Cive*, published in Latin in 1642 and in English in 1651, amplifies the argument sometimes more clearly than *Leviathan*, which appeared in the same year. The three versions therefore became available in English almost simultaneously. They were all written when Hobbes was over fifty, and after the study of Euclid had drawn him to the methods of mathematics and natural science. Politics became for him the highest and most complex part of a system of knowledge which started with the simple propositions of geometry and included in its scope the workings of the human body and the human mind.

Controversy about him began immediately and seems in our own generation to be producing more scholarly works than ever. Some of it perhaps arises from the assumption that his prolific writing, which aimed originally to cover almost every aspect of human and natural affairs, can somehow be reduced to coherence. Hobbes is full of apparent contradictions, and close scrutiny of his work can yield evidence for a good many versions of what he meant – or ought to have meant. Traces of many of the ways of thought he had discarded or drastically modified remained. Hobbes was a scholar, brought up on the uneasy mixture of Christian and Aristotelian concepts that was the standard fare of his kind. Despite his cynicism, complete repudiation of the old apparatus never came easily to him, and it is from his attempts to adapt it to new purposes that many of his difficulties spring. Orthodox Christianity was clearly incompatible both with his method and with his conclusions. The Hobbesian state excluded any division of loyalties: neither a Church, national or universal, nor individual conscience must dispute the state's claim to absolute obedience. 'The law is the publique conscience, by which he hath undertaken to be guided.' His enemies could easily accuse him of atheism. Yet religion occupies a prominent place in his works. He does not frankly repudiate Christianity: having repeatedly led us to the brink of rejection, he indicates practical reasons for going no further. Religion is better than unresolved doubt; the governor of Church and State must be one, and no doctrine he forbids should be taught. 'Points of doctrine concerning the Kingdom of God have so great influence on the Kingdom of Man as not to be determined but by them that under God have sovereign power.'[7] Attempts to show that Hobbes was essentially a Christian, or – more vaguely – was 'in a distinctively Christian tradition' have not found general support. A more persuasive argument against the simple conclusion that he had little use for moral obligations points out his emphasis on the Laws of Nature. These, as set out in *Leviathan*, are rules of behaviour that a reasonable man ought to arrive at in his own interest. They are also the commands of God: one especially, 'that men keep their covenants', raises complex questions of where the line between self-interest and moral obligation can be drawn. But on the claim that divine will, or divine rewards and punishments, are the bases of obligation to obey the laws of human behaviour, Hobbes insists that there can be no 'natural knowledge'. Those that 'know it supernaturally' or believe it because others say they know it, are not arguing from reason.

Hobbes is full of contradictions. It is not in flawless coherence that he triumphs, but in the sheer force of intellect with which he attacks his doubts. Despite his argumentative tone he grapples with problems rather than opponents – though his swift and fatal thrusts at muddle-headed idealists are a constant delight. His style is energetic and purposeful rather than immediately pleasing. He has not Milton's powerful range of language, nor Lilburne's passionate enthusiasm. The sentences are tightly packed with meaning and there is little room for ornament or elegance. Wit and dexterity are always evident; emotional eloquence comes only in occasional moments of anger or horror.

Hobbes was a materialist. He was also a determinist; for he held that the behaviour of the human mind was as predictable as that of any other part of the universe. But he was not an economic determinist. He recognized three main sources of action: greed, vanity, and fear. Men quarrel with each other for 'Gain' or for 'Reputation', or for 'Safety', and 'hereby it is manifest that during the time men live without a common power to keep them all in awe, they are in that condition which is called Warre'.[8] Life is dominated by the fear of violent death, and material or cultural progress is impossible. Nor can there be morality: 'Where there is no common power there is no Law; where no Law, no Injustice. Force and Fraud are in Warre the two cardinall vertues'.[9] The 'state of Warre' is, in short, the worst possible evil, and to escape from it men turn to a lesser evil, the surrender of their freedom to an absolute sovereign. They make a covenant with each other 'to conferre all their power and strength upon one man, or upon one Assembly of men, that they may reduce all their Wills by plurality of voices unto one Will'.[10] Hobbes admits that the 'state of Warre' is not historical. 'I believe it was never generally so, all over the world.' But he has some cogent answers to this objection. The condition exists at all times between nations; and consider the citizen who locks his doors at night: 'does he not as much accuse mankind by his actions as I by my words?' Similarly the covenant is not a historical one, but a symbol of the fact that the power of the sovereign rests not on Divine Right but on consent, given because it is expedient.

The covenant is of course irrevocable. It is a contract between subject and subject, not between sovereign and subject. Once the sovereign exists he must not be resisted merely because he behaves badly – and he probably will – for that would mean a return to the 'state of Warre'. He does not forfeit his power by breaking any body of law, such as a written constitution or the Common Law, for laws proceed only from him and can be made or unmade as he chooses. Only when he fails to maintain his sovereignty, or to preserve the life of the subject, are disobedience and rebellion justified.

So far there are no doubts or qualifications. But on one of the main subjects of the political disputes, Hobbes's answer is equivocal and incomplete. He always admitted the possibility that the sovereign might be an Assembly. He accepts Aristotle's classification of governments as monarchies, aristocracies (meaning any form of representative government), and democracies (where the sovereign body is an assembly of the whole people). He has no doubt about the superiority of monarchy, but the reasons he gives hardly ring true. In *De Cive* he is afraid that the meetings may be so infrequent and irregular as to endanger the existence of the state. In *Leviathan*, though he admits that monarchy has its dangers, he tries to show that a monarch is less likely than an Assembly to subordinate public to private benefits. He gets in some shrewd blows at the smugness of Parliamentarians: the counsellors of a democracy or aristocracy will be 'for the most part those who have been versed more in the acquisition of Wealth than of Knowledge'; an Assembly has more friends and relations than a monarch; secrecy may produce better decisions than publicity. But behind all this there lies the fear that dominates his political thought – the fear of disagreement and strife. Hence it is one of the duties of the sovereign 'that he judge what opinions and doctrines are enemies unto peace, and also that he forbid them to be taught'. He insists that a condition of any government other than monarchy is the acceptance by the minority of the will of the majority; and in monarchy itself there must be no doubts about the succession. When the subject's life is threatened he may, to protect it, resist the sovereign – for the preservation of life comes before all other considerations. Otherwise he should not even protest against the sovereign's decisions. It is not surprising, therefore, that Hobbes rejects the comfortable compromise of a 'limited monarchy' or a 'mixed constitution' – everything, in fact, for which both moderate Royalists and moderate Parliamentarians stood. Political activity for the subject should be in the subordinate 'bodies politic' within the state rather than in matters of sovereignty. Individual liberties 'depend on the Silence of the Law', and their extent is for the sovereign to determine. A Hobbesian state could equally well mean rigid totalitarianism or *laisser-faire*. Stability, he feels, requires that the sovereign must act rationally and justly for the welfare of his subjects. He never fully solves the problems that arise when the sovereign manifestly fails in this.

Hobbes was far too forthright about both his certainties and his doubts to be an accepted theorist of any of the successive governments. He leaves his readers with little sense of hope, or even of full understanding, but rather with the feeling that Leviathan is an ugly and elusive monster who never reveals himself above the deep waters. Yet despite his hatred of muddle and compromise he was on the side that won in the end. Peace with security; protection of property; obedience to the law; the keeping of covenants; conformity in great things and tolerance in small – his demands are what the propertied classes reconciled at the Restoration needed, however repellent the reasons he gave for them. Hobbesian society lay below the smooth surface of Whig society. Hobbesian politics are the politics of the modern state with the hypocrisy removed. He is still worth reading.

NOTES

1. By Edward Sexby and perhaps Silius Titus; the dedication is reprinted in Orwell and Reynolds, *British Pamphleteers*, Vol. I (London, 1948). This also contains extracts from one of the best of the anonymous pamphlets – *Tyranipocrit*. For the history of the pamphlet, see F. F. Madon, *A New Bibliography of Eikon Basilike* (London, 1951), and the article by Professor H. R. Trevor-Roper in *History Today* (1951). *The Political Works of James I*, ed., with introduction, C. H. McIlwain (Cambridge, Mass., 1918).

2. His Pamphlet, *Certain Considerations upon the Duties both of Prince and People*, is reprinted in Somers Tracts, Vol. iv., 316.

3. In *The Resolving of Conscience* (1642).

4. In *The Unlawfulness of Subjects Takying up Armes against their Soveraigne* (1647).

5. The manner is suggested by the titles of some of his other works: *A Whisper in the Ear of Mr. Thomas Edwards; A Still Small Voice*.

6. *The Law of Freedom in a Platform* (1651).

7. *Leviathan* (Everyman edn), 244.

8. *Leviathan*, 64.

9. *Leviathan*, 66.

10. *Leviathan*, 89.

THE HUMANISM OF JOHN BUNYAN

MAURICE HUSSEY

As the technique of popular religious composition evolved in the Middle Ages, it came to embrace a wide range of thought and emotion; soon, all human experience was involved in the oral and written explanation of theology. Religious and political ordinances at the Reformation could not banish traditional ideas from the English mind, so that when John Bunyan came to print his *Pilgrim's Progress* in 1678 he was still unconsciously in touch with the ideas of medieval Catholicism acknowledged by Geoffrey Chaucer and William Langland, to say nothing of the tenets of the Anglican Church accepted and taught by George Herbert. But the conventions which dominate successful religious fiction are not entirely theological. There are practical considerations, and an author is obliged, before embarking upon anything which he visualizes as popular literature, to recognize the nature and sophistication of his audience. It became necessary to him not only to make use of the tone and accent of current speech, but also to reduce the philosophical circumference of his work. Chaucer, Langland, Herbert, Jonson and Shakespeare all share with Bunyan this linguistic qualification; they may at times employ concentrated imagery, but they are equally skilful in the direct colloquial expression of truth. Bunyan has precisely these qualities, and his work, while employing an allegorical method of great integrity, is charged with language pre-eminently suitable for telling legends, fables, and romances besides teaching the faith of Christianity. *Pilgrim's Progress*, with its spiritual subtlety and its popularity of idiom, is at once excellent Puritan propaganda and fine adventure writing; it offers much to literary criticism and to childhood wonderment as well.

A study of the work of John Bunyan reveals not only the religion of an old dispensation but also the predestinarian philosophy of John Calvin. The most insistent of this theologian's demands upon his followers is a scrupulous examination of conscience for signs and

317

proofs of salvation and damnation. Predestination is apparent in *Pilgrim's Progress*, which for this reason cannot be satisfactorily interpreted as another version of the Catholic Morality *Everyman*, whose protagonist indeed is a symbol of mankind as a whole. Christian is one of the Lord's elect, and an individual Christian; those that oppose him are reprobated and consigned to eternal damnation. In Calvin there is an insistence also upon two covenants for two classes of man: the Covenant of Grace for the saved which was the effectual sacrifice of Christ and an immediate passport to paradise; and the Covenant of the Law for the damned which was the standard of the Ten Commandments, a rule of life which was impossible for anyone who lacked direct divine guidance. Symbols of both covenants appear in *Pilgrim's Progress*; without accepting these symbols of the author's intention, no reading of the text can be complete.

Finally, in this preview of Bunyan's art, one needs to notice its heavy debt to reality and the dependence upon autobiography for so many incidents. The author's experience in the Civil War, in lawcourts, in prison, and in the countryside, all appear; more important than these, however, are episodes which depict spiritual striving. This striving is dramatized and given a convincing and objective public form in what may be regarded as a crucial literary experiment. An innocent desire for diversion was admitted at the same time, and all these sources of the author's art enabled him to contribute largely to the growth of the classical novel in this country.

Pilgrim's Progress (1678–84) is an amalgam of religious aspiration and rustic life. Several similarities may be detected between earlier Catholic writings and this allegory, which has influenced all subsequent generations of readers and writers: Langland's *Piers Plowman* (c. 1360–90), Walter Hilton's *Scale of Perfection* (c. 1390), and Guillaume Deguileville's *Pilgrimage of the Soul* (c. 1330). In fact, a strong case has been made that *Pilgrim's Progress* is unconsciously the culmination of a long sequence of ideas and compositions communicated orally from preacher to congregation and from parent to child down the centuries.[1] Biblical reading provided images of pilgrimage such as the wandering of the Children of Israel through the desert, and resounded with the words of Christ: 'I am the way, the truth and the life'. No matter what delays, distractions and difficulties assail him the pilgrim should aspire ever upwards to the Celestial City, the home of grace, and keep his steps on the pathway that will inevitably lead to it. As medieval as the concept of the literary pilgrimage is that of the allegorical dream to which Bunyan was in some sense indebted, consciously or unconsciously. Dante, Chaucer and Langland were among those who had communicated their waking concerns in the medium of dreaming and Bunyan's adaptation of this tradition has its own structural interest. In his practice which was to create a series of episodes that are, as has been said, heaven on the instalment plan, each instalment is complete in itself and rendered intelligible by inbuilt interpretations at some point towards the close. Indeed, every segment, whether a meeting and discussion with a person or an adventure in a man-made or natural environment, is followed up by one of a series of helpers, such as Evangelist, posted on the way to assist at the psychological moment and explain the issues involved to the pilgrims and thus to the readers.

Although much can be established through a study of folk-idiom, we should not use verbal classification as anything more than a starting-point in literary criticism. There is often a danger that we may relegate the language and imagery of a popular writer to the folk-museum along with the metal fiddle and the tinker's irons still preserved in the Bunyan Museum in Bedford. We know, coming to his language, that Bunyan made a deep impression upon sinners precisely by calling them *breeders of lice*, *dirty sows*, or *greedy dogs*, but such colloquiality has little value unless it permeates longer moral passages with aphorisms. The language of the present subject is popular and agricultural, and we find all manner of unusual terms and single words in it: *slithy rob-shop*; *pick-pocket men*; *all on a dung sweat*; *would a had him*; *she all-to-be-fooled me*; the almost Joycean *to get a thing by root of heart*; *made shift to wag along*; short animal tales and farming metaphors and sayings: *loses his sheep for a halfpennyworth of tar* and the ubiquitous *make hay while the sun shines*. From these phrases and the completely frank descriptions of such things as pregnancy and bodily disease, we realize that Bunyan wrote as a man rather than as a gentleman and that his sensibility was of a practical nature.

The term *psychography* has been recently employed for the spiritual biography and Bunyan's example, *Grace Abounding to the Chief of Sinners* (1666), which was apparently written in a period of serious illness, is one of the most distinguished in the language. However, it is so lacking in the normal mundane concerns of the autobiographer that we learn virtually nothing of his native Elstow and his parental home. His wife, whose suffering was to be depicted when Bunyan's Christian left her behind in the tensions of *Pilgrim's Progress* Part One, only for her to establish herself as the central figure of Part Two, is given little space. Her dowry, which included the book to which we shall return, *The Plain Man's Pathway to Heaven*, is the most vivid of her qualities. Other matters of great potential interest are ruthlessly by-passed so that the book is surprisingly lacking in external event. Tantalizingly for a modern reader, Bunyan chose to reduce an extensive military career during the Civil War to a single and rather insensitive sentence. It proves exactly his point: it is a moment in time in which his instinctive action seems to have been divinely guided; but he offers not the least sympathy for the man shown as a surrogate victim:

> This also have I taken notice of with thanksgiving; when I was a soldier, I with others, were drawn out to go to such a place to besiege it; but when I was just ready to go, one of the company desired to go in my room; to which, when I had consented, he took my place; and coming to the siege, as he stood sentinel, he was shot into the head with a musket bullet, and died.

At first, he says, he failed to see the providential message behind this episode and where it might lead him.

The language of *Grace Abounding* is rarely as formal as that paragraph will have suggested. It is commonly dominated by verbs of an intense and tough nature. He explains how he was *hurled*, *tossed*, *tormented*, *forced to fly* or *be consumed*; voices *dart* at him and it was a considerable time before he even asked himself the crucial question for all Puritans: is my life predestined for heaven or hell? Early in his quest he went through the phase of not caring: 'I can but be damned, and if I must be so, I had as good be damned for many sins, as to be damned for few'. Finally, and the reason for the writing of the book in the first place, he turned to a conventional image: 'I saw my gold was in my trunk at home'. It is of such metal as the crowns that Christian sees in the Celestial City: the natural image, it may seem, but one that the anti-royalist Milton sought to avoid in his heaven, showing it instead as one of the products of hell in *Paradise Lost*. Bunyan had no difficulty in accommodating this simple image; it was as natural to him as to suffuse the landscape in and around Bedfordshire in the light of abounding grace when he sought to elaborate the spiritual attestations of hills and mountains that mark the true straight path – what some today might term a *ley-line* – out of this world and into the next.

Some of the personal and local identifications may be lost when they are subsumed into *Pilgrim's Progress* but *Grace Abounding* remains the best commentary upon the allegory. Ideas which are elaborated later often appear in simpler state in the psychography, as in this passage:

> There came flocking into my mind an innumerable company of my sins and transgression, amongst which were at this time most to my affliction, namely my deadness, dulness and coldness in holy duties; my wanderings of heart, of my wearisomeness in all good things, my want of love to God, his ways and people, with this at the end of all, Are these the fruits of Christianity? are these the tokens of a blessed man?

Here we have the identification of sins with people, of the whole of life with allegorical fragments or 'wanderings of the heart'. The concrete style is developed for a simple and illiterate audience, which was expected to observe personifications and identify them in real life, much perhaps as had been the development inside the author's mind when he himself apprehended before realizing their significance; biblical texts emerge as factual imagery and physical experience in this book, rather than as thoughts. A whole gallery of portraits might spring out of this passage, which ends with the characteristic demand for fruits and tokens of salvation, from which a state of spiritual certainty can be achieved when the heart wanderings and the equivocal situations are over.

One of the finest short passages to exemplify the amalgam of rustic and moralist in *Pilgrim's Progress* follows, in the dialogue between Mr Talkative and the Pilgrims. Christian remarks upon the danger of his empty words in these terms:

> His House is as empty as the white of an egg is of savour. There is neither prayer, nor sign of repentance for sin; yea, the brute in his kind serves God far better than he. He is the very stain, reproach and shame of religion, to all that know him; it can hardly have a good word in all that end of the town, where he dwells through him. Thus say the common people that know him. A saint abroad, and a devil at home.

The first analogy here is essentially domestic, yet advanced as a permanent criterion. The words 'kind' and 'shame' retain early connotations, of creation and personal repentance respectively; the culminating epigram is a succinct idiom with a long literary history, to be found in several authors of the century, and clearly indebted for its sharp visualization of the hypocrite to folk tradition. Discussions of this nature in *Pilgrim's Progress* provide effective drama, and they are the result of the author's experience of moral teaching and of popular taste.[2] They represent the summit of Bunyan's Puritan artistry.

It is not necessary to categorize *Pilgrim's Progress* as novel, belated morality, or theological allegory. It is hard to do more than touch upon the qualities of this book in limited space; from such a survey no idea of the vitality of the whole can be conveyed. In places the book is most vigorously related to dramatic speech with its informal movement and sinuous inflection; while in others it rises to didacticism of permanent validity, its tone suggestive of a more academically trained mind. The places of rest in the pilgrimage, such as the halt by the River of Life, are carefully contrived and proclaim artistry as much as any rhetoric or skill in narrative:

> Besides on the banks of this river, on either side, were green trees, that bore all manner of fruit; and the leaves of the trees were good for medicine; with the fruit of these trees, they were also much delighted; and the leaves they eat to prevent surfeits, and other diseases that are incident to those that heat their blood by travels. On either side of the river was also a meadow, curiously beautied with lilies, and it was green all the year long.

A halt of this nature offers spiritual refreshment and creates a store of potential energy; in its use of biblical 'green pastures' there is an artist's handling of light and shade, of tension and relief. The poetic evocation of grace, 'curiously beautified with lilies', is significant also, for it reminds us that the beauties of Puritan literature were never simply aesthetic ones; they always disclose connections with the practical or didactic. They exist to do good, 'to prevent surfeits' or to cure those that 'heat their blood' in experiencing the world. Had this not been the case, a Puritan artist would not have dwelt at length upon them.

At the opening of the narrative Christian (then called Graceless, it should be noticed) deserts his home in the City of Destruction in order to avoid the snares of worldly experience, symbolized by the townsfolk present in the early scenes of both parts of the allegory. Two important incidents may be discussed together: the Slough of

Despond and that of the Wicket-Gate.* The former recapitulates Christian history in the familiar manner later adopted by Jonathan Swift — an admirer of Bunyan — in his *Tale of a Tub*, and is a fine example of a verbal wit rare in one lacking formal education:

> It is not the pleasure of the King that this place should remain so bad; his labourers also have, by the direction of his Majesty's surveyors, been for above these sixteen hundred years, employed about this patch of ground, if perhaps, it might have been mended; yea, and to my knowledge, said he, [Help] here have been swallowed up at least twenty thousand cart-loads; yea, millions of wholesome instructions ... but it is the Slough of Despond still.

This has the concreteness of the descriptions one reads of the state of the roads in medieval England, and the handling of God under the title 'King' and elsewhere the 'Lord of the Manor' brings the allegory down to the life of the seventeenth-century parish most vividly.

The episode which follows is evidence of Bunyan's retention of Catholic formulas. To negotiate the Wicket-Gate successfully demands the same humble submission on the part of the pilgrim as the confessional-box, and the time Christian spends here can legitimately be interpreted as a reference (perhaps unconscious) to that Catholic sacrament:

> ... He knocked therefore, more than once or twice ... At last there came a grave person to the gate, named Good-will, who asked who was there? and when he came? and what he would have?
> CHRISTIAN. Here is a poor burdened sinner. I come from the City of Destruction, but am going to Mount Zion, that I may be delivered from the wrath to come.

Just outside the Wicket-Gate the armies of the devil are massing; as in *The Holy War* they lay siege to Mansoul, and are prepared for a fatal attack upon those who seek to enter with a wrong disposition — the Catholic analogy need not be extended further. The sack of sin becomes more oppressive as the true nature of its contents is realized by the penitent;[3] the manner of its final disappearance is so economically described that it deserves separate discussion.

Between the episodes stands Mr Worldly Wiseman, the first hypocrite to attempt to impose an alien pattern of life upon Christian and the nearest of them all to success. He indicates a turning, where

*Mr Worldly Wiseman, who separates them, was a later addition.

... dwells a gentleman whose name is Legality* a very judicious man, and a man of very good name, that has skill to help men off with such burdens as thine are from their shoulders ... and that which will make thy life the more happy is, to be sure, that thou shalt live by honest neighbours, in credit and good fashion.

Almost all the terms of reference are ambivalent: 'gentleman', 'judicious', 'good', 'honest', and 'happy' have different meanings for a Christian and a tempter, and the pilgrim is too inexperienced to realize the nature of this difference. He accepts the appearance and the name of reality, and turns away until, reaching the foot of Mount Sinai which emits flames as he passes, he finds himself face to face with Evangelist. His mentor upbraids him for deserting the path at the virtual cost of his soul – for the symbol of Sinai with the pressure of the Covenant of the Law behind it would be so interpreted within the theology of Calvin. But for Christian there is better news; as he passes the place of the cross and sepulchre, his sack of sin is taken away and the roll of election is borne to him by the angels:

... upon that place stood a cross, and a little below, in the bottom, a sepulchre. So I saw in my dream, that just as Christian came up with the cross, his burden loosed from off his shoulders, and fell from off his back ... He looked, therefore, and looked again, even till the springs that were in his head sent the waters down his cheeks. Now, as he stood looking and weeping, behold, three Shining Ones came to him and saluted him with 'Peace be to thee'.

The Shining Ones are related to the Angels that stood with Abraham and were accepted in the medieval Church as symbols of the Trinity; here they affirm election which accompanies true grief for sin. Christian is not released from the possibility of error even now; had this been so the book would stop, as would *Hamlet* if Claudius were instantly killed. Both to maintain the narrative and to teach further lessons of humiliation, Bunyan continues to draw spiritual torments from his own experience and clothe them in the external properties of the Valley of Humiliation, the Valley of the Shadow of Death, Vanity Fair, and Doubting Castle.

The Flesh is slow to learn, although the spirit within Christian rapidly appreciates the sinful suggestion in the words of the wayside interlopers. The greatest ordeal to which his weakness leads him, the

*Legality is synonymous with formal social behaviour, with Morality but not Religion – 'he always goes to the town of Morality to church'.

Valley of the Shadow of Death, is directly related to Bunyan's blasphemous verbal automatism which he described in *Grace Abounding*:

> No sin would serve but that; if it were to be committed by speaking such a word, then I have been as if my mouth would have spoken that word, whether I would or no; and in so strong a measure was this temptation upon me that often I have been ready to clap my hand under my chin, to hold my mouth from opening; and to that end also I have had thoughts at other times, to leap with my head downward into some muck-hill hole or other, to keep my mouth from speaking.

The effect of the writing was cathartic, for later he was able to present a similar state impersonally:

> I took notice that now poor Christian was so confounded, that he did not know his own voice; and thus I perceived it. Just when he was come over against the mouth of the burning pit, one of the wicked ones got behind him, and stepped up softly to him, and whisperingly suggested many grievous blasphemies to him, which he verily thought had proceeded from his own mind.

From these passages there can be no doubt of the intensity of Bunyan's experience, nor of the relief from the Devil which was necessary before he could 'place' this situation in calm words: 'I took notice.'

There are other trials ahead, and I would single out the meeting with the lions which are chained, although Christian does not (as one of the elect) need to know this. He goes past, though two others, Timorous and Mistrust, have fallen back most dramatically:

CHRISTIAN. Whither are you going?
MEN. They said, Back! back! and we would have you do so too, if either life or peace is prized by you.

'Life' and 'peace' acceptable to these men would not satisfy Christian; if he accepted their advice – such is the stylization of the writing – he would have identified himself with their retrogressive qualities. As it is, he lives to further his pilgrimage and yet to reach Doubting Castle in which he suffers severely for the capitulation to doubts and despairs which are more terrible because they are so late in the pilgrimage. Giant Despair, his keeper, is a fine comic creation, the product of folk-tales and ballads, and a high tempo is sustained throughout the episode which he dominates. The imprisoned pilgrims escape after a period in which Christian forgets the key of the promises and shows the measure of his despair. The key, when it is finally recalled, goes into the lock 'damnable hard'. At first sight this adjective is another impetus to the narrative, perhaps an imprecation which fell from Christian's lips; on closer inspection it is a grimly ironic pun playing upon the fate from which it releases them, the 'everlasting nay' of damnation; and through one bare word a universe of sinister implication is given to the whole episode.

The allegory is not complete without insistence upon the punishments in store for those who are too full of themselves to attend to God. In Mr By-Ends we meet a more astute member of the tribe of Talkative, whose dialogue repays the closest attention as a perfect revelation of the *parvenu*.[4] Then there is the most plausible Mr Ignorance, whose error lies in demanding the ends without bothering about the means, and who presents himself unqualified at the Celestial City, only to be thrown out like the man without the wedding-garment in the parable (Matthew xxii). There is no occasion to resent Bunyan's handling of him,[5] for the dialogue which passes between Christian and Ignorance is most convincing in its analysis of reprobate error. The submission of Christian already quoted should be compared with the empty prose of this:

> I know my lord's will and I have been a good liver; I pay every man his own; I pray, fast, pay tithes, and give alms, and have left my country for whither I am going.

The parable of the Pharisee and the Publican (Luke xviii) foreshadows this statement. A further source of it was a religious dialogue written in 1601 by the Essex minister Arthur Dent, *The Plain Man's Pathway to Heaven*. In this book – well known to Bunyan – the hero is the Plain Man and the villain a caviller named Antilegon, and as a pair they show a close resemblance to Christian and Ignorance, even down to the dramatic inanity of Antilegon's spiritual disposition:

> I have always served God duly and truly, and had him in my mind. I do as I would be done to. If I go to hell, I shall have fellows and make as good shift as others.

There is no doubt of Dent's displeasure at this, and Ignorance no less deserves his particular punishment for presumption, described with monosyllabic simplicity and finality when angels 'took him up, and carried him through the air to the door that I saw on the side of the hill and put him in there'. Thus the pilgrimage of the two estates of man is concluded. In the process of self-knowledge that Bunyan was steadily inculcating the comparison is vital, and it sums up what the author was seeking to offer when he put a commentary upon his private experience into the hands of the public.

In 1684 there appeared a sequel which brings the deserted wife and family to the Celestial City also. The greater romance-nature of this book suggests a simpler, non-didactic purpose. Dancing and music are more frequent, both folk-song and the art-music of the keyboard, and the rigours of the original journey figure in the sequel only in the manner of some military reminiscence. Its great liveliness extends to the final pages where the last embarkation, in the manner of a happier sixth book to Virgil's *Aeneid*, takes place. From the sequel, most of all, we may refute the arguments of the inhumanity of the Puritans,[6] for in making his own happiness explicit Bunyan has dwelt upon the great joy of the divine presence rather than upon the theological minutiae which in the first pilgrimage tend to predominate. There is, for instance, none of the initial tension from the father's need to abandon his family. Instead, we notice, the sanctity of the family always being at the centre of Puritan moral theology and its attendant didactic literature, Bunyan has supplied the ending of all comic fiction. Family reunion is followed by the establishment of courtship rituals, the foundation of new families and the manifestation of human fertility.

The most 'modern' of Bunyan's writings is *The Life and Death of Mr Badman* (1680), which is cast in the form of a colloquy on urban life and a detailed examination of the habits of Vanity Fair. It is a counterpart to *Pilgrim's Progress* which studies the progress of reprobation in the soul of the protagonist. Mr Badman is a trader whose life is a conglomeration of the rusts of sin. The atmosphere is appropriately changed from that of *Pilgrim's Progress*; false weights, bankruptcy, persecutions, the sordidness and lechery of a market-town are the subjects of an extended homily given by Wiseman to his friend Attentive in the form of a dialogue enlivened by crisp narrative and satirical writing of great fluency and economy.

All the sins of childhood are fathered upon Badman at his arrival in the world, and as he grows more knowledgeable and cunning, his range of sin widens at the same time. The position of apprentices in the mercantile system and the theological justification of that system are the major concerns of conscience in this book. Good masters and bad are equal to young Badman, for his choice is inescapably wrong. The novel proceeds with the birth of illegitimate children and the hypocritical courtship of a religious girl which ends in their unhappy marriage. The consequences are described with devastating plainness:

> Well, to be short, in little time, Mr Badman obtains his desire, gets this honest girl, is married to her, brings her home, makes a feast, entertains her royally, but her portion must pay for all.

The pages in which he brings whores home, with his wife sitting patiently by longing for death, contain further lessons in feminine conduct and are handled with conviction and restraint.

At each turn in the story additional tales, recounted to the joy of the narrators, are introduced to point the moral. One of these, on fornication, will show the fierce pace of sin. In it, a debauchee is faced with his latest bastard child:

> Now there was made in a room hard by a very great fire; so the gentleman* took up the babe, went and drew the coals from the stock, cast the child in and covered it up, and there was an end of that.

More elaborately presented than this is the story of Dorothy Mately, a perjurer who stole a sum from a fellow worker in a sandpit, and on denying the charge was sucked into the ground and suffocated. The description is comic – the lad had opportunely 'laid his breeches by and was at work in his drawers' – and is accompanied with a wealth of circumstantial evidence, exact sums, depths and lengths of time; such verification, in fact, as to compel belief among Dissenters, who distrusted fiction and needed the citation of responsible witnesses to overcome their innate suspicion.† By this realistic reportage the nonconformist middle-classes were brought to accept the novel as a legitimate device of self-improvement, and they clung to it for two hundred years. *Mr Badman*, as a contribution to the development of the novel, was perhaps of greater importance than *Pilgrim's Progress*. The point can be made by referring briefly to the work of Defoe. *Robinson Crusoe* is an account of a physically and spiritually isolated man, and, like many later novels, it depends upon the Calvinist interpretation of the individual conscience displayed in fictional form.

---

*The satirical inflection, damning to courtly society, should be noticed.
†The incident is authenticated from independent sources.

Moll Flanders and *Roxana* owe most to *Mr Badman*, though they lack the traditional firmness of moral character, which Bunyan's novel might have taught his first distinguished successor; as slight compensation they possess the accuracy of detail which commands attention though it cannot replace moral evaluation.

Badman's end displays the working-out of the plan for reprobates. He had shown temporary repentance as the result of an accident, but after the death of his good wife he marries an old whore and sinks still lower in esteem. The ending of this career of loose living is as gentle as that of his wife's: 'Mr Badman died like a lamb, or as they call it, like a chrisom-child, quietly and without fear.' This departure from convention – made more prominent by the juxtaposition in the text of the quiet and holy death of his wife and the flanking description of an account of self-evisceration by one in despair – is made in order to point out the dichotomy between appearance and reality and to provide a final and startling example of it. Nobody could doubt the fate of the dead man; nothing, therefore, can be deduced from a deathbed scene. Bunyan's everyday discernment and his formal theology enrich jointly this most realistic of his writings.

Mr Badman may, finally, be seen as a social document, relevant to the study of the rule of conscience in commercial ethics and practice. Bunyan was in no sense an apologist for capitalist enterprise, although he was no social leveller. The phrase 'grinding the faces of the poor' is employed, and all manner of cheating and oppression from trader and landlord are severely condemned. Nowhere did he speak out more forcibly against Restoration society than in the preface to this novel. A long scholastic section is devoted to bankruptcy, since Badman declared himself broken prematurely in order to reserve stock and a 'hatful of money'. The positive advice offered is that a bankrupt must make honest statements and attempt prompt restitution. The creditor, for his part, must not forget the duty of all men to support their dependants. The bankrupt must in 'Reason, Conscience, and Nature' maintain them. These three terms sum up Bunyan's demands of the whole of society and its intercourse; they comprehend his standards of ethical conduct. In spite of certain similarities, they are further in spirit from the key-words of the age of Pope that ensued – Reason, Truth, Nature, Use, and Sense – than the mere letter admits. A permanent belief in conscience and an insistence upon following all its dictates characterizes Bunyan's advice to mankind. Whether it was in the isolation of the heart or in the traffic of the market-place his instruction was the same, and in two very different books he gave similar advice.

There are many other writings by John Bunyan; they fill three large folio volumes and several more of them are allegorical in method. Only one of these, *The Holy War* (1685), is ever reprinted. It is a work of great ingenuity, and maintains the allegorical form in a manner more complex than in *Pilgrim's Progress*, describing the waxing and waning of grace in Mansoul through encounters between heavenly and diabolical armies for the possession of the fortified city of the soul. A classic like *Pilgrim's Progress* it cannot ever be; it lacks the feeling for 'character' which Bunyan shows at his best, and its procedure admits of no single interpretation. But it shows the author's preoccupation with artistic problems; he was too scrupulous to repeat past successes.

Since his death, the Bunyan tradition has not ceased to grow; many writers have responded imaginatively to the suggestiveness of *Pilgrim's Progress*. Two New Englanders, Nathaniel Hawthorne in *The Scarlet Letter*, *The Blithedale Romance*, and his story *Young Goodman Brown*, and Herman Melville, in *Benito Cereno* and his posthumous *Billy Budd*, have owed their assurance ultimately to the English Calvinists of the seventeenth century. In our own time the most distinctive allegory to stem from the tradition has been *Mr Weston's Good Wine* by T. F. Powys, a great admirer of John Bunyan. All these – and there are many more books which employ the allegorical outline in a mechanical and imitative fashion – are reminders of the power of this long tradition. They are also proof that the Puritanism of the early generations was in accord with the culture, the vigorous speech, and living belief of the country, a belief which had existed for centuries and which was no deterrent to the production of works whose humanism we commonly think to be essentially repugnant to the name and nature of Bunyan's religious persuasion.

NOTES

1. *Literature and the Pulpit in Medieval England* (1933), by G. R. Owst.
2. For further analysis, see Arnold Kettle, *Introduction to the English Novel* (1951), 42–5.
3. cf. 1 above.
4. Further discussion will be found in L. C. Knights, *Drama and the Society in the Age of Jonson* (1937).

5. *The Arraignment of Mr Persecution* (c. 1645) a semi-dramatic pamphlet by Richard Overton and source of the trial scene in Vanity Fair can be cited as evidence that the Puritans did not universally condemn the drama as morally deplorable or the whole art as a sign of damnation. On this topic see Margot Heinemann, *Puritanism and Theatre* (1980).

6. The conflict between Puritanism and humanism in the seventeenth century is analysed by Sir Herbert Grierson in *Cross Currents in the Literature of the Seventeenth Century* (1929).

SAMUEL BUTLER AND *HUDIBRAS*

IAN JACK

Nor is the world so well understood by observation of the little Good that is in it, as the Prodigious variety of Wickednes Folly and Madnes with which it is Possest.

(BUTLER: *Characters and Passages from Note-books*, 344)

Butler (1612–80) took the name of his hero from Spenser, and his great comedy cannot be understood without glancing back to *The Faerie Queene*. In Book II, which is concerned with Temperaunce, Sir Guyon reaches a castle inhabited by three sisters. The youngest loves pleasure, the second moderation, while the third is a sour hater of all delights. Sir Hudibras, who is contrasted with Sans-loy, the wooer of the younger sister, makes his suit to the eldest. In a stanza which throws a great deal of light on *Hudibras* (1662–77), he is described as 'an hardy man',

> Yet not so good of deedes, as great of name,
> Which he by many rash adventures wan,
> Since errant armes to sew he first began;
> More huge in strength, then wise in workes he was,
> And reason with foole-hardize over ran;
> Sterne melancholy did his courage pas,
> And was for terrour more, all armd in shyning bras.
>
> (II. ii. st. 17)

Butler's Hudibras resembles Spenser's in being more famous than he deserves, in having more strength than wisdom, and in being inspired less by true courage than by 'melancholy' (in this context, madness). But by giving his hero this name Butler does not only indicate the main traits of his character: he also states his own attitude to the civil wars and the discontents which led up to them. The suggestion is that the Royalists, or the more extreme among them, bear an affinity to the youngest daughter Perissa and her lover Sans-loy; that the Parliamentary Party may be similarly compared to the eldest daughter and

332

her wooer Hudibras; while the poet himself, and all moderate men, support the 'great rule of Temp'raunce'.

The title is not the only thing about *Hudibras* which reminds one of *The Faerie Queene*. In its whole conception and organization Butler's poem has affinities with Spenser's. The parallel between the adventures of Sir Hudibras and those of the hero of each of the Books of *The Faerie Queene* must have been deliberate. Like one of Spenser's knights, Butler's hero is involved in continual disputes and adventures, and woos a lady. But in all his endeavours he is an un-Spenserian failure.

The fact that Butler was familiar with the Renaissance doctrine of the heroic poem has a bearing on *Hudibras* which is frequently overlooked. Butler knew as well as Spenser or Milton that an allegorical meaning was expected in any long poem, and in fact *Hudibras* has something of the same complexity as *The Faerie Queene*. The strong element of the *roman à clef* has always been recognized; and there is no doubt that the poem was intended to embody a complicated allegory. As each of Spenser's knights represents one of the cardinal virtues, or the striving for that virtue, so Sir Hudibras represents one of the basic vices. John Dennis suggested that *Hudibras* is a satire on hypocrisy. Sir Hudibras is Hypocrisy embodied. Near the beginning of the poem the reader is told that 'Hipocrisie and Non-sence' are in control of Sir Hudibras's conscience; hypocrisy is satirized with particular intensity throughout; and in the brilliant passage, parodying the confessional dialogues and self-communings of the Dissenters, in which Ralpho scares Hudibras into thinking him a supernatural 'Voice', he asks him point-blank:

> Why didst thou chuse that cursed Sin,
> Hypocrisie, to set up in?

To which the knight replies, without demur:

> Because it is the thriving'st Calling,
> The onely Saints-Bell that rings all in.
> (III. i. 1221–4)

Throughout *Hudibras* great emphasis is laid on the difference between profession and performance, outer seeming and inner reality. It would hardly be an exaggeration to say that in this poem every species of human folly and crime is represented as a species of hypocrisy.

Although political satire is the most obvious 'end' of *Hudibras*, therefore, Hazlitt was right when he remarked that Butler 'could not, in spite of himself, narrow his mind / And to party give up what was meant for mankind'. There are many passages where Butler makes no pretence to be limiting his satire to a political party, but attacks lawyers, women, the Royal Society, and pedantry of every kind. If *Hudibras* had been completed it seems likely that every type represented in Butler's prose 'Characters' would have found its niche in a comprehensive 'Anatomy of Melancholy'.

In giving his satire this wide scope Butler was following the tradition of such books as Barclay's *Ship of Fools* and the *Encomium Moriae* of Erasmus. Another writer whose work may have encouraged Butler to widen the scope of his satire was Jonson, for whom he had a great admiration. As in *Volpone* and *The Alchemist*, Jonson's main satire against greed is accompanied and enriched by incidental attacks on other species of folly and sin, so in *Hudibras* hypocrisy is only the principal target. Butler 'in general ridicules not persons, but things', said Hazlitt, 'not a party, but their principles, which may belong, as time and occasion serve, to one set of solemn pretenders or another'. Because Butler was a man of genius, what began as a political burlesque ended as what Dennis truly called a very just satire.

No passage in *Hudibras* is more familiar than that in which Butler ridicules his hero's addiction to rhetoric:

> For *Rhetorick* he could not ope
> His mouth, but out there flew a Trope;
> And when he hapned to break off
> I' th' middle of his speech, or cough,
> H' had hard words, ready to shew why,
> And tell what Rules he did it by.
>
> (I. i. 81–6)

Such satire was thoroughly conventional: one has only to turn to Erasmus to find all the charges that Butler brings against rhetorical pedantry brilliantly deployed by the greatest of all the humanists. What is satirized is not rhetoric itself but the pedantic affectation of rhetoric, fine words and elaborate figures out of season. It would be a serious mistake to suppose that Butler is here rebelling against old attitudes; and it would be equally false to imagine, from his satire on

334

rhetoric, that he himself had no use for it. What Butler wrote of Sprat – 'The Historian of Gresham Colledge, Indevors to Cry down Oratory and Declamation, while He uses nothing else' – is equally true of himself. The point is important because the modern reader, knowing little of decorum and the accepted 'kinds', has a natural tendency to regard *Hudibras* as inspired doggerel and its author as a literary jester who knew no other way of writing. Nothing could be farther from the truth. Butler's other works make it clear that Sir William Temple's description of Rabelais as 'a Man of Excellent and Universal Learning as well as Wit' is no less applicable to him.

It follows that Butler's choice of verse and style was deliberate. The limited value of metrical notations appears in the fact that the same name must be given to the metre of *Hudibras* as to that of Marvell's *To His Coy Mistress* and *The Garden*, as well as many parts of *L'Allegro* and *Il Penseroso*. Like the iambic pentameter, the tetrameter is endlessly adaptable: it is the use that Butler makes of it, the tune that he plays on it, that is significant. What is particularly remarkable is the rushing vigour of *Hudibras*, the unfailing energy of the verse.

Butler's metre cannot usefully be considered in isolation from the other aspects of his idiom, for there is a perfect partnership between his versification and his diction. Even if the verse itself were what is misleadingly termed 'heroic' (iambic pentameters rhyming in pairs), any serious attempt at the 'harmonious numbers' appropriate to heroic verse in the full sense would be ludicrously out of place as an accompaniment to the prosaic diction which is Butler's chosen medium. For this reason Dryden's censure of the metre of *Hudibras* (quoted in part on p. 336) must be read rather as a reflection of his own choice of a suitable metre for satire than as impartial literary criticism.

The characteristic mode of satire in *Hudibras* is that of describing everything in the most undignified manner possible. Satire and the sympathetic feelings are absolutely incompatible. Butler's aim is to kill any sympathy which the reader may feel for the subject of his satire, moving him instead to amusement and contempt. There is nothing indirect in the working of the satire. The method is that of straightforward 'diminution'; the reader is told that the quarrels which led to the Civil War were of no more account than a brawl for a whore, and his acceptance of this view is made inevitable (at least temporarily) by the fact that the whole affair is described in an idiom which ridicules

everything it touches. Butler's subject is as different as possible from
that of the romantic epic poet. Instead of Ariosto's

> Le donne, i cavallier, l'arme, gli amori,
> Le cortesie, l'audaci imprese,

he is concerned with light wenches and prudish viragos, costermon-
gers and fanatics, rudeness in every sense and of every kind. And his
style is equally remote from that of heroic verse. The elementary
principle on which he works is that while many people might sym-
pathize with a *crowd*, no one cares to take sides with a *rout*. The essence
of low satire could not be more simple.

All has not been said of what Johnson called the 'original and
peculiar' diction of *Hudibras* when it has been assigned to the category
of low style. It is remarkably varied. The second paragraph of the
poem, for example, introduces a new element, that of parody:

> A *Wight* he was, whose very sight wou'd
> Entitle him *Mirror of Knighthood*;
> That never bent *his stubborn knee*
> To any thing but *Chivalry*.
>
> (I. i. 15–18 – my italics)

This element of literary satire demands modifications of style which
enhance the variety of the poem.

The critical attitude which inspires the parodies in *Hudibras* is
precisely that which one would expect of Butler, an Augustan conservatism looking back to classical models and suspicious of innovation. The principal targets are such writers of 'romantic' epics as
Ariosto, Spenser, and Davenant. Other unclassical genres which are
parodied include the ballad, the metrical romance of the Middle Ages,
which survived among humble readers during the seventeenth century, and the prose heroic romances so popular in France and England
during Butler's lifetime. Although Butler has his fling at modern
translators, the great classical epics themselves are parodied comparatively seldom.

The literary satire which finds expression in perpetual 'allusions'
throughout *Hudibras* is only one aspect of a comprehensive critique of
the uses and abuses of the English language. No less than Rabelais or
James Joyce, Butler was a fascinated student of language. Odd words
interested him as much as odd ideas. It would not be hard to imagine

him spending an evening with Robert Burton listening to the swearing of the bargees at Folly Bridge. It may be that he had no need to go out of his way to find freaks of language. If there is any truth in the tradition that he was at one time secretary to Sir Samuel Luke, he must have had every opportunity of hearing the latest in cant terms. Perhaps he used some of his numerous notebooks for recording the words he heard. With an intense satiric mastery he culled the language of sectarians and pedants of every sort. *Hudibras* became the receptacle of this wealth of strange words; as a result it has a greater variety of idiom than any other poem in the language.

Yet it would be quite wrong to think of Butler simply as an enthusiast for odd words. He lived in an age of linguistic flux when the native genius of 'the finest of the vernacular tongues' seemed to many good judges to be in peril. Sprat complained that the language had 'receiv'd many fantastical terms, which were introduced by our *Religious Sects* ... and *Translators*'. Dryden returned to this subject time and time again. 'I have endeavoured to write English,' he wrote in his first considerable critical essay, which appeared in the same year as the Second Part of *Hudibras*, 'as near as I could distinguish it from the tongue of pedants, and that of affected travellers. Only I am sorry, that (speaking so noble a language as we do) we have not a more certain measure of it, as they have in France.' In this revival of the Renaissance zeal for ennobling the vernacular, Butler played his own part. 'That Barbarous Canting which those use who do not understand the sense and Propriety of a Language' is continually a target of his satire.

'This Canting runs through all Professions and Sorts of men,' Butler added, 'from the Judge on the Bench to the Beggar in the Stocks'; and he laid all these sources under contribution for his great satire. His use of the special vocabularies of trades and professions may be regarded as a satirical footnote to the dispute about 'terms of art' which raged so fiercely from the early Renaissance onwards. 'The Tearms of all Arts are generally Nonsense,' he wrote in his *Characters*, 'that signify nothing, or very improperly what they are Meant to do, and are more Difficult to be learn'd then the things they are designed to teach.' The cant of lawyers he found even more objectionable than that of astrologers; it is satirized in the language of the practitioner whom Sir Hudibras consults about his complicated affairs. He says that he can find his client plenty of 'Knights of the Post', ne'er-do-wells who live

> [By] letting out to hire, their Ears,
> To Affidavit-Customers:
> At inconsiderable values,
> To serve for Jury-men, or Tales,[a]
> Although retain'd in th' hardest matters,
> Of Trustees, and Administrators.
>
> (III. iii. 729–34)

The affectation of legal terms by the half-educated so common among the Roundheads is unsparingly parodied in the speeches of Sir Hudibras, who delights to give authority to his pronouncements by a judicious smattering of the 'Barbarous French' and Latin of the law. His verbal habits are precisely those which John Eachard censured when he described 'a sort of Divines, who, if they but happen of an unlucky hard word all the week, ... think themselves not careful of their flock, if they lay it not up till Sunday, and bestow it amongst them, in their next preachment'. Like Eachard's preacher, the Knight disdains words 'such as the constable uses' as much as matter 'such as comes to the common market'.

While the diction of *Hudibras* is remarkably varied, it is the astonishing profusion of witty images that distinguishes it most sharply from the common run of burlesques. It is clear from the 'character' of *A Small Poet* and from numerous prose jottings that Butler was keenly interested in the analogical uses of language. Like Bacon's, indeed, his was 'a mind keenly sensitive to all analogies and affinities ... spreading as it were tentacles on all sides in quest of chance prey'. If ever a man was haunted by 'the demon of analogy', it was he.

As one would expect, a very large number of the images in *Hudibras* are of the 'diminishing' sort characteristic of direct satire. The realistic bent of Butler's mind led him to fill his satire with imagery from the most commonplace objects of daily use, 'Out-of-fashion'd Cloaths', bowls, watches that go 'sometime too fast, sometime too slow', 'a Candle in the Socket', and beer 'by Thunder turn'd to Vineger'. He takes his choice from the familiar things of the farmyard and kitchen-hearth, children's games and men's employments. Images from animals are particularly common. Mahomet

> Had Lights where better Eyes were blind,
> As Pigs are said to see the Wind.
>
> (III. ii. 1107–8)

a a legal term.

The Rump Parliament

> With new Reversions of nine Lives,
> Starts up, and, like a Cat, revives.
> (III. ii. 1629–30)

We Dissenters – says one of them – have friends who

> Are only Tools to our Intrigues,
> And sit like Geese to hatch our Eggs.
> (III. ii. 895–6)

Again,

> ... All Religions flock together,
> Like Tame, and Wild-Fowl of a Feather.
> (III. ii. 1455–6)

These are only a few of the animal images from a single canto: to quote more would be tedious. What is remarkable is the effect that Butler achieves. By crowding his poem with similes from animals of 'low' associations like dogs, cats, pigs, and mice he gains an effect of homely caricature. The reader feels that no more is needed to demonstrate the folly of Butler's targets than reference to the store of common sense summed up in the nation's proverbs and homely sayings.

In creating this profusion of imagery Butler was again adapting to the purposes of his own satire a common practice of the Dissenters, who were accused, with justice, of being 'indiscreet and horrid Metaphor-mongers'. 'As for the common sort of people that are addicted to this sort of expression in their discourses,' Eachard complained in 1670, 'away presently to both the Indies! rake heaven and earth! down to the bottom of the sea! then tumble over all Arts and Sciences! ransack all shops and warehouses! spare neither camp nor city, but that they will have them!' Sir Hudibras's proud principle, never to speak 'to Man or Beast, In notions vulgarly exprest', inspires the speeches of many of Butler's characters: in nothing is its meaning more clearly illustrated than in their imagery.

As might be expected, it is not only the Dissenters whose verbal habits are parodied in the imagery of *Hudibras*. A connoisseur of folly in all its forms, Butler was equally amused by the extravagances of the poets of his day, and satirized their commonplace images:

> Some with *Arabian Spices* strive
> To embalm her cruelly alive;

Or *season* her, as *French* Cooks use
Their *Haut-gusts, Buollies,* or *Ragusts*;
Use her so barbarously ill,
To grind her Lips upon a *Mill*,
Until the *Facet Doublet* doth
Fit their *Rhimes* rather than her mouth;
Her mouth compar'd t' an *Oyster's,* with
A row of *Pearl* in't, stead of *Teeth*.

(II. i. 595–604)

Of the prevalent fashions none interested Butler more than the different varieties of the metaphysical idiom, now (in spite of numerous late appearances) past its hey-day. As he turned the pages of such poets as Donne and Cowley and of his friends Davenant and Cleveland, there was nothing that drew his attention more frequently than their bold juxtapositions of ideas. His own relation to the metaphysical poets is never more evident than in some of his images:

His Body, that stupendious Frame,
Of all the World the Anagram,
Is of two equal parts compact
In Shape and Symmetry exact.
Of which the Left and Female side
Is to the Manly Right a Bride.

(III. i. 771–6)

Butler was the first comic poet to invade the territory of metaphysical verse and use with genius the spoils that he found there. More brilliantly than any previous poet, he used 'wit' for the purposes of low satire. As a result he occupies a distinctive place in the evolution of the idioms of English poetry in the later seventeenth century. *Hudibras* was one of the principal channels by which the 'wit' of the earlier part of the century was transmitted to the greatest of the Augustans.

Yet it would be a mistake to think of Butler too narrowly as a satirist. Dennis found 'a vivacity and purity in his Language, *wherever it was fit it should be pure*, that could proceed from nothing but from a generous Education, and from a happy Nature' (my italics). Such a passage as this illustrates what Dennis meant:

For though out-number'd, overthrown,
And by the Fate of War run down;
Their Duty never was defeated,
Nor from their Oaths and Faith retreated.

> For Loyalty is still the same,
> Whether it win or lose the Game;
> True as a Dial to the Sun,
> Although it be not shin'd upon.
>
> (III. ii. 169–76)

This is not 'high style', which would be out of place; but there are no cant terms in these lines, the diction is pure, and the image is handled with a remarkable felicity. The same is true of the *Heroical Epistle of Hudibras to his Lady*, which is not the work of a man completely unskilled in the mode of writing which it parodies. Indeed, *Hudibras* contains a number of passages that would lend distinction to any lyric of the age:

> For as we see th' eclipsed Sun
> By mortals is more gaz'd upon,
> Than when adorn'd with all his light
> He shines in Serene Sky most bright:
> So Valor in a low estate
> Is most admir'd and wonder'd at.
>
> (I. iii. 1051–6)

No 'Caroline lyrist' could do better than this:

> To bid me not to *love*,
> Is to forbid my *Pulse* to move,
>
> (II. i. 343–4)

or excel this image, perhaps the finest of all:

> Like *Indian*-Widows, gone to Bed
> In Flaming Curtains to the Dead.
>
> (III. i. 639–40)

Such a simile reminds one for a moment that Butler was a younger contemporary of Henry King. Occasionally in reading him one hears the rhythms of the Caroline lyric resonant beneath the surface of the verse. A gift for epigram was not the only thing he had in common with Andrew Marvell.

In spite of the 'kinds' there was in the seventeenth century no such hard-and-fast distinction between 'poetry' (conceived of as a serious and, indeed, solemn thing) and 'light verse' as became a commonplace in the nineteenth century. As many of the love poems of the time make clear, verse was a much subtler instrument then than it was later to become. A poet could modulate from one level of seriousness to another in a couplet, or within a single line. Satire and elegy, burlesque and 'the lyric note' were not always mutually exclusive. The best Augustan poetry retains something of this subtlety of tone.

Butler's distinction is twofold. He took over a traditional manner of 'low' writing and used it with a brilliance and variety of effect which were new things, and which led Dennis to call him 'a whole Species of Poets in one'. And, secondly, he differed from earlier burlesque writers in using this amazing idiom 'with a just design, which was to expose Hypocrisie'. So doing, Butler was true to his own ideal of satire: 'A Satyr,' he wrote, 'is a kinde of Knight Errant that goe's upon Adventures, to Relieve the Distressed Damsel Virtue, and Redeeme Honour out of Inchanted Castles, And opprest Truth, and Reason out of the Captivity of Gyants or Magitians' (*Characters*, p. 469). By adapting burlesque to the fundamental requirement of decorum, a worthy and unifying 'end', Butler was able to write one of the greatest comic poems in the language.

NOTE

This essay is an abbreviated version of ch. ii of the author's book, *Augustan Satire: Intention and Idiom in English Poetry 1660–1750* (1952, Oxford paperback, 1966). It is reproduced by permission of the Delegates of the Clarendon Press.

JOHN WILMOT, EARL OF ROCHESTER

V. DE S. PINTO

The last English Court which can fairly be described as a centre of intellectual and artistic culture was the Court of Charles II. The Whig and Puritan tradition, as embodied for example in Macaulay's *History of England*, gave wide currency to the belief that the Restoration courtiers were all corrupt and cynical pleasure-seekers. Many of them certainly deserve this reputation, but modern research has shown that the Whig view is an over-simplification. J. H. Wilson in his admirable study, *The Court Wits of the Restoration*, proves that a number of the more sensational stories which have gone to build up the legend of the Wicked Restoration Courtier are apocryphal: 'About them,' he writes, 'has grown up a considerable body of lurid tradition, nourished by the gossip-mongers of the eighteenth century, and by the errors and credulities of modern biographers.' The young men of the Restoration Court certainly drank hard, indulged in a good deal of sexual promiscuity, made bawdy jokes, and wrote bawdy verses, but their sins seem to have been simply those common to idle young people belonging to a privileged class with money in their pockets in all periods when moral codes have been loosened through the disintegration of traditional beliefs. Many of the courtiers were undoubtedly men of wide culture and creative ability, and there is plenty of evidence of their reading and their interest in literature and the theatre. Dryden's tributes to the civilized quality of their conversation in *An Essay of Dramatic Poesy* (1668) and in the Epistle Dedicatory to *The Assignation* are of great significance and should be used as a corrective to the Victorian tradition of the men with 'foreheads of bronze, hearts like the nether mill-stone, and tongues set on fire of hell'.[1]

Soon after the restoration of Charles II in 1660 a group of literary courtiers, called by Andrew Marvell the 'merry gang', became prominent. They included George Villiers, Duke of Buckingham, Charles Sackville, Lord Buckhurst (afterwards Earl of Dorset), John Sheffield,

Earl of Mulgrave (afterwards Duke of Buckinghamshire), Sir Charles
Sedley, and others. A little later they were joined by Sir George
Etherege, John Wilmot, Earl of Rochester, William Wycherley, and
Henry Savile. These were Pope's 'mob of gentlemen who wrote with
ease', the last English courtier poets, inheritors of a tradition which
went back to Sir Thomas Wyatt and his friends at the Court of Henry
VIII. Their immediate predecessors were Carew, Suckling, and
Lovelace, the poets of the mid-seventeenth century, but something
had been lost which was never quite regained. F. R. Leavis indicated
the nature of this loss with his usual acuteness:

> Charles II was a highly intelligent man of liberal interests, and his mob of
> gentlemen cultivated conversation and the Muses. But that the old fine order,
> ... the 'Court culture', did not survive the period of disruption, exile and
> 'travels' is apparent even in the best things of Etherege, Sedley, Rochester and
> the rest: their finest specimens of the tenderly or cynically gallant or polite lack
> the positive fineness, the implicit subtlety ... in Carew. The cheaper things
> remind us forcibly that to indicate the background of Restoration poetry we
> must couple with the Court, not as earlier the country house, but the coffee-
> house, and that the cofee-house is on intimate terms with the Green-Room.[2]

There is, perhaps, some slight exaggeration or overstatement here.
Some part of the 'old fine order' remained, and there was still an intimate connection between the Court and the country house, as well as
between the Court and the coffee-house, but it is perfectly true that the
richness and subtlety of the courtly culture which produced men like
Sir Henry Wotton, George Herbert, and Thomas Carew did not
survive the Civil War.

The new courtiers were a 'post-war generation' in some ways
rather like the post-war generation of the nineteen-twenties, consciously reacting against the idealisms both of the Puritans and of the old
Cavaliers. Clarendon was shocked by what seemed to him to be their
heartlessness. Their favourite philosopher was Thomas Hobbes of
Malmesbury, author of *Leviathan*, who was a frequent visitor at
Whitehall in the years immediately following the Restoration.
Aubrey tells us that 'order was given that he should have free accesse to
his majesty, who was always much delighted in his witt and smart
repartees'. Hobbes's thorough-going materialism and his rejection of
the 'kingdom of darkness' (superstition and priestcraft) seemed to free
his young disciples from all the inhibitions which were part of the

religiosity that hung like a cloud over their early years. The ideal of the 'merry gang' was the perfect Man of Wit and Fashion, the aesthetic hero, or witty, aristocratic rake already sketched before the Civil War by Fletcher in his comedy *The Wild Goose Chase* and by Sir John Suckling in real life. Sir George Etherege, a prominent member of the group and certainly the most gifted dramatist among them, painted a finished portrait of this character in his most successful play *Sir Fopling Flutter or the Man of Mode* (1676). His hero Dorimant is the ancestor of a long line of witty, attractive rakes in English comedy, which extends from Congreve's Mirabel to Wilde's Lord Goring. Lamb's description of the world of the Comedy of Manners can well be applied to his way of life. It is 'the Utopia of gallantry, where pleasure is duty, and the manners perfect freedom'. Dorimant gets rid of an inconvenient mistress with the grace and poise with which he would change his cravat, and he leads on the absurd Sir Fopling Flutter to display his affectations with the fine touch of a comic artist.

The man on whom the character of Dorimant was said to be based was John Wilmot, second Earl of Rochester, the son of one of the most able Cavalier generals and a pious lady belonging to a famous Puritan family. He seems to have inherited a good share of his father's audacity and some part of his mother's sense of spiritual reality. Educated at Wadham College, Oxford, one of the chief centres of the new scientific movement which led to the establishment of the Royal Society, he was enabled by a generous grant from the King to travel on the Continent for several years and to spend some time studying at the University of Padua. He appeared at Court at Christmas 1664 and at once became the most prominent figure in 'the merry gang'. 'The Court,' we are told by Anthony à Wood, 'not only debauched him; but made him an absolute Hobbist.' Hobbes's *Treatise of Human Nature* had appeared in 1651 when Rochester was a child of three, and his more famous work *Leviathan* in the following year. Rochester probably met the old philosopher, who, as we have seen, was often to be found at Court in the early years of the reign of Charles II. He appears to have accepted Hobbes's doctrines wholeheartedly. '*Pleasure*, therefore, or *delight*', wrote the philosopher in the First Book of *Leviathan*,

is the appearence, or sense of good; and *molestation* or *displeasure*, the appearence, or sense of evil ... Of pleasures or delights, some arise from the sense

345

of an object present; and those may be called *pleasures of sense*, the word *sensual*, as it is used by those only that condemn them, having no place till there be laws.[3]

In other words, the only criterion of good and evil is the presence or absence of sensuous pleasure, and the condemnation of sensuality is a purely artificial inhibition which has no place in nature. To the modern reader Hobbes's philosophy does not seem very favourable to poetry; the universe which it reveals consists of colourless, tasteless, soundless atoms perpetually moving in accordance with mathematical laws. But this was not the aspect of it that appealed to his young disciples of the Restoration Court. They were attracted by its boldness and freshness. It seemed to liberate them from the traditional inhibitions of priestcraft (the 'kingdom of darkness') and to offer a 'scientific' justification for sensuality.

Rochester's mind was essentially serious. He plunged into the experiment of living the complete life of pleasure with the same ardour as that with which Boyle and the *virtuosi* of the Royal Society devoted themselves to the investigation of nature and John Bunyan and George Fox to living according to the Word of God. His extant writings consist of lyrics, satires, a few verse translations, some dramatic fragments, including an unfinished rehandling of Fletcher's tragedy *Valentinian*, an amusing prose lampoon, and a number of letters. His poems are difficult to date, but the earliest, apart from some complimentary verses said to have been written when he was an undergraduate, are probably his lyrics and love poems. These include a handful of love songs which, as Leavis has said, are 'peculiarly individual utterances, with no such relation to convention or tradition as is represented by Carew and Marvell'. Their characteristics are a purity and intensity that only Sedley among his contemporaries approaches in a few lines (never in a complete poem), though he never quite achieves the peculiar lightness and transparency of Rochester's best songs, which, as Sir Herbert Grierson has said, 'might have been written by Burns with some difference'.

A fine poem, almost certainly addressed to his wife, is the expression of a complex mood in which the poet at once regrets his infidelities and also values them, not for themselves, but as a contrast to the only love which brings him happiness.

Absent from thee I languish still,
   Then ask me not, when I return?
The straying Fool 'twill plainly kill,
   To wish all Day, all Night to Mourn.

Dear; from thine Arms then let me flie,
   That my Fantastick Mind may prove,
The Torments it deserves to try,
   That tears my fixt Heart from my Love.

When wearied with a world of Woe
   To thy safe Bosom I retire
Where Love, and Peace, and Truth does flow,
   May I contented there expire.

Lest once more wand'ring from that Heav'n,
   I fall on some base heart unblest;
Faithless to thee, False, unforgiv'n,
   And lose my Everlasting Rest.

This is not the voice of a selfish sensualist but of a tortured realist who has learned from bitter experience that the 'pleasures' of the 'merry gang' soon become 'Torments' and a 'World of Woe'. Such a man is well on the road to a renunciation of Hobbes's utilitarian ethics. Alone among the Restoration Court lyrists, Rochester constantly breaks through the convention of courtly compliment and writes poetry that is dialectical and personal.

The lampoon in verse (usually scurrilous and obscene) was a well-established form of sport at the Court of Charles II,[4] and Rochester was known to his contemporaries chiefly as a writer of 'libels'. His best satires, however, are as different from the verse squibs produced by the other Court wits as his best lyrics are from their songs to Chloe and Phyllis. They are no mere denunciations of individuals, but embody a serious and devastating criticism of all the values of the life of pleasure and fashion into which he had plunged so recklessly. The criticism is all the more effective because it comes from one who is within the society which is criticized and who possesses its virtues of easy sureness of tone and diction and poise of gesture and rhythm. The aesthetic hero, or purely selfish ideal bearing no relation to truth (Etherege's Dorimant), now gives way to the ethical hero, the disillusioned, keen-sighted observer, whose relation to truth is real but entirely negative. In an ironic monologue worthy of Browning and justly praised by Charles Whibley as 'a masterpiece of heroic irony', this observer

shows us *The Maim'd Debauchee* in the likeness of a brave old admiral
'Depriv'd of Force, but prest with Courage still'. This product of a
life of gentlemanly pleasure-seeking foresees his impotent old age
when he will have to content himself with urging on younger men
to the vices which have wrecked his own constitution:

> So when my days of Impotence approach,
>   And I'me by Love and Wine's unlucky chance,
> Driv'n from the pleasing Billows of Debauch,
>   On the dull shore of lazy Temperance.
>
> My pains at last some respite shall afford,
>   While I behold the Battels you maintain:
> When Fleets of Glasses sail around the Board,
>   From whose Broad-Sides Volleys of Wit shall rain.

In his social satires Rochester shows us the obverse of Dorimant's
Utopia of gallantry. He has now come to see that the heaven of the
lusty courtier is precariously constructed over an underworld of
ugliness, cruelty, and filth. The horror of the life of the poor prostitute
in Restoration London is etched with the remorseless power of a
Hogarth in *A Letter from Artemisa in the Town to Cloe in the Country*:

> That wretched thing *Corinna*, who has run
> Through all the sev'ral ways of being undone:
> Cozen'd at first by Love, and living then
> By turning the too-dear-bought cheat on Men:
> Gay were the Hours, and wing'd with joy they flew,
> When first the Town her early Beauties knew:
> Courted, admir'd, and lov'd, with Presents fed;
> Youth in her Looks, and Pleasure in her Bed:
> Till Fate, or her ill Angel, thought it fit
> To make her doat upon a man of Wit:
> Who found 'twas dull to love above a day;
> Made his ill-natur'd jeast, and went away.
> Now scorn'd of all, forsaken, and opprest,
> She's a *Memento Mori* to the rest:
> Diseas'd, decay'd, to take up half a Crown
> Must Mortgage her Long Scarf, and Manto Gown;
> Poor Creature, who, unheard of, as a Flie,
> In some dark Hole must all the Winter lye:
> And want, and dirt, endure a whole half year,
> That, for one month, she Tawdry may appear . . .

There is a substance and a grain in these couplets which express
perfectly the vision of Rochester's searching and sceptical mind and

give the reader a kind of satisfaction which can rarely be obtained from seventeenth-century poetry.

The most memorable of Rochester's satires is the poem which can be fairly described as marking the culmination of his revolt against the values of contemporary English and European society and, indeed, an extension of that revolt to an attack on humanity as a whole. This poem, entitled in the most reliable editions *A Satyr against Mankind*, is suggested by the Eighth Satire of Boileau, reinforced by many suggestions from the essays of Montaigne and particularly from the *Apologie de Raimond Sebond* and from the *Maximes* of La Rochefoucauld. Nevertheless, it is a thoroughly original work stamped with the peculiar strength of Rochester's personality in every line and expressing with an almost terrifying intensity his mood of indignation and disillusionment.

The poem opens with a denunciation of the folly of humanity in preferring 'Reason, an *Ignis fatuus*, in the *Mind*' to sense, the 'light of Nature' (or, as D. H. Lawrence would have said, the 'Intellect' to the 'Blood'). Rochester never created a happier image than his picture of mankind as the lost Traveller who

> Stumbling from thought to thought, falls head-long down
> Into doubt's boundless Sea, where, like to drown,
> Books bear him up awhile, and make him try
> To swim with Bladders of *Philosophy*;
> In hopes still t' o'retake the escaping light,
> The *Vapour* dances in his dazled Sight,
> Till spent, it leaves him to eternal Night.
> Then Old Age, and experience, hand in hand,
> Lead him to death, and make him understand,
> After a search so painful, and so long,
> That all his Life he has been in the wrong.
> Hudled in Dirt, this reas'ning *Engine* lyes,
> Who was so proud, so witty, and so wise ...

Nowhere in the English literature of the seventeenth century has the central dilemma of the age been expressed with such force and precision. In the new mechanico-materialistic universe of Descartes, Hobbes, and the scientists, man is only a 'reas'ning *Engine*' (the phrase is probably suggested by an expression of Robert Boyle).[5] Yet the pitiful creature is, in his own opinion at any rate, proud and witty and wise, and even has the presumption to seek an explanation of a universe which is no longer the divinely planned cosmos of Greek and Christian tradition, but a place where man seems to be little better than an irrelevant accident.

Like most of Rochester's best work the *Satyr against Mankind* is dialectical, dramatic, and witty. It is a dialogue in which the satirist is answered by 'a formal Band and Beard' – in other words, a conventional clergyman, who is pleased enough with his rejection of the 'gibing, gingling knack call'd *Wit*', but shocked by his 'grand indiscretion' in railing at 'Reason and Mankind', which he answers by rather pompous praise of

> Blest glorious *Man*! to whom alone kind *Heav'n*
> An everlasting *Soul* hath freely giv'n; ...

The reply of the satirist is devastating, and expressed with a combination of seriousness and fantastic humour which recalls some of Donne's best work. 'Reason', so far from being the light of heaven, is simply the plaything of idle busybodies. It is a

> busie, puzling stirrer up of doubt,
> That frames deep *Mysteries*, then finds 'em out,
> Filling with frantick Crowds of thinking *Fools*,
> Those rev'rend *Bedlams*, *Colledges*, and *Schools*,
> Borne on whose Wings, each heavy *Sot* can pierce
> The limits of the boundless Universe.
> So charming Oyntments make an Old *Witch* flie,
> And bear a Crippled Carkass through the Skie.

'Right Reason' is something very different. It co-operates with the body instead of condemning it, and

> bounds desires, with a reforming Will,
> To keep 'em more in vigour, not to kill.

If 'Right Reason' can be defended, mankind as a whole is indefensible. The central passage of the poem, a comparison between man and the beasts, is one of the most searching pieces of moral realism in English poetry. It owes much to Montaigne and probably influenced Swift considerably.[6] Rochester is now fighting on another front; it is not the conventional religiosity of the 'formal Band and Beard' which he is attacking now but his own class, the ruling class of Europe, with its obsolete ideal of the predatory warrior:

> Be Judge your self, I'll bring it to the test,
> Which is the basest *Creature, Man*, or *Beast*:
> *Birds* feed on *Birds*, *Beasts* on each other prey;
> But Savage *Man* alone does *Man* betray.
> Prest by necessity, they Kill for Food;
> *Man* undoes *Man*, to do himself no good.
> With Teeth and Claws by Nature arm'd, they hunt
> Nature's allowances, to supply their want:
> But *Man* with smiles, embraces, Friendships, praise,
> Unhumanely his Fellow's life betrays:
> With voluntary pains works his distress;
> Not through necessity, but wantonness.
> For hunger, or for Love they bite or tear
> While wretched *Man* is still in Arms for fear:
> For fear he armes, and is of Armes afraid;
> From fear to fear successively betray'd.
> Base fear, the source whence his best passions came,
> His boasted Honor, and his dear bought Fame:
> The lust of Pow'r, to which he's such a *Slave*
> And for the which alone he dares be brave:
> To which his various Projects are design'd,
> Which makes him gen'rous, affable, and kind.
> For which he takes such pains to be thought wise
> And screws his actions, in a forc'd disguise:
> Leading a tedious life, in Misery,
> Under laborious, mean *Hypocrisie* ...

There is little doubt that it is a passage like this, quite as much as the alleged 'licentiousness' of his poetry, which gave Rochester his traditional evil reputation. He is penetrating the defences of his aristocratic readers and showing the primitive man behind the age-old inhibitions of 'Honour' and 'Fame'.

The nihilism of the *Satyr against Mankind* is slightly mitigated in a curious epilogue appended to it in some editions and possibly added by Rochester as a rejoinder to the Answer to the poem ascribed to a certain 'Reverend Mr Griffith', which appeared shortly after the publication of the broadside edition of the *Satyr* in the summer of 1679. Here it is suggested that, if a man of real integrity ('In *Court*, a just Man, yet unknown to me') could be found, he would be willing to 'recant his paradox'. The description of this ideal, that of the ethical hero, is mainly in negatives and is not very inspiring. The interest of the Epilogue, however, is psychological rather than literary. It shows that Rochester was conscious of the lack of a positive element in his satire and that he was looking for an affirmative answer to his 'obstinate questionings'.

A clue to the kind of experience for which he was striving is to be found in a fragment of a letter to his wife which is, perhaps, the most self-revealing statement in his extant correspondence. In this fragment, he speaks of the 'disproportion 'twixt our desires & what is ordained to content them' and of those who are 'soe intirely satisfyed with theire shares in this world that theire wishes nor theire thoughts have not a farther prospect of felicity & glory'. It was not a system of ethics that Rochester was looking for, but the 'felicity and glory' which he had vainly sought in sensuality and aesthetic experience.

The last act of the drama of Rochester's short life was the famous episode of his conversion. The author of *A Satyr against Mankind*, like the author of *The Waste Land*, was bound ultimately to turn to religion. Rochester had, in Dr Johnson's words, 'blazed out his youth and health in lavish voluptuousness', and his health, which was never robust and which appears to have been undermined by venereal disease early in his career, was failing in the last years of the second decade after the Restoration. Early in 1679 he seems to have been searching for a religious position which he could accept without compromising his intellectual integrity. He consulted the deist Charles Blount, but found little satisfaction in the arid and abstract 'religion of nature' which the seventeenth-century deists (following Lord Herbert of Cherbury) professed. A more fruitful contact was with Gilbert Burnet, afterwards Bishop of Salisbury but then a young Scottish clergyman, who had won a reputation at Court for his frankness, unconventionality, and eloquent preaching. Rochester made his acquaintance in the autumn of 1679 after he had read the first volume of his *History of the Reformation*, which appeared in the spring of that year. In him he found a parson of a kind that he had not met before, a man with a keen and fearless intellect, not a mere conventional mouthpiece of traditional pietism. It must have seemed that he had at last met the sort of hero that he had sketched in the Epilogue to *A Satyr against Mankind*:

> A *Church-Man* who on *God* relyes?
> Whose Life, his Faith, and Doctrine Justifies?

All through the winter of 1679–80 this strangely assorted pair had a series of conversations on religion and ethics which Burnet recorded with admirable fidelity in the short memoir of Rochester which he published soon after the poet's death. At the end of their conversation in the spring of 1680 he seems to have been rationally convinced by Burnet's exposition of Christian ethics, though he had not, in Burnet's words, 'arrived at a full persuasion of Christianity'. It was not till June, when he was lying mortally ill at the Ranger's Lodge at Woodstock, that he found in religion that 'felicity and glory' which he had been seeking for so long.

Like W. B. Yeats in 1914, Rochester had now reached a stage of spiritual development when the life of aesthetic and sensuous pleasure was a 'Fool's coat' (Yeats uses the same image in his poem *A Coat*) and nothing but the naked spirit could satisfy him. Unfortunately, he only lived for five weeks after this experience. We know from the sermon preached by Robert Parsons at his funeral that before his death he was planning to write 'Divine Poetry' and also that he actually dictated in the last weeks of his life. It is probable that two poems printed in one of the early editions[7] of his works are attempts made in the last weeks of his life to express his new conception of the religious hero. Both of them appear to be closely related to the figure of the Suffering Servant in the fifty-third chapter of Isaiah. In one 'Plain Dealing' is shown as a poor country girl driven out of the town and forced to return to the country, where even the rustics refuse to have anything to do with her when they know that she will bring poverty in her train:

> Long time plain dealing in the Hauty Town,
> Wandring about, though in a thread-bare Gown,
> At last unanimously was cry'd down.
>
> When almost starv'd, she to the Countrey fled,
> In hopes, though meanly, she shou'd there be fed,
> And tumble Nightly on a Pea-straw Bed.
>
> But Knav'ry knowing her intent, took post,
> And Rumour'd her approach through every Coast,
> Vowing his Ruin that shou'd be her host.
>
> Frighted at this, each *Rustick* shut his door,
> Bid her begone, and trouble him no more,
> For he that entertain'd her must be poor.

At this grief seiz'd her, grief too great to tell,
When weeping, sighing, fainting down she fell,
Whil's Knavery, Laughing, Rung her passing Bell.

Voltaire rightly called Rochester 'homme de génie et grand poète'. He is not a great poet in the sense that the word can be applied to the professional masters, Milton, Dryden, Pope, and Wordsworth. Judged as works of art, his achievements are those of a brilliant amateur, a handful of exquisite lyrics, and the satires, which, as Leavis has pointed out, have a distinguished place in the 'line of wit' that leads from Donne to Pope. Rochester, however, is one of those poets who are important as daring and original explorers of reality, and his place is with the restless spiritual adventurers such as Marlowe, Blake, Byron, Wilfred Owen, and D. H. Lawrence. Like Byron and Lawrence, he was denounced as licentious because he was a disturbing and outspoken critic of conventional ethics. His poetry expresses individual experience in a way that no other English poetry does between Donne and Blake; it makes us feel what it was like to live in a world which had been suddenly transformed by the new science into a vast machine governed by mathematical laws, where God has become a remote First Cause and man an insignificant 'reas'ning *Engine*'. In his time the great Augostan attempt to found a new orthodoxy based on the Cartesian–Newtonian world-picture was beginning. The Anglo-French civilization of the eighteenth century, the civilization of Voltaire and Diderot, of Addison, Johnson, and Gibbon, came near to achieving the civilized city of good sense, good taste, reason, and common sense, which was the objective of the new orthodoxy. Rochester's glory was that he rejected the new orthodoxy at the very outset, and perceived, as Swift was to perceive after him, that the civilized city of the Augustans, though it might be a resting-place for the human spirit, could very easily become a prison. In the history of English poetic thought his work is an event of major importance. Much of it remains alive in the twentieth century, not for its craftsmanship, but as what D. H. Lawrence called the 'unrestful, ungraspable poetry of the sheer present ... the soul and the mind and body surging at once, nothing left out'.

NOTES

1. Macaulay, *Essay on the Comic Dramatists of the Restoration*. It is true that Macaulay is referring to the characters in the comedies of the period, but part of his argument is that these characters are realistic in the sense that they reflected the ideals of the audience.

2. F. R. Leavis, *Revaluation* (1936), 34.

3. Hobbes, *Leviathan* I, vi. cf. also the statement in I, xiii, that 'the desires, and other passions of man, are in themselves no sin'.

4. For the typical Restoration lampoons, see the various collections of *Poems on Affairs of State* (1689, 1697, 1703, etc.).

5. Boyle called men 'engines endowed with wills'. See E. A. Burtt, *The Metaphysical Foundations of Modern Science* (1925), 176.

6. cf. particularly ch. IV of 'A Voyage to the Country of the Houyhnhms' in *Gulliver's Travels*.

7. *Poems On Several Occasions Written by a late Person of Honour*, London, Printed for A. Thorncome, *1685* (Br. Mus. 11623, a. 37).

ABRAHAM COWLEY

GEOFFREY WALTON

By his extraordinary versatility as poet and prose writer, Cowley (1618–67) forms a living connection between the literature of the early seventeenth century and that of the age of Dryden. An infant prodigy among poets, he began his career as probably the youngest of all the 'sons' of Ben Jonson. In mid career he borrowed extensively from Donne's love poetry. He ended it as a founder of the Royal Society, the leader, though characteristically in retirement, of the literary world and a rival of Butler as a best-seller.[1] It is usual to bracket him with Waller and Denham, or even Dryden, to whom his authority was 'almost sacred', as a reformer of poetry.[2] 'He forsook the conversation, but never the language of the city and the court,' says that typical Restoration divine, Bishop Sprat, in his *Life of Cowley*.[3] He was the effective if not the actual creator of the Pindaric ode. He began the first neo-classic epic in English. His prose and his more classical verse continued to be admired until well into the eighteenth century for what Sprat calls 'the unaffected modesty, the natural freedom and easie vigour, and chearful passions and innocent mirth that appeared in all his manners'. Dr Johnson, after all, thought him 'undoubtedly the best' metaphysical poet;[4] he wrote the kind of metaphysical poetry that the gentleman in the coffee-house and the eighteenth-century common reader could enjoy without undue effort. As Coleridge said, he was a very fanciful poet. In his own way Cowley has notable qualities, especially of tone and accent, and it was largely through him – though Cleveland (1613–58) and Butler (1612–80) contributed to the process – that a stimulating infusion of metaphysical wit was passed on into neo-classic poetry.

His *Ode; Of Wit* provides a series of pointers to the extent of his imaginative range and the quality of his sensibility. He begins with a brief introduction:

> Tell me, O tell, what kind of thing is *Wit*,
>   Thou who *Master* art of it.
> For the *First matter* loves *Variety less*,
> Less *Women* lov't, either in *Love* or *Dress*.
>   A thousand different shapes it bears,
>   *Comely* in thousand shapes appears.
> Yonder we saw it *plain*; and here 'tis now,
> Like *Spirits* in a *Place*, we know not *How*.

Clearly wit implies a mass of varied material in the poet, viewed somewhat frivolously as for ornament or amusement. It is also a mysterious and pervasive spirit in the background. Cowley then proceeds to define wit mainly by negatives:

> 'Tis not a *Tale*, 'tis not a *Jest*
> Admir'd with *Laughter* at a feast,
> Nor florid *Talk* which can that *Title* gain ...
>
> Rather than *all things Wit*, let *none* be there.
>
> 'Tis not when two like words make up one noise;
>   Jests for *Dutch Men*, and *English Boys*.
> In which who finds out *Wit*, the same may see
> In *An'grams* and *Acrostiques Poetrie*.
>   Much less can that have any place
>   At which a *Virgin* hides her face ...
>
> 'Tis not such *Lines* as almost crack the *Stage*
>   When *Bajazet* begins to rage.*
> Nor a tall *Meta'phor* in the *Bombast way*,
>   Nor the dry chips of short lung'd *Seneca*.†
>   Nor upon all things to obtrude
>   And force some odd *Similitude*.

These imply standards of correctness and decorum, literary and social – certain things are 'not done' in poetry – and when Dryden quotes the second passage in the Preface to *An Evening's Love*, the context is strongly social. No serious critic thinks that Donne is characterized by puns and odd similitudes, but nevertheless this disciplined, tidy, and sensible notion seems a long way from Donne's 'giant phansie' which almost burst the bonds of language and was 'longer a knowing than most wits do live', to quote Carew and Jonson. The positive account of wit is equally revealing:

*Turkish ruler as he appears in Marlowe's *Tamburlaine*.
†Latin model for epigrammatic style in prose.

The *Proofs of Wit* for ever must remain.

All ev'ry where, like *Mans*, must be the *Soul*,
And *Reason* the *Inferior Powers* controul.

In a true piece of *Wit* all things must be,
   Yet all things there *agree*.
As in the *Ark*, joyn'd without force or strife,
All *Creatures* dwelt; all *Creatures* that had *Life*.
   Or as the *Primitive Forms* of all
   (If we compare great things with small)
Which without *Discord* or *Confusion* lie,
In that strange *Mirror* of the *Deitie*.

The main emphasis is on '*Reason*', '*agree*', 'without *Discord* or *Confusion*'; we have also been told that the judgement is like a '*Multiplying Glass*', or telescope, to give greater clarity of vision. One now feels that intellectual discipline has been added to the definition, and one may compare Cowley's poem with the severely analytic definition of Hobbes and the later and more genial and discursive definition of Dryden. On the other hand, one has been told that wit is 'like *Spirits* in a *Place*' and later it is compared to 'the *Power Divine*'. Cowley's conception of the poetic imagination would therefore seem to combine the ideas of inspiration and variety of material with those of selection and conscious art. By a certain superficiality and looseness of texture – for none of the ode requires close textual analysis – one sees that he himself lacks the imaginative concentration and tension of the great metaphysicals and, in fact, exemplifies the type of wit he is describing. In this way he is a representative transitional poet.[5]

Cowley did not, however, progress simply from one style to another. His *Hymn to Light*, an impressive but not entirely satisfactory metaphysical work, was written at the end of his life, the *Davideis*, metaphysical in imagery but neo-classic in form, at Cambridge immediately before the Civil War. Much of his best poetry was written about this early time when, as he says in the extremely interesting preface to his folio of 1656, he was 'in the good humour' and had the 'serenity and chearfulness of *Spirit*' necessary 'for a man to write well'. The chief poem of this period is *On the Death of Mr Crashaw*, written in couplets. Cowley celebrates his friend's double character, literary and religious, with sustained and calculated hyperbole. The manner and mood vary considerably paragraph by paragraph from the satiric to the elegaic and the matter-of-fact argumentative. At the end Cowley salutes Crashaw with neo-classic magniloquence and metaphysical ingenuity of analogy:

> Thou from low earth in nobler *Flames* didst rise,
> And like *Elijah*, mount *Alive* the skies.
> *Elisha*-like (but with a wish much less,
> More fit thy *Greatness*, and my *Littleness*)
> Lo here I beg (I whom thou once didst prove
> So humble to *Esteem*, so Good to *Love*)
> Not that thy *Spirit* might on me *Doubled* be,
> I ask but *Half* thy mighty *Spirit* for Me.
> And when my *Muse* soars with so strong a Wing,
> 'Twill learn of things *Divine*, and first of *Thee* to sing.

It is the most emotional, not to say rhapsodic, poem that Cowley wrote – far more so than any of his odes, but the lack of irony in the attitude to his main theme and the simple stately organization show him to be a contemporary of Waller and already practising the kind of literary decorum that one finds in the grandiose elegies and complimentary poems of the Restoration. The elegy *On the Death of Mr William Hervey* is scarcely metaphysical at all except in a few slight touches; it combines a polite, quiet tone and discursive manner with poignant personal feeling. The dramatically ominous and pathetic scene with which Cowley opens the poem illustrates the personal directness of treatment:

> It was a dismal, and a fearful night,
> Scarce could the Morn drive on th' unwilling Light,
> When *Sleep, Death's Image*, left my troubled brest,
>   By something *liker Death* possest.
> My eyes with Tears did uncommanded flow,
>   And on my Soul hung the dull weight
>   Of some *Intolerable Fate*.
> What Bell was that? Ah me! Too much I know.

He gives a (for the time) unusually intimate account of the friendship:

> Ye fields of *Cambridge*, our dear *Cambridge*, say,
> Have ye not seen us walking every day?
> Was there a *Tree* about which did not know
>   The *Love* betwixt us two?
> Henceforth, ye gentle *Trees*, for ever fade;
>   Or your sad branches thicker joyn,
>   And into darksome shades combine,
> *Dark* as the *Grave* wherein my *Friend* is laid.

It is worth drawing attention to the fact, as a sign of the movement of poetic taste in Cowley, that Johnson admired the poem for its naturalness, and that Gray seems to have drawn upon it for an important phrase in the *Elegy*. Compared with both the early metaphysical elegies and the formal elegies of Dryden, informality is its salient quality.

Cowley's *The Mistress* brought him his first contemporary fame and seems to have been considered a kind of *ars amatoria*. He himself eschews any responsibility other than poetic for the collection. These poems belong with the Cavalier lyric; they depend heavily on Donne in dealing with the themes of body and soul and union and separation, but never have the tautness of rhythm and precision of phrase which give these themes realization. There is also an explicit aspiration to emulate Waller. Many of the poems are characterized by mere exaggeration and ingenuity with nothing alive behind them. The successful and amusing ones are – unexpectedly – in the manner of Suckling when he most resembles the Dorsets and the Sedleys who succeeded him. *Discretion, The Frailty, The Waiting-Maid, Honour, The Dissembler, My Dyet* are all in this racy, carefree, conversational manner. *The Rich Rival* has probably the finest management of rhythm and tone:

> They say you're angry, and rant mightilie,
> > Because I love the same as you;
> > Alas! you're very *rich*; 'tis true;
> But prithee Fool, what's that to *Love* and *Me*.
> > You have *Land* and *Money*, let that serve;
> And know you have more by that than you *deserve*.

Thus the intellectual love lyric petered out. The taste in poetry represented by Dryden's jibe that Cowley imitated Donne to a fault in affecting the 'metaphysics' instead of writing of the 'softnesses' of love is not very different from that of his admirer, Sprat, who thought that 'in every copy, there is something of more useful knowledge very naturally and gracefully insinuated'. In both cases conceits and ideas are thought of as something extraneous to the poetry, which expresses – or fails to express – sentiment. Later Johnson remarked in this connection that *The Mistress* might have been 'written by a hermit for penance'. One feels of these poems that it is Cowley's wit in the narrow senses of fanciful ingenuity and humour that survives.

The odes in which Cowley thought he was nearest to Pindar's 'way and manner of speaking' seem, as he himself feared of a translation, little more than a jumble of words. But certain Pindarics, such as *Destinie*, *Life*, and *The Resurrection*, which are really metaphysical poems in loose irregular stanzas, have the same kind of conversational liveliness as the love lyrics and a great virtuosity in conceits, for example:

> We're ill by those *Grammarians* us'd;
> We are abus'd by *Words*, grossly abus'd;
>   From the *Maternal Tomb*,
>   To the *Graves* fruitful *Womb*,
> We call here *Life*; but *Life's* a *name*
> That nothing here can truly claim:
> This wretched *Inn* . . .

Dryden learnt much from these as well as from the more solemn odes. The following stanza from the ode *To the Royal Society* will illustrate Cowley's representative position as thinker as well as the later development of his style:

> Autority, which did a Body boast,
> Though 'twas but Air condens'd, and stalk'd about,
> Like some old Giants more Gigantic Ghost,
>   To terrifie the Learned Rout
> With the plain Magick of true Reasons Light,
>   He chac'd out of our sight,
> Nor suffer's Living *Men* to be misled
>   By the vain shadows of the Dead:
> To Graves, from whence it rose, the conquer'd Phantome
>   fled;
>   He broke that Monstrous God which stood
> In the midst of th' Orchard, and the whole did claim,
>   Which with a useless Sith of Wood,
>   And something else not worth a name.
>   (Both vast for shew, yet neither fit
>   Or to Defend, or to Beget;
>   Ridiculous and senceless Terrors!) made
> Children and superstitious Men afraid.
>   The Orchard's open now, and free;
> *Bacon* has broke the Scar-crow Deitie;
>   Come, enter, all that will,
> Behold rip'ned Fruit, come gather now their Fill.
>   Yet still, methinks, we fain would be
>   Catching at the Forbidden Tree,

> We would be like the Deitie,
> When Truth and Falsehood, Good and Evil; we
> Without the Sences aid within our selves would see;
>   For 'tis God only who can find
>   All Nature in his Mind.

This is poetry with the prose virtues, a vigorous and vivid paragraph. Scholasticism is seen as an absurd and obscene, but still dangerous, Idol of the Tribe which has been overthrown by the great intellectual image-breaker and liberator. The interpretation of the Tree of Knowledge story comes straight from Book I of the *Advancement of Learning*. Cowley like his master felt that for the present enough time and energy had been devoted to the study of Final Causes and the ultimate truths – which still remained true – and that the learned should concentrate on experimental philosophy. The Royal Society was doing this.

Cowley was living in retirement in the country when he wrote this ode at the request of Sprat and Evelyn. There he felt himself, and was felt by others, to be the Horace of his time, and he composed his last work, his *Essays, in Verse and Prose*. The verse, whether in couplets or stanzas, represents a further refinement, in every sense, of his conversational style; the prose is moving towards a lucid modern medium, polite but intimate. In fact, Cowley in his latest work, which earned the admiration of both Pope and Gray, was almost more of a minor Augustan than a seventeenth-century metaphysical, and his attack on '... The Great Vulgar, and the Small'[6] became widely current in eighteenth-century society.

NOTES

1. Contemporary references to Cowley can be studied in Mr Nethercot's 'Cowley's Reputation in England, 1660–1800' (Section 1), *P.M.L.A.*, XXXVIII.

2. Dryden's comments and their context are often illuminating. See *Essays*, ed. W. P. Ker (1900).

3. Sprat's *Life*, *Critical Essays of the XVIIth Century*, ed. Springarn (1908–9), Vol. II, gives an extremely interesting and valuable survey of his work and personality – one must allow, of course, for the obituary eulogy.

4. Metaphysical poetry was not congenial to Dr Johnson, but his severe, reasoned criticism should be considered.

5. T. S. Eliot interprets the ode rather differently in 'A Note on Two Odes of Cowley' in *XVIIth Century Studies Presented to Sir H. Grierson* (1938). Chapter

II of my *Metaphysical to Augustan* (1955) contains a comparison with the relevant passages of Hobbes and Dryden.

6. Bishop Hurd's *Select Works of Cowley* (1772) contains a note that this phrase had become part of the language and gives other interesting indications of eighteenth-century taste in Cowley.

PART IV

APPENDIX

COMPILED BY MAURICE HUSSEY
AND ROBERT WILCHER

FOR FURTHER READING AND REFERENCE

The Historical and Social Setting

Literature and the Arts

AUTHORS AND WORKS

E.	Everyman edition
W.C.	World's Classics edition
ed., edn	edited, edition
rev.	revised edition
repr.	reprinted
b.	born
d.	died
fl.	flourished
c.	circa
?	probably

Under each author, the aim has been to list first a standard biography (if any), second one or more standard editions, and third a selection of books and chapters for further study.

FOR FURTHER READING AND REFERENCE

The Historical and Social Setting

I. GENERAL AND POLITICAL HISTORIES

Lord Clarendon *History of the Rebellion* (1702–4; ed. W. D. Macray, 6 vols, Oxford, 1888; selections ed. G. Huehns, w.c., 1955, rev. H. R. Trevor-Roper, Oxford, 1978)

Hobbes, Thomas *Behemoth or the Long Parliament*, ed. F. Tönnies (London, 1899; rev. 1969)

May, Thomas *The History of the Parliament of England* (Oxford, 1854)

Ashton, R. *The English Civil War* (London, 1978)

Aylmer, G. E. *The King's Servants: The Civil Service of Charles I, 1625–1642* (London, 1961; rev. 1974)

Aylmer, G. E. *The Struggle for the Constitution: 1603–1689* (London, 1963)

Aylmer, G. E. *The State's Servants: The Civil Service of the English Republic, 1649–1660* (London, 1973)

Brunton, D. and Pennington, D. H. *Members of the Long Parliament* (London, 1954)

Davies, G. *The Early Stuarts, 1603–1660* (Oxford, 1937; rev. 1959)

Fletcher, A. *The Outbreak of the English Civil War* (London, 1981)

Fletcher, A. *Reform in the Provinces* (New Haven, 1986)

Graves, M. A. R. and Silcock, R. H. *Revolution, Reaction and the Triumph of Conservatism: English History 1558–1700* (Auckland, 1984)

Hexter, J. H. *The Reign of King Pym* (Cambridge, Mass., 1941)

Hill, C. *The Century of Revolution, 1603–1714* (London, 1961; rev. 1980)

Hirst, D. *The Representative of the People? Voters and Voting in England under the Early Stuarts* (Cambridge, 1975)

Hirst, D. *Authority and Conflict: England 1603–1658* (London, 1986)

Hutton, R. *The Restoration 1658–67* (Oxford, 1985)

Kenyon, J. P. *The Stuart Constitution* (Cambridge, 1966)

Kenyon, J. P. *Stuart England* (Penguin, 1978)

Manning, B. *The English People and the English Revolution 1640–1649* (London, 1976)

Ogg, D. *England in the Reign of Charles II* (Oxford, 1934; rev. 1956)

Russell, C. *Parliaments and English Politics* (Oxford, 1979)

Starkey, D. et al. *The English Court: From the Wars of the Roses to the Civil War* (London, 1987)

Underdown, D. *Royalist Conspiracy in England 1649–1660* (New Haven, 1960)

Underdown, D. *Pride's Purge: Politics in the Puritan Revolution* (Oxford, 1971)

Underdown, D. *Revel, Riot and Rebellion: Popular Politics and Culture in England 1603–60* (Oxford, 1985)

Wedgwood, C. V. *The King's Peace: 1637–1641* (London, 1955)

Wedgwood, C. V. *The King's War: 1641–1647* (London, 1958)

Woolrych, A. *Commonwealth to Protectorate* (Oxford, 1982; rev. 1986)

Woolrych, A. *Soldiers and Statesmen: The General Council of the Army and its Debates, 1647–1648* (Oxford, 1987)

Worden, B. *The Rump Parliament* (Cambridge, 1974)

Zagorin, P. *The Court and the Country* (London, 1969)

II. SOCIAL AND ECONOMIC BACKGROUND

Gardiner, D. *The Oxinden Letters, 1607–42* (London, 1933)

Harrison, G. B. *Jacobean Journals* (I, London, 1941; II, Michigan, 1958)

Houlbrooke, R. (ed.) *English Family Life 1565–1716: An Anthology from Diaries* (Oxford, 1988)

McClure, N. E. *The Letters of John Chamberlain* (Philadelphia, 1939)

Peacham, H. *The Compleat Gentleman* (1622; ed. G. S. Gordon, Oxford, 1906)

Schofield, B. (ed.) *The Knyvett Letters* (Norfolk Record Society, 1949)

Smyth, J. (ed.) *The Berkeley Manuscript* (c. 1618; ed. Sir John Maclean, 3 vols., London, 1883)

Thirsk, J. and Cooper, J. P. (eds.) *Seventeenth-Century Economic Documents* (Oxford, 1972)

Wilson, T. (the younger) *The State of England, A.D. 1600* (ed. F. J. Fisher, Camden Miscellany XVI, 1936)

Ashley, M. *Life in Stuart England* (London, 1964; rev. 1967)

Ashton, R. *The Crown and the Money Market, 1603–1640* (Oxford, 1960)

Burton, E. *The Jacobeans at Home* (London, 1962)

Campbell, M. *The English Yeoman under Elizabeth and the Early Stuarts* (New Haven, 1942; rev. 1959)

Cliffe, J. T. *The Puritan Gentry* (London, 1984)

Cliffe, J. T. *Puritans in Conflict* (London, 1988)

Cressy, D. *Literacy and the Social Order* (Cambridge, 1980)

Durston, C. *The Family in the English Revolution* (Oxford, 1989)

Everitt, A. M. *The Community of Kent and the Great Rebellion* (Leicester, 1966)

Fisher, F. J. *Essays in the Economic and Social History of Tudor and Stuart England* (Cambridge, 1961)

Fletcher, A. A. *A Country Community in Peace and War: Sussex, 1600–1660* (London, 1975)

Fraser, A. *The Weaker Vessel: Woman's Lot in Seventeenth-Century England* (London, 1984)

Hill, C. *Society and Puritanism in Pre-Revolutionary England* (London, 1964)

Hill, C. *The World Turned Upside Down* (London, 1972)

Hill, C. *The Experience of Defeat* (London, 1984)

Hoskins, W. G. *The Midland Peasant* (London, 1957)

Laslett, P. *The World We Have Lost* (London, 1965; rev. 1971)

Lindley, K. *Fenland Riots and the English Revolution* (London, 1982)

MacFarlane, A. *The Origins of English Individualism* (Oxford, 1979)

McGrath, P. *Merchants and Merchandise in Seventeenth-Century Bristol* (Bristol, 1955)

Morrill, J. S. *The Revolt of the Provinces: 1630–1650* (London, 1976)

Notestein, W. *The English People on the Eve of Colonisation, 1603–1630* (London, 1954)

Pattern, J. *English Towns, 1500–1700* (Folkestone, 1978)

Pearl, V. *London and the Outbreak of the Puritan Revolution* (London, 1961)

Reay, B. (ed.) *Popular Culture in Seventeenth-Century England* (London, 1985)

Slater, M. *Family Life in the Seventeenth Century* (London, 1984)

Spufford, M. *Small Books and Pleasant Histories: Popular Fiction and Its Readership in Seventeenth-Century England* (London, 1981)

Stone, L. *The Crisis of the Aristocracy* (Oxford, 1965; abridged edn 1967)

Stone, L. *Social Change and Revolution in England, 1540–1640* (Oxford, 1965)

Stone, L. *The Family, Sex and Marriage in England, 1500–1800* (London, 1977)

Stoye, J. *English Travellers Abroad, 1604–1667* (London, 1952)

Supple, B. *Commercial Crisis and Change 1600–1642* (Cambridge, 1959)

Tawney, R. H. *Religion and the Rise of Capitalism* (London, 1926; Penguin, 1938)

Trevelyan, G. M. *Illustrated Social History of England* (3 vols., 1949–52; Penguin, 1954)

Wrightson, K. *English Society, 1580–1680* (London, 1982)

III. INTELLECTUAL BACKGROUND: RELIGION, SCIENCE, AND EDUCATION

Aylmer, G. E. (ed.) *The Levellers in the English Revolution* (London, 1975)

Bacon, Francis *The Advancement of Learning* (1605; W.C., 1906; E., 1915)

Chandos, J. (ed.) *In God's Name: Examples of Preaching in England 1534–1662* (London, 1971)

Erskine-Hill, H. and Storey, G. (eds.) *Revolutionary Prose of the English Civil War* (Cambridge, 1983)

Haller, W. (ed.) *Tracts on Liberty in the Puritan Revolution, 1638–1647* (3 vols., New York, 1934; repr. 1965)

Haller, W. and Davies, G. (eds.) *The Leveller Tracts, 1647–53* (New York, 1944; repr. Gloucester, Mass., 1964)

Hobbes, Thomas *Leviathan* (1651; E., 1914, repr. 1965; Penguin, 1968, rev. 1981)

Knachel, P. A. (ed.) *Eikon Basilike* (New York, 1966)

More, P. E. and Cross, F. L. (eds.) *Anglicanism: The Thought and Practice of the Church of England, Illustrated from the Religious Literature of the Seventeenth Century* (London, 1935)

Patrides, C. A. (ed.) *The Cambridge Platonists* (London, 1969; Cambridge, 1980)

Seymour-Smith, M. (ed.) *The English Sermon: Vol. I 1550–1650* (Cheadle, 1976)

Smith, N. (ed.) *A Collection of Ranter Writings* (London, 1983)

Bennett, H. S. *English Books and Readers 1603–40: A Study in the History of the Book Trade* (Cambridge, 1970)

Brailsford, H. N. *The Levellers* (ed. C. Hill, London, 1961)

Butterfield, H. *The Origins of Modern Science 1300–1800* (London, 1949, rev. 1957)

Capp, B. S. *The Fifth Monarchy Men* (London, 1972)

Collinson, P. *The Religion of Protestants, 1559–1625* (Oxford, 1982)

Costello, W. T. *The Curriculum at Seventeenth-Century Cambridge* (Cambridge, Mass., 1958)

Curtis, M. *Oxford and Cambridge in Transition, 1558–1642* (London, 1959)

Davis, J. C. *Fear, Myth and History: The Ranters and the Historians* (Cambridge, 1986)

Dures, A. *English Catholicism, 1558–1642* (Harlow, 1983)

Firth, K. R. *The Apocalyptic Tradition in Reformation Britain: 1530–1645* (Oxford, 1979)

Fussner, F. S. *The Historical Revolution: English Historical Writing and Thought, 1580–1640* (London, 1962)

Hill, C. *The Intellectual Origins of the English Revolution* (London, 1965)

Jones, R. F. *Ancients and Moderns* (Washington, 1936)

Lamont, W. M. *Godly Rule: Politics and Religion, 1603–60* (London, 1969)

Lyons, Sir H. *The Royal Society* (London, 1944)

Macpherson, C. B. *The Political Theory of Possessive Individualism* (Oxford, 1962)

McAdoo, H. R. *The Spirit of Anglicanism* (London, 1965)

McGee, J. S. *The Godly Man in Stuart England* (New Haven, 1976)

McGregor, J. F. and Reay, B. (eds.) *Radical Religion in the English Revolution* (Oxford, 1984)

Merton, R. K. *Science, Technology and Society in Seventeenth-Century England* (New York, 1938; repr. 1970)

Morgan, J. *Godly Learning: Puritan Attitudes towards Reason, Learning, and Education, 1560–1640* (Cambridge, 1986)

Morton, A. L. *The World of the Ranters* (London, 1970)

New, J. F. H. *Anglican and Puritan: The Basis of their Opposition, 1558–1640* (London, 1964)

Nicolson, M. H. *The Breaking of the Circle* (Evanston, 1950; rev. New York, 1960)

O'Day, R. *The English Clergy: The Emergence and Consolidation of a Profession, 1558–1642* (Leicester, 1979)

Packer, J. W. *The Transformation of Anglicanism, 1643–1660* (Manchester, 1969)

Parker, D. *Familiar to All: William Lilly and Astrology* (London, 1975)

Parry, G. *The Seventeenth Century: The Intellectual and Cultural Context of English Literature, 1603–1700* (London, 1989)

Powicke, F. J. *The Cambridge Platonists* (London, 1926)

Prest, W. R. *The Inns of Court under Elizabeth I and the Early Stuarts* (London, 1972)

Reay, B. *The Quakers and the English Revolution* (New York, 1985)

Schochet, G. J. *Patriarchalism in Political Thought* (Oxford, 1975)

Seaver, P. S. *The Puritan Lectureships* (Stanford, 1970)

Shapin, S. and Schaffer, S. *Leviathan and the Air-Pump: Hobbes, Boyle, and the Experimental Life* (Princeton, 1985)

Shapiro, B. J. *Probability and Certainty in Seventeenth-Century England: A Study of the Relationships between Natural Science, Religion, History, Law, and Literature* (Princeton, 1985)

Trevor-Roper, H. R. *Catholics, Anglicans and Puritans* (London, 1987)

Vickers, B. (ed.) *English Science, Bacon to Newton* (Cambridge, 1987)

Walzer, M. *Revolution of the Saints* (London, 1965)

Watkins, O. C. *The Puritan Experience* (London, 1972)

Webster, C. (ed.) *The Intellectual Revolution of the Seventeenth Century* (London, 1974)

White, H. C. *English Devotional Literature (Prose 1600–40)* (Madison, Wis., 1931)

Wilson, J. F. *Pulpit in Parliament* (Princeton, 1969)

Woodhouse, A. S. P. *Puritanism and Liberty* (London, 1938; rev. 1974)

Yule, G. *The Independents in the English Civil War* (Cambridge, 1958)

IV. MEMOIRS AND BIOGRAPHIES

Aubrey, John *Brief Lives*, ed. O. L. Dick (London, 1949; Penguin, 1972)

Bamford, F. (ed.) *A Royalist's Notebook, The Commonplace Book of Sir John Oglander of Nunwell, 1622–1652* (London, 1936)

Baxter, Richard *The Autobiography of Richard Baxter* (1696; abridged edn by J. M. Lloyd Thomas, London, 1925; repr. E., 1931 and 1974)

Briggs, K. M. (ed.) *The Last of the Astrologers: Mr William Lilly's History of His Life and Times from the Year 1602 to 1681* (Folklore Society, 1974)

Burnet, G. *History of My Own Times* (1723; ed. O. Airy, 2 vols., Oxford, 1897)

Cavendish, Margaret *The Life of William Cavendish, Duke of Newcastle* (1667; ed. C. H. Firth, London, 1886; repr. E., 1915)

Lord Clarendon *Life* (2 vols., Oxford, 1857)

Coates, W. H., Young, A. S. and Snow, V. F. (eds.) *The Private Journals of the Long Parliament 3 January to 5 March 1642* (New Haven, 1982)

D'Ewes, Simonds *The Autobiography and Correspondence of Sir Simonds D'Ewes*, ed. J. O. Halliwell (2 vols., London, 1845)

Evelyn, John *Diary*, ed. E. S. de Beer (Oxford, 1959; E., 1907)

Fox, George *The Journal of George Fox* (1694; E., 1924)

Herbert of Cherbury, Lord Edward *The Life of Edward, First Lord Herbert of Cherbury, Written by Himself*, ed. J. M. Shuttleworth (Oxford, 1976)

Holles, Gervase *Memorials of the Holles Family* (Camden Series, 1937)

Hutchinson, Lucy *Memoirs of the Life of Colonel Hutchinson* (E. 1908, rev. 1968; ed. J. Sutherland, Oxford, 1973)

Loftis, J. (ed.) *The Memoirs of Anne, Lady Halkett, and Ann, Lady Fanshawe* (Oxford, 1979)

Smith, D. Nichol (ed.) *Characters from the Histories and Memoirs of the Seventeenth Century* (Oxford, 1918)

Sorlien, R. P. (ed.) *The Diary of John Manningham of the Middle Temple, 1602–1603* (Hanover, N. H., 1976)

Verney, F. P. and M. M. *Memoirs of the Verney Family during the Seventeenth Century* (4 vols., London, 1892–9)

Walton, Izaak *Lives* (1640–78; W.C., 1927)

Warwick, Sir Philip *Memoirs of the Reign of King Charles I* (London, 1813)

Adair, J. *A Life of John Hampden: The Patriot (1594–1643)* (London, 1976)

Adamson, J. H. and Follard, H. F. *Sir Harry Vane (1613–1662)* (London, 1973)

Ashley, M. *Charles II: The Man and the Statesman* (London, 1971)

Ashley, M. *General Monck* (London, 1977)

Ashley, M. *Charles I and Oliver Cromwell* (London, 1987)

Carlton, C. *Charles I: The Personal Monarch* (London, 1984)

Fraser, A. *Cromwell, Our Chief of Men* (London, 1973)

Gibb, M. *John Lilburne the Leveller* (London, 1947)

Gregg, P. *Free-born John* (London, 1961)

Hamilton, E. *Henrietta Maria* (London, 1976)

Hill, C. *God's Englishman: Oliver Cromwell and the English Revolution* (London, 1970; Penguin, 1972)

Hulme, H. *The Life of Sir John Eliot* (London, 1957)

Huxley, G. *Endymion Porter* (London, 1959)

Jacob, J. R. *Henry Stubbe: Radical Protestantism and the Early Enlightenment in England* (London, 1983)

Lockyer, R. *Buckingham* (London, 1981)

Marriott, J. *Life and Times of Lucius Cary, Viscount Falkland* (London, 1907)

Mathew, D. *Sir Tobie Mathew* (London, 1950)

Mathew, D. *James I* (London, 1967)

Ralph, P. L. *Sir Humphrey Mildmay, Royalist Gentleman* (New Brunswick, 1947)

Smith, G. R. *Without Touch of Dishonour: The Life and Death of Sir Henry Slingsby (1602–1658)* (Kineton, 1968)

Trevor-Roper, H. R. *Archbishop Laud* (London, 1940; rev. 1962 and 1988)

Walker, E. C. *William Dell: Master Puritan* (Cambridge, 1970)

Wedgwood, C. V. *Thomas Wentworth, First Earl of Strafford* (London, 1961)

Wilson, J. *Fairfax: General of Parliament's Forces* (London, 1985)

V. REFERENCE BOOKS AND HISTORIES OF
LITERATURE

Briggs, J. *This Stage-Play World: English Literature and its Background: 1580–1625* (Oxford, 1983)

Bush, D. *English Literature in the Earlier Seventeenth Century* (Oxford, 1945; rev. 1962)

The Cambridge History of English Literature, Vols. IV, VII, VIII (1907–16; repr. 1932)

Donker, M. and Muldrow, G. M. *Dictionary of Literary Rhetorical Conventions of the English Renaissance* (Westport, 1982)

Heninger, S. K., Jr *English Prose, Prose Fiction, and Criticism to 1660: A Guide to Information Sources* (Detroit, 1976)

King, B. *Seventeenth-Century English Literature* (London, 1982)

Patrides, C. A. and Waddington, R. B. (eds.) *The Age of Milton: Backgrounds to Seventeenth-Century Literature* (Manchester, 1981)

Rivers, I. *Classical and Christian Ideas in English Renaissance Poetry* (London, 1979)

Ruoff, J. E. *Handbook of Elizabethan and Stuart Literature* (London, 1976)

Sutherland, J. *English Literature of the Late Seventeenth Century* (Oxford, 1969)

Watson, G. (ed.) *The New Cambridge Bibliography of English Literature: Vol. I 600–1660* (Cambridge, 1974)

The Year's Work in English Studies (annual survey of literary research, published by the English Association since 1919)

VI. CONTEMPORARY CRITICISM

Atkins, J. W. H. *English Literary Criticism: The Renascence* (London, 1947)

Hamilton, K. G. *The Two Harmonies: Poetry and Prose in the Seventeenth Century* (Oxford, 1963)

Korshin, P. J. *From Concord to Dissent: Major Themes in English Poetic Theory 1640–1700* (Menston, 1973)

Sasek, L. A. *The Literary Temper of the English Puritans* (Baton Rouge, 1961)

Spingarn, J. E. (ed.) *Seventeenth-Century Critical Essays* (3 vols., Oxford, 1908–9)

Tayler, E. W. (ed.) *Literary Criticism of Seventeenth-Century England* (New York, 1967)

Tuve, R. *Elizabethan and Metaphysical Imagery* (Chicago, 1947)

Vickers, B. W. *Classical Rhetoric in English Poetry* (London, 1970)

Wallerstein, R. *Studies in Seventeenth-Century Poetic* (Madison, Wis., 1950)

VII. MUSIC AND THE VISUAL ARTS

Finney, G. L. *Musical Backgrounds for English Literature: 1580–1650* (New Brunswick, 1962)

Ford, B. (ed.) *The Cambridge Guide to the Arts in Britain*, vol. 4, *The Seventeenth Century* (Cambridge, 1989)

Hagstrum, J. H. *The Sister Arts* (Chicago, 1958)

Hind, A. M. *Engraving in England in the Sixteenth and Seventeenth Centuries* (3 vols., Cambridge, 1952)

Jorgens, E. B. *The Well Tun'd Word: Musical Interpretations of English Poetry 1597–1651* (Minneapolis, 1982)

Le Huray, P. *Music and the Reformation in England, 1549–1660* (London, 1967; Cambridge, 1978)

Mellers, W. *Harmonious Meeting: A Study of the Relationship between English Music, Poetry, and Theatre, c. 1600–1900* (London, 1965)

Mercer, E. *English Art, 1553–1625* (Oxford, 1962)

Parry, G. *The Golden Age Restor'd: The Culture of the Stuart Court 1603–42* (Manchester, 1981)

Spink, I. *English Song, Dowland to Purcell* (London, 1974)

Strong, R. *The English Icon: Elizabethan and Jacobean Portraiture* (London, 1969)

Summerson, J. *Architecture in Britain, 1530–1830* (Penguin, 1953; rev. 1958)

Waterhouse, E. K. *Painting in Britain, 1530–1790* (Penguin, 1953)

Whinney, M. *Sculpture in Britain, 1530–1830* (Penguin, 1964)

Whinney, M. and Millar, O. *English Art, 1625–1714* (Oxford, 1957)

Woodfill, W. L. *Musicians in English Society from Elizabeth to Charles I* (Princeton, 1953)

VIII. POETRY AND PROSE: GENERAL STUDIES AND COLLECTED ESSAYS

Numbers in brackets after the names of some critics are to facilitate reference in the Author bibliographies that conclude this Appendix.

Aers, D., Hodge, B. and Kress, G. (eds.) *Literature, Language and Society in England 1580–1680* (Dublin, 1981)

Allen, D. C. *Image and Meaning* (Baltimore, 1960; rev. 1968)

Alvarez, A. *The School of Donne* (London, 1961)

Beilin, E. V. *Redeeming Eve: Women Writers of the English Renaissance* (Princeton, 1987)

Bennett, J. *Five Metaphysical Poets* (Cambridge, 1934; rev. 1964)

Bottrall, M. *Every Man a Phoenix* (London, 1958)

Boyce, B. *The Theophrastan Character in England* (Cambridge, Mass., 1947; London, 1967)

Brooks-Davies, D. *The Mercurian Monarch: Magical Politics from Spenser to Pope* (Manchester, 1983)

Bush, D. *Mythology and Renaissance Tradition in English Poetry* (Minneapolis, 1932; New York, 1957)

Clark, I. *Christ Revealed* (Gainesville, 1983)

Cruttwell, P. *The Shakespearean Moment* (London, 1954; New York, 1960)

Daiches, D. *The King James Version of the English Bible* (Chicago, 1941)

Delany, P. *British Autobiography in the Seventeenth Century* (London, 1969)

de Mourgues, O. *Metaphysical, Baroque and Précieux Poetry* (Oxford, 1953)

Ebner, D. *Autobiography in Seventeenth-Century England* (The Hague, 1971)

Eliot, T. S. *Selected Essays* (London, 1932; rev. 1951)

Erskine-Hill, H. *The Augustan Ideal in English Literature* (London, 1983)

Farley-Hills, D. *The Benevolence of Laughter* (London, 1974)

Farmer, N. K., Jr *Poets and the Visual Arts in Renaissance England* (Austin, 1984)

Fish, S. E. (ed.) (1) *Seventeenth-Century Prose* (New York, 1971)

Fish, S. E. (2) *Self-Consuming Artifacts* (Berkeley, 1972)

Freeman, R. *English Emblem Books* (London, 1948)

Gilman, E. B. (1) *The Curious Perspective: Literary and Pictorial Wit in the Seventeenth Century* (New Haven, 1978)

Gilman, E. B. (2) *Iconoclasm and Poetry in the English Reformation* (Chicago, 1986)

Goldberg, J. (1) *James I and the Politics of Literature* (Baltimore, 1983)

Goldberg, J. (2) *Voice Terminal Echo: Postmodernism and English Renaissance Texts* (London, 1986)

Gordon, I. A. *The Movement of English Prose* (London, 1966)

Grundy, J. *The Spenserian Poets* (London, 1969)

Halewood, W. H. *The Poetry of Grace* (New Haven, 1970)

Helgerson, R. *Self-Crowned Laureates* (Berkeley, 1983)

Hill, C. (1) *Puritanism and Revolution* (London, 1958)

Hill, C. (2) *Collected Essays of Christopher Hill: Vol. I Writing and Revolution in Seventeenth-Century England* (Brighton, 1985)

Hobby, E. *Virtue of Necessity: English Women's Writing 1649–1688* (London, 1988)

Jose, N. *Ideas of the Restoration in English Literature, 1660–71* (Cambridge, Mass., 1984)

Keast, W. R. (ed.) *Seventeenth-Century English Poetry* (New York, 1962; rev. 1971)

Knights, L. C. *Public Voices: Literature and Politics* (London, 1971)

Knott, J. R., Jr *The Sword of the Spirit: Puritan Responses to the Bible* (Chicago, 1980)

Kupersmith, W. *Roman Satirists in Seventeenth-Century England* (London, 1985)

Lewalski, B. K. *Protestant Poetics and the Seventeenth-Century Religious Lyric* (Princeton, 1979)

Lord, G. de F. *Classical Presences in Seventeenth-Century English Poetry* (New Haven, 1987)

Love, H. (ed.) *Restoration Literature: Critical Approaches* (London, 1972)

McCanles, M. *Dialectical Criticism and Renaissance Literature* (Berkeley, 1975)

McClung, W. A. *The Country House in Renaissance Poetry* (Berkeley, 1977)

McKeon, M. *The Origins of the English Novel 1600–1740* (Baltimore, 1987)

Malekin, P. *Liberty and Love: English Literature and Society, 1640–1688* (London, 1981)

Marcus, L. S. *The Politics of Mirth* (Chicago, 1986)

Martz, L. L. (1) *The Poetry of Meditation* (New Haven, 1954; rev. 1962)

Martz, L. L. (2) *The Paradise Within* (New Haven, 1964)

Martz, L. L. (3) *The Wit of Love* (Notre Dame, 1970)

Mazzeo, J. A. *Renaissance and Seventeenth-Century Studies* (New York, 1964)

Miner, E. (1) *The Metaphysical Mode from Donne to Cowley* (Princeton, 1969)

Miner, E. (2) *The Cavalier Mode from Jonson to Cotton* (Princeton, 1971)

Miner, E. (ed.) (3) *The Restoration Mode from Milton to Dryden* (Princeton, 1974)

Mitchell, W. F. *English Pulpit Oratory from Andrewes to Tillotson* (London, 1932; repr. New York, 1962)

Nevo, R. *The Dial of Virtue* (Princeton, 1963)

Norbrook, D. *Poetry and Politics in the English Renaissance* (London, 1984)

Palmer, D. J. and Bradbury, M. (eds.) *Stratford-upon-Avon Studies*, Vol. XI: *Metaphysical Poetry* (London, 1970)

Parfitt, G. *English Poetry of the Seventeenth Century* (London, 1985)

Parry, G. *Seventeenth-Century Poetry: The Social Context* (London, 1985)

Patterson, A. M. *Censorship and Interpretation: The Conditions of Writing and Reading in Early Modern England* (Madison, Wis., 1984)

Peterson, D. L. *The English Lyric from Wyatt to Donne* (Princeton, 1967)

Raspa, A. *The Emotive Image: Jesuit Poetics* (Fort Worth, 1983)

Richmond, H. M. *The School of Love: The Evolution of the Stuart Love Lyric* (Princeton, 1964)

Rivers, I. *The Poetry of Conservatism 1600–1745* (Cambridge, 1973)

Rostvig, M-S. *The Happy Man: Vol. I 1600–1700* (Oslo, 1954; rev. 1962)

Salzman, P. *English Prose Fiction 1558–1700* (Oxford, 1985)

Schleiner, L. *The Living Lyre in English Verse from Elizabeth through the Restoration* (Columbia, 1984)

Scoular, K. *Natural Magic* (Oxford, 1965)

Seelig, S. C. *The Shadow of Eternity* (Lexington, 1981)

Selden, R. *English Verse Satire 1590–1765* (London, 1978)

Sharpe, K. *Criticism and Compliment: The Politics of Literature in the England of Charles I* (Cambridge, 1987)

Sharpe, K. and Zwicker, S. N. (eds.) *Politics of Discourse: The Literature and History of Seventeenth-Century England* (Berkeley, 1987)

Sinfield, A. *Literature in Protestant England 1560–1660* (London, 1983)

Slights, C. W. *The Casuistical Tradition in Shakespeare, Donne, Herbert, and Milton* (Princeton, 1981)

Sloane, M. C. *The Visual in Metaphysical Poetry* (Atlantic Heights, 1982)

Smith, A. J. *The Metaphysics of Love* (Cambridge, 1985)

Southall, R. *Literature and the Rise of Capitalism* (London, 1973)

Stewart, S. *The Enclosed Garden* (Madison, Wis., 1966)

Summers, J. H. *The Heirs of Donne and Jonson* (London, 1970)

Swardson, H. R. *Poetry and the Fountain of Light* (London, 1962)

Turner, J. G. *The Politics of Landscape* (Oxford, 1979)

Walton, G. *Metaphysical to Augustan* (Cambridge, 1955; New York, 1971)

Webber, J. *The Eloquent 'I'* (Madison, Wis., 1968)

White, H. C. *Metaphysical Poets* (New York, 1936)

Wilding, M. *Dragon's Teeth: Literature in the English Revolution* (Oxford, 1987)

Willey, B. *The Seventeenth-Century Background* (London, 1934; Penguin, 1962)

Williamson, G. (1) *The Senecan Amble* (London, 1951)

Williamson, G. (2) *The Proper Wit of Poetry* (Chicago, 1961)

Wilson, F. P. *Seventeenth-Century Prose* (Berkeley, 1960)

AUTHORS AND WORKS

Collections and Anthologies: (i) Verse

Auden, W. H. and Pearson, N. H. (eds.) *Elizabethan and Jacobean Poets* (Penguin, 1977)

Cain, T. G. S. (ed.) *Jacobean and Caroline Poetry* (London, 1981)

Clayton, T. (ed.) *Cavalier Poets* (Oxford, 1978)

Gardner, H. (ed.) *The Metaphysical Poets* (Penguin, 1957)

Greer, G. *et al.* (eds.) *Kissing the Rod: An Anthology of Seventeenth-Century Women's Verse* (London, 1988)

Grierson, Sir H. *Metaphysical Lyrics and Poems of the Seventeenth Century* (Oxford, 1921; repr. 1959)

Grierson, Sir H. and Bullough, G. (eds.) *The Oxford Book of Seventeenth-Century Verse* (Oxford, 1934)

Hollander, J. and Kermode, F. *The Literature of Renaissance England* (New York, 1973)

Howarth, R. G. (ed.) *Minor Poets of the Seventeenth Century* (E., 1931; rev. 1953)

Hunter, W. B., Jr (ed.) *The English Spenserians* (Salt Lake City, 1978)

Hussey, M. (ed.) *Poetry 1600–1660* (London, 1981)

Lewalski, B. K. and Sabol, A. J. (eds.) *Major Poets of the Earlier Seventeenth Century* (New York, 1973)

Martz, L. L. (ed.) *The Meditative Poem* (New York, 1963)

Parfitt, G. A. E. (ed.) *Silver Poets of the Seventeenth Century* (E., 1974)

Partridge, A. C. *The Tribe of Ben* (London, 1966)

Saintsbury, G. (ed.) *Minor Poets of the Caroline Period* (3 vols., Oxford, 1905–21)

Wilmott, R. (ed.) *Four Metaphysical Poets* (Cambridge, 1984)

(ii) Prose

Ferry, A. D. (ed.) *Religious Prose of Seventeenth-Century England* (New York, 1967)

Lamont, W. and Oldfield, S. *Politics, Religion and Literature in the Seventeenth Century* (E., 1975)

Lievsay, J. L. (ed.) *The Seventeenth-Century Resolve: A Historical Anthology of a Literary Form* (Lexington, 1980)

Muir, K. (ed.) *Elizabethan and Jacobean Prose 1550–1620* (Penguin, 1956)

Novarr, D. (ed.) *Seventeenth-Century English Prose* (New York, 1967)

Smith, D. N. (ed.) *Characters of the Seventeenth Century* (Oxford, 1918)

Ure, P. (ed.) *Seventeenth-Century Prose 1620–1700* (Penguin, 1956)

Vickers, B. (ed.) *Seventeenth-Century Prose* (London, 1969)

White, H. C., Wallerstein, R. C., Quintana, R. and Chambers, A. B. (eds.) *Seventeenth-Century Verse and Prose: I 1600–1660* (New York, 1951; rev. 1971)

Authors

To avoid unnecessary duplication in the Author bibliographies, relevant material in books listed in Section VIII above is indicated by the critic's name and (where appropriate) a number in brackets.

ANDREWES, LANCELOT (1555–1626): Preacher and scholar in divinity; b. London; Merchant Taylor's School; Pembroke, Cambridge; Fellow and Master; D.D. 1588. Royal chaplain to both Elizabeth and James I. Rhetorical manner of preaching much admired. Advanced through different bishoprics to that of Winchester, 1619. Served on Hampton Court Conference of theologians, 1604, and collaborated on translation of Authorized Version of Bible, 1611.

Life by P. A. Welsby (London, 1958)

Works ed. J. Bliss and J. P. Wilson (11 vols., London, 1841–54; rev. Oxford, 1843–60)

Selected Sermons ed. G. M. Story (Oxford, 1967)

See M. F. Reidy, *Bishop Lancelot Andrewes* (Chicago, 1955)

   T. A. Owen, *Lancelot Andrewes* (Boston, 1981)

   Essays in Eliot, Fish (1), Mitchell

BACON, FRANCIS, first Baron Verulam and Viscount St Alban (1561–1626): Philosopher, lawyer, and statesman; b. York House, Strand, London; Trinity College, Cambridge, 1573–5; Gray's Inn, 1576; attached to

English Ambassador to France, 1577–9; on death of father, 1579, entered legal and political career; began main scientific work, 1603; Solicitor-General, 1607; Attorney-General, 1613; Lord Chancellor, 1618; Baron, 1618; Viscount, 1621; deposed from office on charges of bribery, 1621; thereafter devoted himself to writing and to scientific research.

Life by J. J. Epstein (Athens, Ohio, 1977); by J. O. Fuller (London, 1981)

Works (including *Life and Letters*) ed. Spedding, Ellis, and Heath (14 vols., London, 1857–74; repr. New York, 1968); abridged edn J. M. Robertson (London, 1905)

The Philosophy of Francis Bacon 1603–1609 ed. B. Farrington (Liverpool, 1964) includes English versions of three early scientific works not translated by Spedding

Selected Works ed. F. H. Anderson (New York, 1960) and A. Johnston (London, 1965)

Advancement of Learning ed. G. W. Kitchin (E., 1915; repr. 1973); ed. A. Johnston, with *New Atlantis* (Oxford, 1974; repr. 1980)

Essays ed. M. Kiernan (Oxford, 1985); ed. J. Pitcher (Penguin, 1986)

Henry VII ed. R. Lockyer (London, 1971)

Novum Organum ed. T. Fowler (Oxford, 1878; rev. 1889)

See F. H. Anderson, *The Philosophy of Francis Bacon* (Chicago, 1948)

L. Jardine, *Francis Bacon: Discovery and the Art of Discourse* (Cambridge, 1975)

A. Quinton, *Francis Bacon* (London, 1980)

P. Rossi, *Francis Bacon: From Magic to Science*, trans. S. Rabinovitch (London, 1968)

B. W. Vickers, *Francis Bacon and Renaissance Prose* (Cambridge, 1968)

B. W. Vickers (ed.) *Essential Articles for the Study of Francis Bacon* (Hamden, 1968; London, 1972)

K. R. Wallace, *Francis Bacon on the Nature of Man* (Urbana, Ill., 1967)

H. B. White, *Peace among the Willows: The Political Philosophy of Francis Bacon* (The Hague, 1968)

C. Whitney, *Francis Bacon and Modernity* (New Haven, 1986)

BEAUMONT, JOSEPH (1616–99): Poet and divinity scholar; b. Hadleigh, Suffolk; Peterhouse, Cambridge, 1631; ejected from fellowship at Peterhouse for Royalist sympathies, 1644; retired to Hadleigh, where he wrote his epic poem, *Psyche*, published 1648; married 1650, and resided on wife's property at Tatington Place, Suffolk, where he composed most of his minor poems; Master of Peterhouse, 1663; regius divinity professor at Cambridge, 1674.

> *Complete Poems in Latin and English* ed. A. B. Grosart (2 vols., Edinburgh, 1880; repr. New York, 1967)
>
> *Minor Poems* ed. E. Robinson (London, 1914)

BROWNE, SIR THOMAS (1605–82): Author and physician; Winchester and Broadgate Hall, Oxford; M.A., 1629; took M.D. at Leyden, 1634; *Religio Medici* written during period of leisure, published without his permission, 1642, and reissued with his sanction, 1643; settled as doctor in Norwich, 1637; published *Pseudodoxia Epidemica* (*Vulgar Errors*), 1646; inspired by discovery of funeral urns near Norwich to write *Urne Buriall*, 1658; knighted on royal visit to Norwich, 1671.

> *Works* ed. G. Keynes (6 vols., London, 1928–31; Vols. V and VI, *Miscellaneous Works and Correspondence*, repr. with corrections, 1946; new edn in 4 vols., London, 1964; also appearing in part as *Selected Writings*, 1968)
>
> *Major Works* ed. C. A. Patrides (Penguin, 1977)
>
> *Pseudodoxia Epidemica* ed. R. H. A. Robbins (2 vols., Oxford, 1981)
>
> *Religio Medici and Other Writings* ed. C. H. Herford (E., 1906; repr. 1965)
>
> *Religio Medici, Hydriotaphia, and The Garden of Cyrus* ed. R. H. A. Robbins (Oxford, 1972)
>
> See J. Bennett, *Sir Thomas Browne* (Cambridge, 1962)
>
> F. L. Huntley, *Sir Thomas Browne* (Ann Arbor, 1962)
>
> L. Nathanson, *The Strategy of Truth* (Chicago, 1967)
>
> C. A. Patrides (ed.) *Approaches to Sir Thomas Browne* (Columbia, 1982)
>
> Essays in Bottrall, Fish (1 and 2), Webber, Wilding, Willey, Wilson

BROWNE, WILLIAM (1591–1643?): Poet; b. Tavistock; Exeter College, Oxford; Inns of Court; best known for his pastoral poems in imitation of Spenser, *The Shepheards Pipe* (1614) and *Britannia's Pastorals* (1613–16).

> *Poems* ed. G. Goodwin (2 vols., London, 1894)
>
> See J. Grundy, *The Spenserian Poets* (London, 1969)

BUNYAN, JOHN (1628–88): Author and preacher; b. Elstow, Bedfordshire; son of tinker; followed father's trade from early age till enlisted in Parliamentary army; married *c.* 1648 and returned to trade as tinker; made acquaintance of Gifford, head of Baptist community of Bedford, 1653; after death of wife *c.* 1656 achieved reputation as preacher throughout Bedfordshire; first published work, *Some Gospel-truths Opened*, 1656; remarried *c.* 1659; imprisoned as unlicensed preacher, 1660, and spent most of next twelve years in prison; wrote many books and tracts during imprisonment, including *Grace Abounding* (1666) and *The Pilgrim's Progress* (published 1678); on release from prison preached all over country; published cautionary tale, *Life and Death of Mr Badman* (1680) and second part of *The Pilgrim's Progress* (1684).

Life by W. Y. Tindall (New York, 1934); by M. Furlong (London, 1975)

Grace Abounding (E., 1953, repr. 1984; ed. W. R. Owens, Penguin, 1987)

The Holy War ed. R. Sharrock and J. F. Forrest (Oxford, 1980)

Life and Death of Mr Badman (E., 1953; repr. 1984; ed. J. F. Forrest and R. Sharrock, Oxford, 1988)

Miscellaneous Works general ed. R. Sharrock (10 vols., Oxford, 1976–87)

The Pilgrim's Progress ed. J. B. Wharey (Oxford, 1928; rev. R. Sharrock, 1960); (W.C., 1902, repr. 1984; E., 1954, repr. 1985; Penguin, 1970)

See C. W. Baird, *John Bunyan: A Study in Narrative Technique* (New York, 1977)

E. B. Batson, *John Bunyan: Allegory and Imagination* (London, 1984)

R. L. Greaves, *John Bunyan* (Abingdon, 1969)

C. Hill, *A Turbulent, Seditious and Factious People: John Bunyan and his Church* (Oxford, 1988)

U. M. Kaufmann, *The Pilgrim's Progress and Traditions in Puritan Meditation* (New Haven, 1966)

N. H. Keeble (ed.), *John Bunyan: Conventicle and Parnassus* (Oxford, 1988)

V. Newey (ed.), *The Pilgrim's Progress: Critical and Historical Views* (Liverpool, 1980)

R. Sharrock, *John Bunyan* (London, 1954; repr. 1968)

Essays in Bottrall, Ebner, Fish (1 and 2), Freeman, Knott, Southall, Webber

BURTON, ROBERT (1557–1626): Churchman, psychologist, prose-writer; b. Lindley, Leicestershire; Brasenose College; Christ Church, Oxford, where he remained for rest of his life. *Anatomy of Melancholy*, a collection of observations and anecdotes about the state of melancholy attributed to 'Democritus Junior', published 1621 and later revised and extended; *Philosophaster*, a Latin play, acted 1618.

Anatomy of Melancholy ed. F. Dell and P. Jordan-Smith (New York, 1927, repr. 1955); ed. H. Jackson (3 vols., E., 1932; repr. 1961); ed. T. C. Faulkner, N. K. Kiessling and R. L. Blair (Oxford, 1989)

See L. Babb, *Sanity in Bedlam* (East Lansing, 1959)

B. G. Lyons, *Voices of Melancholy* (London, 1971)

M. Mulhauser, *Burton's Anatomy of Melancholy* (London, 1959)

Essays in Fish (1 and 2), Webber, Wilson

BUTLER, SAMUEL (1612–80): Satirist; son of prosperous Worcestershire yeoman; King's School, Worcester; possibly Gray's Inn; never at university, but greatly learned; in household of Countess of Kent; acquainted with Selden; considered painting as a career; clerk to various county magistrates; secretary to Earl of Carbery and steward of Ludlow Castle, 1661; *Characters*, 1667–9 (published 1759); *Hudibras*, rhymed satire on Puritans, begun before Restoration (three parts, 1662, 1663, 1677); secretary to Duke of Buckingham, whom he probably helped with *The Rehearsal*; pension from King, 1677; died of consumption.

Works ed. A. R. Waller and R. Lamar (3 vols., Cambridge, 1905–28)

Characters ed. C. W. Daves (Cleveland, 1970)

Hudibras ed. J. Wilders (Oxford, 1967)

Hudibras Parts I and II and Selected Other Writings ed. J. Wilders and H. de Quehen (Oxford, 1973)

Prose Observations ed. H. de Quehen (Oxford, 1979)

See I. Jack, *Augustan Satire* (Oxford, 1952; repr. 1966)

G. R. Wasserman, *Samuel Butler* (Boston, 1976)

Essays in Farley-Hills, Love, Miner (3), Selden, Wilding

CAREW, THOMAS (1595?–1640?): Poet; son of lawyer; Merton College, Oxford, 1608; B.A., 1611; Middle Temple, 1612; favourite of Charles I; became one of the Court poets; friend of Lovelace, Suckling, Davenant; reputation for dissipation; secretary to Sir Dudley Carleton, ambassador to Italy, 1613–15; accompanied Lord Herbert of Cherbury to France, 1619; wrote masque, *Coelum Britannicum*, in collaboration with Inigo Jones, 1634.

> *Poems* ed. R. Dunlop (Oxford, 1949)
> *Minor Poets of the Seventeenth Century* ed. R. G. Howarth (E., 1931; rev. 1953)
> See L. Sadler, *Thomas Carew* (Boston, 1979)
>> E. I. Selig, *The Flourishing Wreath* (New Haven, 1957)
>> Essays in Farmer, Martz (3), McClung, Sharpe and Zwicker, Summers

CARTWRIGHT, WILLIAM (1611–43): Poet, dramatist, and preacher; b. near Tewkesbury; Westminster; Christ Church, Oxford, 1628; M.A. 1635; took holy orders; literary work much admired by contemporaries, including Jonson; contributed poem on Jonson to *Jonsonus Virbius*, 1638; favourite of Charles I, who wore mourning for him when he died of fever.

> R. C. Coffin, *The Life and Poems of William Cartwright* (Cambridge, 1918)
> *Plays and Poems* ed. G. B. Evans (Madison, Wis., 1951)

CAVENDISH, MARGARET, Duchess of Newcastle (1623?–73): Poet, essayist, biographer, and dramatist; b. near Colchester, Essex; daughter of Sir Thomas Lucas, landed gentleman; maid of honour to Queen Henrietta Maria, 1643–5; married William Cavendish, Marquis and subsequently Duke of Newcastle, in Paris, 1645; lived with him in exile in Paris, Rotterdam, and Antwerp until 1660; after Restoration lived with her husband in the country; regarded as eccentric because of her interest in experimental philosophy and her literary activities; best known as a writer for her account of her own life and a biography of her husband (1667).

> Life by D. Grant (London, 1957)
> *Life of William Cavendish, Duke of Newcastle, to which is added, The*

- *True Relation of my Birth, Breeding and Life* ed. C. H. Firth (London, 1886; rev. 1920)

Poems and Fancies, 1653 ed. G. Parfitt (Menston, 1972)

See G. D. Meyer, *The Scientific Lady in England* (Berkeley, 1955)

    M. Reynolds, *The Learned Lady in England 1650–1760* (Boston, 1920)

    H. Smith, *Reason's Disciples: Seventeenth-Century English Feminists* (Urbana, Ill., 1982)

    V. Woolf, *The Common Reader* (New York, 1925)

EARL OF CLARENDON (EDWARD HYDE) (1609–74): Historian and statesman; Magdalen College, Oxford, 1626; barrister of Middle Temple, 1633; one of Falkland's circle at Great Tew; friend of Jonson, Digby, Carew, Selden and Waller; one of opposition leaders till 1641, when he refused to go whole way with reformers in Long Parliament; Chancellor to Charles I, 1643; one of guardians of Prince of Wales (later Charles II) and followed him to Scilly and Channel Islands where he began *History*, c. 1646; organizer and policy maker of exiled Court; became Lord Chancellor at Restoration but was dismissed, 1667, and went to France where he completed *History* and wrote *Life of Edward, Earl of Clarendon*.

Life by Sir H. Craik (2 vols., London, 1911)

History of the Rebellion ed. W. D. Macray (6 vols., Oxford, 1888; repr. 1958)

Selections from History and Life ed. G. Huehns (w.c., 1955; rev. Oxford, 1978)

See R. W. Harris, *Clarendon and the English Revolution* (London, 1983)

    R. Ollard, *Clarendon and his Friends* (London, 1987)

    B. H. G. Wormald, *Clarendon: Politics, History and Religion* (Cambridge, 1951; rev. Chicago, 1977)

Essays in Hill (1), Knights

CLEVELAND, JOHN (1613–58): Poet; b. Loughborough; son of a Royalist clergyman; Christ's College, Cambridge, 1627; Fellow of St John's, 1634; M.A., 1635; studied law; ejected by Parliament, 1645; joined Royalist forces at Oxford; promoted to office of judge-advocate; composed witty political satires; acted as tutor to Cavalier families after defeat of King; imprisoned by authorities for three months, 1655; poems include an elegy on Edward King, Milton's 'Lycidas'.

Poems ed. J. M. Berdan (New Haven, 1911)

Poems ed. B. Morris and E. Withington (Oxford, 1967)

See L. A. Jacobus, *John Cleveland* (Boston, 1975)

COWLEY, ABRAHAM (1618–67): Poet and essayist; b. London; son of stationer and bookseller; wrote first volume of poetry at age of fifteen while at Westminster; Cambridge; became Fellow of Trinity College, but was ejected by Puritans, 1644; cipher secretary to Henrietta Maria *c.* 1647; contemporary reputation established by love poems in *The Mistress*, 1647; worked for Royalist cause at Oxford and Paris; imprisoned by Cromwell as spy; in later years, lived in retirement in country, studying medicine and botany and writing *Essays in Verse and Prose* (published 1668); one of first members of Royal Society.

Life by A. H. Nethercot (London, 1931; New York, 1967)

Complete Works ed. A. B. Grosart (2 vols., Edinburgh, 1881; repr. New York, 1967)

English Writings ed. A. R. Waller (2 vols., Cambridge, 1905–6; repr. 1967)

Silver Poets of the Seventeenth Century (E., 1974)

The Civil War ed. A. Pritchard (Toronto, 1973)

See R. B. Hinman, *Abraham Cowley's World of Order* (Cambridge, Mass., 1960)

D. Trotter, *The Poetry of Abraham Cowley* (London, 1979)

Essays in Alvarez, Jose, Nevo, Patterson, Rostvig, Schleiner, Walton

CRASHAW, RICHARD (1612–49): Poet; b. London; son of Puritan rector; Charterhouse; Pembroke, Cambridge; Fellow of Peterhouse, 1637; expelled as Anglican, 1643; became Catholic *c.* 1645; friend of Cowley; went to Paris *c.* 1645 and to Italy *c.* 1648; at death held minor post at Cathedral of Holy House of Loreto.

Poetical Works ed. L. C. Martin (Oxford, 1927; rev. 1957)

Complete Poetry ed. G. W. Williams (New York, 1972)

Silver Poets of the Seventeenth Century (E., 1974)

See M. F. Bertonasco, *Crashaw and the Baroque* (Alabama, 1971)

T. F. Healy, *Richard Crashaw* (Leiden, 1987)

P. A. Parrish, *Richard Crashaw* (Boston, 1980)

R. T. Petersson, *The Art of Ecstasy* (London, 1970)

M. E. Rickey, *Rhyme and Meaning in Richard Crashaw* (New York, 1961; repr. 1973)

R. Wallerstein, *Richard Crashaw* (Madison, Wis., 1935; repr. 1959)

A. Warren, *Richard Crashaw: A Study in Baroque Sensibility* (Louisiana, 1939; London, 1957)

G. W. Williams, *Image and Symbol in the Sacred Poetry of Richard Crashaw* (Columbia, 1963)

R. V. Young, *Richard Crashaw and the Spanish Golden Age* (New Haven, 1982)

Essays in Alvarez, Bennett, de Mourgues, Farmer, Keast, Martz (3), Parry, Raspa, Schleiner, Sloane, Summers, White

DAVENANT, SIR WILLIAM (1606–68): Poet and dramatist; b. Oxford; son of tavern keeper; Magdalen Hall, Oxford; in service of Duchess of Richmond and later of Fulke Greville; many friends at Court; succeeded Ben Jonson as poet laureate, 1638; also wrote several plays produced before Civil War; knighted at Siege of Gloucester, 1643; after Royalist defeat accompanied Court to France where began most important non-dramatic poem *Gondibert* and published *Discourse on Gondibert* with Hobbes's *Answer*, 1650; captured while sailing to America on royal mission, 1650, and imprisoned in Tower till 1654; wrote and produced plays for semi-private performance during Protectorate, including *The Siege of Rhodes* (first British opera), 1656; after Restoration became manager of own theatre company.

Life by M. Edmond (Manchester, 1987)

Gondibert ed. D. L. Gladish (Oxford, 1971)

Shorter Poems and Songs ed. A. M. Gibbs (Oxford, 1972)

See C. M. Dowlin, *Sir William Davenant's Gondibert: Its Preface and Hobbes' Answer* (Philadelphia, 1935)

A. Harbage, *Sir William Davenant, Poet Venturer* (Philadelphia, 1934)

A. H. Nethercot, *William Davenant* (Chicago, 1938; repr. 1967)

DENHAM, SIR JOHN (1615–69): Poet; b. Ireland, where father was chief Baron of Exchequer; Trinity College, Oxford; Lincoln's Inn; poetry anticipates Restoration period, though most of it written before 1660; most famous poem, *Cooper's Hill* (1642, but subsequently revised) employs meditation on landscape as vehicle for observations on political situation just before Civil War; regarded by Restoration critics as one of pioneers of new versification.

Life by B. O Hehir, *Harmony from Discords* (Berkeley, 1968)

Poetical Works ed. T. H. Banks (New Haven, 1928; rev. 1969)

Silver Poets of the Seventeenth Century (E., 1974)

See B. O Hehir, *Expans'd Hieroglyphicks: A Critical Edition of Cooper's Hill* (Berkeley, 1969)

  E. R. Wasserman, *The Subtler Language* (Baltimore, 1959)

  Essays in Malekin, Rostvig, Turner

DIGBY, SIR KENELM (1603–65): Autobiographer, poet and philosopher; member of wealthy Catholic family; son of Sir Everard Digby, who was executed for his part in Gunpowder Plot against James I; imprisoned in Winchester House for activity against Parliament, 1642; one of Sir Thomas Browne's first readers and published *Observations upon Religio Medici*, 1643; autobiography, written 1628, is interesting as social history and as narrative prose; also wrote two philosophical *Treatises* (1645) and an essay *Concerning Spenser*; 'Son of Ben Jonson', whose works he edited.

Loose Fantasies ed. V. Gabrieli (Rome, 1968)

Observations upon Religio Medici ed. R. B. Waddington (Menston, 1973)

Private Memoirs ed. Sir N. H. Nicolas (London, 1827)

See E. W. Bligh, *Sir Kenelm Digby and his Venetia* (London, 1932)

  R. T. Petersson, *Sir Kenelm Digby* (London, 1956)

DONNE, JOHN (1572–1631): Poet and priest; son of prosperous iron-monger; educated as Catholic; Hart Hall, Oxford, 1584; Lincoln's Inn, 1592; known in London as 'a great visitor of ladies, a great frequenter of plays, a great writer of conceited verses'; in Essex's expedition to Cadiz, 1596, and to the Azores, 1597; friend of Sir Henry Wotton and of Jonson; wrote most of *Satyres and Elegies* and probably many of *Songs and Sonets*, 1592–8; became Anglican *c.* 1598; private secretary to Lord Keeper Egerton, 1598; dismissed by Egerton, 1601, because of marriage to Anne More, niece of Egerton's wife; spent next ten years in poverty, with no regular occupation, at Mitcham, writing many of verse-letters, the rest of the *Elegies* and *Songs and Sonets* and the first religious poems;

published two *Anniversaries*, 1611 and 1612, and wrote some of prose works, including *Biathanatos*, about this time; ordained, 1615; chaplain to James I, 1615; Divinity Reader at Lincoln's Inn, 1616; established reputation as preacher; Dean of St Paul's 1621–31; during this last period wrote *Devotions* and rest of *Divine Poems* and sermons.

Life by R. C. Bald (Oxford, 1970)

Poems ed. Sir H. Grierson (2 vols., Oxford, 1912; abridged edn 1929)

Complete Poetry and Selected Prose ed. J. Hayward (London, 1929; rev. 1962)

Complete English Poems ed. A. J. Smith (Penguin, 1974)

Selected Prose ed. H. Gardner and T. Healy (Oxford, 1967)

Selected Prose ed. N. Rhodes (Penguin, 1987)

Anniversaries ed. F. Manley (Baltimore, 1963)

Biathanatos ed. M. Rudick (New York, 1982); ed. E. W. Sullivan II (Newark, 1984)

Devotions upon Emergent Occasions ed. J. Sparrow (Cambridge, 1923); ed. A. Raspa (Quebec, 1975; repr. Oxford, 1987)

Divine Poems ed. H. Gardner (Oxford, 1952; rev. 1978)

Elegies and Songs and Sonnets ed. H. Gardner (Oxford, 1965)

Epithalamions, Anniversaries and Epicedes ed. W. Milgate (Oxford, 1967; rev. 1979)

Essays in Divinity ed. E. M. Simpson (Oxford, 1952)

Ignatius his Conclave ed. T. S. Healy (Oxford, 1969)

Paradoxes and Problems ed. H. Peters (Oxford, 1980)

Satires, Epigrams and Verse Letters ed. W. Milgate (Oxford, 1967)

Sermons ed. G. R. Potter and E. M. Simpson (10 vols., Berkeley, 1953–62; repr. 1985)

Songs and Sonnets ed. T. Redpath (London, 1956; rev. 1983)

See J. Carey, *John Donne: Life, Mind, Art* (London, 1981)

T. Docherty, *John Donne, Undone* (London, 1986)

D. L. Guss, *John Donne, Petrarchist* (Detroit, 1966)

M. T. Hester, *Kinde Pitty and Brave Scorn: John Donne's Satyres* (Durham, N.C., 1982)

R. E. Hughes, *The Progress of the Soul* (London, 1969)

J. B. Leishman, *The Monarch of Wit* (London, 1951; rev. 1962)

B. K. Lewalski, *Donne's 'Anniversaries' and the Poetry of Praise* (Princeton, 1973)

W. R. Mueller, *John Donne: Preacher* (Princeton, 1962)

U. Nelly, *The Poet Donne: His Dialectic Method* (Cork, 1969)

A. C. Partridge, *John Donne: Language and Style* (London, 1979)

J. R. Roberts (ed.), *Essential Articles for the Study of John Donne's Poetry* (Hamden, 1975)

M. Roston, *The Soul of Wit* (Oxford, 1974)

A. F. Marotti, *John Donne: Coterie Poet* (London, 1986)

P. G. Pinka, *This Dialogue of One* (Alabama, 1982)

W. Sanders, *John Donne's Poetry* (Cambridge, 1971)

W. Schleiner, *The Imagery of John Donne's Sermons* (Providence, 1970)

T. G. Sherwood, *Fulfilling the Circle* (Toronto, 1984)

E. M. Simpson, *A Study of the Prose Works of John Donne* (Oxford, 1924; rev. 1948)

A. J. Smith (ed.), *John Donne: Essays in Celebration* (London, 1972)

J. Webber, *Contrary Music* (Madison, Wis., 1963)

Essays in Aers *et al.*, Alvarez, Bennett, Cruttwell, Erskine-Hill, Farmer, Fish (1), Gilman (2), Keast, Lewalski, Martz (1 and 3), Mazzeo, McCanles, Palmer and Bradbury, Parry, Peterson, Selden, Slights, Sloane, Southall, Webber, White

DRUMMOND, WILLIAM (1585–1649): Poet; aristocratic background; M.A., Edinburgh University; travelled on Continent; good linguist; led leisured and cultured life at estate of Hawthornden; leader of 'literary' life in Edinburgh; wrote courtly poem 'Forth Feasting' to commemorate visit of King James to Scotland, 1617; visited by Ben Jonson, 1619, and made notes of their conversation.

Life by D. Masson (1873; repr. New York, 1969)

Conversations in *Works of Ben Jonson, Vol. I* ed. C. H. Herford and P. Simpson (Oxford, 1925); also in *Ben Jonson: Complete Poems*, ed. G. Parfitt (Penguin, 1975)

Poetical Works ed. L. E. Kastner (2 vols., Manchester, 1913)

Poems and Prose ed. R. H. Macdonald (Edinburgh, 1976)

See *The Library of Drummond of Hawthornden* ed. R. H. Macdonald (Edinburgh, 1973)

EARLE, JOHN (1600?–65): Character-writer, poet, scholar, and clergyman; Merton College, Oxford; Fellow, 1619; won fame by publication of *Microcosmographie*, 1628, which drew many of its 'characters' from university life; one of Falkland's circle at Great Tew; chaplain to Lord Chamberlain; tutor to Prince of Wales and adviser to Charles I; after Restoration became Dean of Westminster, then Bishop of Worcester and finally Bishop of Salisbury.

> *Microcosmography* ed. H. Osborne (London, 1933); ed. A. S. West (London, 1951)
>
> See D. Nichol Smith, *Characters of the Seventeenth Century* (Oxford, 1918)
>
> Essay in Boyce

FILMER, SIR ROBERT (c. 1588–1653): Political writer; b. Kent into landed family; Trinity College, Cambridge, 1604; Lincoln's Inn; acquainted with Selden, Donne, George Herbert, Walton; imprisoned in Leeds Castle, Kent, 1643; wrote *Patriarcha* (published 1680) before Civil War in defence of absolutism and divine right of kings; involved in controversy over monarchy, 1647–8.

> *Patriarcha and Other Political Works* ed. P. Laslett (Oxford, 1949)
>
> See J. Daly, *Sir Robert Filmer and English Political Thought* (Toronto, 1979)
>
> Essay in Malekin

FLETCHER, GILES (c. 1585–1623): Poet; b. Cambridge; son of Dr Giles Fletcher, poet-ambassador, cousin of John Fletcher, dramatist; made first literary appearance with his brother in Cambridge Miscellany, *Sorrow's Joy*, 1603; disciple of Spenser; B.A., Trinity College, Cambridge, 1606; Reader in Greek, 1615; published most important poem, *Christ's Victorie and Triumph*, 1610; became rector of Alderton, Suffolk, 1619.

> *Poetical Works of Giles and Phineas Fletcher: Vol. I* ed. F. S. Boas (Cambridge, 1909; repr. 1970)
>
> *English Works* ed. L. E. Berry (Madison, Wis., 1964)
>
> *The English Spenserians* ed. W. B. Hunter (Salt Lake City, 1976)
>
> See F. S. Kastor, *Giles and Phineas Fletcher* (Boston, 1980)
>
> Essay in Grundy

FLETCHER, PHINEAS (1582–1650): Poet and clergyman; son of Dr Giles Fletcher, brother of poet, Giles Fletcher; Eton and King's College, Cambridge; B.A., 1604; M.A., 1608; rector of Hilgay, Norfolk, 1621–50; published Spenserian poem, *The Purple Island*, 1633; works of both Fletchers very fashionable when Milton went to Cambridge and had some influence on him.

Poetical Works of Giles and Phineas Fletcher ed. F. S. Boas (2 vols., Cambridge, 1909; repr. 1970)

The English Spenserians ed. W. B. Hunter (Salt Lake City, 1976)

See F. S. Kastor, *Giles and Phineas Fletcher* (Boston, 1980)

A. B. Langdale, *Phineas Fletcher, Man of Letters, Science and Divinity* (New York, 1937)

Essay in Grundy

FULLER, THOMAS (1608–61): Clergyman and writer; b. Aldwinkle, Northamptonshire; son of rector; Queens' College, Cambridge; M.A., 1628; published *The History of the Holy War*, 1639, and *The Holy State and the Profane State*, 1642; chaplain to Royalist troops during Civil War; after Royalist defeat, lost all clerical appointments and retired to Exeter where he wrote *Good Thoughts in Bad Times*, 1645, and *Good Thoughts in Worse Times*, 1647; one of first English writers to support himself by his pen; published *Church History*, 1655, and *History of the University of Cambridge*, 1659; after Restoration published *Mixed Contemplations in Better Times*, 1660, and became chaplain to Charles II; greatest work, *The History of the Worthies of England*, published posthumously, 1662.

Life by W. Addison (London, 1951)

A Collection of Sermons, 1656 ed. E. McCutcheon (Menston, 1973)

The History of the Worthies of England ed. P. A. Nuttall (3 vols., London, 1840; repr. 1965)

The Holy State and the Profane State ed. M. G. Walten (2 vols., New York, 1938)

Worthies of England abridged edn J. Freeman (London, 1952)

See W. E. Houghton, *The Formation of Thomas Fuller's Holy and Profane States* (Cambridge, Mass., 1938)

Essay in Mitchell

HABINGTON, WILLIAM (1605–54): Poet; b. Worcestershire; Catholic gentleman; educated in France; wrote *Historie of Edward the Fourth* (1640) and one play, *The Queene of Arragon* (1640), in addition to his volume of poetry, *Castara* (1634/5), composed in honour of Lucy Herbert, who became his wife; final version of *Castara* (1640) included four prose 'characters'.

 Poems ed. K. Allott (Liverpool, 1948)
 See essay in Rostvig

HALL, JOSEPH (1574–1656): Character-writer, poet, and clergyman; b. Ashby de la Zouch; Emmanuel College, Cambridge, 1589; Puritan leanings; verse satires, 1597; published first English collection of 'characters', 1608; Bishop of Exeter, 1627; defended episcopacy against Milton, 1641; Bishop of Norwich, 1641; silenced 1643.

 Life by T. F. Kinloch (London, 1951); by F. L. Huntley (Cambridge, 1979)

 Works ed. P. Hall (12 vols., Oxford, 1837–9)

 Poems ed. A. Davenport (Liverpool, 1949)

 Another World and Yet the Same: Bishop Hall's Mundus alter et idem trans. and ed. J. M. Wands (New Haven, 1981)

 Heaven upon Earth and Characters of Vertues and Vices ed. R. Kirk (New Brunswick, 1948)

 See R. A. McCabe, *Joseph Hall: A Study in Satire and Meditation* (Oxford, 1982)

 L. D. Tourney, *Joseph Hall* (Boston, 1979)

 Essay in Boyce

HARRINGTON, JAMES (1611–77): Republican theorist; aristocratic background; Trinity College, Oxford; spent some time in service of Elector Palatine; visited Rome and Venice; in service of Charles I at Holmby and on Isle of Wight; published *The Commonwealth of Oceana*, 1656, outlining a plan for an ideal republic in opposition to Hobbes's *Leviathan*; also wrote *Aphorisms Political*, 1659, and *Political Discourses tending to the introduction of a free commonwealth in England*, 1660; formed Rota club for political discussion, 1659–60; imprisoned in Tower, 1661.

 Political Writings ed. C. Blitzer (New York, 1955); ed. J. G. A. Pocock (Cambridge, 1977)

Oceana ed. S. B. Lidjegren (Heidelberg, 1924)

See C. Blitzer, *An Immortal Commonwealth* (New Haven, 1960)

I. Grimble, *The Harrington Family* (London, 1957)

H. F. R. Smith, *Harrington and his Oceana* (Cambridge, 1914)

Essay in Hill (1)

HERBERT OF CHERBURY, EDWARD, LORD (1583–1648): Poet, philosopher, historian and diplomat; b. Eyton-on-Severn, nr Wroxted; son of Sir Richard Herbert and eldest brother of George Herbert; University College, Oxford, 1596; at Court, 1600; travelled abroad, 1608–10; friend of Jonson, Donne and Carew; employed on diplomatic missions, 1619–24; published *De Veritate*, 1624; baron of Cherbury, 1629; aimed at neutrality in Civil War, during which he wrote autobiography; submitted to Parliament and received pension, 1645.

De Religione Laici ed. H. R. Hutcheson (New Haven, 1944)

De Veritate trans. M. H. Carre (Bristol, 1937)

Life of Edward, First Lord Herbert of Cherbury, Written by Himself ed.
   J. M. Shuttleworth (Oxford, 1976)

Poems ed. G. C. Moore Smith (Oxford, 1923)

Minor Poets of the Seventeenth Century (E., 1931; rev. 1953)

See R. D. Bedford, *The Defence of Truth* (Manchester, 1979)

   Essays in Bottrall, Cruttwell, Farmer, Willey

HERBERT, GEORGE (1593–1633): Poet and priest; b. Montgomery Castle; son of Sir Richard Herbert and brother of Lord Herbert; early contacts with Donne who was one of mother's friends; Westminster School; Trinity College, Cambridge; early dedication to religious verse; distinguished scholar and able musician; Public Orator at Cambridge, 1619–27; abandoned worldly ambitions to become deacon, 1625, and priest, 1630; rector of Bemerton, nr Salisbury, 1630–33; many of poems in *The Temple* (published posthumously, 1633) written or revised during three years at Bemerton; prose work, *A Priest to the Temple*, published 1652.

Life by A. M. Charles (Ithaca, 1977)

Works ed. F. E. Hutchinson (Oxford, 1941)

Poems ed. H. Gardner (W.C., 1961); ed. C. A. Patrides (E., 1974); ed.
   L. L. Martz (with Vaughan's Poems) (Oxford, 1986)

See H. A. R. Asals, *Equivocal Predication* (Toronto, 1981)

D. Benet, *Secretary of Praise* (Columbia, 1984)

S. Fish, *The Living Temple* (Berkeley, 1978)

C. Freer, *Music for a King* (Baltimore, 1972)

B. L. Harman, *Costly Monuments: Representations of the Self* (Cambridge, Mass., 1982)

A. D. Nuttall, *Overheard by God* (London, 1980)

C. A. Patrides (ed.), *George Herbert: The Critical Heritage* (London, 1983)

M. E. Rickey, *Utmost Art* (Kentucky, 1966)

J. R. Roberts (ed.), *Essential Articles for the Study of George Herbert's Poetry* (Hamden, 1979)

A. Stein, *George Herbert's Lyrics* (Baltimore, 1968)

R. Strier, *Love Known: Theology and Experience* (Chicago, 1983)

J. H. Summers, *George Herbert: His Religion and Art* (London, 1954)

R. Tuve, *A Reading of George Herbert* (London, 1952)

G. E. Veith, *Reformation Spirituality: The Religion of George Herbert* (Lewisburg, 1985)

H. Vendler, *The Poetry of George Herbert* (Cambridge, Mass., 1975)

Essays in Allen, Alvarez, Bennett, Clark, Fish (2), Freeman, Goldberg (2), Halewood, Keast, Lewalski, Martz (1), McCanles, Palmer and Bradbury, Parry, Schleiner, Seelig, Slights, Sloane, Summers, Swardson, White

HERRICK, ROBERT (1591–1674): Poet and clergyman; b. Cheapside, London; son of goldsmith; apprenticed to uncle, Sir William Herrick, prosperous London goldsmith, 1607–13; took two degrees at St John's College, Cambridge; friend of Jonson and the Court wits; became rector of Dean Prior, Devonshire, 1629; dismissed by Puritan government, 1647, and restored, 1662; published *Hesperides* and *Noble Numbers*, 1648.

Life by F. W. Moorman (1910; repr. New York, 1970)

Poetical works ed. L. C. Martin (Oxford, 1956); ed. J. M. Patrick (New York, 1963)

See R. H. Deming, *Ceremony and Art* (The Hague, 1974)

R. B. Rollin, *Robert Herrick* (New York, 1966)

R. B. Rollin and J. M. Patrick (eds.), '*Trust to Good Verses': Herrick Tercentenary Essays* (Pittsburgh, 1978)

Essays in Farmer, Marcus, McClung, Parry, Rostvig, Schleiner, Summers, Swardson

HOBBES, THOMAS (1588–1679): Philosopher; b. Malmesbury; son of Wiltshire parson; learnt Latin and Greek at age of six; Magdalen Hall, Oxford, 1603; B.A., 1608; tutor and companion to second and third Earls of Cavendish family; friends included Harvey, Bacon, Cowley, Davenant, Jonson, Waller and Selden; travelled on Continent and made friends with Gassendi and Galileo; fled to Paris after meeting of Long Parliament, 1640; after publishing *Leviathan*, 1651, was accused of atheism and returned to England where similar charges were made; was involved for many years in religious controversies; protected from Clarendon and Church party by Charles II who granted him pension of £100; retired to country estates, 1675.

Life by C. Hinnant (Boston, 1977)

Behemoth or the Long Parliament ed. F. Tönnies (London, 1899; rev. 1969)

De Cive ed. H. Warrender (2 vols., Oxford, 1983)

Elements of Law, Natural and Politic ed. F. Tönnies (London, 1899; rev. 1969)

Leviathan ed. M. Oakeshott (Oxford, 1946); ed. J. Plamenatz (London, 1962); ed. C. B. Macpherson (Penguin, 1968; rev. 1981); (E., 1914; repr. 1965)

See J. Bowle, *Hobbes and His Critics* (London, 1951)

D. P. Gauthier, *The Logic of Leviathan* (London, 1969)

M. M. Goldsmith, *Hobbes' Science of Politics* (London, 1966)

J. Hampton, *Hobbes and the Social Contract Tradition* (Cambridge, 1986)

D. Johnston, *The Rhetoric of Leviathan: Thomas Hobbes and the Politics of Cultural Transformation* (Princeton, 1986)

M. Oakeshott, *Hobbes on Civil Association* (Oxford, 1975)

R. S. Peters, *Hobbes* (Penguin, 1956; rev. 1967)

D. D. Raphael, *Hobbes: Morals and Politics* (London, 1977)

T. Sorrell, *Hobbes* (London, 1986)

T. A. Spragens, Jr, *The Politics of Motion* (London, 1973)

H. Warrender, *The Political Philosophy of Hobbes* (Oxford, 1957)

J. W. N. Watkins, *Hobbes's System of Ideas* (London, 1965; rev. 1973)

S. S. Wolin, *Hobbes and the Epic Tradition of Political Theory* (Los Angeles, 1970)

Essays in Hill (1), Malekin, Southall, Willey

JONES, INIGO (1573–1652): Architect and designer; b. London into poor Welsh family; apprenticed to a joiner; influence of Palladio and others during tours of Italy in 1601 and 1613 led to his becoming the first innovative Renaissance figure in English architecture; Surveyor-General to James I and Charles I from 1615; designer of stage and costume for Court masques (usually with Ben Jonson as literary collaborator) 1605–40; among few surviving buildings, Banqueting Hall, Whitehall, and Queen's House are masterpieces, and his contribution to Wilton House, Wiltshire, is most important outside London; began rebuilding St Paul's and much town planning in London until Civil War intervened and royal patronage ceased; satirized by Jonson; his architectural style was not fully established or followed until the eighteenth century.

Life by J. Summerson (Penguin, 1966)

Literary texts associated with Jones and all his masque designs appear in S. Orgel and R. Strong (eds.) *The Theatre of the Stuart Court* (2 vols., California, 1973)

See J. Lees-Milne, *Age of Inigo Jones* (London, 1953)

J. Orrell, *The Theatres of Inigo Jones and John Webb* (Cambridge, 1985)

P. Palme, *The Triumph of Peace* (Stockholm, 1956)

JONSON, BEN (1572–1637): Poet, dramatist and critic; b. Westminster; son of minister; Westminster School; bricklayer; soldier on Continent; returned to England *c.* 1592; working for Henslowe *c.* 1597; friend of Selden, Bacon, Chapman and Fletcher; patrons included Countess of Bedford, Countess of Rutland, Sir Robert Sidney and the Earl of Pembroke; published poems with masques and plays, 1616; from 1616 granted pension by James I as 'King's poet'; visited William Drummond of Hawthornden, who recorded their conversations, 1619; quarrel with Inigo Jones, his collaborator on Court masques, 1630; wrote last laureate verses, 1635; regarded as leader among London poets until his death when they extolled his memory in *Jonsonus Virbius*, 1638.

Life by R. Miles (London, 1986); by D. Riggs (Cambridge, Mass., 1989)

Works ed. C. H. Herford and P. and E. Simpson (11 vols., Oxford, 1925–52); VIII contains Poems and Prose Works, XI the commentary on the poems.

Poems ed. G. B. Johnston (London, 1954); ed. W. B. Hunter (New York, 1963); ed. I. Donaldson (Oxford, 1975); ed. G. Parfitt (Penguin, 1975)

Epigrams and The Forest ed. R. Dutton (Manchester, 1984)

See R. Dutton, *Ben Jonson* (Cambridge, 1983)

> J. K. Gardiner, *Craftsmanship in Context: The Development of Ben Jonson's Poetry* (The Hague, 1975)
>
> D. C. Judkins, *The Non-Dramatic Works of Ben Jonson* (Boston, 1982)
>
> J. G. Nichols, *The Poetry of Ben Jonson* (London, 1969)
>
> G. A. Parfitt, *Ben Jonson, Public Poet and Private Man* (London, 1976)
>
> R. S. Peterson, *Imitation and Praise in the Poems of Ben Jonson* (New Haven, 1981)
>
> W. Trimpi, *Ben Jonson's Poems* (Stanford, 1962)
>
> Essays in Helgerson, Keast, Marcus, McClung, Norbrook, Parry, Patterson, Southall, Walton

KING, HENRY (1592–1669): Poet and clergyman; b. Buckinghamshire; son of bishop; Westminster School; Christ Church, Oxford; B.A., 1611; M.A., 1614; wrote elegy on Sir Walter Ralegh, 1618; wrote 'The Exequy' on death of wife, *c.* 1624; friend of Donne and Jonson and wrote elegies on both of them; Bishop of Chichester, 1642; ejected by Puritans, 1643; wrote elegy on Charles I; restored to bishopric at Restoration.

Poems ed. M. Crum (Oxford, 1965)

See R. Berman, *Henry King and the Seventeenth Century* (London, 1964)

> Essay in Summers

KNEVET, RALPH (1601–72): Poet; b. Norfolk, into a branch of the great Knyvett family; Peterhouse, Cambridge, 1616; published *Stratioticon*, a poetic discourse on military discipline, 1628; served Paston family in some capacity, possibly tutor or chaplain; published a pastoral play,

Rhodon and Iris, 1631; completed manuscript of continuation of Spenser's *Faerie Queene*, 1635; travelled to Italy with William Paston, 1638–9; worked on manuscript collection of devotional lyrics in imitation of George Herbert, *A Gallery to the Temple*, during 1640s; became rector at Lyng, in Norfolk, 1652, where he continued till his death.

  Shorter Poems ed. A. M. Charles (Columbus, 1966)

  See M. W. Merchant, *Essays and Studies*, Vol. XIII (1960)

LILBURNE, JOHN (1615–57): Leveller leader; son of Durham squire; apprenticed to London draper; accused before Star Chamber of printing and circulating unlicensed books, 1637; imprisoned 1638–40; fought for Parliament, 1642–5; refused to take covenant, 1645, and wrote *England's Birthright Justified* while in prison; wrote pamphlets criticizing army leaders, 1648–9; imprisoned in Tower, charged with treason and acquitted, 1649; banished by special Act of 'Rump' Parliament, 1652–3; on return to England refused to promise compliance with government and was confined in Jersey and Guernsey and at Dover Castle till 1655; became Quaker.

  Life by M. A. Gibb (London, 1947); by P. Gregg, *Free-Born John* (London, 1961)

  England's Birthright Justified in W. Haller, *Tracts on Liberty in the Puritan Revolution*, Vol. III (New York, 1934) and in G. E. Aylmer, *The Levellers in the English Revolution* (London, 1975)

  England's New Chains Discovered in Aylmer (ibid.) and in H. Erskine-Hill and G. Storey, *Revolutionary Prose of the English Civil War* (Cambridge, 1983)

  The Legal Fundamental Liberties of the People of England and other pamphlets in W. Haller and G. Davies, *The Leveller Tracts* (New York, 1944)

  A Worke of the Beast in W. Haller, *Tracts on Liberty*, Vol. II

  See H. N. Brailsford, *The Levellers and the English Revolution* (London, 1961)

  J. Frank, *The Levellers* (New York, 1955)

  Essay in Webber

LOVELACE, RICHARD (1618–*c*. 1657): Poet and Cavalier; b. Woolwich (?); member of old Kentish family; Charterhouse School; Gloucester Hall,

Oxford; M.A., 1636; joined Court; in Scottish expedition, 1639; poems very popular with contemporary wits and poets; friends included Carew, Marvell, Henry Lawes and Charles Cotton; imprisoned for supporting 'Kentish Petition', 1642; joined Charles I at Oxford, 1645; fought for French king, 1646; imprisoned for seven weeks, 1648–9; while in prison prepared collection of his poems, *Lucasta*, for publication; died in poverty, having consumed his fortune in Cavalier cause.

Poems ed. C. H. Wilkinson (Oxford, 1930)

Minor Poets of the Seventeenth Century ed. R. G. Howath (E., 1931; rev. 1953)

See C. H. Hartmann, *The Cavalier Spirit and its Influence on the Life and Work of Richard Lovelace* (London, 1925)

M. Weidhorn, *Richard Lovelace* (New York, 1970)

Essays in Allen, Farmer, Keast

MARVELL, ANDREW (1621–78): Poet and politician; b. Hull; son of clergyman of Puritan sympathies; Hull Grammar School (?); Trinity College, Cambridge; B.A., 1638; travelled abroad, 1642–6; wrote 'An Horatian Ode upon Cromwell's Return from Ireland', 1650; tutor to daughter of Lord Fairfax at Nun Appleton House, Yorkshire, 1651–3, when probably wrote some of most famous lyrics, including 'Upon Appleton House' and 'The Garden'; tutor to William Dutton, ward of Cromwell, 1653; friends included Lovelace, James Harrington and Milton; Milton's colleague in Latin Secretaryship, 1657; defended Milton, 1660; M.P. for Hull, 1659–78; wrote satirical and polemical prose and some verse satires, including *Last Instructions to a Painter*, after Restoration.

Life by P. Legouis (Oxford, 1965); by J. D. Hunt (London, 1978)

Poems and Letters of Andrew Marvell ed. H. M. Margoliouth (2 vols., Oxford, 1927; rev. P. Legouis and E. E. Duncan-Jones, 1971)

Complete Poetry ed. G. de F. Lord (New York, 1968; repr. E., 1984); ed. E. S. Donno (Penguin, 1972)

The Rehearsal Transpros'd: Parts I and II ed. D. I. B. Smith (Oxford, 1971)

Selected Poetry and Prose ed. R. Wilcher (London, 1986)

See A. E. Berthoff, *The Resolved Soul* (Princeton, 1970)

M. C. Bradbrook and M. G. Lloyd Thomas, *Andrew Marvell* (Cambridge, 1940)

R. L. Brett (ed.), *Andrew Marvell: Essays on the Tercentenary of his Death* (Oxford, 1979)

J. Carey (ed.), *Andrew Marvell: A Critical Anthology* (Penguin, 1969)

W. L. Chernaik, *The Poet's Time: Politics and Religion in the Work of Andrew Marvell* (Cambridge, 1983)

R. L. Colie, *'My Ecchoing Song'* (Princeton, 1970)

E. S. Donno (ed.), *Andrew Marvell: The Critical Heritage* (London, 1978)

K. Friedenreich (ed.), *Tercentenary Essays* (Hamden, 1977)

D. M. Friedman, *Marvell's Pastoral Art* (London, 1970)

R. I. V. Hodge, *Foreshortened Time* (Cambridge, 1978)

J. Klause, *The Unfortunate Fall* (Hamden, 1983)

J. B. Leishman, *The Art of Marvell's Poetry* (London, 1966)

C. A. Patrides (ed.), *Approaches to Marvell* (London, 1978)

A. M. Patterson, *Marvell and the Civic Crown* (Princeton, 1978)

M. Stocker, *Apocalyptic Marvell* (Brighton, 1986)

H. E. Toliver, *Marvell's Ironic Vision* (New Haven, 1965)

J. M. Wallace, *Destiny his Choice: The Loyalism of Andrew Marvell* (Cambridge, 1968)

R. Wilcher, *Andrew Marvell* (Cambridge, 1985)

Essays in Allen, Alvarez, Bennett, Eliot, Farley-Hills, Gilman (1), Goldberg (2), Hill (1), Jose, Keast, Lord, Malekin, Marcus, Martz (3), McCanles, Sharpe and Zwicker, Wilding

MILTON, JOHN (1608–74): Poet, pamphleteer and Puritan administrator; b. London; son of prosperous scrivener; spent childhood in household which was Puritan, yet cultured and humanist; St Paul's School, 1620?–25?; Christ's College, Cambridge, 1625; wrote 'On the Morning of Christ's Nativity', 1629; abandoned original intention to take holy orders because could not bring himself to submit to discipline of Church; lived at Horton, Buckinghamshire, 1632–8, reading widely in preparation for career as poet; *Comus* produced 1634 at Ludlow Castle by Henry Lawes, the musician; contributed pastoral elegy, 'Lycidas', to volume commemorating Edward King, former fellow-student at Cambridge, 1638; travelled in Italy, France and Switzerland, 1638–9, but returned to England because of threat of Civil War; spent next twenty years teaching and pamphleteering on behalf of ecclesiastical, civil, and political liberties; married Mary Powell, member of Cavalier family, 1642; on her desertion wrote treatises on divorce; published *Areopagitica*, 1644, in defence of a free press; published English and Latin poems, 1645; reunited with wife, 1645, till her death, 1652; Latin Secretaryship to Commonwealth Government, 1649; wrote treatises defending regicide; became completely blind, 1652; married Katherine Woodcock, 1656, and deplored her death in a sonnet, 1658; working on *Paradise Lost c.* 1658; published pamphlets warning of dangers of return to monarchy, 1659–60; prosecuted at Restoration but escaped with nominal imprisonment; married Elizabeth Minshull, 1663, and retired from public life; published *Paradise Lost*, 1667, and *Paradise Regained* and *Samson Agonistes*, 1671.

Life by D. Bush (London, 1965); by W. R. Parker (2 vols., Oxford, 1968); by A. N. Wilson (Oxford, 1983)

H. Darbishire (ed.), *The Early Lives of Milton* (London, 1932)

J. M. French (ed.), *Life Records* (5 vols., New Brunswick, 1949–58)

Works ed. F. A. Patterson *et al.* (20 vols., New York, 1931–40); abridged edn, *The Student's Milton* (New York, 1930; rev. 1933)

Poetical Works ed. H. Darbishire (London, 1958); ed. B. A. Wright (E., 1956; rev. 1980); ed. J. T. Shawcross (New York, 1963); ed. D. Bush (Oxford, 1966); ed. J. Carey and A. Fowler (2 vols., London, 1968)

Complete Prose Works gen. ed. Don M. Wolfe (8 vols., New Haven, 1953–82)

Selected Prose ed. M. W. Wallace (W.C., 1925); ed. K. M. Burton (E., 1958); ed. C. A. Patrides (Penguin, 1974)

Complete Poems and Major Prose ed. M. Y. Hughes (New York, 1957)

See A. E. Barker, *Milton and the Puritan Dilemma* (Toronto, 1942)

B. M. Berry, *Process of Speech: Puritan Religious Writing and 'Paradise Lost'* (Baltimore, 1976)

F. C. Blessington, *'Paradise Lost' and the Classical Epic* (Boston, 1979)

D. F. Bouchard, *Milton: A Structural Reading* (London, 1974)

J. B. Broadbent, *Some Graver Subject* (London, 1960)

C. C. Brown, *John Milton's Aristocratic Entertainments* (Cambridge, 1985)

A. Burnett, *Milton's Style* (London, 1981)

S. Davies, *Images of Kingship in 'Paradise Lost'* (Columbia, 1983)

S. Davies, *The Idea of Woman in Renaissance Literature* (Brighton, 1986)

J. G. Demaray, *Milton and the Masque Tradition* (Cambridge, Mass., 1968)

J. G. Demaray, *Milton's Theatrical Epic* (Cambridge, Mass., 1980)

W. Empson, *Milton's God* (London, 1961; Cambridge, rev. 1981)

A. Ferry, *Milton's Epic Voice* (Cambridge, Mass., 1963)

S. Fish, *Surprised by Sin: The Reader in 'Paradise Lost'* (London, 1967)

R. M. Frye, *Milton's Imagery and the Visual Arts* (Princeton, 1978)

H. Gardner, *A Reading of 'Paradise Lost'* (Oxford, 1965)

C. Grose, *Milton and the Sense of Tradition* (New Haven, 1988)

J. Halkett, *Milton and the Idea of Matrimony* (New Haven, 1970)

C. Hill, *Milton and the English Revolution* (London, 1977)

J. S. Hill, *John Milton: Poet, Priest and Prophet* (London, 1979)

M. Y. Hughes (gen. ed.), *A Variorum Commentary on the Poems of John Milton* (4 vols., 1970–75)

C. Hunt, *'Lycidas' and the Italian Critics* (New Haven, 1979)

G. K. Hunter, *Paradise Lost* (London, 1982)

W. B. Hunter (gen. ed.), *A Milton Encyclopedia* (9 vols., Lewisburg, 1979–83)

J. R. Knott, Jr, *Milton's Pastoral Vision* (Chicago, 1971)

J. B. Leishman, *Milton's Minor Poems* (London, 1969)

B. K. Lewalski, *Milton's Brief Epic* (Providence, 1966)

B. K. Lewalski, *'Paradise Lost' and the Rhetoric of Literary Forms* (Princeton, 1985)

C. S. Lewis, *A Preface to 'Paradise Lost'* (London, 1942)

A. Low, *The Blaze of Noon* (New York, 1974)

L. L. Martz, *Poet of Exile* (New Haven, 1980)

A. Milner, *John Milton and the English Revolution* (London, 1981)

A. K. Nardo, *Milton's Sonnets and the Ideal Community* (Nebraska, 1979)

M. Nyquist and M. W. Ferguson (eds.), *Re-Membering Milton: Essays on the Texts and Traditions* (New York, 1987)

C. A. Patrides (ed.), *Milton's 'Lycidas': The Tradition and the Poem* (New York, 1961; rev. Columbia, 1983)

C. A. Patrides, *Milton and the Christian Tradition* (Oxford, 1966)

C. A. Patrides (ed.), *Milton's Epic Poetry* (Penguin, 1967)

J. Peter, *A Critique of 'Paradise Lost'* (London, 1960)

M. Pointon, *Milton and English Art* (Manchester, 1970)

F. T. Prince, *The Italian Element in Milton's Verse* (Oxford, 1954)

M. A. Radzinowicz, *Toward 'Samson Agonistes': The Growth of Milton's Mind* (Princeton, 1978)

B. Rajan, *The Lofty Rhyme* (London, 1970)

H. Rapaport, *Milton and the Postmodern* (Lincoln, Neb., 1983)

C. Ricks, *Milton's Grand Style* (London, 1963)

M. Roston, *Milton and the Baroque* (London, 1980)

R. M. Schwartz, *Remembering and Repeating: Biblical Creation in Paradise Lost* (Cambridge, 1989)

J. T. Shawcross (ed.), *Milton: The Critical Heritage* (London, 1970)

J. T. Shawcross (ed.), *Milton 1732–1801: The Critical Heritage* (London, 1972)

A. Stein, *The Art of Presence* (Berkeley, 1977)

J. H. Summers, *The Muse's Method* (London, 1962)

E. M. W. Tillyard, *Milton* (London, 1930; rev. 1966)

R. Tuve, *Images and Themes in Five Poems by Milton* (Cambridge, Mass., 1958)

A. J. A. Waldock, *'Paradise Lost' and Its Critics* (Cambridge, 1947)

J. M. Webber, *Milton and his Epic Tradition* (Seattle, 1979)

J. A. Wittreich, *Interpreting 'Samson Agonistes'* (Princeton, 1986)

A. S. P. Woodhouse, *The Heavenly Muse* (Toronto, 1972)

Essays in Aers *et al.*, Fish (1 and 2), Gilman (2), Goldberg (2), Helgerson, Jose, Knott, F. R. Leavis (*Revaluation*, London, 1936; Penguin, 1964), Lord, Malekin, Marcus, Martz (2), McCanles, Miner (3), Norbrook, Parry, Sharpe and Zwicker, Slights, Southall, Swardson, Webber, Wilding

MORE, HENRY (1614–87): Poet, philosopher and theologian; b. Lincolnshire; son of Calvinist and Cavalier family; Eton; Christ's College, Cambridge, 1631, where he met Whichcote and younger Platonists; M.A. and Fellow, 1639; took orders but declined preferment and devoted life to study, writing and conversation; published *Philosophical Poems*, 1647; published *An Antidote against Atheism*, 1652, and from then on wrote mainly prose; friends and correspondents included Cudworth and other Platonists, Descartes and Jeremy Taylor.

Complete Poems ed. A. B. Grosart (Edinburgh, 1878; reissued 1969)

Philosophical Poems ed. G. Bullough (Manchester, 1931)

Philosophical Writings ed. F. I. Mackinnon (New York, 1925)

See J. Hoyles, *The Waning of the Renaissance 1640–1740* (The Hague, 1971)

A. Lichtenstein, *Henry More* (Cambridge, Mass., 1962)

Essays in Rostvig, Willey

OVERBURY, SIR THOMAS (1581–1613): Character-writer; second edition of poem, *A Wife now the widow of Sir Thomas Overbury*, included twenty-two prose characters (later expanded) attributed to Overbury 'and other learned gentlemen his friends'; died in mysterious circumstances, possibly murdered.

The Overburian Characters ed. W. J. Paylor (Oxford, 1936)

See W. McElwee, *The Murder of Sir Thomas Overbury* (London, 1952)

D. Nichol Smith, *Characters of the Seventeenth Century* (Oxford, 1918)

B. White, *Cast of Ravens* (London, 1965)

Essay in Boyce

OVERTON, RICHARD (fl. 1642–63): Leveller, pamphleteer and satirist; attacked bishops in *Lambeth Fayre*, 1642; published *Mans Mortalitie*, 1644, which was followed by establishment of sect called 'soul sleepers'; wrote tracts signed 'Martin Marpriest' attacking Westminster Assembly of Divines, 1646; wrote *Remonstrance of Many Thousand Citizens* in defence of imprisoned Lilburne, 1646; imprisoned for defence of Lilburne, 1646–7; imprisoned in Tower with other Leveller leaders, 1649; escaped to Flanders, 1655, and obtained commission from Charles II; last Leveller to carry on struggle – imprisoned 1659 and 1663.

A Remonstrance of Many Thousand Citizens and *The Araignement of Mr Persecution* in W. Haller, *Tracts on Liberty in the Puritan Revolution*, III (New York, 1934)

An Appeal from the Degenerate Representative Body in D. M. Wolfe, *Leveller Manifestoes of the Puritan Revolution* (New York, 1944)

Mans Mortalitie ed. H. Fisch (Liverpool, 1968)

See J. Frank, *The Levellers* (Cambridge, Mass., 1955)

PHILIPS, KATHERINE (1631–1664): Poet; b. London; daughter of John Fowler, merchant; educated at fashionable boarding school in Hackney; became second wife of James Philips of the Priory, Cardigan, 1647; two children, born 1647 and 1656; became centre of a society of friendship, including Sir Edward Dering and Jeremy Taylor, in which she was known as Orinda; earliest printed verses prefixed to works by Henry Vaughan and William Cartwright, 1651; translation of Corneille's *Pompée* performed in Dublin, 1663; unauthorized edition of her miscellaneous poems printed 1664; died of smallpox in Fleet Street; the verses of 'the matchless Orinda' were collected and published posthumously, 1667; *Letters of Orinda to Poliarchus* (Sir Charles Cotterel) printed 1705.

Poems in G. Saintsbury (ed.), *Minor Poets of the Caroline Period*, I (Oxford, 1905)

See P. W. Souers, *The Matchless Orinda* (Cambridge, Mass., 1931)

Essays in Hobby, Rostvig

QUARLES, FRANCIS (1592–1644): Poet and prose writer; b. Romford, Essex; son of Queen Elizabeth's surveyor-general for victuals of the navy; graduated from Christ's College, Cambridge, 1608; Lincoln's Inn; published a series of biblical paraphrases and meditations in verse during 1620s; acquainted with Phineas Fletcher and Drayton; private secretary to James Ussher, Archbishop of·Armagh, in Dublin, 1629; more verses followed, including a poetic romance, *Argalus and Parthenia*, 1629, and *Divine Poems*, 1633; retired to Roxwell, in Essex, he prepared his most famous work, *Emblems Divine and Moral*, 1635, a collection of allegorical engravings accompanied by explanatory verses; during 1630s he worked on a series of allegorical pastorals, later published as *The Shepheards Oracles* (1646), in which he examined the current state of religion; in his last years, despite the Puritan cast of his mind, he supported the King's cause in a series of pamphlets, three of which were reissued posthumously under the title, *The Profest Royalist*, 1645.

Complete Works ed. A. B. Grosart (3 vols., Edinburgh, 1880–81; repr. New York, 1967)

Hosanna or Divine Poems and *Threnodes* ed. J. Horden (Liverpool, 1960)

See essays in Freeman, Gilman (2)

RANDOLPH, THOMAS (1605–35): Poet and dramatist; b. Northamptonshire; son of steward to Edward, Lord Zouch; Westminster School; Trinity College, Cambridge; great admirer of Jonson to whom he wrote 'Gratulatory to Mr Ben Jonson for his Adopting him to be his Son'; friend of Shirley and Digby; wrote pastorals, elegies and epithalamia; also wrote five plays.

Poems and Amyntas ed. J. J. Parry (New Haven, 1927)

Poems ed. G. Thorn Drury (London, 1929)

See I. Mullick, *The Poetry of Thomas Randolph* (Bombay, 1974)

ROCHESTER, JOHN WILMOT, EARL OF (1647–80): Poet, wit, satirist, courtier, libertine; b. Ditchley, Oxfordshire; succeeded to earldom, 1658; Wadham College, Oxford; travelled on Continent, 1661–5; studied at Padua; at Court, 1665; fought in war against Dutch, 1665–6; favourite of Charles II, by whom frequently banished from Court and pardoned; most notorious of group of noble rakes; Paris, 1669; patron of poets, including Dryden; *Satyr against Mankind, c.* 1675–6; wrote amorous and obscene lyrics; conversations with Burnet, 1677–80; serious illness, 'conversion', public recantation, June 1680.

Life by V. de Sola Pinto (London, 1935; rev. 1962)

Collected Works ed. J. Hayward (London, 1926)

Letters ed. J. Treglown (Oxford, 1980)

Poems ed. D. M. Vieth (New Haven, 1968); ed. K. Walker (Oxford, 1984)

Some Passages of the Life and Death of John, Earl of Rochester (1680), by Gilbert Burnet (Menston, 1972)

See D. Farley-Hills, *Rochester's Poetry* (London, 1978)

D. Farley-Hills (ed.), *Rochester: The Critical Heritage* (London, 1972)

D. H. Griffin, *Satires Against Man: The Poems of Rochester* (Berkeley, 1973)

J. Treglown (ed.), *Spirit of Wit: Reconsiderations of Rochester* (Oxford, 1982)

J. H. Wilson, *The Court Wits of the Restoration* (Princeton, 1948)
Essays in Farley-Hills, Hill (2), Keast, Love

SUCKLING, SIR JOHN (1609–42): Poet, dramatist and courtier; b. Twicken-
ham, Middlesex; son of important Court official; Trinity College,
Cambridge; travelled in France and Italy; fought in Germany under
Gustavus Adolphus; returned to England, 1632, and joined Court circle
where acquired reputation for wit and dissipation; took part in expedition against Scots, 1639; began writing, 1637 – poetry notable for
lightness and humour rather than for depth of feeling or polish; wrote
four plays, mainly interesting today for their contemporary allusions;
took part in abortive Royalist conspiracy to free Earl of Strafford, 1641;
escaped to France where, according to Aubrey, he poisoned himself.

Works ed. A. H. Thompson (London, 1910; reissued, 1964); ed. T.
Clayton and L. A. Beaurline (2 vols., Oxford, 1971)
Minor Poets of the Seventeenth Century (E., 1931; rev. 1953)
Poems and Letters from MS ed. H. Berry (London, Ont., 1960)
See C. L. Squier, *John Suckling* (Boston, 1978)
Essay in Summers

TAYLOR, JEREMY (1613–67): Priest and writer; b. Cambridge; son of
barber; Cambridge, 1626; B.A., 1630–31; M.A., 1633–4; Fellow of
Caius College, *c.* 1633; took orders; preaching impressed Laud who sent
him to Oxford where became Fellow of All Souls, 1636; chaplain to
Laud; published *Sermon upon the Anniversary of the Gunpowder Treason*,
1638; taken prisoner by Parliamentary forces, 1645; on release settled at
Golden Grove, Carmarthenshire, as teacher and as chaplain to second
Earl of Carbery; wrote *The Rule and Exercises of Holy Living*, 1650, and
The Rule and Exercises of Holy Dying, 1651; Bishop of Down and Connor,
1661.

Works (including *Life*) ed. R. Heber (15 vols., London, 1822; rev.
C. P. Eden, 10 vols., 1847–54; reissued, 1968)
The Golden Grove: Selected Passages from . . . Jeremy Taylor ed. L. P.
Smith (Oxford, 1930)
See H. T. Hughes, *The Piety of Jeremy Taylor* (London, 1960)
F. L. Huntley, *Jeremy Taylor and the Great Rebellion* (Ann Arbor,
1970)

H. B. Porter, *Jeremy Taylor: Liturgist* (London, 1979)
Essay in Mitchell

TRAHERNE, THOMAS (1637–74): Poet, prose writer and cleric; b. Hereford; son of a shoemaker; Oxford; served parish of Credenhill in Herefordshire until 1669 when he retired to Teddington as chaplain to Sir Orlando Bridgeman; writings, mainly of later years, develop heretical idealism and pantheism which he harmonized with more conventional faith; little of his work was known until twentieth century; mainly devotional poetry and meditative prose.

Life by G. I. Wade (Princeton, 1944)

Centuries, Poems and Thanksgivings ed. H. M. Margoliouth (2 vols., Oxford, 1958)

Poems, Centuries and 3 Thanksgivings ed. A. Ridler (Oxford, 1966)

See A. L. Clements, *The Mystical Poetry of Thomas Traherne* (Cambridge, Mass., 1970)

R. D. Jordan, *The Temple of Eternity* (New York, 1972)

K. W. Salter, *Thomas Traherne: Mystic and Poet* (London, 1964)

S. Stewart, *The Expanded Voice* (San Marino, 1970)

Essays in Clark, Lewalski, Love, Martz (2), Parry, Seelig, Sloane, Webber, White

VAUGHAN, HENRY (*c.* 1622–95): Poet, prose writer and physician; b. Newton-by-Usk, Brecknockshire; member of old and distinguished Welsh family; Jesus College, Oxford, 1638; studied law in London; took some part in Civil War on Royalist side; practised medicine in later life in Brecknockshire; began literary career by writing secular poetry, published 1646 and 1651; experienced religious conversion *c.* 1648; two volumes of *Silex Scintillans* (1650 and 1655) reflect spiritual experiences of committed Royalist and Anglican under Puritan dispensation of new Commonwealth.

Life by F. E. Hutchinson (Oxford, 1947)

Works ed. L. C. Martin (Oxford, 1914; rev. 1957)

Poems ed. F. Fogle (New York, 1965); ed. A. Rudrum (Penguin, 1976); ed. L. L. Martz (with Herbert's Poems) (Oxford, 1986)

See T. O. Calhoun, *Henry Vaughan: The Achievement of Silex Scintillans* (Newark, 1981)

NOTES ON CONTRIBUTORS

FRANK W. BRADBROOK Died 1983. Senior Lecturer in English, University College of North Wales, Bangor. Author of *Jane Austen: Emma* (1961) and *Jane Austen and her Predecessors* (1966); editor (with James Kingsley) of *Jane Austen: Pride and Prejudice* (1970).

JOHN BROADBENT Formerly Professor in the School of English and American Studies, University of East Anglia, Norwich. Author of *Poetic Love* (1964), audio-tapes on Milton and Shakespeare, general editor of *The Cambridge Milton* (1973), and editor of *Signet Classic Poets of the 17th Century* (1974).

L. A. CORMICAN Formerly Principal of St Patrick's College, University of Ottawa. Contributed essays on 'Medieval Idiom in Shakespeare' and 'Shakespeare and his Contemporaries' to *Scrutiny* 1950–51.

MARJORIE COX Formerly Lecturer in Modern History, University of Manchester. Author of 'Sir Roger Bradshaigh and the Electoral Management of Wigan, 1695–1747', *Bulletin of the John Rylands Library*, vol. 37 and (with L. A. Hopkins) of *A History of Sir John Deane's Grammar School, Northwich* (1975).

R. G. COX Died 1981. Reader in English Literature, University of Manchester. Author of articles and reviews in *Scrutiny*, *The Times Literary Supplement*, *The Sewance Review* and other periodicals; editor of *Thomas Hardy: The Critical Heritage* (1970).

D. J. ENRIGHT Writer, formerly university teacher. Publications include *Shakespeare and the Students* (1970), *The Alluring Problem: An Essay on Irony* (1986), and *Collected Poems 1987*; editor of *A Choice of Milton's Verse* (1975), *Rasselas* (1976), *The Oxford Book of Contemporary Verse 1945–1980* (1980) and *The Oxford Book of Death* (1983).

MAURICE HUSSEY Formerly Lecturer in English at the Cambridge College of Arts and Technology. Author of *Chaucer's World* (1967) and *The World of Shakespeare and his Contemporaries* (1971); editor of *English Poetry, 1600–1660* (1981).

IAN JACK Professor of English, University of Cambridge. His books include *Augustan Satire* (1952), *English Literature 1815–1823* (1963), *Keats and the Mirror of Art* (1967), *Browning's Major Poetry* (1973); general editor of the Clarendon Edition of the novels of the Brontës.

ODETTE DE MOURGUES Died 1988. Professor of French and fellow of Girton College, Cambridge. Author of *Metaphysical, Baroque and Précieux Poetry* (1953), *O Muse, Fuyante Proie . . . Essai sur la Poésie de La Fontaine*

R. Garner, *Henry Vaughan* (Cambridge, 1959)

E. Holmes, *Henry Vaughan and the Hermetic Philosophy* (Oxford, 1932)

E. C. Pettet, *Of Paradise and Light* (Cambridge, 1960)

J. F. S. Post, *Henry Vaughan: The Unfolding Vision* (Princeton, 1982)

A. Rudrum, *Henry Vaughan* (Univ. of Wales, 1981)

A. Rudrum (ed.), *Essential Articles for the Study of Henry Vaughan* (Oxford, 1987)

J. D. Simmonds, *Masques of God* (Pittsburgh, 1972)

N. K. Thomas, *Henry Vaughan: Poet of Revelation* (Worthing, 1986)

Essays in Allen, Alvarez, Bennett, Clark, Halewood, Hill (2), Lewalski, Martz (1 and 2), Parry, Rostvig, Seelig, Sloane, Summers, White

WALLER, EDMUND (1606–87): Poet; b. Hertfordshire; son of wealthy country gentleman; Eton; King's College, Cambridge; M.P. from age of sixteen; frequent visitor to Penshurst, home of Sidneys; published first collection of poems, 1645; popular with all Courts – wrote panegyrics on Charles I, Cromwell, Charles II and Prince of Orange; greatly admired by contemporaries, who regarded him, with Denham, as one of pioneers of new Augustan versification.

Poems ed. G. Thorn Drury (2 vols., London, 1905)

Silver Poets of the Seventeenth Century (E., 1974)

See A. W. Allison, *Toward an Augustan Poetic* (Lexington, 1962)

W. L. Chernaik, *The Poetry of Limitation* (New Haven, 1968)

Essay in Farmer

WALTON, IZAAK (1593–1683): Biographer; b. London; son of shopkeeper; self-educated; one of Donne's parishioners; literary life began when he became friend of Sir Henry Wotton, who commissioned him to collect material for life of Donne, which was prefixed to Donne's *Sermons*, 1640; published *Life of Sir Henry Wotton*, 1651; wrote *The Compleat Angler* in retirement and published it 1653; published *Life of George Herbert*, 1670, and *Life of Sanderson*, 1678.

The Compleat Angler ed. J. Buchan (W.C., 1935; rev. J. Buxton, 1982); ed. M. Bottrall (E., 1962); ed. J. Bevan (Oxford, 1983)

Lives ed. G. Saintsbury (W.C., 1927; repr. 1962)

See J. Bevan, *Izaak Walton's The Compleat Angler: The Art of Recreation* (Brighton, 1988)

   M. Bottrall, *Izaak Walton* (London, 1955)

   J. Butt, *Biography in the Hands of Walton, Johnson and Boswell* (Berkeley, 1966)

   J. R. Cooper, *The Art of 'The Compleat Angler'* (Durham, N.C., 1968)

   D. Novarr, *The Making of Walton's 'Lives'* (New York, 1958)

WINSTANLEY, GERRARD (1609–after 1660): Leader of Diggers; became prominent, 1649, as leader of party of men who tried to set up model community at St George's Hill, Surrey, asserting right of common people to claim land without paying rent; published tracts on subject of communal ownership and on religious questions; buried as a Quaker.

Works ed. G. H. Sabine (New York, 1941)

Selections ed. L. D. Hamilton (London, 1944)

The Law of Freedom and Other Writings ed. C. Hill (Penguin, 1973; reissued, Cambridge, 1983)

See T. W. Hayes, *Winstanley the Digger* (Cambridge, Mass., 1970)

   W. Schenk, *Concern for Social Justice in the Puritan Revolution* (London, 1947)

   Essay in Knott

WITHER, GEORGE (1588–1667): Poet and pamphleteer; b. Bentworth, Hampshire; Magdalen College, Oxford, 1604; Lincoln's Inn, 1615; friend of Drayton and William Browne; wrote elegies, epithalamia, and satires; committed to prison for offending the authorities with *Abuses Stript and Whipt*, 1613; while in prison he wrote pastorals, *The Shepherd's Hunting* (published 1615); in trouble with authorities again over *Wither's Motto*, 1621; became a convinced Puritan; raised a troop of horse for Parliament in 1642 and rose to rank of major; supported Commonwealth and Protectorate; later writing consists of pious exercises (*Halelujah*, 1641; *Emblemes, Ancient and Moderne*, 1635) and political diatribes or panegyrics ('The Protector. A Poem', 1655) in verse and prose; imprisoned 1660–63 for writings offensive to authorities.

Poems ed. F. Sidgwick (2 vols., London, 1902)

A Collection of Emblemes, Ancient and Moderne (1635) ed. R. Freeman (Columbia, 1975)

See C. S. Hensley, *The Later Career of George Wither* (The Hague, 1969)

   Essays in Grundy, Hill (2)

WROTH, LADY MARY (c. 1586–after 1640): Eldest daughter of Robert Sidney, first Earl of Leicester; married Sir Robert Wroth, 1604; often at Court; patroness of Jonson, Chapman, Wither; money troubles after husband died in 1614 leaving estate in debt; in 1621 published a pastoral romance, *Urania*, in imitation of Sir Philip Sidney's *Arcadia*; appended to volume is a collection of poems, entitled *Pamphilia to Amphilanthus*, containing first sonnet sequence in English which saw romantic love from a woman's point of view; book withdrawn from sale because reflections on courtiers gave offence.

Poems ed. J. A. Roberts (Baton Rouge, 1983)

See M. N. Paulissen, *The Love Sonnets of Lady Mary Wroth* (Salzburg, 1982)

(1962), *Racine, or the Triumph of Relevance* (1967) and *Two French Moralists* (1978).

DONALD PENNINGTON Fellow and tutor in Modern History, Balliol College, Oxford; formerly Reader in History, University of Manchester. Books include *Members of the Long Parliament* (with D. Brunton, 1954) and *Seventeenth-Century Europe* (1970).

GILBERT PHELPS Free-lance writer, lecturer and broadcaster. Author of *The Russian Novel in English Fiction* (1956), *A Survey of English Literature* (1965) and *A Short Guide to the World Novel* (1988). His eight novels include *The Winter People* (1963), *The Old Believer* (1973) and *The Law Road* (1975).

THEODORE REDPATH Fellow of Trinity College, and formerly Lecturer in English at Cambridge University. Editor of *The Sons and Sonets of John Donne* (1956, 1983, Pbk 1987) and (with W. G. Ingram) *Shakespeare's Sonnets* (1964, 1978). Author of *The Young Romantics and Critical Opinion 1807–24* (1975).

IAN ROBINSON Formerly Senior Lecturer in English-Language and Literature, University College of Swansea, and Director of the Brynmill Press Ltd. Best-known publications are *The Survival of English* (1973) and *The New Grammarians' Funeral* (1975).

W. W. ROBSON Masson Professor of English Literature, University of Edinburgh. Author of *Critical Essays* (1966), *The Definition of Literature* (1982) and *A Prologue to English Literature* (1986).

VIVIAN DE SOLA PINTO Died 1969. Was Professor of English Literature at Southampton and Nottingham Universities. His literary criticism ranged from the Restoration poets through William Blake to D. H. Lawrence and includes *Rochester: Portrait of a Restoration Poet* (1935) and *Enthusiast in Wit* (1962). His last book, *The City that Shone* (1969), was an autobiography.

ROY STRONG Director of the National Portrait Gallery (1967–73) and the Victoria and Albert Museum (1973–87). His many books on the life and art of Tudor and Early Stuart England include *The Cult of Elizabeth* (1977), *The Renaissance Garden of England* (1979), *Henry, Prince of Wales and England's Lost Renaissance* (1986) and *Gloriana's Portraits of Queen Elizabeth* (1987).

GEOFFREY WALTON Formerly Professor of English at Ahmadu Bello University, Zaria, Nigeria, the University College of Ghana and at Makerere University College. He is the author of *Metaphysical to Augustan* (1955) and *Edith Wharton: A Critical Interpretation* (1970).

ROBERT WILCHER Lecturer in English, University of Birmingham. Editor of *Andrew Marvell: Selected Poetry and Prose* (1986); author of *Andrew Marvell* (1985) and of articles on seventeenth-century literature in *Shakespeare Survey*, *Critical Quarterly*, *Renaissance and Modern Studies*, *Southern Review*, *Cahiers Elisabethains*, and other periodicals.

INDEX